*For my undergraduate professors
at Georgia Southern University,
especially Zia Hashmi and Hew Joiner.*

The African Stakes of the Congo War

The African Stakes
of the Congo War

EDITED BY JOHN F. CLARK

First published in hardcover in 2002 by PALGRAVE MACMILLAN™
First PALGRAVE MACMILLAN™ paperback edition: October 2004
175 Fifth Avenue, New York, N.Y. 10010 and
Houndmills, Basingstoke, Hampshire, England RG21 6XS.
Companies and representatives throughout the world.

PALGRAVE MACMILLAN is the global academic imprint of the Palgrave
Macmillan division of St. Martin's Press, LLC and of Palgrave Macmillan Ltd.
Macmillan® is a registered trademark in the United States, United Kingdom and other
countries. Palgrave is a registered trademark in the European Union and other
countries.

ISBN 1-4039-6723-7

Library of Congress Cataloging-in-Publication Data
The African Stakes of the Congo War / edited by John F. Clark.
    p.   cm.
    Includes bibliographical references and index.
    ISBN 0-312-29550-2 (cloth)
    ISBN 1-4039-6723-7 (paperback)
    1. Congo(Democratic Republic)—History—1997-   2. Political violence—Congo
(Democratic Republic)   3. Congo (Democratic Republic)—History—1960–1997.
I. Clark, John Frank.

DT658.26.A36   2002
967.5103'3—dc21

                                                                        2002024196

A catalogue record for this book is available from the British Library.

Design by Letra Libre, Inc.

First PALGRAVE MACMILLAN™ paperback edition: October 2004

10 9 8 7 6 5 4 3 2 1

Printed in the United States of America.

CONTENTS

List of Acronyms

ADF	Allied Democratic Forces (Uganda)
ADFL	Alliance des Forces Démocratiques pour la libération du Congo-Zaire (Alliance of Democratic Forces for the Liberation of Congo-Zaire)
ANC	African National Congress (South Africa)
ANC	Armée Nationale Congolaise
BBC	British Broadcasting Corporation
CAR	Central African Republic
COMESA	Common Market for East and Southern African States
CNN	Cable News Network
DFA	Department of Foreign Affairs (South Africa)
DRC	Democratic Republic of Congo
DTI	Department of Trade and Industry (South Africa)
ECOWAS	Economic Community of West African States
FAR	Forces Armées Rwandaises (Rwandan Armed Forces)
FAC	Forces Armées Congolaises (Congolese Armed Forces) (since 1997)
FAZ	Forces Armées Zaïroises (Zairian Armed Forces) (under Mobutu)
FDD	Front pour la Défense de la Démocratie (Burundi)
FIS	Front Islamique de Salut (Islamic Salvation Front) (Algeria)
FLC	Front de Libération du Congo (Congolese Liberation Front)
FLN	Front de Libération Nationale (National Liberation Front) (Algeria)
FLEC	Front for the Liberation of the Enclave of Cabinda (Congo-Brazzaville)
FLS	Front Line States
FRELIMO	Frente de Libertação de Mozambique (Liberation Front of Mozambique)
HCR	Haute Conseil de la République (High Council of the Republic) (Zaire)
IFIs	International Financial Institutions (World Bank and International Monetary Fund)
IMF	International Monetary Fund
ISDSC	Inter-State Defence and Security Committee (Zimbabwe)
JMC	Joint Military Council (of Lusaka Agreement)
LRA	Lord's Resistance Army (Uganda)
MIBA	Minière de Bakwanga (Bakwanga Mines)

MLC	Mouvement pour la Libération du Congo (Movement for the Liberation of Congo)
MNC	Mouvement National Congolaise (Congolese National Movement)
MONUC	Mission d'Organisation Nations Unis au Congo (United Nations Mission to the Congo)
MPLA	Movimento Popular de Liberação de Angola (Popular Movement for the Liberation of Angola)
MPR	Mouvement Populaire de la Révolution (Popular Movement of the Revolution) (Zaire)
NEPAD	New Partnership for Africa's Development
NRA	National Resistance Army (Uganda)
NRM	National Resistance Movement (Uganda)
OAS	Organization of American States
OAU	Organization of African Unity
OECD	Organization for Economic Cooperation and Development
POLISARIO	Frente Popular para la Liberación de Seguia el-Hamra y Río de Oro (Popular Front for the Liberation of Seguia el-Hamra and Río de Oro) (Western Sahara)
PNP	Parti National du Progrès (Congo) (National Progress Party)
PRP	Parti de la Révolution Populaire (Congo)
RENAMO	Resistencia Naçional Moçambicana (Mozambican National Resistance)
RCD	Rassemblement Congolaise pour la Démocratie (Congolese Rally for Democracy)
RCD-ML	RCD—Mouvement de Libération (RCD—Liberation Movement)
RPA	Rwandan Patriotic Army
RPF	Rwandan Patriotic Front
SADC	Southern African Development Community
SACU	Southern African Customs Union
SPLA	Sudanese People's Liberation Army
SWAPO	South West African People's Organization
UDPS	Union pour la Démocratie et le Progrès Social (Union for Democracy and Social Progress) (Zaire and DRC)
UNHCR	United National High Commission for Refugees
UNITA	União Nacional para a Independência Total de Angola (National Union for the Total Independence of Angola)
UPDF	Uganda People's Defence Forces
ZANLA	Zimbabwe African National Liberation Army
ZDF	Zimbabwe Defence Forces
ZIPRA	Zimbabwe People's Revolutionary Army

AFRICA

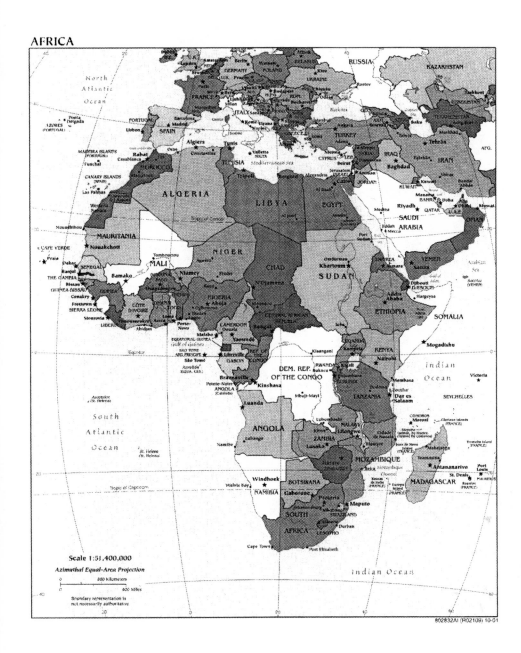

Scale 1:51,400,000

Azimuthal Equal-Area Projection

0   800 Kilometers

0   800 Miles

Boundary representation is
not necessarily authoritative

802832AI (R02109) 10-01

Democratic Republic of the Congo

—————— International boundary

— · —— · — Province boundary

★ National capital

⊛ Province capital

·—·—·— Railroad

·········· Road

*Kinshasa (Ville de Kinshasa) has
status equal to that of a province.

0   100   200 Kilometers

0   100   200 Miles

Mercator Projection

Preface

This volume has its origins in a conference entitled "Conflict and Peace-Making in the Great Lakes Region" that took place in Entebbe, Uganda, from 10–12 July 2000. I was able to take a leading role in the organization of that conference thanks, in the first place, to a U.S. Fulbright scholar program grant to lecture and conduct research at Makerere University for the 1999–2000 academic year. Accordingly, my first thanks go to the Fulbright Africa program, which made possible a marvelous year for me at Makerere. I specifically wish to thank Ms. Debra Egan for her kindness, advice, and support during the application process. When the American Center in Kampala approached me in early 2000 about the possibility of organizing a conference before the end of my tenure in Uganda, I urged them to make conflict and peacemaking in the Great Lakes the conference theme. Thanks to the inexhaustible energy of Ms. Sara Stryker, then deputy public affairs officer at the center, we were able to organize a very satisfying and successful conference on the topic in a few scant months. Sara and Ms. Dorothy Ngalombi, the center's cultural officer, took primary administrative responsibility for the conference, while I oversaw its academic aspects. The three-day conference featured three major addresses, thirty-five paper presentations, and the participation of some one hundred other invited guests. I am profoundly grateful to the American Center for having provided me with the opportunity to organize this conference.

Among the most successful aspects of the conference were the three special addresses given on the three successive days. The keynote address was given by Professor M. Crawford Young, who graciously returned to Kampala expressly for this purpose. The lecture served brilliantly to situate the current conflicts of the Great Lakes in their historical and continental context. An expanded and revised version of his presentation appears as chapter 2 in this volume. A special evening lecture entitled "Reflections on the Conflict in the Great Lakes Region" was presented at the end of the second day by Professor Mahmood Mamdani, formerly of Makerere University and now head of African Studies at Columbia University. Mamdani's sophisticated and theoretical analysis of the origins of the Rwanda conflict stimulated much discussion among his former colleagues and his compatriots at large over the ensuing weeks. Finally, John Stremlau, a former high-ranking U.S. State Department official, generously traveled up from his post in the International Relations Department at Witwatersrand University to give the closing address. His presentation on "Ending Africa's Wars," taken partly from his recent *Foreign Affairs* article, proved a most articulate and fitting end to the conference. I thank each of these speakers for their inspired oratory and for traveling to the Entebbe conference.

Among the final participants in this project, seven were presenters or participants in the Entebbe conference. Aside from Professor Young and myself, Chris

Landsberg (South Africa), Augusta Muchai (Kenya), Martin Rupiya (Zimbabwe), and Thomas Turner (then based in Tunisia) all made presentations at the conference. Their chapters herein, as well as my own, are revisions of the papers that we originally presented at the conference. Jude Murison, who was a nonpresenting participant at the conference in Entebbe, has also contributed a chapter to this volume. She worked with some assistance from Mr. Mauro de Lorenzo, yet another conference observer. I wish to thank all of the participants in this conference, particularly my former colleagues at Makerere, for their encouragement and support. I wish to single out Dr. Charles Bwana, then head of the Political Science Department at Makerere, Ms. Genevieve Kyarimpa, and Mr. Phillip Kasaija for their special efforts and unfailing support. Finally, I wish to thank three of my former Makerere University students, Joseph Mpanga, Hippo Twebaze, and Philip Asavia, for their hard work at the conference. Such fine young persons certainly provide much hope for the future of Uganda and Africa at large.

I also wish to thank two of the conference participants who are not contributors to this volume. First, I thank my fellow Fulbright scholar at Makerere, Professor Bill Herrin of the University of the Pacific. Bill's good humor and tremendous love of Uganda sustained me emotionally, and his expert culinary skills physically, during my Fulbright year in Uganda. Second, I wish to thank Professor Will Reno, my former colleague now of Northwestern University, for his good humor and tirelessness in traveling to Entebbe (while en route to Kyrgystan!). Will presented a marvelously researched and provocative paper at the conference and spiced every session with his wit and insight. His bargaining skills in the Kampala markets, honed over years of experience in West Africa, were also unsurpassed.

I also thank the other contributors to this volume, whom I have recruited here in the United States. All of them have had to produce their contributions in a much more rapid fashion than the conference participants, and all did so with little complaint. I was particularly pleased that two scholars of Congolese origin, Mungbalemwe Koyame and Osita Afoaku, agreed to participate in the final stages. I also especially appreciate Timothy Longman, who has devoted most of his career as a scholar to relating accurately and dispassionately the painful story of post-Habyarimana Rwanda. Both he and Thomas Turner contributed to a previous volume that I coedited with David Gardinier. I thank them, along with Kevin Dunn, for their loyalty and good patience.

In the publication of this volume, I was most fortunate to have the opportunity to work with the excellent staff at Palgrave press. Acquisitions editor Ella Pearce demonstrated faith in the project from the beginning and assisted me in many different aspects of the book. Production editor Annjeanette Kern oversaw the all-important production phase of the book with great diligence and tolerated my queries and pleas for help with equanimity. Jen Simington and Erin Chan carried out their work as copy editors with great skill and efficiency, improving the final product in a myriad of small details. My sincere thanks go to all four of them.

Special thanks are reserved for my wife, Janie Valdes. Having spent six months of my Fulbright fellowship with me in Uganda, Janie now not only understands my passion for Africa but shares it as well. We will both always treasure our months of "ordinary life" together in Uganda, and holidays in Tanzania. In the case of this volume, Janie provided more than her usual reflexive encouragement and emotional support.

She also gave freely of her own time to help us with innumerable aspects of the organization of the Great Lakes conference.

This volume is dedicated to my undergraduate professors at Georgia Southern University, where I earned my bachelor's degree in 1986. Actual teaching at a university is rarely an easy task, and normally it brings little recognition or reward. Yet many of my undergraduate professors at Georgia Southern devoted themselves completely to nurturing all of the students in their charge. They did so, I think, as much for the sheer joy of teaching as for the meager paychecks. Through their example, I saw that one could live well and honorably as a professor, and I made that my life's goal at the age of twenty. Thanks in part to their dedication and support, I have been able to realize that calling. Among those who inspired me were David Speak and Lane Van Tassell, from the Political Science Department; Sally Gershman (now deceased) and Vernon Egger, from the History Department; and John Humma from the English Department. I wish to single out two, however, for special appreciation: Hew Joiner, the director of the Bell Honors program, whose devotion to scholarly enquiry, work ethic, and unsentimental spirit of humanity have made him a model for his students; and Zia H. Hashmi, professor emeritus of political science, whose enormous devotion to teaching and scholarship, as well as his poise, professionalism, and integrity, were an inspiration to all of his students, and especially to me.

John Clark, Miami, October 2001

CHAPTER I

Introduction

CAUSES AND CONSEQUENCES
OF THE CONGO WAR

JOHN F. CLARK[1]

This volume represents the first effort to collect together a wide-ranging set of essays on the motivations and strategies of the many actors involved in the current war in the Democratic Republic of Congo (DRC). It also contains several chapters on the consequences of the war for ordinary citizens, regimes, and states. Like most collections of essays on a topic, it contains much more intermediate level analysis than it does abstract theory. Nonetheless, it has been designed ultimately to steer the reader's intellectual efforts toward theoretical reflection on the Congo war. In the end, the Congo war will be of interest not only to students of Africa's politics and international relations, but to political scientists and social theorists studying state-building in "newer" states, international conflict on the peripheries of world politics, and many other theoretical issues of politics that go beyond Africa.

Of course, the Congo war is of interest to laypersons and generalists, as well as to those seeking to think theoretically about political phenomena. There has been a stream of recent popular works on Congo covering everything from the horrors of Belgian colonialism to the unglamorous final demise of the Mobutu regime over its last years in power.[2] There has also been a recent revival of scholarly, as well as popular, interest in the assassination of Patrice Lumumba in 1961.[3] As ordinary observers of human frailties, cruelties, and heroism, we cannot help but be fascinated by Congo and its travails; as moral beings, we cannot help but be gravely concerned with the unspeakable human suffering that has resulted from the recent war, as well as Congo's other postcolonial traumas.

This introduction, however, seeks to provide a guide to more theoretical considerations. It presents several some of the various theoretical approaches that will help frame future debates over the meaning of the Congo war. It does so by raising a series of questions about the evolution of politics in the DRC and the sources and manifestations of the Congo war. Each should be of interest to theorists studying similar phenomena in other parts of Africa or other regions of the world. The various contributions to this volume are referred to in the course of these discussions to illuminate the theoretical issues to which they speak.

The first theoretical question about the Congo war is simply, "Why has the war occurred, and what does this possibly tell us about the evolution of African politics and international relations?" There are three fundamentally different perspectives on this question that direct our attention to different bodies of literature. The first perspective sees the Congo war largely as an issue of state collapse, succeeded by a scramble of unscrupulous neighbors for the lush spoils left unguarded and unclaimed. It is well appreciated that many things were against Congo in the quest for peaceful development at its independence. Belgian colonial rule had done precious little, of course, to prepare the Congolese to govern a modern state, and it was not unpredictable that they would fail. The nature of the grant of independence itself, and the ensuing scramble for influence among the United States, the Soviet Union, and the former colonizer, both demonstrated the severe weaknesses of the postcolonial state and further undermined its limited prospects for success. In this context, the long and ruinous rule of Mobutu Sese Seko only represents another revolution of the cycle. The form of nondevelopmental authoritarianism he practiced certainly reflected the incapacities of Congo's administrative inheritance, but it also made it likely that his successors would have little prospect of sparking a more virtuous cycle of development and liberal reform. In terms of political economy, the internal logic of Mobutu's "extractive state" was such that it evolved inexorably toward collapse.[4] Mobutu's rule also both reflected and reinforced a culture of arbitrariness, oppression, and violence in Congo's public life that has not been overcome. This internal cycle of oppression of Congo is well summarized in chapter 3 by Mccalpin in this volume.

Crawford Young's chapter 2, by contrast, puts the current Congo crisis in the historical perspective of the region and, in so doing, raises the possibility that the species of war that we now observe in Congo is part of a larger, continental trend. He argues that the current varieties of internal war all across Africa have a different set of motivations than earlier generations of warfare. In particular, the anti-imperial and socialist revolutionary campaigns of the past have entirely disappeared, while regional secessionist movements have been much more rare, the unique case of Eritrea excepted. These have been replaced primarily with different varieties of warlordism, motivated either by the lure of controlling natural resources or by the timeless lust for power, local or national. Young's work here thus extends some of the more empirical work on collapsed states in Africa that appeared during the 1990s[5] and begins to make some theoretical generalizations.

If indeed the kind of violence and disorder that we are now witnessing in Congo is part of a larger trend, one may ask, what broad social processes or developments have given rise to the new trend? The answer leads us to a second perspective on the question of the Congo war, one that emphasizes how recent changes in international policies may have impacted the stability of African states. One aspect of these changes, alluded to by Young, is the conspicuous transformation in the functioning of world economic processes, often lumped together with many corresponding social changes under the popular label "globalization." These transformation in economic processes have, among other things, made the conduct of business between the corporations of the developed world and nonstate actors (including warlords) ordinary events in Sub-Saharan Africa.[6] Such practices were much less common in the past, and they may have given rise to new forms of warmaking and more frequent state "collapse." Another part of the explanation, also referenced by Young, is equally evident, but no less strong in interpretive power: the virtual withdrawal of American support for the Mobutu regime after the end of the Cold War and of both superpowers from Africa in general. The initial collapse of the Somali state in 1991, for instance, appears to have much to do with the withdrawal of American support and little with the internal trajectories of its politics.

In the case of Congo, these two explanations compete, but the second provides far more explanatory power than the first. Since Mobutu was largely a creature of the Cold War, it is no surprise that his control over the state waned after 1989; indeed, some might think it remarkable that he survived the end of the Cold War as long as he did. That the Mobutu regime did survive in power until 1997 suggests, however, that the real bases for its insistence were not entirely external. Mobutu was quite capable in deploying charismatic, even "esoteric," and domestic economic instruments in support of his power, as well. The withdrawal of American support in the early 1990s was nonetheless a psychological blow to the regime, given the widespread belief within Zaire that the United States and other outside forces largely determined the state's trajectory. Materially, it was the withdrawal of the assistance of the international financial institutions (i.e., the International Monetary Fund and World Bank—IFIs) that sparked the collapse of the copper industry, and economy at large, in Congo.[7] As the state's copper revenues shrank over the first few years of the 1990s, the material basis for the state evaporated. But the withdrawal of the IFIs from Zaire resulted more from a strategic calculation that the Mobutu regime was no longer necessary than from a politico-economic one that the Mobutu regime lacked the will and capacity for effective economic management. The latter fact had already been evident for over fifteen years by 1990.

The end of the Cold War also helps explain the relative lack of interest on the part of the United States in negotiating a settlement that would have left post-Mobutu Congo more stable. Likewise, the emergent Franco-American rivalry in central Africa in the early 1990s, felt much more strongly on the French side, also helps explain why the Western powers did not develop a common strategy for post-Mobutu Congo.[8] Indeed, France and the United States appeared to be rivals to most Africans witnessing Mobutu's final fall in May 1997 at the hands of rebels backed by "anglophile" Uganda and Rwanda.

These developments in Congo unfolded, of course, in an emerging new economic environment mentioned just above. Yet it is far from clear how the allegedly sinister forces of "globalization" had any bearing on the course of the Mobutu regime or the Zairian state. For many Africanists, the most troubling component of this bundle of economic trends includes the vigorous application of structural adjustment programs to African economies in exchange for debt relief by the IFIs. The result in Zaire, however, was *not* enduring structural adjustment but rather a general economic collapse, mostly of Mobutu's domestic making. While "globalization" generally implies an increasing dependence on foreign private capital for developing states, the opposite was the case in Zaire: The few remaining foreign capital investments in Zaire were being withdrawn in the early 1990s.[9] Only a very few "buccaneer" capitalists, mostly mining interests, were still engaged in some investment in Zaire by this time. Less adventuresome investors, meanwhile, were sensibly awaiting the restoration of a functioning state in Zaire before risking investment. It is true that the mining companies were doing business with Laurent Kabila in the period after August 1996 before he had taken power, which may have speeded the end of the Mobutu regime, but this phenomenon occurred in the very late stages of the Mobutu regime, at a moment when the dictator's fate was already sealed.

Both of these sources of explanation for the dissolution of state power in Congo, and its failure to be restored rapidly, reflect *normative* changes in world politics as well.[10] Both the rather laissez faire attitude of the major powers toward state collapse and the predatory, disruptive behavior of business dealing in natural resources in Africa may be manifestations of an emergent ideology that shuns regulation and collective management of social problems on the continent. If so, the new norms for Africa run exactly opposite those that have been manifest in Eastern Europe and other regions. Perhaps a cynical kind of international "triage" is now being practiced that has written off the possibility of real African development, at least in some regions, while simultaneously insisting on African openness to Western business. Another, kinder, explanation for Western inaction in Zaire, both before and during the collapse of the Mobutu regime, is simply that the main Western states in Zaire could not envision a plan for the unfortunate country that would plausibly restore it to political and economic health.

The third broad perspective on the question of why the war in Congo has occurred directs our attention not to the literature on state collapse but to that on foreign policy making in the states intervening in Congo. This perspective views the war not as a result of internal collapse but as primarily the result of external intervention. Afoaku's chapter 7 in this volume demonstrates quite clearly that the main rebel groups now fighting inside Congo are largely the creation of the outside interveners. His work thereby focuses our attention on the external interveners and their goals. While the group of Jean-Pierre Bemba may have more indigenous support than the two factions of the Rassemblement Congolais pour la Démocratie (RCD), it is extremely doubtful that it would have flourished without the protective umbrella, aid, and logistical support of the Ugandan army. This perspective points out that Congo's weakness may be a "permissive condition," but it was scarcely an efficient cause. Congo's relative weakness vis à vis its neighbors, even including its inability to prevent insurgency groups from operating from its territory, cannot alone explain the current war. From this perspective, one must look inside the intervening, neighboring states for an explanation for the Congo war.

If we look outside Congo itself for the sources of the war, and into the politics of the neighboring states, what is it about their political development, we might ask, that makes them interventionist? To this question, several different kinds of answers have been given. One of the most fascinating and coherent is that offered by Mohammed Ayoob via his theory of "subaltern realism," a theory that could apply to states of "inferior rank" anywhere on the peripheries of world politics.[11] Ayoob makes a compelling case that classical realism provides great insights into both domestic politics and international relations in the third world. He argues that the contemporary leaders of developing states are emulating the leaders of European states in the early modern period. Their main goal, like that of their European predecessors, is to build up their states in terms of their economic strength, administrative capacity, and military power. In so doing, war fighting and intervention in neighboring states is often a logical part of the process.[12] Ayoob, like Machiavelli and Hobbes, the political philosophers of early modern Europe, takes it for granted that domestic and foreign policies are inextricably intertwined, and both part of the nationalist goal of state-building. Among the interveners in Congo, the ones that seem to fit Ayoob's model best are Uganda and, possibly, Zimbabwe. In the Ugandan case, President Yoweri Museveni appears to have been building up the economy and military prowess of the Ugandan state since his rise to power in 1986. Given the vast amounts of natural resources and wealth that have flowed from Congo into Uganda since 1998, one might perceive the invasion and occupation to be part of a rational plan to build the Ugandan economy at Congo's expense.[13] In chapter 9 my analysis suggests otherwise, however.

A perspective closely related to that of Ayoob sees a developing state's military intervention into a neighbor as an issue of what David calls "leadership survival in the face of domestic threats."[14] I have developed this argument elsewhere, particularly for African states, and identified the concept of "regime security" as a key to understanding their foreign policy behavior.[15] One may agree with Ayoob that domestic politics are the key to the foreign policies of domestic states without conceding that rulers are actually building up state capacities. In many African states, individual rulers have frequently appeared to be all-consumed with the business of merely staying in power, even as the capacity of the states they ruled was collapsing around them. Mobutu himself is a prime example of this phenomenon. Thus, intervention abroad may have more to do to with personal and family enrichment, or political advantage against internal political challenges, than it does with building state capacities. This is the view that many analysts have of Zimbabwe's intervention in Congo, although Rupiya's chapter 6 in this volume supports the official view that Zimbabwe came to the defense of a victim of foreign aggression in the context of a broader Southern African Development Community (SADC) decision. Whatever Zimbabwe's original reasons for the intervention, however, the outcome of its intervention has been enrichment for several of Mugabe's cronies and impoverishment for the Zimbabwean state (as argued in both Rupiya's chapter 6 and Koyame and Clark's chapter 12).

Similarly, foreign intervention may be designed to bolster regime security against insurgencies based in neighboring states. This source of intervention and counter-intervention in Africa's international relations has been salient in both the Cold War and post-Cold War periods.[16] Classical realists had no difficulty understanding the hostility of the rulers of fragile states toward their neighbors who have wished them ill for any number of reasons. René Lemarchand has unconsciously deployed precisely this variety of old-fashioned power political analysis to the foreign policies of the states of the Great Lakes region recently with great success.[17] That the goals and ambitions of Yoweri Museveni, Paul Kagame, and Pierre Buyoya were not generally shared by their countrymen was of no particular relevance to Lemarchand's analysis, just as the gap between the goals of Lorenzo deMedici and those of Florence's citizens in the sixteenth century was of little matter to Machiavelli. Even in the far more benign environment of southern Africa after apartheid, Khadiagala has acknowledged " . . . new conflicts have overshadowed the broadening of institutional ties."[18] All of these analyses suggest that the security of regimes remains of paramount concern, and a motive force behind foreign policy when regimes are really threatened. Although they do not use this language explicitly, the analyses of Longman (chapter 8, on Rwanda) and of Turner (chapter 5, on Angola) both broadly support this point of view.

If classical realism draws our attention to the intersection of domestic politics and foreign policy for the states neighboring Congo, the structural variety of realism again draws it back to changes in the international system. [19] For these changes have created a new environment in which the formulation of foreign policy of African states must take place. According to the introductory essays in two recent volumes on foreign policy making in Africa, this new international environment is having an important influence on the nature of the foreign policies now being made in African states.[20] We noted above that recent changes in the international system have affected the internal stability of African states, but they have equally affected the context of foreign policy making. Superpower involvement in Zaire and Angola during the 1970s and 1980s served as a brake on the direct intervention of the two states in each other's affairs (the 1977 and 1978 Shaba invasions notwithstanding). As in Eastern Europe, the withdrawal of the Soviet Union from central Africa and the reduction of American commitments in the region seems to have stimulated interstate confrontations and intervention.

Other changes in the international system, not involving the superpowers and their orientations, have also altered the context of foreign policy making. As noted above, France, which could perhaps be counted a "great power" in the African context, generally tried to "rationalize" its presence in Central Africa during the 1990s. That is, France has sought to reduce the costs of its involvement in the region while maintaining its political influence and economic interests. Among the steps it has taken as a result was the closure of its former base in the Central Africa Republic. Meanwhile, France's ironclad support for the former regimes of Mobutu Sese Seko and Juvénal Habyarimana cost it political influence in the mid-1990s that is only slowly being restored. These developments, too, have increased the uncertainty in the domestic political stability and international relationships of the states in the region. In the absence of great power guarantees, all of the states of the region seem more predisposed to overt intervention to achieve international aims.

One might also consider the impact of recent increases in the sensitivity of the international community to ethnic cleansing and genocide. Unlike the previous considerations, all generated by realist observations about the trajectory of the global system, this consideration is generated by the liberal sensitivity to changes in community morals. In the past, episodes of mass killing (though not, admittedly, genocide itself) only had a short-term impact on Western policy in various world regions, including the Great Lakes. In the case of Rwanda, though, Western guilt about its inaction at the time of the 1994 genocide exerts a decisive—and somewhat perverse—influence over the policies of the Western powers in the region. Just as the Museveni regime is forgiven its trespasses because of its "good" economic policies, the Kagame regime is forgiven because it represents the physical protection for Rwanda's shrunken Tutsi minority. The physical protection for the Tutsi it represents, the West is constantly reminded, was not provided by the international community in 1994.

Liberals are attuned to other changes in both African domestic politics and international affairs that provide a different theoretical perspective on the origins of the Congo war. Liberals have long noted, of course, that democratic states virtually never fight wars against one another, even if they do intervene frequently in the affairs of their nondemocratic neighbors.[21] At least one scholar has recently suggested that the same logic may apply in the African context. Schraeder has argued that "The Cold War's end and the process of democratization have significantly affected the

formulation and implementation of Francophone West African foreign policies."[22]
This analysis implies that the strengthening of democratic institutions would pacify
the foreign policies of African states, too, vis à vis democratic neighbors. Even if this
logic is universal, however, it appears to have little relevance in Central Africa and
the Great Lakes, since none of the countries in the region is remotely "democratic."
Although Uganda has some well-functioning liberal institutions, including its parliament and judiciary, and merits recognition as a more liberal and stable polity than,
say, Angola or Rwanda, its interventionism has been scarcely less vigorous. Whatever
its shortcomings in the way of explanation, though, this perspective does suggest a
long-term solution for the conflicts of the region: democratization. Insofar as an
opening of the political space in Congo was made a precondition for foreign withdrawal under the Lusaka Agreement, this perspective has been integrated into the
peacemaking efforts of the region.

The context of foreign policy making has also been changed by the new prominence of the IFIs in Africa since the 1980s, and by the general ideological trend
against state involvement in economics, domestic or interstate. This observation is
most likely to be made by those from the "globalist," or radical, camp in international
relations. Consider, for instance, the constraints and incentives on Uganda's foreign
policies created by these developments. First, the United States' condemnation of
Uganda's blatantly illegal occupation of a large part of Congolese national territory
has been mild because Uganda is a "model pupil" of the World Bank in its economic
reforms. The United States and the other Western economic powers (excluding
France, perhaps) have a stake in the continuing success of Ugandan economic reform, if the wisdom of structural adjustment is to be confirmed. This removes a potential constraint on Ugandan behavior vis à vis its neighbors. Second, Uganda's
balance of trade and external accounts are somewhat improved by the flow of ill-
gotten gains from Congo through Uganda's economic space.[23] Although the IFIs
have fretted about increases in Uganda's military budget, any improvement in its finances serves to keep the IFIs at bay.

On the other hand, the Mugabe regime in Zimbabwe has been swimming up-
stream against the flow of ideological history. More important than Mugabe's
rhetoric, though, has been his frightful mismanagement of the Zimbabwean economy and his recent efforts to distract Zimbabweans from their domestic economic
and political misery by targeting the country's white landowners as scapegoats for
the country's problems. As a result, the IFIs have withdrawn their economic support
for Zimbabwe and put the Mugabe government under additional pressure to withdraw from Congo. In chapter 6, Rupiya defends the intervention of Zimbabwe in
Congo, invoking both liberal norms and radical critiques in the process. Echoing the
official Zimbabwean view of the state's intervention in the conflict, Rupiya argues
for the legality and legitimacy of the counterintervention of a group of states sanctioned by SADC. He contrasts this policy with the Rwanda and Uganda's prior intervention, backed by a coalition of Western powers and the IFIs. In evoking this
extra-Africa backing, Rupiya implicitly pits the capitalist and interventionist West
against the defenders of African sovereignty.

A second major theoretical question about the Congo war is whether it will lead
to state-building for the intervening states or nation-building for Congo. On this
question, the realists (in both the political and economic realms) are split, while liberals and radicals have characteristic views. Ayoob's recent theory, mentioned above,

has explained wars on the periphery in terms of state-building efforts, and therefore must predict that wars will in fact strengthen states; my own view, in favor of "regime security" as the central concern of national leaders, is that foreign intervention may, on the contrary, represent a *cost* to be borne by the intervening state. Likewise, most liberals can only doubt that war is likely to lead to stronger states or development in general, and they generally lament the fighting as a waste of resources better spent elsewhere. Critical-minded theorists are also unlikely to believe that war is likely to lead to strengthen states or societies; instead, they are more interested in the profits that the wealthy and powerful have gained from the fighting. In the cases of Uganda and Zimbabwe, these profits are not inconsiderable, but neither are the costs of war. Chapter 13 by Koyame and Clark was prepared to provide some empirical basis for systematic reflection on the overall economic consequences of the war.

The question of nation-building in Congo is more complicated still. On one hand, whatever activities the state might undertake in building a national consciousness have been indisputably disrupted. Such activities would include building a physical infrastructure to link the country together and strengthening state-level institutions, including the army. Such institutions often serve to transform the identities of the individuals whom they enmesh, such that their local consciousness is displaced by a national one. Meanwhile, the fact that some of the rebel movements, notably that of Jean-Pierre Bemba, appear to have a regional basis is likely to reinforce regional, rather than national, identities in the minds of many Congolese citizens. On the other hand, the experience of foreign intervention has, perversely, done much to bring the Congolese together: If there is one thing that the great majority of Congolese agree on—even the Banyamulenge, who are allegedly shielded from harm—it is that the occupation of eastern Congo by Rwanda (and Uganda) is an intolerant affront to their national greatness and unity.

A final theoretical question raised indirectly by the Congo war concerns the very nature of states in Africa (and elsewhere on the periphery). Critical theorists and post-structuralist thinkers have engaged this question most intensively, but they are far from reaching any consensus about the meaning of the state, or sovereignty, in Africa. For instance, Grovogui insists that "post-colonial sovereignty" in Africa does *not* constitute "a historical deviation from Western norms," heavily criticizing Robert Jackson for suggesting otherwise.[24] On the other hand, Kevin Dunn insists that the concept of the state needs to be " problematized" for Africa; he goes on "to question the use of the state as the primary unit of analysis in I R [international relations]."[25] Without having acknowledged it, these two scholars have generated the beginnings of a debate about the appropriateness of Western concepts to the analysis of politics in Africa.

The chapters in this volume address such issues only indirectly, but several do contain arguments and information that could well become ammunition in these abstruse debates. Notably, the chapters on refugees and arms trafficking in the Great Lakes region raise issues about the continuing influence and relevance of African states. Murison's chapter on refugees demonstrates the extent to which large groups of essentially stateless persons can heavily influence the politics and economics of a region. Critical theorists and constructivists are certain to seize upon the complex and multiple identities of refugee populations as evidence that traditional academic concepts fail to capture and understand the patterns of interstate politics that impact far more on ordinary persons than national leaders. Likewise, Muchai's analysis of arms trafficking (chapter 10) raises questions about whether the states of the Great Lakes are in the grip of nongovernmental forces that they can no longer control. Certainly, the diffusion of arms to myriad nonstate groups during the course of the Congo war has created a context in which not only states, but also coherent insurgencies, have control over the means of violence.

The chapters that lie ahead are intended to provide the raw material for debates such as these outlined here. Those that explore the role of the relevant states (and their governing regimes) are intended to help us understand how the "interests" of these actors came to be constructed before and during the two recent Congo wars. Those that examine the nonstate actors and phenomena serve to remind us that the decisionmaking of national leaders is conditioned by the human and physical resources at their disposal. Together, all of the chapters invite us to consider the trajectories of sociopolitical development in Africa and the larger meaning of the current struggle now unfolding in Congo.

NOTES

1. I wish to thank Crawford Young for providing an extended commentary to me on this introduction, though the responsibility for remaining errors of fact or interpretation is entirely my own.
2. See Adam Hochschild, *King Leopold's Ghost: A Story of Greed, Terror, and Heroism in Colonial Africa* (New York: Houghton Mifflin, 1998), and Michela Wrong, *In the Footsteps of Mr. Kurtz: Living of the Brink of Disaster in Mobutu's Congo* (New York: HarperCollins, 2001).
3. Ludo De Witte, *The Assassination of Patrice Lumumba*, trans. Ann Wright and Renée Fenby (London: Verso, 2001).
4. On the trajectories of the state in Zaire as a function of Mobutu's rule, see John F. Clark, "The Extractive State in Zaire," in Leonardo Villalon and Philip Huxtable, eds., *Critical Juncture: The African State Between Disintegration and Reconfiguration* (Boulder, CO: Lynne Rienner, 1997): 109–125.
5. See for example, I. William Zartman, ed., *Collapsed States: the Disintegration and Restoration of Legitimate Authority* (Boulder, CO: Lynne Rienner, 1995).
6. See, inter alia, William Reno, "External Relations of Weak States and Stateless Regions in Africa," in Gilbert M. Khadiagala and Terrence Lyons, eds., *African Foreign Policies: Power and Process* (Boulder, CO: Lynne Rienner, 2001).
7. I am indebted to Crawford Young for reminding me of these points.
8. On this issue, see Peter J. Schraeder, "Cold War to Cold Peace: Explaining U.S.-French Competition in Francophone Africa," *Political Science Quarterly* 115, no. 3 (2000): 395–421.
9. In fact, much as Mobutu's critics may have perceived him to be a product of foreign capital forces, Zaire never attracted a great deal of foreign investment, especially in comparison with its enormous potential for profits. For the view that Mobutu was a product of foreign capital forces, see Jacques Depelchin, *From the Congo Free State to Zaire, 1885–1974: Towards a Demystification of Economic and Political History*, trans. Ayi Kwei Armah (London: Codesria, 1992), and David Gibbs, *The Political Economy of Third World Intervention: Mines, Money and U.S. Policy in the Congo Crisis* (University of Chicago Press, 1991). For evidence on the lack of Western investment in Zaire, see Crawford Young, "The Zaïrian Crisis and American Foreign Policy," in Gerald J. Bender, James S. Coleman, and Richard L. Sklar, eds., *African Crisis Areas and U.S. Foreign Policy* (Berkeley: University of California Press, 1985), 214–219. For an explicit rejoinder to Depelchin and Gibbs, see Clark, "The Extractive State in Zaire."

10. On this point, also see the work of Grovogui, who writes about the West's moral construction of "sovereignty" in the African context. In some sense, the changing patterns of internal war in Africa, and the Western responses to them, may reflect changes in African "regimes of sovereignty." Siba N. Grovogui, "Sovereignty in Africa: Quasi-Statehood and Other Myths in International Theory," in Kevin C. Dunn and Timothy M. Shaw, eds., *Africa's Challenge to International Relations Theory* (New York: Palgrave, 2001), 31.

11. Mohammed Ayoob, "Subaltern Realism: International Relations Theory Meets the Third World," in Stephanie G. Neumann, ed., *International Relations Theory and the Third World* (New York: St. Martin's Press, 1998), 45.

12. Interestingly, in some of Ayoob's earlier work, he emphasizes that attempts at territorial aggrandizement may *weaken,* rather than strengthen, the intervening state. I thank Crawford Young for pointing this out to me.

13. William Reno, "Stealing like a Bandit, Stealing like a State" (paper presented to the Department of Political Science, Makerere University, Uganda, 14 April 2000).

14. Steven R. David, "The Primacy of Internal War," in Stephanie G. Neumann, ed., *International Relations Theory and the Third World* (New York: St. Martin's Press, 1998), 87.

15. John F. Clark, "Foreign Policy Making in Central Africa: The Imperative of Regime Security in a New Context," in Gilbert M. Khadiagala and Terrence Lyons, eds., *African Foreign Policies: Power and Process* (Boulder, CO: Lynne Rienner, 2001).

16. John F. Clark, "Realism, Neo-Realism and Africa's International Relations in the Post–Cold War Era," in Kevin C. Dunn and Timothy M. Shaw, eds., *Africa's Challenge to International Relations Theory* (New York: Palgrave, 2001).

17. René Lemarchand, "Foreign Policy Making in the Great Lakes Region," in Gilbert M. Khadiagala and Terrence Lyons, eds., *African Foreign Policies: Power and Process* (Boulder, CO: Lynne Rienner, 2001).

18. Gilbert M. Khadiagala, "Foreign Policy Decisionmaking in Southern Africa's Fading Frontline," in Gilbert M. Khadiagala and Terrence Lyons, eds., *African Foreign Policies: Power and Process* (Boulder, CO: Lynne Rienner, 2001), 132.

19. On this point, see again the work of David, "The Primacy of Internal War."

20. Stephen Wright, "The Changing Context of African Foreign Policies," in Wright, ed., *African Foreign Policies* (Boulder, CO: Westview, 1999), and Gilbert M. Khadiagala and Terrence Lyons, "Foreign Policy Making in Africa: An Introduction," in Khadiagala and Lyons, eds., *African Foreign Policies: Power and Process* (Boulder, CO: Lynne Rienner, 2001). Also see Timothy M Shaw and Julius E. Nyang'oro, "Conclusion: African Foreign Policies and the Next Millennium: Alternative Perspectives, Practices, and Possibilities," in Khadiagala and Lyons, eds., *African Foreign Policies: Power and Process* (Boulder, CO: Lynne Rienner, 2001).

21. One classic statement of this phenomenon is Michael Doyle, "Liberalism and World Politics," *American Political Science Review* 80 (1986), 1151–70.

22. Peter J. Schraeder, "New Directions in Francophone West African Foreign Policies," in Gilbert M. Khadiagala and Terrence Lyons, eds., *African Foreign Policies: Power and Process* (Boulder, CO: Lynne Rienner, 2001), 60–61.

23. On this point, see Reno, "Stealing like a Bandit, Stealing like a State."

24. Grogovui, "Sovereignty in Africa," 30.

25. Kevin C. Dunn, "MadLib #32: The Blank African State: Rethinking the Sovereign State in International Relations Theory," in Kevin C. Dunn and Timothy M. Shaw, eds., *Africa's Challenge to International Relations Theory* (New York: Palgrave, 2001), 49.

PART I

The Congo War in Context

CHAPTER 2

Contextualizing Congo Conflicts

ORDER AND DISORDER IN POSTCOLONIAL AFRICA

CRAWFORD YOUNG

INTRODUCTORY REMARKS: ANALYTICAL PURPOSES

Africa, Frantz Fanon famously remarked, has the shape of a pistol, with Congo-Kinshasa[1] resembling the trigger housing. The violence implicit in the metaphor aptly captures the tumultuous events afflicting a significant part of Africa in the 1990s; the pistol, however, rather than pointing toward Antarctica, aims its fire inwards. Some twenty-four of the fifty-three states on the continent have experienced sustained civil strife during the last decade,[2] and two significant interlocked zones of civil warfare spilling across borders have emerged: one stretching from the Horn of Africa in a southwestward arc to Angola and the two Congos, and the other extending along the West African coast from Liberia to Senegal. At the turn of the twenty-first century, Congo had become the veritable epicenter of conflict in Africa, with involvement of six neighboring armies and four internal ones, plus smaller fragments spinning off.

The object of this chapter is to provide a context for the following ones, which explore diverse aspects of the complex Congo conflicts since 1996 and their African implications. The thesis I wish to advance is that the intractability of the crisis and the larger challenges it poses to civil order in Africa more broadly must be understood in the framework of a number of novel factors conditioning internal warfare that appear in the 1990s. Some of these phenomena reflect broader changes in the international environment and are encountered in other world regions. A number, however, are particular to the patterns of state crisis facing African countries. Gurr, for example, in his arresting finding that the incidence of civil wars has significantly decreased during the 1990s in the world at large, acknowledges that Africa is the major exception.[3]

The human costs of civil conflict in Africa are immense. The Rwandan 1994 genocide and its aftermath took well over a million lives (800,00 to a million in the initial genocide, plus 300,000 Hutu refugees, militia and civilian, slaughtered in

Congo in 1997); at least 200,000 lives were lost in Burundi since the 1993 coup ousted an elected, Hutu-dominated government; and there have been an estimated 1.7 million Congo fatalities since 1998 attributable to the dislocations of internal war, to mention only the Great Lakes cases. The crossborder spillover effect of civil conflicts threatens stability and hopes for sustainable development in adjoining states as well as those torn by violence.

To achieve the aim of contextualizing the current Congo conflicts, I will first re-visit patterns of armed challenge to state instances, beginning with the terminal colonial period in the 1950s. Through this historical excursion, the gradual trans-formation of parameters of conflict may be illuminated. The chapter then turns to identify those dimensions of contemporary conflict that make their initial appear-ance or become salient only in the last decade. Appraisal of the balance between con-tinuity and rupture will then serve as introduction to the chapters that follow.

The colonial state in its final phases had largely succeeded in its hegemonical pretensions, enforcing its writ throughout its territorial domain and maintaining a civil order largely undisturbed until the rise of armed national liberation move-ments, beginning in Algeria in 1954.[4] In overcoming the often tenacious and de-termined resistance to colonial occupation, the colonial state successfully disarmed the population. In an Africa almost entirely administered by European powers, acquisition of weapons more lethal than spears or muskets was virtually impossible. The remarkable sustained boom of the 1950s put dramatically en-hanced resources in the hands of the state, permitting a reinforcement of the sometimes skeletal framework of administrative presence throughout the terri-tory. As well, for the first time in the colonial period, there was a swift expansion of the previously minimal social infrastructure of schools, clinics, and roads. The 1950s were the sole colonial decade when a substantial increase in real wages oc-curred, along with the opening of new opportunities for a ramifying educated elite. Thus, in most of Africa, at the point of departure of this analysis, the late colonial state bore a reasonable resemblance to the Weberian model of stateness: it exercised effective domination over its territorial domain and had a monopoly on the legitimate use of coercion.[5]

INITIAL FORMS OF AFRICAN CIVIL DISORDER

Anticolonial nationalism rapidly developed in the 1950s, challenging the colonial order. In the great majority of cases, the weapons of nationalist organizers were in-ternal political agitation and skillful recourse to an international audience and diplo-matic realm increasingly hostile to the colonial system. The greater adventure of armed challenge to the metropolitan powers was neither necessary nor easily feasi-ble. In Congo, for example, the critical episodes that so shook a once-invincible colonial administration ("Bula Matari," or crusher of rocks, in popular parlance[6]) were the leaderless, spontaneous convulsion of the January 1959 Kinshasa (Leopoldville) riots and the spread of civil disobedience in such key regions as Lower Congo, Kwilu, and Maniema later that year. The international and domestic politi-cal costs of seeking to crush the turbulent, hydra-headed anticolonial movement in Congo were beyond contemplation. A suddenly deflated and demoralized colonizer conceded immediate independence in January 1960.

In a pair of cases, Kenya (1952--57) and Cameroon (1955--60), rebellion against colonial authority in the 1950s took a violent though ultimately unsuccessful form, necessitating the dispatch of regular troops from metropolitan forces. In both these instances, armed uprising accelerated evolution toward independence but was contained and subdued by the reinforced colonial security forces. The uprisings were fatally weakened by a lack of weapons, military knowledge and skills, and their dependence on specific ethnic groups for support (Kikuyu and closely related Meru and Embu in Kenya, Bassa and Bamileke in Cameroon). As well, the rebels were surrounded by other territories still under colonial rule; transborder operation and sanctuary were impossible.[7]

In five cases, national liberation movements, confronting an adversary that categorically rejected decolonization, launched armed struggles that defined the independence combat (Algeria, Guinea-Bissau, Angola, Mozambique, Zimbabwe). These liberation struggles, inspired by the success of protracted anticolonial insurrection in Vietnam and Indonesia, had a relatively coherent strategic vision. Prolonged combat was expected, the polarizing impact of which would gradually mobilize growing fractions of the population. Well-developed doctrines of guerrilla warfare, in which Chinese experience played a formative part, informed insurgent action. Actual military defeat of large and well-equipped colonial armies was improbable, but indefinite survival of the guerrilla forces was feasible. In all cases, active support, including sanctuary and facilitation of arms flow, was available from nearby or neighboring states. Although ethnic difference played some part in the dialectic of struggle, in defining lines of division among competing liberation groups (Angola, Zimbabwe), or delineating zones of maximum guerrilla support (Mozambique, Guinea-Bissau), the shared discourse of anticolonial nationalism diminished the saliency of these cleavages. Liberation movements benefited from an increasingly supportive international environment, in terms of active diplomatic backing in world forums, some financial backing (especially from the Nordic states), and military training and arms supply from the former Soviet bloc. Fellow African states supplied external office facilities, passports, and plane tickets for key insurgent operatives. At moments when the purely military situation appeared hopeless, liberation movements drew crucial psychological sustenance from the certainty that historical process operated to their advantage and that eventual triumph was inevitable.

In the final analysis, the survival capacity of the guerrilla movements was decisive; no colonial army was defeated, and in the Algerian and Angolan cases the uprising was all but contained by the metropolitan army. The nationalist capacity to persist in a struggle that might not be ever completely lost but could not be decisively won, however, finally weakened imperial resolve. By the time it did, those leading the insurrection had acquired a standing with the populace that made the terms of settlement evident, with the exception of Angola.

Four other liberation struggles merit note. In two cases, Western Sahara and Eritrea, a territorial identity defined by a colonial domain served as unifying ideology for a revolt against annexation by an African state (Morocco and Ethiopia). In both instances, invocation of *uti possidetis* doctrines of territorial succession commanded only partial and ambiguous international support, as the annexing states were African. Western Sahara insurgents did have important sanctuary and support from Algeria, and their Eritrean counterparts could operate with transit facilities through Sudan. Despite the more unfavorable international environment, both liberation movements built very high levels of support among their populations and survived for a quarter century and three decades respectively.[8]

The other two cases, Namibia and South Africa, fall somewhat outside our comparative field. Although both liberation movements, the South West African People's Organization (SWAPO) and the African National Congress (ANC), had military aims, the decisive struggle was for the mobilization and active engagement of civil society, and for the leveraging of the global opprobrium attached to the apartheid regime at the level of international diplomacy. The level of internal armed conflict was always minimal, and thus supplies no comparative tissue relating to the Great Lakes crises.

In the initial postcolonial years, violent civil conflicts were relatively infrequent. In most countries, successor elites inherited a state apparatus that by inertial force sustained its hegemonic grip and was amply resourced. Independence opened access to new sources of development assistance, relatively generous in the moment of enthusiasm attending new statehood. The momentum of state expansion from the 1950s could be at first maintained, and even accelerated. In a number of countries, but by no means all, anticolonial mobilization had earned a legitimation for the postindependence rulers that was initially robust. The few armed civil conflicts that erupted early in the postindependence period had four sources: botched decolonization, separatist movements, early state failure, and racial oppression (in southern Africa). Each of these conflict patterns will be examined in turn.

Two instances of derelict decolonization management stand out: those of Angola and Congo. In the Angola instance, the Portuguese simply withdrew in November 1975, without having negotiated any succession formula engaging the three major liberation movements, the Movimento Popular de Libertação de Angola (Popular Movement for the Liberation of Angola—MPLA), Frente Nacional de Libertaçao de Angola (National Front for the Liberation of Angola—FNLA), and União Nacional para a Independência Total de Angola (National Union for the Total Independence of Angola—UNITA). The final colonial governors tilted ideologically toward the Marxist-Leninist orientation of the MPLA, whose power seizure in the wake of Portuguese flight was informally facilitated. The real ideological gap between the three movements was relatively shallow, but the Cold War atmosphere then prevailing drew external partners into the fray in a fashion sustaining the illusion of a doctrinal abyss between the three: Cuba and the Soviet Union for the MPLA, Congo and the United States for FNLA, and South Africa for UNITA. Beyond the imported Cold War dimension, the conflict in its early stages drew upon internal cleavages. The MPLA base was built on urban intellectuals, the Luanda mulatto and *assimilado* elite, leftist whites, and the Kimbundu hinterland, whose evangelical patron was the Catholic Church. The FNLA was mostly Kongo, with important connections to the large Angolan Kongo diaspora in Kinshasa. UNITA drew its support above all from Ovimbundu country and disinherited parts of the southeast. The FNLA and UNITA had close connections with different Protestant missions.

After independence, though FNLA soon vanished as an active player, the combat between MPLA and UNITA became far more ferocious, as both sides were equipped with heavy arms by their external patrons. Over time, the very large resources generated by oil and diamond exports became almost entirely devoted to sustaining the civil war. The end of the Cold War and South African apartheid brought the withdrawal of the external patrons, but by this time the warring parties had war machines sustainable by their own endeavors. The ideological patina that once gave a semblance of doctrinal meaning to the combat evaporated, with Soviet and Cuban withdrawal and MPLA abandonment of official Marxism-Leninism. Emblematic of the changing nature of the conflict was the metamorphosis of UNITA leader Jonas Savimbi, in Western press terminology, from "freedom fighter" to "warlord." Over time as well, the Angolan civil war developed the array of pathologies comparable to the broader African 1990s pattern; neither contending movement at this juncture has much real support from a populace brutalized, pauperized, and traumatized by a quarter century of unending war and insecurity. Control of the traffic in high value resources (oil and diamonds) permits the warring parties to ignore the disengagement of their political clientele and the overwhelming popular desire for peace.[9]

The chaos attending the Congo power transfer represented an abdication of a different sort. Belgium concluded by late 1959 that its administrative grip on the colony was fast eroding, that a dispatch of metropolitan troops to Congo was politically inconceivable, and that Belgium was too weak to withstand international pressures. The only exit, it then appeared, was concession to the maximum demand of the fragmented nationalists: immediate independence. With the colonial army still in the command of an entirely European officer corps, and only three Africans among the 4,600 persons occupying the top three ranks in the civil service,[10] the calculation was that nominal independence might be granted while the colonial establishment retained effective control during an extended institutional transition after formal power transfer. Known as the "pari congolais," this wager on the improbable comity between boisterous youthful nationalists and a conservative colonial bureaucracy lasted five days; then, within a week, the army mutinied and its European officers were expelled, the overwhelming majority of the Belgian administrators fled, and the wealthiest province, Katanga, seceded with Belgian encouragement.

After an initial wave of violence, mainly the depredations of mutinied soldiers, the inertial hold of the colonial order reasserted itself in most of the country. As well, a United Nations peacekeeping force, numbering 20,000 at its peak, was on its way within a fortnight of independence. Sustained armed confrontation was mainly limited to the secessionist zone of Katanga, where a youth militia (including future president Laurent Kabila) soon emerged to challenge the secession and its intimate links with Belgium and the Katanga colonial establishment, although by the end of 1960 a rival central government was established in Kisangani with its own armed detachments, and a second separatist regime was proclaimed in the diamond-producing zones of South Kasai. Almost everywhere the replacement of the Belgian administrators in the central and provincial institutions by erstwhile clerks, and similar processes at the prefectoral echelons of regional administration, brought a marked deflation in state capacity. This was cushioned at first by the almost uninterrupted action of the Catholic and Protestant missions, which managed much of the social infrastructure, and the colonial corporations. However, after the UN withdrawal, completed in 1964, state deflation and its consequences paved the way for the 1964--65 Congo rebellions, to which I return below.

A second pattern of postcolonial conflict is represented by secessionist movements. Although there were a number of separation claims in the early independence years, for the most part these came from small clusters of disaffected elites who lacked an established political base and had undertaken no organizational preparations to give effect to their sovereignty declarations. Two serious separation movements arose, however, with strong popular backing: Biafra and southern Sudan.[11]

In the Biafran instance, the proclaimed independence in 1967 built upon the federal structure of the Nigerian first republic. The eastern region of Nigeria provided the territorial frame; its intact administrative structure supplied a structural vessel for separation. In the period of deepening ethnic tensions within the armed forces following a 1965 military coup, the army itself had become unscrambled, and the eastern personnel were at the disposition of the secession. The actual warfare thus pitted two segments of the national army, both augmented by rapid new recruitment, against one another in the mode of classic interstate warfare; the Nigerian Federal army, only 10,000 at the moment of independence, was inflated to 150,000 by the end of the 1967--70 civil war.[12] Although the French provided some support to the secession, and four African states (Côte d'Ivoire, Gabon, Tanzania and Zambia) broke ranks to recognize Biafra, the strong antipathy of the international system at that time to state breakup, and the robust Organization of African Unity (OAU) doctrine on the intangibility of existing frontiers, sharply limited external backing.[13] The ultimate defeat of the secession was complete, and the post-conflict national reconciliation policy was effective in preventing any reconstitution of former Biafra soldiers into rogue militia or flow of their weapons into the hands of the disaffected; thus the civil war left no after-effects of violent disorder.

The southern Sudan revolt, in contrast, decanted into what more than four decades later remains an inextricable morass of violence. The trauma began a few months before 1956 independence, with the mutiny of the Equatoria Corps, an army unit whose ranks were southern and officers mostly northern; a number of the initial mutineers became the first generation of insurgents. The driving force in southern insurrection was the failure of the northern elites, who dominated and defined anticolonial nationalism, to acknowledge the cultural divide that separated a north for which Arabism and Islam were the prime talismans of an asserted national identity, and a south whose multiple ethnic selves and religious sensibilities were deeply threatened by such dominant visions.[14] The always-marginal southern voice in Khartoum was all but silenced by 1960, many southern elites sought refuge abroad, and a congeries of insurgent groups took form. In this initial stage, although separation was an implicit program for many, the disunity among both exiles and insurgents, the complex template of ethnic and regional consciousness-shaping alignments, and the dispersed character of resistance to Khartoum inhibited articulation of a clear platform for southern salvation. Even though, in the early stages, southern insurrection had little access to arms or external support, a weakly implanted northern administration exercised only limited control over the area, whose insurgent disposition was sustained by the same fear of cultural annihilation that inhabited part of Igboland during the Nigerian civil war.

A settlement was reached in 1972, granting a degree of autonomy to the southern region and providing substantial cultural reassurance. However, in 1983, Islamism in a more intransigent form was reinstituted as master discourse of Sudanese identity, reinforced in 1989 by a power seizure by the radical Islamist movement, the National Islamic Front, emanation of the Muslim Brotherhood. Rebellion broke out again, this time in more unified and organized fashion, with the Sudanese People's

Liberation Army (SPLA) under the leadership of John Garang. The SPLA official platform called for a reconception of Sudan as a secular state with Arabhood demoted to regional consciousness; thus secularized and de-ethnicized, Sudan could provide a nationhood in which the south could share. Secession, however, remained an implicit option, and, for that matter, the real preference of much of its following. The SPLA now enjoyed far more international support and sustenance than the earlier generation of insurgents. Though the implacable Islamism of Khartoum tended to isolate it, especially after 1989, Garang until 1991 could rely upon sanctuary in Ethiopia and a substantial arms supply.

In 1991, leadership conflicts and a Dinka-Nuer rivalry produced a split in the SPLA at the same time that the overthrow of the Mengistu Haile Meriam regime in Ethiopia resulted in an expulsion of SPLA bases. These developments permitted Khartoum to accelerate an emerging strategy of "southernizing" the war, by arming diverse groups opposed to the Garang SPLA and encouraging marauding and plundering excursions largely directed at civil populations. Although the SPLA found alternative bases, especially in Uganda, and the arms flow into the south escalated, the nature of the violence altered and became an integral part of the 1990s African pathologies of disorder. Increasingly, a permanent insecurity of civil populations produced popular disengagement from the armed contenders, whose action became devoid of social meaning or purpose. Hutchinson and Jok give compelling summation of the metamorphosis from an imagined redemption either through a reinvention of Sudan or southern separation into an abyss of inexplicable and endless violence and total insecurity:

> As local codes of inter- and intra-ethnic warfare have twisted and collapsed beneath the weight of AK-47 rifles and the heavy blows of rival southern military leaders, ordinary Nuer and Dinka men and women have been forced the reassess the social bases of their personal and collective security. And of the many thorny issues requiring rethinking, one of the most fundamental and far-reaching concerned the nature, significance and scope of their ethnic affiliations. On the one hand, this has witnessed the violent rise of "ethno-nationalist" ideologies on previously unimaginable scales within both groups. On the other hand, whatever sense of ethnic unity these groups fostered in the context of continuing political rivalries . . . has been repeatedly shattered from within. Break-away warlords intent on carving out their own domains of military dominance have fractured and destroyed countless local communities.[15]

A third pattern of postcolonial civil strife may be traced to an early version of state failure. The two prime instances are the complex series of revolts that, for a time, all but obliterated the Chad state from 1979 to 1982, and the Congo rebellions of 1964 and 1965. In the Chad case, although this territory was one of the more improbable candidates for the nation-state model, five years of inept misrule by Ngarta Tombalbaye and egregious oppression of the arid and desert north passed before rebellion was provoked. With the dismissal and arrest of key Muslim northern ministers in 1963, political exclusion of the north was complete. Insensitive, oppressive, and predatory behavior of the southern cadres sent to replace French administrators in the north added fuel to the fire, and rebellion broke out in 1965, which, even with episodic commitment of French troops, could not be quelled until 1982, when a northern leader, Hissein Habre, emerged as a compromise ruler ending three years of virtual state collapse. During the period of maximum confused disorder, from

1975 to 1982, a multiplication of armed militia spun off from the main military factions in a manner presaging the 1990s pattern. As well, another precursor was the first emergence of the term "warlord" to characterize the various factional leaders. In the words of Robert Buijtenhuis, by 1977 "war became an industry, a career, and a way of life, as much for the grass-roots rebels as for their leaders." Buijtenhuis adds, "This happened, however, to the detriment of the rural communities that had to bear the brunt of very oppressive 'revolutionary' fiscal policies. Local populations became the victims of arbitrary acts perpetrated by armed young men with no respect whatsoever for law or for traditional moral standards. Under these circumstances, the magical saying: *"je suis combattant"* . . . became a kind of *laissez-passer,* entitling an individual to anything and everything."[16] Strikingly, throughout the basic postulate shared by all contenders was that the unitary, centralized state-as-nation was the imperative framework for resolution.[17]

Congo-Kinshasa was the theater for the other conflict born of precocious state failure. The Congo rebellions, though multiple, cohered around a single discourse of betrayal of independence by imperialist intervention and the martyred memory of the radical nationalism incarnated by the assassinated first prime minister, Patrice Lumumba. Around the theme of a necessary "second independence," insurgents eliminated a central government presence for some months in the northeast quadrant of the country and some parts of the Kwilu district in the southwest. The dramatic deflation of state authority attending a decolonization gone awry, analyzed earlier, was cushioned initially by the security and logistic presence of the UN peacekeeping force throughout the country. The UN withdrawal, and final exclusion of most Lumumbist followers from the Kinshasa regime by late 1963, led to the decision by a number of key Lumumbists in October 1963 to launch an armed uprising. Regime complexion in neighboring Congo-Brazzaville and Burundi offered initial bases for this enterprise. The weakened condition of state fabric, unusual in the 1960s but widespread in the 1990s, permitted a rapid snowballing expansion of rebel forces, especially in the east.

The Kwilu rebel pocket stood out for the ideological coherence of its revolutionary discourse and the didactic ambitions of its leader, Pierre Mulele. Mulelist discourse offered a simplified version of Maoist doctrine and a class exegesis identifying the social enemy as the white collar agents of the state regional administration and their counterparts serving the missions and palm plantation enterprises. Mulele drew together a closely bonded guerrilla following of a few thousand and a larger village support base, which held the national army at bay for several months. Its fatal weakness, beyond the poverty of its armament and isolation from external supply, was an ethnic encapsulation within Pende and Mbundu groups, resulting from the ethnic subtexts read by neighboring groups into its message of social revolution.

The eastern rebellions were far more fragmented, with a looser amalgam of radical nationalist language. Manipulation of a supernatural discourse, promising insurgents invulnerability to government bullets if ritual immunization was obtained and attendant taboos respected, helped motivate young rebels to march against state garrisons. Sharing the same belief system, the weakly disciplined and inadequately led national army on innumerable occasions simply fled without resistance. An unrestrained social anger among the marginalized youth who filled the rebel ranks led to massacres of many thousands of state personnel and others classified as "intellectuals" in the towns overrun. Unlike the Mulele insurgents, based in rural redoubts, the eastern rebels seized the urban centers without any project or capacity to govern them.

Thus, the insurgents were soon victims of their own initial success. In the phase of rapid expansion, armories and vehicles were captured and new recruits added with each new town capture. However, rebel columns quickly reached locations where the Lumumba symbolism resonated less strongly and where they were perceived as alien; as well, national army units became reinforced with mercenaries. Torn by leadership conflicts and deepening disorganization in the zones overrun, rebel forces fell apart before advancing mercenary-spearheaded columns, guided by Belgian and American officers and intelligence operatives.

The legacy of the rebellions was of signal importance for a couple of decades subsequent. Particularly for the regions affected, the rebellions became a collective nightmare, an incubus whose memory long supplied a legitimating disposition for the project of restoration of a strong, centralized, unitary state on the colonial model proposed by President Mobutu after his power seizure in November 1965. Untold thousands had perished at the hands of either the rebels or the national army. Thousands more had fled into the forest to avoid the violence that had become daily fare. Mobutu long invoked the recollection of not only the rebellions, but the entire 1960--65 period as a "pagaille," a disorderly shambles, from which he had saved a nation whose "very existence was threatened . . . from the exterior and the interior" with a social, financial, and political situation that was "catastrophic."[18]

A number of contrasts between the civil wars of the earlier periods and those of the 1990s merit note. The nature of external involvement was radically different, with Belgium and the United States playing limited but decisive roles. Though a belated effort was made by some radical African states—Egypt and Algeria in particular—and the Communist bloc to provide some arms to the insurgents, this gesture was far too late, and had to pass through Sudan, where much of the shipment was captured by southern Sudanese rebels. The rebel militia were not only poorly armed but were lacking any leadership with military knowledge and skills. Beyond confiscation of vehicle parks and liquid resources in banks and commercial establishments in captured towns, insurgents had no notion as to how their insurrection could be financed. Some gold seized from inventories of the Belgian-managed Kilo-Moto mines in the northeast found its way to Uganda, but the sophisticated resource exploitation operations that mark militias of the 1990s were far in the future.[19] Finally, the political language accompanying the rebellions drew upon the purposive visions of anticolonial nationalism, whose full restoration through a "second independence" was a promise that had genuine resonance.

A final form of postcolonial strife, chronologically more recent but still belonging to an immediate postindependence period, issued from South African destabilization policies, undertaken in earnest after 1980. The independence of Zimbabwe in that year sharpened the preexisting conflict between South Africa and the newly independent territories formerly ruled by Portugal. Theories of counter-revolutionary warfare, developed by the French army in Algeria, became absorbed into South African security force doctrine.[20]

The victims of the new South African "total strategy" for repulsing liberation forces were primarily Angola and Mozambique. The primary instruments for pursuit of this goal were opposition militia: UNITA in Angola and Resistencia Naçional Moçambicana (Mozambican National Resistance—RENAMO) in Mozambique.

The tragic destructiveness of the Angolan civil war was discussed earlier. In Mozambique, RENAMO, originally created under the tutelage of the settler Rhodesian security forces, came under South African sponsorship in 1980. An important part of its operations consisted of economic sabotage: railroads, oil pipelines, and other infrastructure. Raids by South African security forces also hit infrastructure targets. As well, these destructive actions drove a million Mozambicans into refugee camps in Malawi. The failings of the Afro-Marxist project of the ruling Frente de Libertação de Mozambique (Liberation Front of Mozambique—FRELIMO) further deepened the impasse; by the late1980s, generalized insecurity affected a large part of the population, which FRELIMO could neither protect nor feed.

CIVIL CONFLICT BEFORE THE 1990S: DISTINCTIVE ASPECTS

Before I turn to the 1990s, a number of observations may be drawn from this review of earlier patterns of disorder. First, and of particular importance, organizers of violent movements and their external partners had purposive agendas rooted in widely respected moral discourses. In the earliest phases, these were national liberation struggles, employing the unifying and territorial discourse of anticolonial mobilization. Leaders of such movements well recognized the improbability of defeat of colonial armies, which had vastly superior numbers and armament; their survival depended upon a capacity to create a popular base. The other kinds of movements examined, to one degree or another, had a project in mind, whether separation or a second independence, which implied the necessity of seeking a constituency for the political ends in mind.

Second, the global environment and the determinants of external involvement in African conflicts were still shaped by the Cold War and marked by interventionist habits of the extra-African world. The interpretive grid through which the major powers constructed their understanding of civil strife in Africa was framed by the Cold War and erected upon zero-sum premises. An African conflict outcome that advantaged one side automatically was a net loss for the other. Conversely, within Africa doctrines the supreme value of state sovereignty, and the sanctity of nonintervention, remained paramount. These principles were contravened on occasion; the Somali army invaded Ethiopia in pursuit of a pan-Somali dream in 1977, at a moment when Ethiopia appeared vulnerable. This initiative was repulsed by Cuban and Soviet forces rallying by Cold War logic behind the newly Marxist-Leninist Ethiopian regime. Tanzania, provoked beyond endurance by the tyrannical escapades of Idi Amin and his occupation of some Tanzanian territory, sent its army, along with a force of Ugandan exiles, to drive Amin from power in 1979. Gabon allowed its territory to be used as a transit for war supplies for Biafra, and Ethiopia openly provided rear bases and sanctuary for the SPLA from 1983 to l991. Libya occupied the Aouzou strip in northern Chad for more than a decade beginning in 1973, and occupied other parts of the country in 1980--81 and 1983--87 in support of diverse opposition militia.[21] But these instances were the exception rather than the rule, and far more frequent was meticulous respect for an African international normative doctrine of nonintervention.

Civil populations often suffered the consequences of combat in their vicinity but were only infrequently the direct target. In some instances, such as the Congo rebellions of 1964–65, segments of the population defined as social enemies (the white collar "intellectual") by insurgents, or as rebel supporters by the national army, were victimized in large numbers. Civil casualties were extensive in the Nigerian civil war, especially as a result of starvation and other dislocations of war. But the scale, intensity, and duration of the insecurity confronting large sectors of the populace as a consequence of civil conflict rarely approximated what lay in store in the 1990s.

Over time, modern weapons gradually became more available in informal markets and to insurgent groups. Before the 1990s the primary exceptions were the Biafrans, fighting as a conventional army and UNITA, beneficiary of a large-scale supply of heavy weapons through the 1980s, primarily from South Africa, and after the 1986 repeal of the Clark Amendment openly from the United States. But movements such as the first- and early second-generation southern Sudan rebels, or the 1964 Congo insurgents, had only limited arms supplies.

NEW PATTERNS OF VIOLENT CIVIL CONFLICT IN THE 1990S

We may now turn to the crucial changes in the 1990s. Fundamental was the transformation of the international order marked by the collapse of the Soviet Union in 1991. Even in the 1980s, Soviet motivations for an activist African policy were waning. Disillusionment grew with the prospects for Afro-Marxism and the prospects for the once-widely touted noncapitalist road to development. The resolution of the Namibian decolonization question in 1989, accompanied by the withdrawal of Cuban troops from Angola and the subsequent demise of the apartheid regime in South Africa, weakened Cold War reflexes in American policy. With the genuine resolution of the Mozambican civil war, the illusory accord in Angola in 1992, and the 1991 American-brokered dissolution of the Afro-Marxist Mengistu regime in Ethiopia, U.S. preoccupations with Soviet activity in Africa finally dissolved.

Within Africa, profound mutations in the language of conflict took place. Marxism-Leninism vanished from regime discourse. The independence of Namibia and Eritrea, and the final death of apartheid in South Africa, brought the era of national liberation struggle to a close. The Western Sahara issue remained alive, to be sure, but its violent phase was long past, active struggle was dormant, and deep engagement with the issue was limited to Morocco as the de facto annexing state and Algeria as patron of the exiled Frente Popular para la Liberación de Seguia el-Hamra y Río de Oro (Popular Front for the Liberation of Seguia el-Hamra and Rio de Oro— POLISARIO). The long era of ideological primacy for national liberation struggle, which opened with the beginning of the Algerian liberation war in 1954, had ended.

In its place came newly salient and highly divisive tropes of solidarity. A militantly Islamic regime seized power by military coup in Sudan in 1989. The legitimating claim that it was the incarnation of the anticolonial revolution that had long justified single party rule by the Front de Libération Nationale (National Liberation Front—FLN) in Algeria lost its credibility in a wave of urban protest in 1988; the competitive elections beginning in 1991 were on the verge of bringing the Islamist Front Islamique de Salut (Islamic Salvation Front—FIS) to power when the military intervened to forestall this outcome in January 1992. The result has been a decade of violence, both repeated massacres of civil populations by fragments of the Groupe Islamique Armé and lethal ripostes by the national army. The religious line of division in a Nigeria almost evenly

divided between Muslims and Christians, of little consequence in the early independence years, had come to rival ethnicity as a polarizing cleavage by the 1990s. In 1993
in Burundi and especially 1994 in Rwanda, the genocidal risks in total escalation of
zero-sum ethnic conflicts became clear.

A framing factor in the threats to civil order, less noted in the 1980s than the
overexpanded and underperforming character of states often seen by the citizenry
as oppressive and predatory,[22] was the corrosion of stateness in many parts of the
continent. A few analytical voices had suggested by the 1980s that state sovereignty
in Africa was in good part only a fiction of the international juridical order, that
African states were merely "quasi-states."[23] But events of the 1990s brought force-
fully home the serious weakening of the state fabric in many African polities. Most
dramatically revelatory was the actual full collapse of states in Liberia in 1990 and
Somalia in 1991. By 1992, Sierra Leone had all but ceased to function as a recogniz-
able state.[24] In Congo-Kinshasa, by 1994, former Assistant Secretary of State for
African Affairs Herman Cohen observed, "To say that [Congo-Kinshasa] has a government today would be a gross exaggeration."[25] The Mobutu regime had a tenuous
grip on Kinshasa, the remote presidential palace in Gbadolite, the central bank, and
some flow of diamond receipts; by 1994, the World Bank had ceased including
Congo-Kinshasa data in its statistical tables, and the International Monetary Fund
had expelled the country.

More frequent than actual collapse is a pervasive weakening of the fabric of stateness, or some degree of state failure. As Jennifer Widner argues, for a number of
African states the crucial question of the 1990s was less the sustainability of democratization or economic reform than state effectiveness itself: "Parallel political authorities—warlords, kingdoms, new religious groups—often make stronger claims
on obedience than do nation-states and compete with nation-states as centers of
revenue collection and regulation. Pervasive personal insecurity, a result of the
spread of cheap and therefore "democratic" weaponry such as grenades, AK-47s, and
land mines, undermines norms that support savings, maintenance, and investment.
At issue in these cases is not policy per se but the every existence of states."[26]

State weakening was a cumulative process, at first not visible to the naked eye.
The two decades of steady economic decline, beginning in the 1970s, brought con-
tracting revenue flows in tandem with a continuing momentum of state expansion;
the initial temptation was recourse to external borrowing or use of development assistance loans, a major source of the debt crisis evident by 1980. The structural adjustment programs forced upon African states by the international financial
organizations and Western donor community were, for an extended period,
founded upon unrealistic premises about the early beneficial effects of the "therapy"
and the foreign investment flows that would underwrite recovery. African states in
turn only partially applied economic reform measures. Regimes declined to wean
themselves from diversion of resources, to sustain neopatrimonial networks deemed
essential to survival, and to privilege security expenditures over social outlays. Unsustainable public sector wage bills were managed by devaluing the real value of civil
service salaries in preference to force reductions, and not infrequently by permitting
salary arrearages to build up. These measures in turn brought increasing demoral-
ization to public servants and the imperative necessity for state employees to find
supplementary income through additional employment or other means to survive.
Those social services most prized by ordinary citizens—education and health service

in particular—experienced sharp declines in availability or the necessity of informal payments for access. These patterns inevitably took their toll on the legitimacy of states and their practical capacity to govern their territories.

By way of prelude to the syndrome of civil conflict in the 1990s, a novel mode of regime displacement opened in 1979, with the overthrow of Idi Amin in Uganda by a polyglot force of Ugandan exiles spearheaded by the Tanzanian army. In contrast to a military coup, in which extant security forces remain intact, the standard form of regime change in the autocratic decades was forceful government overthrow from the periphery or the outside, resulting in a dissolution of the existing army, whose personnel flee to neighboring states or their home communities, with their arms entering hidden caches or informal markets. Uganda was a paradigmatic case; Amin's former soldiers turned up as reconstituted militia in northwest Congo-Kinshasa and southern Sudan, and Karimojong warriors emptied well-stocked armories at Moyo and Kotido, producing a dramatic escalation of lethal forms of cattle raiding.[27] Similar kinds of regime change then followed in Chad (1990), Liberia (1990), Ethiopia (1991), Somalia (1991), Rwanda (1994), Congo-Kinshasa (1996), and Congo-Brazzaville (1997); everywhere the consequences were similar and opened the door to violent militias far better armed than insurgents in the past.

The increase in black market weaponry was huge, abetted by several sources. Ethiopia and Somalia had two of Africa's largest armies in 1991 when their regimes dissolved and their weaponry vanished into the informal economy. The multiplication of armed conflicts motivated aggressive weapons acquisitions by embattled regimes, a fraction of which leaked into parallel markets or opposing militia; Angola and Sudan were especially dramatic examples. A combination of imploded and bankrupt states and vast weapons stockpiles made such countries as Bulgaria, Ukraine, and the Russian Federation major suppliers of official and unofficial arms markets in Africa, though western arms merchants were by no means passive bystanders.

The dissolution of existing armies made available not only foot soldiers of rebellion but experienced officers who learned their trade at the finest military training centers in the United States, Britain, France, China, and elsewhere. This cadre of officers with sophisticated military knowledge gave a fighting capacity to contemporary insurgents that bears no relationship to that, say, of the 1964 Congo rebels. A Malian colonel, in a military academy paper, makes the interesting point that Tuareg insurgency in northern Mali, crushed with great brutality in the early 1960s, could not be defeated when a second uprising broke out at the beginning of the 1990s. The new factor: leading the uprising were several veterans of the anti-Soviet warfare in Afghanistan, whose experience and skills made the guerrillas far more formidable. Negotiated settlement rather than military victory was the necessary option.[28]

Contemporary insurgents have developed an ability to sustain themselves through traffic in high value resources under their control. Emblematic of the changing patterns of insurgent war finance is Angola. Through the 1980s, UNITA forces operated in areas of southern Angola devoid of such resources; their needs were met by access to South African, American, and some other supply and funding. In the 1990s, UNITA, now shorn of Cold War support, shifted its military operations to the diamond fields and found a lucrative means of sustaining itself. Charles Taylor in Liberia was another pioneer in the use of illicit trade in diamonds and timber to fund insurgency, serving as tutor and mercantile intermediary for his Sierra

Leone satellite movement, the Revolutionary United Front (RUF). All the Congo-Kinshasa armed factions since 1998 have financed their operations in this manner. So also, in large measure, have the foreign armies supporting one or another of the factions (Rwanda, Uganda, Burundi, Zimbabwe, Angola, and Namibia).

Such a mode of war finance has important repercussions for the nature of the militia. Any motivation to seek popular support evaporates; having responsibility for servicing populations only dissipates resources better used in pursuit of warfare. The key object is control of the resource source; responsibility for a civil population becomes a needless burden.[29] Violence, in such circumstances, becomes an end in itself, lending some credence to the controversial Chabal-Daloz thesis that African politics is essentially defined by an "instrumentalization of disorder."[30]

Thus in the 1990s there appeared a rogue's gallery of violent militia who enjoyed virtually no popular base, but yet were able to sustain their insurgency virtually indefinitely. Many examples of this pathology dotted the continent. The RUF in Sierra Leone was a prime instance; its innumerable atrocities directed at civil populations in its zones of operations bore stark witness to its normlessness. So also were the Allied Democratic Forces (ADF) and Lord's Resistance Army (LRA) in Uganda.[31] Increasingly, movements that once enjoyed substantial regional support, such as the SPLA in Sudan or UNITA in Angola, became indistinguishable from other warlord militia, their former popular base disaffected by the unending violence and total insecurity. The four warring factions in Congo-Kinshasa fell in this category; all were led by individuals who had been out of the country for many years, while the internal opposition to the Mobutu regime remained marginalized, voiceless, and paralyzed.

The absence of popular backing, indeed the bitter animosity felt toward the insurgent militia in zones where they operated, frequently made recruitment of adult soldiers difficult. Another central element in the violence syndrome of the 1990s was the widespread practice of abducting children, who through brutalization, terror, and drugs were transformed into child soldiers. This practice emerged in Mozambique in the mid-1980s, as RENAMO lost some of its South African support after the 1984 Nkomati agreement between the South African and Mozambican governments.[32] Child soldiers became essential to the RUF in Sierra Leone, the LRA and ADF in Uganda, and were widely used in Congo-Kinshasa.[33] Once abducted and isolated from kin and community, inspired by the promise of supernatural immunization against bullets and drugs, the child soldier was a fearsome warrior. They also became aware that their villages would not welcome them back. Adolescent boys were feared as violent sociopaths, and girls were irreparably damaged by sexual abuse and exposure to AIDS.

Child soldiers were not always indispensable. The urban slums and refugee camps also provided a supply of unemployed, impoverished, and disaffected youths. The violent ethnoregional militia that ravaged Congo-Brazzaville in 1993, then again in 1997, sprang from such milieux. The 1997 wave of property destruction, looting, and killing took an officially estimated 10,000 to 15,000 lives. Although the violence subsided when Denis Sassou-Nguesso seized power with Angolan military backing in 1997, the cultural pathologies generated by these rampages of violent ethnopolitical militia tended to become enrooted. As Bazenguissa-Ganga argues, " . . . an analysis of the violence of the period, considered in terms other than as a dysfunctioning of the democratic process, can reveal much about the way in which political practice in Congo has been transformed. This amounts to a redefinition of common social experience and popular conceptions of social status, the true subject of the various conflicts which have been so tragically militarized."[34]

Dramatic new technologies of communication enhanced the capabilities of militia operating in remote locations. Cellular phones connected warlords with the global media and arms merchants. The possibility of instant media access and feasibility of swift long-distance transactions added further novel elements to the repertoire of insurgency.

Finally, as civil conflicts persisted over decades in such pivotal instances as Angola and Sudan, the patterns of disorder spilled across borders in ways that made resolution far more complex. Whereas in previous decades intervention frequently came from outside Africa, driven by Cold War logic or, in the French case, the dictates of *francophonie* and a French-protected *pré carré*, in the 1990s the external world drew back from involvement in African conflicts. In its place came a much more active African disposition to intervene militarily, primarily arising from two very distinct motivations. On the one hand, the absolutist doctrines of sovereignty and the sacralization of nonintervention dominant in OAU norms before 1990 gave way to notions of humanitarian intervention and African peacekeeping responsibilities. Emblematic of this altered perspective was the Nigerian deployment in Liberia in 1990, ostensibly on behalf of the Economic Community of West African States (ECOWAS), and subsequent dispatch of Nigerian troops to Sierra Leone and Angola on peacekeeping missions. Also fitting this pattern was the decision of Zimbabwe, Angola, and Namibia to answer the appeal of President Kabila, addressed to the Southern African Development Community (SADC), for military aid to confront Rwandan and Ugandan armed forces entering his country as sponsors of the Rassemblement Congolais pour la Démocratie (Congolese Rally for Democracy—RCD) rebels.

On the other hand, the new willingness to intervene was for security-driven reasons of state. The crucial Rwandan and Ugandan intervention in Congo-Kinshasa, in both 1996–1997 and 1998 onward, was indisputably motivated by the continued operations from Congo territory of former Rwandan army and *Interahamwe* Hutu militia, held responsible for the 1994 genocide. Ugandan and Burundian military deployments in Congo were similarly motivated, at least in part, by the operation of insurgent factions from Congolese bases.[35] The sharp Sudanese escalation of its weapons supply to the LRA in 1994 was clearly tied to frustration over Ugandan sanctuary for SPLA action. Senegal intervened in Guinea-Bissau in 1998 in good measure because restive elements in the Guinea-Bissau military had been suspected of providing arms and sanctuary for Casamance rebels. Angolan intervention in Congo-Kinshasa since 1996, and Congo-Brazzaville since 1997, arose from the determination to deny external facilities to UNITA.

These new rules of crossborder engagement lent a singular intractability to conflicts such as those of Sierra Leone and Congo-Kinshasa. In the latter, each of the six African states with military forces deployed in 2000 had a distinct roster of security or other preoccupations. Finding the least common denominator among these conflicting agendas, while simultaneously providing minimal satisfaction to the four domestic military factions as well as a civil society entirely unrepresented in the armed confrontation requires a solomonic wisdom.

<u>*CONCLUDING REFLECTIONS*</u>

By way of conclusion, several observations emerge from this exegesis of civil disorder in Africa. A sea change in the world order in the 1990s has altered the basic texture of the linkages between Africa and the global system of states as well as the international normative domain. At the same time, a gradual weakening of the fabric of stateness occurred in many African countries, a product of the prolonged economic crisis beginning in the 1970s and the delegitimation of patrimonial autocracy as a mode of rule. Democratization and economic reform, however indispensable, have not as yet provided a universal remedy for state weakness.

These broad transformations have increased the vulnerability of African states to civil conflict. Meanwhile, armed challengers to public order have acquired new capabilities in the 1990s. In a number of cases, regime displacement has resulted in a dissolution of existing security forces, dispersing to the four corners of the continent trained soldiers, skilled officers, and abundant weapons. Throughout the continent, even in the many countries free of dissident armed militias, ready availability of lethal weapons at bargain prices transforms the balance of force between government security establishments and disaffected armed bands, or even apolitical criminals. So also do new communication technologies and the exploitation of child soldiers.

The smuggling of resources of high value relative to their bulk, very limited in colonial times, became a significant pattern by the late 1960s. However, mercantile exploitation of such commodities by warlords assumed importance only in the 1990s; "blood diamonds" are a new phenomenon. Rebel groups such as UNITA, the RUF, or the three Congo-Kinshasa rebel fragments acquired a survival capacity rendering them largely independent of any need for local support.

The contrast with earlier patterns of armed conflict is sharp. Gone are the mobilizing discourses of radical anti-imperial nationalism and the dreams of socialist transformation. Some protagonists, such as Ernest Wamba of the RCD-Bunia, may have been inspired by a commitment to genuine democratization. However, one struggles in vain to perceive any ennobling vision in such warlords as Fodoy Sankoh, Joseph Kony, Charles Taylor or Jonas Savimbi.

This retrospective on earlier forms of armed conflict in postwar Africa and focus upon the forms of patterned violence particular to the 1990s provide a sobering context for reflection on the magnitude of the challenge for finding a formula for a stable peace in Congo-Kinshasa and the Great Lakes region. But equally evident are the terrible human costs of a prolongation of the regional pattern of low-intensity warfare dating from the Rwandan Patriotic Front invasion of its homeland from Uganda in 1990. The banalization of insecurity, the diffusion of a youth culture of violence, and the creation of a vicious circle of fear and vengeance are the inevitable products of a perpetuation of the conflict. Resolution in Congo cannot lie in the military triumph of any of the contenders. In some adapted form, only democratization can offer an acceptable exit from impasse. This in turn opens a possibility (not a certainty) of a state capable of connecting to an emergent civil society, a precondition for restoring a public economy and breaking the cycle of relentless impoverishment that set in during the 1970s.

1. Congo-Kinshasa has borne several official designations since its 1960 independence. From 1971 to 1997, the country was rebaptised as Zaire by former president Mobutu Sese Seko. Upon his May 1997 seizure of power, with the crucial armed backing of Rwanda, Angola, and Uganda, and self-proclamation as president, Laurent Kabila resurrected an earlier designation of his country as the "Democratic Republic of the Congo." Since the "democratic" designation is a grotesque misrepresentation of political practice, save only for the briefest moment at the beginning of the 1960s, I resort to earlier common convention and employ the designation of "Congo-Kinshasa" or simply "Congo" for the entire postindependence period. The other Republic of Congo will be always be labeled "Congo-Brazzaville."

2. Algeria, Angola, Burundi, Central African Republic, Chad, Comoros, Congo-Brazzaville, Congo-Kinshasa, Ethiopia, Ghana, Guinea, Guinea-Bissau, Liberia, Mali, Morocco/Western Sahara, Mozambique, Niger, Nigeria, Rwanda, Senegal, Sierra Leone, Somalia, Sudan, and Uganda.

3. Ted Robert Gurr, "Ethnic Warfare on the Wane," *Foreign Affairs* 79, no. 3 (May/June 2000): 52–64.

4. Crawford Young, *The African Colonial State in Comparative Perspective* (New Haven: Yale University Press, 1994), 182–217.

5. Not all analysts agree on this point. For a work stressing the weakness of the colonial state, as well as its precolonial and postcolonial predecessors and successors, see Jeffrey Herbst, *States and Power in Africa: Comparative Lessons in Authority and Control* (Princeton: Princeton University Press, 2000). For a discussion of stateness, see the chapters by Mark R. Beissinger and Crawford Young in *Beyond State Crisis? Africa and Post-Soviet Eurasia in Comparative Perspective* (Washington: Wilson Center Press, forthcoming).

6. For the origins and meaning of the "Bula Matari" label for Belgian colonial rule, see Crawford Young and Thomas Turner, *The Rise and Decline of the Zairian State* (Madison: University of Wisconsin Press, 1985), 30–37.

7. Among an abundant literature, for Kenya Carl G. Rosberg and John Nottingham, *The Myth of Mau Mau: Nationalism in Kenya* (New York: Frederick A. Praeger Publishers, 1966), remains a basic work. See also David F. Gordon, *Decolonization and the State in Kenya* (Boulder, CO: Westview Press, 1986). On Cameroon, see in particular Richard A. Joseph, *Radical Nationalism in the Cameroun* (Oxford: Clarendon Press, 1977), and Victor T. Le Vine, *The Cameroons from Mandate to Independence* (Berkeley: University of California Press, 1964).

8. Substantial literature exists for the Eritrean struggle; Ruth Iyob, *The Eritrean Struggle for Independence: Domination, Resistance, Nationalism, 1941–1993* (Cambridge: Cambridge University Press, 1995) provides one definitive study; on the Ethiopian side, see also Dawit Wolde Giorgis, *Red Tears: War, Famine and Revolution in Ethiopia* (Trenton: Red Sea Press, 1989). On the Western Sahara, see John Damis, *Conflict in Northwest Africa: The Western Sahara Dispute* (Stanford: Hoover Institution Press, 1983), and Tony Hodges, *Western Sahara: The Roots of a Desert War* (Westport: Lawrence Hill & Company, 1983).

9. Particularly valuable on the early stages of the Angolan conflict is John A. Marcum, *The Angolan Revolution*, 2 vols. (Cambridge: MIT Press, 1969, 1978). For thoughtful treatment of the Angolan crisis in both historical and contemporary perspective, see Linda Heywood, *Contested Power in Angola: 1840s to the Present* (Rochester: University of Rochester Press, 2000).

10. Crawford Young, *Politics in the Congo* (Princeton: Princeton University Press, 1965), 402.

11. Eritrea, often termed an example of secession, is better classified as a national liberation movement, accepting its own doctrinal self-definition as a former colony abusively annexed by a neighboring African state.

12. On the Nigerian army, see Robin Luckham, *The Nigerian Military* (Cambridge: Cambridge University Press, 1971); Theophilus Olatunde Odetola, *Military Politics in Nigeria* (New Brunswick: Transaction Books, 1978); and Jiri Peters, *The Nigerian Military and the State* (London: Tauris Academic Studies, 1997).

13. See especially John Stremlau, *The International Politics of the Nigerian Civil War 1967–1970* (Princeton: Princeton University Press, 1977); Crawford Young, "Comparative Claims to Political Sovereignty: Biafra, Katanga, Eritrea," in Donald Rothchild and Victor A. Olorunsola, eds., *State Versus Ethnic Claims: African Policy Dilemmas* (Boulder, CO: Westview Press, 1983), 199–232.

14. Francis M. Deng gives masterful analysis of the inner essence of the Sudan north–south division in *War of Visions: Conflict of Identities in the Sudan* (Washington: Brookings Institution, 1995).

15. Sharon Elaine Hutchinson and Jok Madut Jok, "Gendered Violence and the Militarization of Ethnicity: A Case Study from South Sudan," typescript, 2001. See also Jok and Hutchinson, "Sudan's Prolonged Second Civil War and the Militarization of Nuer and Dinka Ethnic Identities," *African Studies Review* 42, no. 2 (1999): 125–145. The invaluable earlier Hutchinson monograph, *Nuer Dilemmas: Coping with Money, War and the State* (Berkeley: University of California Press, 1996), shows the significant but far more limited impact of the first civil war.

16. Robert Buijtenuis, "Chad in the Age of the Warlords," in David Birmingham and Phyllis M. Martin, *History of Central Africa: The Contemporary Years since 1960* (London: Longman, 1998), 29–30.

17. Abderahman Dadi, *Tchad: L'état retrouvé* (Paris: L'Harmattan, 1987), 14. See also Robert Buijtenhuis, *Le Frolinat et les révoltes populaires du Tchad, 1965–1976* (The Hague: Mouton, 1978), Gali Ngothe Gatta, *Tchad: Guerre civile et désaggrégation de l'état* (Paris: Présence Africaine, 1985), and Sam C. Nolotshungu, *Limits of Anarchy: Intervention and State Formation in Chad* (Charlottesville: University Press of Virginia, 1996).

18. Young and Turner, *Rise and Decline of the Zairian State*, 42.

19. On the Congo rebellions, see especially Catherine Coquéry-Vidrovitch, Alain Forest, and Herbert Weiss, *Rébellions-Révolution au Zaire 1963–1965*, 2 vols. (Paris: L'Harmattan, 1987); Benoit Verhaegen, *Rébellions au Congo* (Brussels: Centre de Recherche et d'Information Socio-Politiques, 1966, 1969); and Crawford Young, "Rebellion and the Congo," in Robert I. Rotberg and Ali A. Mazrui, eds., *Protest and Power in Black Africa* (New York: Oxford University Press, 1970), 969–1011.

20. On this phenomenon and its impact, see Joseph Hanlon, *Beggar Your Neighbours: Apartheid Power in Southern Africa* (Bloomington: Indiana University Press, 1986), and Margaret Hall and Tom Young, *Confronting Leviathan: Mozambique since Independence* (Athens: Ohio University Press, 1997).

21. Bernard Lanne, *Tchad-Libye; La querelle des frontières* (Paris: Editions Karthala, 1982).

22. See, for example, Jaean-François Bayart, *L'Etat au Cameroun* (Paris: Presses de la Fondation Nationale des Sciences Politiques, 1979); Comi M. Toulabor, *Le Togo sous Eyadema* (Paris: Karthala, 1986); Thomas M. Callaghy, *The State–Society Struggle: Zaire in Comparative Perspective* (New York: Columbia University Press, 1984); and Young and Turner, *Rise and Decline of the Zairian State*.

23. This argument was first made by Robert H. Jackson and Carl G. Rosberg, "Why Africa's Weak States Persist: The Empirical and the Juridical in Statehood," *World Politics* 35 (October 1982): 1–24, then elaborated by Jackson in *Quasi-States: Sovereignty, International Relations, and the Third World* (Cambridge: Cambridge University Press, 1990).

24. William Reno, *Corruption and State Politics in Sierra Leone* (New York: Cambridge University Press, 1995) and *Warlord Politics and African States* (Boulder, CO: Lynne Rienner Publishers, 1998).

25. Herbert Weiss, "Zaire: Collapsed Society, Surviving State, Future Polity," in I. William Zartman, *Collapsed States: The Disintegration and Restoration of Legitimate Authority* (Boulder, CO: Lynne Rienner Publishers, 1995), 157.

26. Jennifer A. Widner, "States and Statelessness in Late Twentieth-Century Africa," *Daedalus* 124, no. 3 (summer 1995): 129.

27. Mustafa Mirzeler and Crawford Young, "Pastoral Politics in the Northeast Periphery in Uganda: AK-47 as Change Agent," *Journal of Modern African Studies* 38, no. 3 (2000): 407–430.

28. Lt. Col. Kalifa Keita, "Conflict and Conflict Resolution in the Sahel: The Tuareg Insurgency in Mali," pamphlet, Strategic Studies Institute, U.S. Army War College, May 1998.

29. This logic of mercantile insurgency is well captured by Reno, *Warlord Politics.*

30. Patrick Chabal and Jean-Pascal Daloz, *Africa Works: Disorder as Political Instrument* (Oxford: James Currey, 1999).

31. On the LRA, see Heike Behrend, "The Holy Spirit Movement's New World: Discourse and Development in Northern Uganda," in Holger Bernt Hansen and Michael Twaddle, eds., *Developing Uganda* (Oxford: James Currey, 1998), 245–253; Ruddy Doom and Koen Vlassenroot, "Kony's Message: A New *Koine?* The Lord's Resistance Army in Northern Uganda," *African Affairs* 98 (1999): 5–36; Robert Gersony, "The Agony of Northern Uganda: Results of a Field-Based Assessment of the Civil Conflicts in Northern Uganda," (Kampala: USAID, 1997). Sallie Simba Kayunga examines both movements in "The Impact of Armed Opposition on the Movement System," in Justus Mugaju and J. Oloka-Onyango, eds., *No-Party Democracy in Uganda: Myths and Realities* (Kampala: Fountain Publishers, 2000), 109–126.

32. Hall and Young, *Confronting Leviathan,* 167–170.

33. See the eloquent testimonials by former Sierra Leone child soldiers in Krijn Peters and Paul Richards, "Youths in Sierra Leone: 'Why We Fight,'" *Africa* 68, no. 2 (1998): 183–210.

34. Remy Bazenguissa-Ganga, "The Spread of Political Violence in Congo-Brazzaville," *African Affairs* 98 (1999): 54.

35. Clark's chapter 9 in this volume makes a persuasive case for a different explanation in the Ugandan instance. I believe, however, that in the initial choice to intervene the security imperative played an important role, even if other motivations developed as the intervention expanded in scope and reach.

CHAPTER 3

Historicity of a Crisis

THE ORIGINS OF THE CONGO WAR[1]

JERMAINE O. MCCALPIN

INTRODUCTION

C ongo is a physically imposing country nestled in the heart of Africa. It is the continent's second largest country, rich in natural resources such as copper, cobalt, diamonds, and gold. It is also home to the Congo River and Inga dams, which could be meaningful sources of hydropower if they were properly utilized. Given its natural resource base and sheer size, Congo stands likely to be an engine of development for central Africa. Congo's grandeur and potential for greatness, however, have been besmirched by a recent history of crisis. The contemporary crisis to which I allude is powerful because it has economic and social dimensions as well as political ones, leaving Congo in a bewildering—but not irreversible—situation.

The configuration of the contemporary Congolese polity is not to be viewed as simply the general disorder that has come to characterize African states but rather as a direct result of crosscutting influences in its particular history.[2] The current situation represents the superimposition of an overdeveloped, extractive, and predatory state upon the vestiges of traditional societies and an ethnic mosaic. This in turn has served to complicate Congo's present as well as its future.[3] Nonetheless, my focus in this chapter will be the origins (historicity) of Congo crisis beginning in 1996 and not the crisis itself, although the crisis inevitably serves as a backdrop to any contemporary discussion. The fundamental assertion of this chapter is that the crisis was not a sudden or unlikely outcome, given Congo's history. Nonetheless, given these predisposing conditions, the crisis was still not an inevitable outcome.

The crisis in the Congo cannot be understood as an event in isolation; it is the result of a series of postcolonial tragedies that exacerbated the legacies of a harsh colonialism and a miscalculated independence. First, the strength of these legacies made the Congo crisis very likely, even if they did not make it inevitable. To argue that legacies made present occurrences inevitable, and therefore unavoidable, would be too deterministic. Second, this crisis is not only consequential for Congo, but for neighboring states, as well. It has the potential of spreading throughout central Africa especially because of the series of crises set off by political maneuvers to manipulate interethnic tensions in neighboring countries. Indeed the crisis has implications for security and stability throughout Africa. Finally, the historical development of crisis and conflict in contemporary Africa is not a neat, linear process. Congo appears to be an appropriate case study of the nature and types of conflicts that are bedeviling Africa today.[4] Along with Liberia and Sierra Leone, Congo appears to be portending all the unfortunate symptoms of failing states, where the rule of law is subverted by a "khakistocracy" of warlords and other such antidemocratic forces.

In order to adequately examine the assertions of this chapter, I will discuss Congo's development through a set of historical stages, from the era of King Leopold's Congo through Belgian colonialism to the postcolonial era, developing several key ideas in the process. The first was the era of the personal possession of King Leopold between 1885 and 1908, and its implications for posterity. The Belgian colonial era with its enormous impact on Congolese society followed. Finally, a disjointed and hasty independence of the Congo worsened the effects of the colonial state. This crisis of independence created an auspicious occasion for Mobutu Sese Seko to emerge and to consolidate his regime. The regime made itself ubiquitous and held Congo together in what I choose to call "ordered chaos." Mobutu's coup d'état also represented the failure of the Congolese political elite to construct a coherent state that would have contained, if not solved, the problems of ethnicity and regionalism. When this fragile but expansive state began to crumble in the 1990s, all the bombs that had laid buried, bombs like ethnic tensions and the pent up frustrations of poverty and underdevelopment, detonated into conflict in 1996--97. This conflict eventually toppled the regime. In none of the stages described had a prodemocratic political culture been allowed to emerge. One can only wait in cautious optimism to see whether the current war and its end will lay the basis for a resurgent Congo, or whether the tragedies of colonialism and independence will continue to exercise their negative influences over Congo's future.

THE IMPOSITION OF ALIEN RULE

Congo has had contact with the external world since the fifteenth century, when Portuguese explorers navigated the Congo River.[5] These early contacts laid the basis for trade among the Portuguese, Arabs, and the BaKongo people. What was clear from all the trading, however, was that Congo would be exploited for its economic potential. These exchanges with the outside world also laid the basis for a fragmented society shaped by the complexities of ethnic divisions and dependent economic relations. Rivalries developed along the trading posts, and some ethnic groups were afforded more access to trade than others. This provided the context for future competitions among ethnic groups in their bid to access and obtain the scarce resources. The slave and ivory trade flourished for over two centuries and continued until the late nineteenth century, when a new and more intense phase of contact with Europe began.

Henry Morton Stanley was asked by King Leopold to continue the explorations of David Livingstone into the Congo interior and along the great Congo River.[6] He spent three years in Congo doing so and then returned to Europe in 1877. King Leopold, on hearing of the natural resource potential of Congo, became interested in a "scientific exploration" of Congo. He hired Stanley under the guise of explorer for the Survey Committee of the Upper Congo. After those three years Congo quickly became the personal property of the King.[7] This action prompted the Conference of Berlin of 1884--85 where it was formally acknowledged that Congo was King Leopold's personal possession, setting off the "scramble for Africa."

In 1885 this personal property of King Leopold became the "Congo Free State." Leopold's ambition was intrinsically the exploitation of Congo's natural resources for economic gain. The native Congolese were in conflict over these resources and eventually Congo Free State became the colonial extractive state. The fragmented territory was united through force and repression as the extant villages and kingdoms became absorbed into Congo Free State.

The administration of Congo Free State, based on exploitation and extraction, had by 1906 divided Congo into fifteen provinces, and each became the administrative responsibility of a "commissar." These units were arbitrarily defined, beginning what became one of Congo's chronic problems: the arbitrariness of internal borders and the attendant problems for ethnic relations and interactions. The creation of a monolithic state destroyed the native polities, but not the ethnopolitical identity on which they were based. Meanwhile, Leopold's state developed the monopoly on trade. This exclusion of the natives cannot be ignored, as it reemerges in the colonial era, when a native economic elite was neither encouraged nor even allowed to develop on its own. A national political consciousness was nonexistent and a unified political culture did not emerge. Access to the state once more became a fierce competition that pitted ethnic groups in a hostile interaction for scarce resources.

Due to epidemic, famine, and state-sanctioned violence between 1887 and 1905, the population of Congo Free State plummeted to half of what it had been in precolonial times.[8] It became obvious that the brutality of Congo Free State could not be ignored. Through pressure from his European *compères,* Leopold proposed cosmetic reform and social improvements after 1905; however, by 1906 there was no substantive change. In a move that was to usher in the close of the Leopoldian era in Belgium, the Free State finally became an official colony of Belgium in 1908, rather than remain the personal property of the king.

The new Belgian administration vowed to never repeat the abuse and exploitation of Leopold. Yet this was hardly likely in light of the fact that Congo still remained "a pearl of great price." The administration of the territory became even more bureaucratic, and the extraction of natural wealth continued in a more efficient, if less brutal, manner. The legacy of bitter tensions between ethnic communities was evident in the Belgian Congo; the erstwhile rival groups renewed their competition for access to the colonial machinery. The prospects of building a cohesive colony seemed illusory.

The native chiefs who attempted to reassert their authority were forced to submit to the administration or were undermined through the Belgian selection of chiefs and other local colonial officials. The Belgians governed through a highly effective bureaucratic administration and divided the country accordingly. By 1933 Congo was redivided into six provinces: Katanga (Elizabethville), Kasai (Luluaborg), Kivu (Bukavu), Orientale (Stanleyville), Équateur (Coquilhatville), and Lower Congo (with the capital in Leopoldville).[9] However, it was paradoxical that even amid this effective colonial administration there were provinces with a nominal degree of autonomy from the centralized state. Katanga and Kasai consistently thwarted the ideal of a unitary colony. It is this potential for secession that would become real in the postcolonial crisis of 1960–65.

The Road to Independence

The Congolese continued to be excluded from the administration of their colony even as the colonial state expanded into and regulated a great many aspects of their lives. Nonetheless, through the work of missionaries and their schools, a native educated elite began to emerge. In no direct way, however, was this native class being prepared to take up the mantle of leadership. The importance of World War II as a force of change impacting on colonial policy was significant. Many Congolese were in Europe during the war and remained there to be educated. This exposure to Europe and education prompted the emergence of the *évolués* (civilized individuals); they began to seek equal treatment with Europeans as well as a stake in the future of Congo. By the early 1950s the *évolués* began to petition the Belgian colonial administration for reforms in government, political leadership, and office as well as for access to the scarce resources of the state. At this point, however, Belgium gave no sign of being ready to surrender Congo.[10]

By 1954 a number of political organizations emerged, but they never truly operated on the national level, developing instead along regional and ethnic lines. This development was to set in motion the manipulation of ethnicity for political gain. Namely, the competition for access to the state and its resources were ethnopolitically generated. In 1955 and 1956, the Belgian law professor A. J. van Bilsen published *A Thirty Year Plan for the Political Independence of Belgian Africa*, reflecting the recalcitrance of the Belgian administration to consider independence. I cannot resist the temptation to ask what would have happened if the Belgian Congo had not been given independence until later (if not even 1985, as proposed). The Belgian dilemma is best captured by Arthur House, who wrote, "Belgium was not prepared to grant independence and neither was Congo prepared to receive it, but at the same time they feared the consequences of not doing so."[11] The incipient political elite (*évolués*) saw this as too long a wait for their accession to the political kingdom. Particularly, the Alliance des Bakongo (Abako, an ethnic party of the Bakongo) demanded negotiations for an immediate independence. In response the Belgians finally allowed the first municipal elections to be held in 1957.

Though inchoate and fragile, political organizations did begin to mobilize the populace; it was primarily on the basis of ethnicity in the absence of a statewide political consciousness. At the time, this appeared to be the only plausible route for accessing the scarce resources of the state. In the context of immediacy, no coherent or concrete political ideologies developed to garner support; in their place were the charismatic churnings of independence and promises of ethnic emancipation and prosperity. It was, however, two major events in 1958 and 1959 that prompted Belgium to seriously consider independence. The first was that just across the river in Congo-Brazzaville, President Charles De Gaulle delivered a speech on the proposed independence of Francophone Africa; this directly stimulated greater demands for independence in the Belgian Congo. The Fanonian metaphor of a "dying colonialism" is apt.[12] The administration was losing its control over particular regional centers, and of greatest concern was the capital, Leopoldville, and the mineral-rich Katanga province. The second was more pronounced; in 1959 riots broke out in the capital and though by then an unanticipated independence seemed inevitable, the reality of the situation was the fact that Belgium had not been developing any concrete plan for a transfer of power to a native political class. The dilemma was obvious: Congo was not politically or administratively prepared for independence, neither was Belgium ready to grant independence, but most paradoxically, independence now seemed inevitable.

In 1960 Belgium convened a roundtable conference in Brussels to discuss Congolese independence. The plan was to grant independence within six months. The parliamentary democracy model of the metropole was to be transferred to the independent Congolese state. It was a plan that essentially grafted (alien) European political institutions onto a polity whose sole contemporary political experience had been colonial authoritarianism. In no way were the nascent Congolese politicians prepared to operate such alien political machinery.

National elections were slated for May 1960, and a month later independence was to be granted. A constitution, the Loi Fondamentale (Supreme Law), was also drafted and approved by the Brussels authorities. It was to be the basis of the social and political order of the new state. Even with these epic political changes unfolding, gradualism rather than immediacy appeared to be the vision of Belgian decolonization policy.

The Belgian administration encouraged the creation of political parties. Three important ones emerged, though their bases were still ethnically centered. The Mouvement National Congolaise (National Congolese Movement—MNC), led by Patrice Lumumba, appeared to be the party with the most broad-based appeal, though its support was concentrated in the leader's home areas, East Kasai and Orientale. The aforementioned Abako, headed by Joseph Kasavubu, had its constituent support in the capital and the rest of the Lower Congo region. The third was the Parti National du Progrès (National Progressive Party—PNP), which was a coalition of ethnic-based parties that had the support base of native chiefs, and was led by Paul Boyla; its regional support center was in the Equateur province. This last party also had the firm backing of the colonial authorities.

In May 1960 the founding national elections were held. Given the lack of concrete political organizations and the diversity of political interests competing for access, a plethora of parties (forty to be exact) fielded candidates. As expected, the voting took place considerably along ethno-regional lines, since ethnicity represented the only politically salient basis for political mobilization at the time. No party won an absolute majority, but Lumumba's MNC won 24 percent (33) of the Assembly's 137 seats and emerged with a plurality of seats. The elections thus confirmed that it was the only party that had any semblance of a national constituency. Given this narrow triumph, however, strategic political alliances became inevitable.

Another reality that the elections confirmed was that the independence for which the political parties campaigned was not a widely understood concept, and consequentially no one group captured the legitimacy necessary for national government of an independent Congo.[13] Lumumba had to enter into an alliance with Kasavubu's Abako in order to form a government to accede to independence. This was to prove an uneasy alliance. In their erstwhile political campaigns they had exhibited clashing, almost irreconcilable views on how to organize the state after independence. It was unlikely that a divided coalition could provide the new state with a government of national unity. Nonetheless Lumumba was named prime minister and Kasavubu president of Congo. With two weeks left for formal independence, the alliance and political leadership began to sway. The birth pangs of the independent Congolese state were sharp, and an uneasy quietude hung over Congo. On the official Independence Day of 30 June 1960, the unwieldy coalition government led the country into an uncertain independence.

CONGO'S FIRST REPUBLIC: 1960 TO 1965

Independence Day was a momentous occasion not because it was a positive turning point but because it was the starting point in a series of subsequent crises.[14] Agreement is almost universal as to the serious miscalculation that the mode of independence represented on Belgium's part.[15] When King Baudouin and Prime Minister Eyskens transferred the reins of power to Congolese leadership, the birth of the new nation was confirmed. Lumumba's forthright speech highlighting oppression, slavery, and exploitation by the Belgians, however, dampened the celebrations. It reinforced the sentiment of a hastily conceived independence that had ignored many issues that needed to be addressed for the new nation. The absence of a confident and state-wide political culture and incipient political elite, along with barely suppressed ethnic rivalries, seemed to cloud the horizon of a new and prosperous Congo.

Apart from the legacy of a colonial state apparatus, there was nothing preparatory about independence. The ethnic constituencies, whose rivalries were salient in the elections, would now be in open contest for political access, and the fissures of regionalism remained in evidence. Within a week of independence, the new nation was held hostage by a Congolese army mutiny. Congolese soldiers in the Force Publique (the army) mutinied, and violence broke out. It was prompted when Belgian army chief General Emile Janssens, the last Belgian commander-in-chief, unabashedly told his troops that independence meant no real changes for the military, or society at large, effectively saying that the Belgians would still be in charge. News of this local incident in Leopoldville spread rapidly throughout the rest of the country, precipitating further mutinies. The violence had set in motion a dangerous and disappointing post-independence trajectory. The promise of independence was obliterated by the reality of a fragile and disjointed nation confronting a metropole that still hoped to dominate it. As elsewhere in Africa and across the postcolonial world, independence promised much but appeared to deliver little in its immediate aftermath.[16]

Although Congolese constituted the entire enlisted ranks, a swift effort was made to add them to the officer corps of the Force Publique. However, by then the situation had already escalated to crisis proportions. The European population was targeted by some of the mutinous troops. The sudden departure of the Belgian army commanders meant that the Force Publique would be ineffective against the chaos. Belgium intervened to protect its nationals by deploying troops from its base in Congo and sending others from Europe. The Congolese government, however, interpreted this action as a contravention of independent Congo's nascent sovereignty. A second woe also soon befell Congo: With the departure of many Belgians from

Congo, a swift exodus of capital followed. The Belgians had a strong presence in agriculture and commerce, and the economy was to instantly feel the effect of the withdrawal of their human and financial capital. According to one estimate, the Belgian population, which totaled 110,000 in 1959, fell to approximately 80,000 at independence, and then fell even more dramatically to 20,000 by 1961, by which time the majority of the remaining expatriates were in the mineral rich and prosperous Katanga province.[17] It was also consequential that there was no native economic class to replace the Belgians who left in the exodus.

The political leaders of the young nation requested the United Nations' assistance with "the provision of international military for the protection of the national territory against the present external (Belgian) aggression which was a threat to international peace."[18] In so doing, they brought this peripheral crisis to international attention, and in the process, the Soviet Union, the United States, and the UN, as well as Belgium, soon became external players. Before the UN could arrive, the province of Katanga, under Moïse Tshombe, seceded from Congo on 11 July. This was not an unforeseen development as Katanga, along with Kasai, was known to be dominated by secessionist politicians and their parties. Katanga's secession was also part of Belgium's plan to preserve its capital investments in a Congo headed by a staunch anti-imperialist leader. The UN arrived four days later but appeared unable to expedite the withdrawal of the Belgian troops, who had by now insulated their interests in Katanga from the crisis in the rest of Congo. Lumumba accused the UN of not only dragging its feet but of supporting the desires of western imperialists. It was at that point, in deep frustration, that he courted the Soviet Union for assistance. In hindsight this was to be Lumumba's fatal mistake.

Politically, the Congolese government was to move into the "reign of chaos" that would last for the next four years. The courting of the Soviet Union by Lumumba angered Kasavubu, who soon ordered Lumumba's dismissal and the appointment of Joseph Ileo as prime minister. Lumumba attempted to obviate his dismissal, but it was already too late; the fragile alliance had been broken. After only a month of independence, political uncertainty was rising steadily in Congo. Before the appointment of Ileo could take effect, a hitherto silent broker, Col. Joseph Desiré Mobutu (later Mobutu Sese Seko), army chief of staff and former Lumumba ally, staged a peaceful coup. He assured the country that the army was only neutralizing Kasavubu and Lumumba and would set up a provisional government led by the College des Commisaires, made up of Congolese university graduates and others who had studied in Belgium.

Mobutu made it clear that this government was only provisional and would dissolve itself as soon as the political uncertainty was resolved. Mobutu ordered the arrest of Lumumba, contending that he had incited the military to mutiny. Lumumba eluded capture, however, and went under UN protection. He was subsequently arrested in the fall of 1960 while trying to leave the UN guard. He was taken to Thysville in late December, and after an escape attempt he was transferred from Thysville to Elizabethville under the pretext that he was being invited to return to leadership. But in January 1961, Tshombe's forces, with the approval of several western governments, killed Patrice Lumumba. It remains inconclusive as to the nature of support for the assassination of Lumumba, but even if the trigger was pulled by Tshombe's forces, it was nonetheless the fulfillment of Belgium's and America's desire to eliminate a perceived threat to the stability and anticommunist ideal they had for Africa.[19] They believed that to eliminate such threats was to register victories for Africa's fledgling polities. The first head of government of independent Congo had fallen victim to the chaotic political climate and the parochial interests of Western powerbrokers who saw him as a threat.

Although Lumumba had been eliminated from the political arena, his supporters and his cause remained strong. Antoine Gisenga, one of Lumumba's lieutenants, mounted political and military opposition efforts against the regime in power. Gisenga's political vehicle of opposition was the Parti Solidaire Africaine (African Solidarity Party—PSA). At this point Congo seemed even more irreversibly fragmented than before.[20] The country even had two capitals: Stanleyville had been brought under Gisenga's control and claimed as Congo's real capital. Katanga and Kasai had seceded under Tshombe and Albert Kalonji (the elected head of Kasai), respectively. The UN moved promptly to a series of talks attempting reunification. Most UN officials felt, rightfully so, that the reunification of Congo was indispensable to the stability of Congo as a whole. In January of 1963 the Katangan secession came to an end, and the secessionist leader Tshombe fled into exile. The end of the Katangan secession did not, however, quiet all of the storms in Congo. A new government under the neutral deputy Cyrille Adoula had come to power but was operating under a cloud of political uncertainty. As a result political breakdown once again seemed likely. A weak central government began to concede to pressure from the provinces, whose number had increased from six to twenty-one.[21] Facing unbearable opposition, Adoula resigned and a political vacuum reemerged in Congo.

In July 1964 Tshombe returned to Congo from exile and took charge of a new government formed by Kasavubu. The Loi Fondamentale adopted at independence was replaced with a new constitution, at which time the country was also renamed Democratic Republic of Congo. The new government and constitutional reform hardly signaled the end of political rivalries and ambitions, however. In less than three months, another uneasy and fragile alliance had crumbled. Kasavubu calculated that a dismissal of Tshombe, now considered a threat to his rule, would be a political panacea. Kasavubu thus dismissed Tshombe and appointed Evariste Kimba to his post. He was due to assume his position in November of 1965, but before he could do so the canny Mobutu, recognizing the window of opportunity that the political conflict had created, again seized power in a coup d'état. On 25 November 1965, Mobutu declared himself president. It was the end of the first Republic and a chaotic five years for the new nation. Independence had meant fragmentation, conflict, chaos, and economic collapse, while the postcolonial political elite had proven itself incapable of leading. Under the First Republic the actors constantly changed places, but a type of neocolonial rule was instituted.

Given the terminal colonial experience, as well as a miscalculated independence, crisis was at least very likely, if not inevitable. Congo was granted independence without the necessary construction of a national political consciousness. The rule of the inexperienced political elite that led the country into independence had intensified the possibility of a collapse of the Congolese state. The political culture of the native political class remained nearly as authoritarian as that of the colonial rulers. The main additions to their political culture were the practices of ethnoregional and patrimonial politics. They proved to be more concerned with political advantage than with the construction a coherent and functional state. The problems of ethnic and regional identities, rather than being mitigated by the postcolonial political class, were exacerbated.

Could Mobutu the army chief become the statesman to lead Congo out of this postcolonial crisis? He had promised on his accession to office that he only intended to stay as interim president for five years; once national unity and order were restored, he promised, he would step aside. In doing so, Mobutu papered over the problem of ethnoregionalism while perfecting patronage politics to a fine art. Importantly, Mobutu moved to consolidate his rule and imposed his own order on the chaos that had been characteristic of Congolese politics.

ORDERED CHAOS AND THE MOBUTU YEARS: 1965 TO 1997

The claim that the patterns that would come to characterize Mobutu's rule of Congo were established during the early period of 1964 to 1967 is profoundly accurate.[22] In the early Mobutu years, however, it was clear that Mobutu was the leader of Congo, but it was less certain as to the direction in which Congo would be going.[23] The first five years of independence did not entirely foreshadow the decades of stagnation, ethnic conflict, and secession to come, nor the political instability and weak state apparatus. Congo had not fulfilled its potential to be the engine of economic growth in central Africa, but at this juncture, some still held out hope that the country might play such a role in the coming years.

Mobutu moved to consolidate his power, and he brought some measure of order to the chaos by restoring nominal stability and restoring the state apparatus. Before he did this, however, he ensured that he recast them in such a way to ensure his personal control.[24] In a much larger sense, however, the coup of 1965 represented a failure, specifically the failure of the politico-administrative class of postcolonial Zaire to find a consensual political formula for the new nation.[25] They had allowed political ambitions rather than Congo's political future to be their raison d'étre, and Congo was to suffer hard and long as a result. This observation points as much to Congo's defective, authoritarian political culture as to Mobutu as the real source of Congo's perpetual crises. One cannot help but recognize how Mobutu's survival was intricately dependent upon the continued existence of this culture of authoritarianism and patrimonial predatory practices. If the combination of these habits and practices had evolved, then his regime would have ended much sooner than it did.

The major problem to be overcome by the Mobutu regime was the deficit of legitimacy. Mobutu established his own network within the politicobureaucratic sector in a bid to develop a secure economic base for his regime.[26] Between 1965 and 1973, the first phase of his rule, Mobutu made some key moves that would give his regime a gloss of legitimacy as well as a much-needed measure of order and stability. He established a puppet legislature that he believed would provide legitimacy for his regime without presenting any real challenge to his policies and political maneuvers. In a policy that may have been the only silver lining of the Mobutuist regime, he took steps intended to stem the country's pervasive ethnic conflict.[27] He calculated that most of the ethnic conflicts had been centered on the plethora of small, ethnically based provinces, and in 1967 he began moving toward the consolidation of these small units into larger administrative ones.[28] This was a critical maneuver on Mobutu's part. The ethnic cleavages that had been exacerbated by a miscalculated independence and had plunged Congo into chaos were by the late 1960s under control. It was the subsequent decline in central power years later that precipitated the crisis of 1996.

The next step was to politicize the provincial legislatures. Mobutu developed an elaborate centralized state under which the provincial governments became just administrative expressions. In effect, he had eliminated the middlemen of the state, the ethnoregional political leaders who had mobilized around ethnicity.[29] By 1967 Mobutu's regime moved to single party rule with the founding of his Mouvement Populaire de la Revolution (Popular Movement of the Revolution—MPR). The justification for this step, common in Africa at the time, was that the superfluity of political parties had divided the country after independence. The MPR became the country's dominant political institution, and the state had become Mobutu's much as it had been Leopold's in an earlier era. In 1970, presidential elections were held and Mobutu was "elected" for a seven-year term. Political order was maintained through centralized control and an elaborate security apparatus, employing torture, clandestine imprisonment, and assassination. Meanwhile, the state employed ideological indoctrination, religious repression, and corruption of the judiciary to supplement these harsher activities.[30] Between 1965 and 1967 there were over six major uprisings against the regime, but all were violently and successfully suppressed. Civilian and military opposition were not distinguished.

According to Michael Schatzberg, an extraordinary personalization of political rule resulted, a cult of personality flourished. It was an effort to provide an ideological foundation for the regime, which in the late 1960s was asserted as "authentic nationalism."[31] At various times this ideological rhetoric was broadcast under the labels of "nationalism," "authenticity," and even "Mobutisme." The raison d'être of this ideology was to indigenize the ideals of state control inherited from Belgium in Zaire and to distract attention from the state's failure to provide for a more egalitarian and democratic socioeconomic system.[32]

The most austere manifestation of this Zairian nationalism was the "Zairianization" measures of November 1973. These measures provided Mobutu with the wherewithal to patronize his loyal supporters and build a patrimonial basis of support among his cronies. In the early 1970s Zaire appeared to be attracting investments because of its mineral and natural resource potential (including copper, diamonds, and hydroelectricity), but with Mobutu's nationalization policy, Zaire was to become the architect of its own destiny. It was to become an insular, nationalized economy. He seized the large enterprises of the foreign business and agricultural sector and simply handed them over to his *compères*. Lacking any economic savvy, these "acquirers" looted and destroyed the enterprises with which they were entrusted, driving the national economy into headlong decline. In the political realm, Mobutu, the "father of the Zairian family" and the putative repository of truth, began to change the country's place names, and in 1971 Congo itself was renamed Zaire. The move was claimed as an act of African authenticity, although "Zaire" was actually a Portuguese corruption of a local word. The state and Mobutu were presented to the population as the epitome of national independence.

Unfortunately for the Congolese, the name change did nothing to stem the headlong decline of the plummeting economy. Nondevelopment had become a signal feature of the Mobutu regime by 1974; after only a few months of "Zairianization," the economy was comatose. The measures had destroyed the commercial supply of goods and the channels of distribution. The second and more consequential effect was that the acquirers of former European businesses fired remaining Zairian workers and hired their own relatives and others of their ethnic stock. This renewal of ethnic-based access to the state and its economy and resources was to have serious consequences in the years to come. The state was losing revenue because acquirers looted capital stocks for short-term gain while avoiding the payment of excise taxes. It is paradoxical that, although Mobutu had made remarkable efforts to unite the country during his early years in power, he neither built a political consensus nor embarked on any real economic development efforts.

By 1974 the Mobutu regime was beginning to experience a serious crisis that was soon exacerbated by declining terms of trade. The price of copper, the major Zairian natural resource being exploited at that time, was selling for U.S.\$3,380 per metric ton at the beginning of 1974, but in just three and a half months it had fallen to U.S.\$1,350 per ton. The political and economic crises were also exacerbated in 1975 with the outbreak of Angolan civil war. The fighting had caused the mining prosperity of the Shaba region to decline. The crisis of Shaba was indicative of the economic plight of Zaire in general and of a political regime that, though authoritarian and having the appearance of cohesion and control, was weakening.

The economic decline was glaring. By 1978 real wages had declined and the price of goods had risen to ten times what they had been in 1964.[33] The GNP per capita that had stood at U.S.\$360 in 1978 fell to U.S.\$150 (in constant 1987 dollars) in 1989. This decline seemed even more dramatic in light of the fact that Zaire had such a great natural resource endowment. Despite the richness of Zaire's mineral assets, economic mismanagement and political exploitation had completely stymied economic growth. Potential for growth and the reality of Zaire's nondevelopment had diverged. It was the mass of semi-urban and rural people who were most affected as they had the least access to the state and its resources. World Bank economic indicators were most discouraging. The exchange rate for the Zaire fell from U.S.\$1.00 to Z\$0.50 in 1974 to a rate of U.S.\$1.00 to Z\$496.99 in 1990. Domestic inflation was also beginning to pick up, the average inflation rate between 1980 and 1987 being 53.5 percent, with 1987 setting a record rate of 106.5 percent for the year.[34] This trend foreshadowed the price percentage increases that would be measured in the thousands during the 1990s. Between 1976 and 1986, Mobutu had negotiated seven stabilization schemes under the IMF. The economic recession caused the rise and flourishing of a second, informal economy that diverted productive national growth potential. While Zaire's finances were still good enough for the country to get loans, the Mobutu regime also borrowed some U.S.\$10 billion from international lenders. Mobutu had mortgaged Zaire's future and had to refinance loans merely to service already existing debts by the end of the 1970s.[35]

By the early 1980s Mobutu's regime was widely recognized as a "kleptocracy," with public funds and resources being used for private gain rather than for national investment. The president himself was the biggest culprit, having redirected massive revenue into personal accounts. In spite of the obvious deterioration of the Zairian economy and social infrastructure, Mobutu maintained power. By 1990 the presidency accounted for 80 percent of government expenditure, while agriculture accounted for only 11 percent.[36] By that same year Mobutu controlled over U.S.\$3 billion, his control of the output of state-run mining firms alone having added U.S.\$1 billion to his political resources.[37] The economic trends meant that Zaire's political and economic renaissance would be delayed. A poor and underdeveloped country with an authoritarian regime seemed entirely unlikely to develop a strong democratic and progressive economic ethic. Meanwhile, Mobutu rhetorically espoused an anticommunist stance, maintaining Western support and sponsorship; the Reagan administration in the United States continued to hail Mobutu as an American friend and example for central Africa.

The Mobutu regime had proven to be characteristic of the previous postcolonial regimes in Zaire. It had neither rescued the country from stagnation and underdevelopment nor had it encouraged or allowed the creation of a climate for political change and development. The promises made to Congo in 1965 by Mobutu had been forfeited. The dedicated politicoadministrative class necessary to the development of an effective and democratic polity was lacking, and in its place was a corrupt and abusive cadre of leaders who were more corrupt than they had been in the immediate postindependence years. By 1990 Zaire had, in effect, seen no real political or economic development since Mobutu's seizure of power in 1965. Yet the crisis of 1990 did not immediately produce a strong new leader, unlike that of 1960 to 1964.

It was changing international political circumstances that served to undermine the hegemony of the Mobutu regime, and lead to yet another era in Zaire's history.

THE UNRAVELING STATE 1990 TO 1997

The year 1990 was to also signal the genesis of what one could call the "unraveling state."[38] Mobutu was to a face serious challenge to his regime, beginning with the end of the Cold War. As the Cold War ended, western states moved to put pressure on Mobutu for political and economic reform, and the IFIs curtailed their remaining programs. France cut its aid in 1991 to one-third of what it had been in 1988--1989, and the World Bank broke relations with Mobutu after the misappropriation of nearly U.S.$500 million from state-run copper mines. Economic decline prompted by constantly falling copper prices and strikes in the civil service and military were forcing Mobutu to reconsider his options.

In April 1990 Mobutu was forced to make political concessions. The legalization of independent opposition parties and the creation of a multiparty democratic system were announced. Although elections were not held as promised, Mobutu agreed to a coalition government with the popular Etienne Tshisekedi. Tshisekedi, who hailed from the historically problematic province of Kasai Orientale, was a former stalwart of the regime who had become its fiercest and most determined critic since 1981. This political aperture did not just signal the renaissance of political factions but more importantly heralded the end of the centralized patronage network. Access to the state became even more highly contested.[39] Meanwhile, Zaire's leading supporters—France, Belgium, and the United States—continued to reduce their diplomatic presence. In light of the unrelenting political and economic instability, and Mobutu's failure to follow up on his promises, aid was finally suspended. Mobutu formed a succession of "transitional" governments as political chaos took hold. As a means to configure a new political formulation, a (putatively) "sovereign" national conference was allowed to convene in 1991 in order to examine the possibilities and initiate the imperative of a new structure. The mandate of the conference was to reconstruct the failed political institutions of the Second Republic and preside over a return to multiparty politics.

In August of 1992 the Sovereign National Conference drafted La Chatre de la Transition (Transition Charter) to replace the constitution. Under the charter, Mobutu was to relinquish control of public finances, foreign affairs, and defense. The conference, which had declared itself "sovereign," voted overwhelmingly to restore Tshisekedi to the post of prime minister, the latter having been discharged in early 1992. Ethnic rivalries soon reemerged in this politically charged environment. The dismissal of Nguza Karl-I-Bond as prime minister provoked clashes in Kasai and Shaba between Nguza's Lunda and Tshisekedi's Luba ethnic groups. In 1993 Nguza declared that Shaba would not recognize Tshisekedi's authority. According to one author, this development was strangely reminiscent of Shaba's demands for independence from Kinshasa in 1960.[40]

Mobutu's crisis management strategy contributed to the ultimate collapse of his regime. In 1992 he purchased currency notes from a German company to pay troops who were threatening mutiny. This was a contravention of the determination of the national conference, which had ordered that Tshisekedi should take responsibility for fiscal and monetary policy. The result was hyperinflation, and the Zaire declined to Z $110 million to the U.S. dollar by 1993.[41] The unpaid army had declined dramatically, from 70,000 in 1983 to only 20,000 by the mid-1990s.[42] Mobutu decentralized the military in an effort to let the army accumulate its own revenue. Each of the six new units rivaled each other for the scarce resources throughout the country. The patrimonial regime had descended to its most banal: economic accumulation through warlord politics and a politico-economic culture of kleptocracy.[43] Zaire was crippled by a regime that had no real concern for the society's development and failed to look beyond its own survival.

This unraveling state had once again become "the shadow theater of ethnicity."[44] The Luba of Shaba were having their property sequestered and many were deported from Shaba to Kasai, where they had lived for generations.[45] Other groups perpetrated attacks on immigrants of Rwandan origin (largely Tutsi) in North Kivu. Ethnoregional contestation was proving once again to be significant in the breakdown of African states and regimes. It was particularly detrimental for Zaire because of its proximity to the states of the Great Lakes. Warring Hutu and Tutsi identity groups in eastern Congo, Rwanda, and Burundi lived in such close proximity that their conflicts frequently spilled across international borders. This was particularly the case after Rwanda's genocide of 1994. After the flood of Hutu refugees poured into Zaire in late 1994, Mobutu was in desperate need of some survival strategy if he was to continue in power. Both the state and society were in a state of disorder, but this was the result of a deliberate strategy rather than mere anarchy.[46]

Mobutu was at work constantly to co-opt the Haute Conseil de la Republique (High Council of the Republic—HCR), the transitional body put in place by the national conference. Mobutu's forces in the HCR formed an alliance with alleged "neutrals," which allowed Mobutu to appoint another old baron of the regime, Kengo wa Dondo, to the post of prime minister in 1994. Kengo's appointment only staved off the rising disorder for a short while, however. Zaire was soon in the midst of a political crisis reminiscent of the crises of the immediate postindependence period. My tabulation reveals that there were over fourteen prime ministers (but only two presidents, including Mobutu) between 1960 and 1990. The instability characteristic of the frequent change in heads of government is telling. The political realm was unstable, and it was only the existence of an authoritarian president that prevented total state collapse. Paradoxically, it was the decline of the same formerly strong, authoritarian president that also helped to account for state collapse.

The refugee crisis facing all of the states bordering Rwanda and Burundi also affected Zaire and the Mobutu regime. Several hundred thousand people fleeing ethnic conflict in Rwanda had taken refuge in Zaire since 1994. Meanwhile, Mobutu had begun a policy of expulsion against people of the indigenous Banyamulenge (largely Tutsi) heritage, mainly to create a scapegoat for Zaire's many problems and to distract the attention of the populace from the real source of their misery. Nonetheless, he had regained a small measure of confidence from his external supporters by the humanitarian acceptance of refugees.

Although it appeared superficially that Mobutu had regained political supremacy after 1994, Zaire was still unraveling. It had a hard outer layer but a fragile inner core; the core of support for Mobutu had long eroded. The periphery, although not having total autonomy from the center, was not effectively under its control either. The regime had grown too weak to monitor the outer layer of the state (i.e., regional centers). The weakness of the Zairian state was now extended into the crucial domain of physical control over the regions.

In May 1995 general elections were cancelled in Zaire, but the opposition forces continued to gain strength.[47] The multiplicity and diversity of interests of political groups and the ethnopolitical struggles that helped to cause the descent into civil war immediately after independence were re-emerging.[48] Mobutu continued to lose his grip on Zaire, but in the end, it was sickness that proved to be his most formidable nemesis, as the dictator was diagnosed with prostate cancer. It was within this setting that Mobutu was caught unawares by an insurrection movement that began in the fall of 1996.

In the over three decades of Zaire's independence the only constant had been patrimonialism, authoritarianism, and political decline. Neither a political culture strong enough to build democracy nor an opposition strong enough to oppose an authoritarian regime had emerged. This period of the unraveling state (1990–96) reaffirmed the postcolonial political instability and lack of a national consciousness. In the absence of a formidable alternative to the Mobutu regime, the Zairian state reached very near to the point of collapse.

THE FINAL COLLAPSE OF THE MOBUTU REGIME

By early 1996 the Zairian state was being challenged by a fierce rebellion of the Banyamulenge people.[49] During the next few months, the Alliance des forces démocratiques pour la libération du Congo-Zaire (Alliance of Democratic Forces for the Liberation of Congo—ADFL) led by Laurent Kabila, declared war on the already-beleaguered Mobutu regime. Kabila had originally been "spokesperson" for the group, and it is unclear as to how he emerged as its leader. Initially the ADFL was composed of five temporary allies: a Banyamulenge militia, the Marxist-oriented People's Progressive Party (which was more a political organization than a party), a Kuba militia group from the southeast of Kasai, a Shaba group drawn from the over half million Luba who fled Shaba to Kasai, and a Kissasse group, which included the Mai-Mai warriors.[50] Kabila, a long-time revolutionary and leader of the group, was putatively inspired by Lumumba's principles but sought to first and foremost topple Mobutu's regime to take power for himself. It was this goal, rather than any deep concern for the restoration of the Zairian state, that was at the heart of the rebellion. The rebellion had developed during Mobutu's prolonged absence while seeking medical treatment in Europe. His absence had left a political vacuum in Kinshasa and a lack of leadership to deal with the crisis.

The rebel forces advanced from the east of Zaire and within a month had occupied a significant portion of eastern Zaire as the crumbling Zairian army fled in the process. The advance was intensifying the displacement of over a million refugees between Zaire and Rwanda. The spread of disease and starvation, along with causalities of war, created a great humanitarian crisis for the entire Great Lakes region. The ADFL, with the support of Rwanda, Uganda and Angola, continued its advance to Kinshasa. The Zairian state had all but disappeared by the time the ADFL reached Kinshasa in May 1997. Its borders had proved porous and the regime's security was (literally) under fire because of the lack of an effective army.[51] Given its heavy Tutsi and Banyamulenge leadership, the ADFL also attacked Hutu refugees both on the fringes of the Rwandan border and deep inside Zaire, where they had fled. The villagers in the provinces near Kinshasa supported Kabila, and the unpaid army had little power of resistance.

In December of 1996 Mobutu returned to Zaire after a prolonged absence for medical treatment. He quickly moved to take the reins of power. After a series of military maneuvers, the Zairian Armed Forces was somewhat strengthened and began mounting a counteroffensive. The ADFL, with the heavy support of Ugandan and Rwandan troops, soon regained initiative, however, and continued its march to the capital. By January 1997 the Kabila-led forces had seized gold mines in the east and were gaining ground; in a few more weeks they were at Goma and then Kisangani. The Zairian army was not able to put up a significant challenge and by May 1997 Mobutu, recognizing the imminent overthrow of his regime, fled to Moroccan exile. That same month, Kabila and his bedraggled forces took control of Kinshasa.

Within days Kabila had renamed Zaire the Democratic Republic of Congo, and declared himself president. This signaled not just the overthrow of a regime but Kabila's putative intention to undertake a thoroughgoing reformulation of the structures of the state. Nonetheless, it soon became clear that Kabila shared Mobutu's penchant for political control, patrimonialsim, and ethnic politics. This was hardly surprising given that he, too, was a product of Zaire's political culture. The state was more fragile than ever but had not altogether collapsed. Kabila's "revolution" brought with it high expectations among the people for both political freedom and economic improvement. Yet in the months that followed Kabila was only able to restore the functioning of the state to a modest level. In his initial months in office, Kabila introduced a new currency and maintained its stability over several more months. His regime also initially suppressed the predations that the army might have exacted against the civilian population. Well before the beginning of the second Congo war, however, it had become clear that Kabila was more interested in building a network of key supporters through the time-tested Mobutuist methods than he was in assuring the genuine economic development of the country.

LEGACIES AND CONCLUSIONS

The Congo crisis and war discussed in this volume did not erupt spontaneously but were the tragic result of colonial legacies and postcolonial nondevelopment. The war's longevity will largely be determined by the renaissance and the transformation of political consciousness (or lack thereof) in the Congolese political class and population at large. The absence of a unified and healthy political culture in Congo, as well as an absence of alternatives to authoritarian rule, made continuation of crisis after Mobutu a likely outcome. Pragmatism is not pessimism, however; this chapter was never meant to overemphasize the determining influence of Congo's colonial legacy, or of Mobutu's rule, though such legacies have proven difficult to overcome in Africa and elsewhere. Rather, it was the manipulation and exacerbation of these legacies by Kabila and his allies that proved detrimental to Congo after May 1997. In effect, the current crisis represents the unsurprising legacy of Congo's tragic colonization and the venal rule that followed it in the postcolonial period.

The Mobutu regime, rather than mitigating the legacies of these colonial developments, exacerbated them and helped to account for the longevity of dysfunctional political forms in the country. Congo must not be seen as an eternally tragic case, since it is not entirely beyond a renaissance. Nonetheless, there exist some essential conditions if this is to take place. First, a strong democratic political culture must be built or encouraged, most likely by a particularly charismatic local leader, and likely with the benevolent assistance of outside forces. We must acknowledge that the challenge of this proposition is huge in the absence of a broad class of citizens who could advocate for democratic development, but it is nonetheless indispensable to Congo's political reemergence. Second, political and regime imperatives must be made secondary to systematic economic development. All of the regimes of postcolonial Congo have been more concerned with regime survival than with giving to Zaire a functional political system or self-renewing economy.

The current crisis must be seen not only as a weakness of postcolonial African states but also as an opportunity to overcome or lessen the influence of the colonial experience on the contemporary. Congo's challenge in dealing with this crisis is also Africa's challenge.[52] The colonial legacy cannot be eluded, but it can be mimimized with strong political leadership and a transformation of the existing political culture.

NOTES

1. Accompanying the many postcolonial regimes have been several name changes for the country once called the Belgian Congo. Following independence it was renamed the Republic of Congo. By 1964 it became known as the Democratic Republic of Congo. In 1971, under Mobutu, it was once again renamed, this time as Zaire. In 1997 Kabila chose to revert the name back to the Democratic Republic of Congo.
2. Winsome J. Leslie, *Zaire: Continuity and Political Change in an Oppressive State* (Boulder, CO: Westview Press, 1993), 5.
3. These three metaphors are powerful images of the development of the postcolonial state in Africa. For greater elucidation, see John Clark, "The Nature and Evolution of the State in Zaire," *Studies in Comparative International Development* 32, no. 4 (1998): 3–23. Mahmood Mamdani and Robert Fatton also offer critical insights. See Fatton's *Preda-*

tory Rule in Africa (Boulder, CO: Lynne Reiner Press, 1992), and Mamdani's, *Citizen and Subject* (Princeton: Princeton University Press, 1995).

4. The second chapter in this volume, by Crawford Young, most perspicaciously captures this point.

5. Leslie, *Zaire*, 5.

6. For a superb overview of the whole remarkable period of European exploration and early colonization, written for a popular audience, see Adam Hochschild, *King Leopold's Ghost: A Story of Greed, Terror, and Heroism in Colonial Africa* (New York: Houghton Mifflin, 1998).

7. Leslie, *Zaire*, 8.

8. Jan Vansina in his introduction to Daniel Vangoweghe, *Du Sang sur les Lianes* (Brussels: Didier Hatier, 1986), cited in Hochschild, *King Leopold's Ghost*, 233.

9. Leslie, *Zaire*, 25.

10. Michael Schatzberg, *Mobutu or Chaos? The US and Zaire, 1960–90* (Washington: University Press of America, 1991), 10.

11. Arthur House, *The U.N. in the Congo: The Political and Civilian Efforts* (Washington: University Press of America, 1978), 6–10.

12. Frantz Fanon, *A Dying Colonialism* (New York: Grove Press, 1965).

13. House, *The U.N. in the Congo*, citing Jules Gérard-Libois and Benoit Verhagen, eds., *Congo 1960*, vol. 1 (Brussels: Centre de Reserche et d'Information Socio-Politque, 1961), 206–66. *Congo 1960*, vividly describes the events leading up to independence as a hasty and disjointed affair that the Congolese population had not fully understood. See House, *The U.N. in the Congo*, 256–66. For more detailed accounts in English, see Crawford Young, *Politics in the Congo: Decolonization and Independence* (Princeton: Princeton University Press, 1965), and René Lemarchand, *Political Awakening in the Belgian Congo* (Berkeley: University of California Press, 1964).

14. Leslie, *Zaire*, 20.

15. See Rajeshwar Dayal, *Mission for Hammarskjold: The Congo Crisis* (Princeton: Princeton University Press, 1976), 2, as well as Schatzberg, *Mobutu or Chaos?*, 11.

16. This was the reflection given by a fellow student after having heard the elder African statesman Ali Mazrui speak at a lecture I was privileged to attend at the University of the West Indies, Mona, Jamaica, 1997.

17. Leslie, *Zaire*, 21.

18. Dayal, *Mission for Hammarskjold*, 6–7.

19. For a recent and thoroughly documented recent account that blames Belgian officials for this infamous assassination, see Ludo De Witte, *The Assassination of Patrice Lumumba*, trans. Ann Wright and Renée Fenby (London: Verso, 2001).

20. Leslie, *Zaire*, 23–5.

21. Ibid.

22. Sean Kelly, *America's Tyrant: The CIA and Mobutu of Zaire* (Washington D.C.: University Press of America, 1993), 193.

23. For a surprisingly positive assessment of Mobutu's early years by a deeply informed scholar who subsequently became a Mobutu critic, see Jean-Claude Willame, *Patrimonialism and Political Change in the Congo* (Stanford, CA: Stanford University Press, 1972); also see Crawford Young and Thomas Turner in *The Rise and Decline of the Zairean State* (Madison: University of Wisconsin Press, 1985); the Young and Turner volume is the definitive work on the Mobutu regime through the mid-1980s.

24. Schatzberg, *Mobutu or Chaos?*, 32.

25. Guy Gran argues this point most convincingly in "An Introduction to Zaire's Permanent Development Crisis," in Gran, ed., *Zaire: The Political Economy of Underdevelopment* (New York: Praeger Press, 1979), 58.

26. See Ibid., 59 as well as Young and Turner, *Rise and Decline*, 281–306.

27. On this point, see Colette Braeckman, *Le dinosaure: Le Zaïre de Mobutu* (Paris: Fayard, 1992), 191.
28. Schatzberg, *Mobutu or Chaos?*, 32.
29. On this point, see particularly Thomas Callaghy, *The State-Society Struggle: Zaïre in Comparative Perspective* (New York: Columbia University Press, 1984).
30. The definitive source on Mobutu's mode of oppression is Michael G. Schatzberg, *The Dialectics of Oppression in Zaïre* (Bloomington: Indiana University Press, 1988).
31. Schatzberg, *Mobutu or Chaos?*, 34.
32. Gran, "An Introduction," 58.
33. Jean Philippe Peemans and Jean-Marie Wautlet, *Accumulation and Non-Development in Zaïre 1960–80* (Louvain: University of Louvain Press, 1981), 227.
34. Schatzberg, *Mobutu or Chaos?*, 39.
35. Ibid., 40.
36. Banque du Zaire, *Rapport annuel,* cited in William Reno, *Warlord Politics and African States* (Boulder, CO: Lynne Reiner Press, 1998): 154.
37. Ibid., 155.
38. My conversations with John Clark while writing this chapter prompted my adoption of the concept of the unraveling state. It is a state that is declining in its capacity for enforced order because the fabric of power and authority is unraveling, due to decline in public support and economic recession, among other things. For a discussion about when the "critical juncture" in the decline of the Zairian state was reached, see John F. Clark, "The Extractive State in Zaire," in Leonardo Villalon, ed., *Critical Juncture: The African States Between Disintegration and Reconfiguration* (Boulder, CO: Lynne Rienner, 1997), 112–15.
39. Clark, "The Nature and Evolution of the State in Zaire," 3–6.
40. Leslie, *Zaire,* 174.
41. Reno, *Warlord Politics,* 159.
42. Kisangani Emizet, "Zaire after Mobutu: A Potential Case of Humanitarian Emergency" (paper from the World Institute for Development Economic Research Seminar, Helsinki 6–8 October, 1996), 6.
43. William Reno argues that "warlord politics" had become characteristic of failing African states; see the introduction to his *Warlord Politics,* 3–15.
44. Jean Francois Bayart, *The State in Africa* (London: Longman, 1993), conceptualizes the African state as a stage where ethnic rivalries are often played out. The state is the site and seat of power, domination, and accumulation.
45. On this episode, and on the evolution of ethno-regional identities and clashes in Congo in general, see John F. Clark, "Ethno-Regionalism in Zaire: Roots, Manifestations and Meaning," *Journal of African Policy Studies* 1, no. 2 (1995): 23–45.
46. Reno, *Warlord Politics,* 161.
47. Edgar O'Ballance, *The Congo–Zaire Experience 1960–98* (London: Macmillan Press, 2000), xviii-xix.
48. Ibid., 50.
49. The Banyamulenge are Congolese citizens of Tutsi origin, having migrated to the Mulenge mountain area sometime in the distant past.
50. Ibid., 165–6.
51. Filip Reyntjens, "The Second Congo War: More than a Remake," *African Affairs* 98 (1999): 241.
52. Ibid., 242.

PART II

The Post-Mobutu Regimes in Congo and Their Supporters

CHAPTER 4

A Survival Guide to Kinshasa

LESSONS OF THE FATHER,
PASSED DOWN TO THE SON

KEVIN C. DUNN[1]

When Laurent Désiré Kabila's forces drove out the remaining vestiges of Mobutu Sese Seko's crumbling thirty-year-old dictatorship in May 1997, a mood of uncertainty prevailed both within Zaire and the international community. Zairians had suffered for over three decades while Mobutu, supported by various international actors such as the United States, France, and Belgium, had bled the country dry. It has been estimated that Mobutu and his close friends pillaged between U.S.$4 billion and U.S.$10 billion of the country's wealth, siphoning off up to 20 percent of the government's operating budget, 30 percent of its mineral export revenues, and 50 percent of its capital budget.[2] Zaire's formal economy had shrunk by more than 40 percent between 1988 and 1995. Its foreign debt in 1997 was around U.S.$14 billion. At U.S.$117, its 1993 per capita gross domestic product was 65 percent lower than its 1958 pre-independence level.[3] While there was little disagreement about how bad the past was, there were few willing to place bets on the future. Kabila was a relative unknown, having spent much of Mobutu's reign as a small-time career rebel ensconced in the east and engaged in gold smuggling and the occasional armed attack. When Kabila's rebels took the capital, Kinshasa, and Kabila proclaimed himself president of the country—renamed the Democratic Republic of Congo (DRC)—few foreign observers were sure if he would be a savior or a successor to Mobutu's dictatorial ways.

On 16 January 2001, after less than four years in power, Laurent Kabila was assassinated by a member of his own presidential bodyguard. In his brief reign, Kabila had seen the country collapse into another war. This time, the war involved at least three rebel groups, five major intervening (or invading) regional states, a handful of other neighboring states drawn into the fray, and a wide array of international actors, most of whom attempted to reap the financial benefits of the ongoing conflict. As this civil war (perhaps a misnomer given that its roots lay in a foreign invasion) progressed, Kabila was frequently portrayed as either "Mobutu redux" or a messiah for national unity. In fact, he was neither. Despite clear dictatorial and repressive tactics,

Kabila was not Mobutu. Nor was the regional and international context Kabila found himself in anything like the Cold War context of Mobutu's heyday. However, if there was anything clearly "Mobutuesque" about Kabila, it was his ability to survive against the odds—at least initially. This chapter will analyze the strategies Kabila employed for remaining in power. As will be clear, these strategies helped facilitate Congo's descent into violence and fragmentation. They also eventually proved counterproductive for Kabila, as he was gunned down by one of the men entrusted with ensuring his personal survival.

This chapter divides the Kabila era into two stages. First, it focuses on his ascension, installation, and consolidation of power, covering the outbreak of the anti-Mobutu rebellion in 1996 to the beginning of the rebellion against Kabila's own regime that began in 1998. In so doing, it evaluates Kabila's record during his first year in power, focusing on the strategies he used to survive. Stage two involves the political, diplomatic, and military strategies of the Kabila government after the outbreak of the second rebellion. While some of Kabila's survival strategies remained the same, he was forced to employ new ones and enlist a different set of friends for the defense of his regime. At the time of his death, Kabila was embarking on a third stage. In fact, it seems that his assassination may have been prompted by resistance to this third stage. Now that Joseph Kabila has assumed office, this chapter will conclude with an estimation of the short-term and long-term implications of his father's survival strategies, as well as a discussion of Joseph Kabila's own strategies.

STAGE ONE: THE INSTALLATION OF KABILA

Unlike other "new leaders" in Africa who spent years to win their revolutions—thirty in the case of Issaias Afwerki's Eritrean revolution, six for Yoweri Museveni's Uganda, and four for Paul Kagame's Rwanda—Kabila's rebellion took less than a year to topple Mobutu's regime.[4] While it is certainly true that Kabila had been a career rebel for more than three decades, he had not spent that time creating a vision or strategy for a new Congo. Rather, he ruled a small mountainous corner of eastern Zaire, where he engaged in mineral smuggling, often with the blessing and connivance of Mobutu's local strongmen.

Kabila was born in Likasi, Katanga, in 1939 to a Luba father and Lunda mother. His roots were in the Manono Zone of northern Katanga. After the Katangan secession in 1960, Kabila became actively involved in the fighting against Moise Tshombe's secessionist forces, serving as a "deputy commander" of the Balubakat party's youth wing, the Jeunesses Balubakat. By 1962, he was appointed to the North Katanga provincial assembly and served as chief of cabinet for Minister of Information Ferdinand Tumba. He established himself as a supporter of Prosper Mwamba Ilunga and hardline Lumumbists. When the Lumumbists formed the Conseil National de Libération (CNL), Kabila was sent to the eastern Congo to assist in the organization and promotion of revolution, especially in the provinces of Kivu and North Katanga. In 1965, he was running rebel operations across Lake Tanganyika from Kigoma, Tanzania. He continued this work after the CNL was succeeded by the Conseil Suprême de la Révolution (Supreme Council of the Revolution—CSR) in 1965. It was during this time that a Cuban expeditionary force, led by Ché Guevera, briefly joined Kabila's rebels. The Cubans, however, became deeply disillusioned by what they considered to be the ineptness and disorganization among the Congolese, and left after a few months.[5]

In 1967, Kabila and some of his remaining supporters withdrew into the mountains of South Kivu, in the Fizi-Baraka area, where they founded the Parti de la Révolution Populaire (Party of the Popular Revolution—PRP). Over the next few decades, Kabila and his followers created a minor fiefdom in the region, featuring collective agriculture, rudimentary Marxist-Leninist re-education, extortion and exploitation, and mineral smuggling. The PRP operated with the knowledge of the local Zairian army in Kivu. Reportedly, the local garrison commanders would trade munitions with Kabila's forces for a cut of their extortion and robbery operations. By the late 1970s and early 1980s, Kabila had become a successful trader and smuggler in East Africa, maintaining homes in Dar-es-Salaam and Kampala, where he reportedly encountered Yoweri Museveni, future leader of Uganda. Museveni and former Tanzanian president Julius Nyerere would later introduce Kabila to Paul Kagame of Rwanda. These connections proved fortuitous for Kabila when the Ugandan and Rwandan regimes began looking for a Congolese face to put on their intervention into Mobutu's Zaire.[6]

The immediate roots of the Rwandan and Ugandan intervention can be traced back to the early 1990s, when Mobutu's regime increasingly fanned the flames of ethnic hatred in the eastern part of Zaire. Succumbing to domestic and international pressure, Mobutu called a Sovereign National Conference in 1991. One of the many results of the national conference was the exposure of numerous tensions in Zairian society, not the least of which stemmed from ethnicity and social identity. Representatives from North and South Kivu provinces in the eastern part of the country used the national conference as a forum to attack the Kinyarwanda speakers in the regions, referred to as Banyarwanda and Banyamulenge, respectively. The Kivu representatives sought to rescind the citizenship of these groups under the 1981 Zairian Nationality Act and force them to return to Rwanda and Burundi. This highlighted ongoing and complex tensions in the Great Lakes region, most of which related to issues of identity and access to land. By 1993, armed groups began attacking Banyarwanda in North Kivu. Soon, the killings were in full swing, paralleling actions in neighboring Rwanda. By mid-1994, thousands were dead in North Kivu and thousands more had sought refuge in Rwanda and South Kivu.[7]

On 6 April 1994, a plane carrying Rwandan president Habyarimana and Burundian president Ntaryamira was shot down over the Rwandan capital of Kigali. This provided the spark for several months of killing and fighting, now commonly referred to as the 1994 Rwandan genocide.[8] The hundred-day killing spree resulted in the murder of around 800,000 Rwandans, the overthrow of the Rwandan government by Paul Kagame's Rwandan Patriotic Front (RPF), and the exodus of over 2 million Rwandans to refugee camps inside Zaire. These refugees were a mix of civilians, Interahamwe (the militia largely held responsible for the genocide), and members of the defeated Rwandan army (Forces Armées Rwandaises—FAR). The refugee camps quickly became controlled by the Interahamwe and FAR. Over the next two years, these groups (with the blessing of Mobutu's central government and regional strongmen) reorganized and rearmed. Soon, they began launching attacks from the camps into neighboring Rwanda and against the Banyamulenge in South Kivu. After their requests for assistance were ignored by the international community, the

Rwandan government and local Banyamulenge decided to take matters into their own hands by attacking their attackers.

Forming a Rebel Alliance

The *Interahamwe* and FAR forces operating from the refugee camp bases stepped up their attacks on the local Banyamulenge in 1995 and 1996. The citizenship question for this group remained a volatile issue. On 7 October 1996, the governor of South Kivu announced that all Banyamulenge had to leave the country in a week. While this event is often cited as the spark that ignited the uprising, the rebellion had been planned as early as July or August 1996, if not earlier. The rebels launched a multi-prong attack against the refugee camps, *Interahamwe,* and Zairian army (Forces Armées Zaïroises—FAZ). The rebels quickly moved from south to north, gaining control of the 300 miles of Zaire's eastern frontier and capturing the cities of Uvira on 24 October, Bukavu on 30 October, and Goma on 1 November. The refugee camps were attacked and disassembled. An enormous human wave moved westward, made up of refugees, *Interahamwe,* and FAZ, all of whom were fleeing from the advancing rebels.[9]

Largely orchestrated by the Kagame regime in Rwanda, the rebels were actually a loose alliance of several opposition forces. The four primary groups were Kabila's PRP, the Conseil de la Résistance pour la Démocratie (CRD) led by André Kisasse Ngandu, the Mouvement Révolutionnaire pour la Libération du Zaire (MRLZ) led by Masasu Ningaba, and the Alliance Démocratique des Peuples (ADP) led by Déogratias Bugera. These forces were united under the label Alliance des Forces Démocratiques pour la Libération du Congo-Zaire (ADFL). At the center of this union was a shaky alliance between Kabila's rebels and the CRD. Initially, it was reported that Kabila was the spokesman for the coalition, with André Kisasse Ngandu as its military commander. However, Kisasse Ngandu was killed early on in the campaign under mysterious circumstances, and Kabila became increasingly portrayed as the ADFL's leader.[10]

At first, most Zairian's dismissed Kabila's leadership position as a transparent effort by Rwanda and Uganda to give the rebellion a "Zairian" face. The ADFL was initially unpopular with the majority of the population because of its image as a Tutsi-dominated foreign creation. The rebellion was given a major boost within Zaire when the popular opposition leader Étienne Tshisekedi publicly defended Kabila and the rebels against this xenophobia.[11] This would prove to be ironic, given the subsequent souring of Kabila and Tshisekedi's relationship. Over the next few months, Zairians began to accept Kabila due to his rhetorical claims of historic legitimacy as a rebel leader, their own desire to be "liberated," and the dawning realization that Mobutu's days were numbered.

However, the populace's initial perception of the ADFL as a foreign invention turned out to be correct. In July 1997, Kagame admitted what had been long believed to be the truth: Rwanda had planned and directed the rebellion. In a surprisingly frank interview with the *Washington Post,* Kagame stated that the Rwandan government had decided in 1996 that the threat from the refugee camps in Zaire had to be eliminated. The Rwandan government sought out Zairian opposition groups such as the PRP to help fight against Mobutu and provide a Zairian cover to the operations. Kagame even confirmed that Rwandan troops and officers were at the forefront of the rebellion.[12]

Surviving through the Kindness of Friends

By April 1997, Kabila's rebels and their Rwandan comrades had gained control of the mineral-rich provinces of Kasai and Shaba, thus robbing Mobutu and his power elite of a major economic lifeline. As they moved toward Kinshasa, Angolan government troops poured across the border to assist them in the overthrow of Mobutu, who was being aided by the Angolan rebel group UNITA (União Nacional para a Independência Total de Angola). By 17 May 1997, Kinshasa had fallen and Mobutu and his entourage had fled. Soon afterward, Kabila proclaimed himself the new president, renamed the country the Democratic Republic of Congo (DRC), reintroduced the flag and the currency unit originally adopted at independence, banned political parties, and began to consolidate his power.

Initially, Kabila's strategy for survival was to rely heavily upon regional and international support. Of particular importance was his dependence on Rwanda, Uganda, and Angola. The Angolan government proved to be extremely valuable to Kabila, both in their assistance in capturing Kinshasa and in providing essential logistical support. The Angolans' involvement was largely aimed at delivering what they hoped would be a deathblow to the UNITA rebels by cutting off their supply lines, driving them out of their Zairian rear bases, and ousting their longtime benefactor, Mobutu. The Museveni regime also proved to be extremely important in Kabila's ascension to power. Museveni provided military assistance, in large part to deny the Allied Democratic Forces (ADF), the Lord's Resistance Army (LRA), and the West Bank Nile Front (WBNF) the use of Zairian territory as rear bases for the destabilization of Uganda. Yet, it was the Rwandan regime of Paul Kagame that was the primary force behind the ADFL and their victory over Mobutu. Not only did Rwanda provide troops, logistical support, and material, but many of the Banyamulenge fighters had received their training when fighting with the RPF in Rwanda since 1990 (just as many of the RPF soldiers had earlier received their training fighting alongside Museveni's troops).

Once in power, Kabila continued to rely heavily on Rwandan assistance and protection. As Peter Rosenblum wrote, "any visitor to the seat of the government in Kinshasa—the Intercontinental Hotel—would have been struck by the presence of Rwandan soldiers and businessmen, most of whom did little to hide their origins. Then there were Kabila's 'bodyguards'—'six tall, English-speaking gentlemen,' as one visitor described them—not Zairian and not necessarily there to protect him."[13] Evidence of the extent to which Kabila depended upon his RPF benefactors became clear when the United Nations attempted to launch an investigation into reported human rights abuses during the war against Mobutu.

As UN Secretary-General Kofi Annan moved to set up the investigation team, Kabila's government insisted that they look at the events of the previous year in context of the 1994 massacres in Rwanda and the decades of Mobutu's dictatorship. The UN agreed, but Kabila put up other obstacles. Since he was generally regarded as the liberator of Congo, Kabila enjoyed an initial honeymoon period with most of the international community. This was clearly the reason why Kofi Annan was overly willing to accommodate Kabila's demands, and Annan made numerous concessions to placate Kabila. Kabila then attempted to thwart the investigation by insisting that the mission await a parallel investigation by the Organization of African Unity, denying the investigators the ability to buy tickets, and staging local protests to disrupt their work.

Despite these impediments, on 24 August 1997, a team of UN investigators arrived in Kinshasa to begin investigating the fate of Hutu refugees reportedly massacred during the rebellion. In a preliminary report, Roberto Garreton, the initial leader of the UN investigation, concluded that the massacres of Rwandan refugees were planned and systematic, and he identified 40 massacre sites in eastern Congo. Most human rights observers and relief workers in the region confirmed that there had been massive human rights violations and over 100,000 Rwandan refugees murdered. Finally, in March 1998, the investigators and forensic experts withdrew. By that time, international interest had turned elsewhere and the investigation collapsed.

Importantly, Kabila and his troops were not the focus of the investigation. Rather, most of the investigation revolved around the actions of the Rwandan military forces operating with the ADFL. Circumstantial evidence suggested that Rwandan soldiers and officers were on the spot where the massacres occurred. It was largely believed that these massacres were carried out against Hutu refugees—many of whom were believed to be *Interahamwe* and FAR members—as retribution for the 1994 genocide. Rather than allow the UN to investigate these human rights abuses, which probably would have done little to discredit his own regime, Kabila was steadfast in his opposition. This was done to protect his Rwandan backers, despite the fact that Kabila's resistance to the investigation depleted the substantial reserve of international goodwill toward his regime. Yet, given the extent to which Kabila was dependent upon his RPF backers, he had little choice but to resist.

Kabila's resistance to the UN was emboldened by signals being sent from Washington, D.C. The United States paid only minor lip service to the charges of human rights abuses during the anti-Mobutu rebellion. This was clearly due to the established connections the RPF regime had with Washington, D.C. Since Kagame's victory in 1994, the United States had become his primary supporter in the international community, as it was with Museveni's Uganda. The United States had provided counterinsurgency training to the Rwandan army and, according to Kagame's *Washington Post* interview, was aware of Rwanda's intentions to attack the refugee camps in Zaire.[14]

During the early stages of the rebellion, the United States was one of its clearest supporters. Indeed, the United States was involved in Kabila's rebellion from the very beginning. As François Ngolet writes, "these links were evident when an American diplomat, Dennis Hankins, the political official in Kinshasa, went to the rebel headquarters in Goma. Hankins's visit was followed by the United States ambassador in Kigali, Peter Whaley, who frequently visited Kabila in Goma, at a moment when the rebels' strategy moved from a regional insurgency to the drive to overthrow Mobutu."[15] The United States sent other officials to visit Kabila as well. At a time when the ADFL was still seen as suspect by most Zairians, the head of the U.S. Committee for Refugees, Roger Winter, visited Kabila in eastern Zaire and praised the rebels, suggesting that they were being warmly received by the local population.[16]

Once Kabila came to power, the United States continued its support. As Kabila's initial honeymoon became tarnished with calls for a UN investigation into reported human rights violations, the Clinton administration declared its sympathy with Kabila's assertion that the UN and human rights organizations were trying to impose "Western values" on Africa. As one U.S. official stated, "We have to respect the African point of view."[17] The United States chose to downplay the situation publicly, even distorting the number and plight of the refugees remaining in Zaire to divert criticism away from Kabila and his Rwandan backers. Most importantly, U.S. officials reportedly instructed Kabila not to cooperate with the UN investigations of the massacres.[18] Because of their defense of Kabila's intransigence to the UN investigation, one observer noted at the time that "not since the 1980s, when the two were colliding over Central America, has the relationship between the U.S. government and the international human-rights community been as acrimonious as it is today over U.S. policy in the Congo."[19] The United States initially supported Kabila for several reasons: to exploit natural resources, to contain Islamic fundamentalism in east Africa, and to extend its influence in central Africa.[20] The extension of its influence was seen as a direct challenge to the waning Francophone power in the region.

Not surprisingly, France was resistant to the Kabila rebellion. As the ADFL and their Rwandan backers swept across Zaire, France publicly called for a multinational force to intervene for "humanitarian" reasons. However, most observers believed that France was more interested in propping up Mobutu than rescuing civilians—much as they had done in Opération Turquoise, when they attempted to stall an RPF victory by protecting the retreat of the former Rwandan government, its army, and the *Interahamwe*. As Kabila's rebellion gathered strength, Paris argued that Mobutu was the only leader that could "save Zairians from themselves and the inevitable ethnic blood bath that would follow."[21] However, France's legitimacy within the region and the international community had already been severely compromised. Despite the will to intervene, France's past record and damaged reputation meant that its hands were tied. Even the French press openly questioned the government's humanitarian motives and viewed Mobutu as a lost cause.[22]

The initial French resistance to and U.S. support of Kabila signaled how dramatically the balance of power in central Africa had shifted in the wake of the 1994 Rwandan genocide. Beforehand, Paris enjoyed tremendous influence in the region. By the mid-1990s, however, Francophone influence had been replaced by the Anglophone influence of Kampala, Uganda—and its American patron in Washington, D.C. The victory of the RPF in Rwanda and the ADFL in Zaire/Congo further alienated Paris in the region and elevated U.S. influence.[23] Kabila was deftly able to exploit U.S. interest in the region for his own survival, particularly in terms of accessing financial resources.

Kabila courted the international economic community, and they him. Even before Kinshasa had fallen, Kabila's finance minister, Mawampanga Mwana, was meeting with dozens of businessmen in Lubumbashi, including representatives from Goldman Sachs, First Bank of Boston, Morgan Grefell, and other economic investors.[24] The United States was instrumental in facilitating these connections. Indeed, North American mining corporations were quick to reach out to Kabila. American Mineral Fields (AMF), a mining firm based in Hope, Arkansas (the hometown of then-president Bill Clinton), approached Kabila and organized contacts. In fact, most of the contracts with Western speculative companies had been signed with Mobutu's Kengo government. However, given the rebels' advance into mineral-rich areas, Kabila was able to reap the benefits of these agreements. The AMF and Canadian-owned Tenke Mining Corp.—which had been awarded a contract for cobalt and copper exploitation by the Kengo government—reportedly began supplying millions of dollars to the ADFL, along with transport for Kabila's troops.[25] After coming into office, Kabila and his mining administration sought to squeeze as much money as possible from U.S., Canadian, Australian, and South African mining companies.[26]

Yet, Kabila's connections to Western multinationals, and his ability to reap the personal benefits of conducting business with them, were offset by a rather cautious stance taken by the international financial institutions (IFIs). At a meeting in Paris on 5 September 1997, the World Bank and the International Monetary Fund (IMF) stated that the disbursement of much-needed aid would be tied to certain conditionalities. Primary among these was the requirement of a coherent plan from the Kabila government for the realization of democracy and human rights, as well as the revival of the economy.[27] This position by the IFIs was in interesting contrast to their position vis à vis Mobutu, in which they allowed vast amounts of money to disappear into the black hole of the dictator's pockets. It is estimated that the World Bank, the IMF, and bilateral donors gave over U.S.$8.5 billion in loans and grants to Zaire between 1970 and 1994. Despite the tough stand of the IFIs to his new government, Kabila was gambling that international aid donors would not want to punish the man who got rid of Mobutu.

The High Price Of Friendship: Distrusted at Home

From the outset of the ADFL rebellion, Kabila relied more on his foreign backers than he did on domestic support. Indeed, the survival strategies displayed by Kabila in his first few months of rule were markedly external-oriented, with little attempt to garner domestic support beyond rhetorically positioning himself as the liberator of Congo. His relationship with the established opposition and civil society groups are particularly instructive.

When the ADFL rebels captured Kinshasa and ended Mobutu's reign, many were cautiously optimistic that this victory would enable a true opening of political space for opposition parties and civil society groups. But this was not to be. On 28 May 1998, Kabila issued a one-page decree establishing the new constitutional order and granting nearly absolute power to the president. The next day, he was sworn into office. In his inaugural speech, Kabila dismissed the work of the 1991–92 Sovereign National Conference and, by extension, Étienne Tshisekedi's (leader of the Union pour la Démocratie et le Progrès Social–UDPS) claim to the post of prime minister. Kabila attacked the local opposition leaders and dismissed the demand for immediate elections. In this speech, Kabila also said: "Let's stop talking about democracy and elections. We are not going on with the preceding regime, but we are building a new state built on new values."[28] Kabila then announced that a commission would write a new constitution by October 1998, with a referendum on its adoption by December. Legislative and presidential elections would follow in April 1999. Yet, these and other deadlines were soon missed.

As Peter Rosenblum correctly points out, Kabila could not have accepted the work of the Sovereign National Conference without accepting Tshisekedi as prime minister.[29] To do so would have undermined his own authority. Yet, the Sovereign National Conference itself had been manipulated by Mobutu and its defenders were not above suspicion. As Edouard Bustin has aptly observed, few of the established domestic opposition leaders could "pride themselves on having kept their hands clean, or never having supped with the devil."[30] Aware that his survival depended on his external backers and not on a domestic power base, Kabila could not allow

Tshisekedi and other opposition leaders a political opening without putting his own future at risk. After being snubbed by Kabila, Tshisekedi attacked him for being a dictator, stating: "I call on the people to resist with all their strength and energy. He is not president. He is just a candidate for president."[31] Kabila refused to sit by quietly. In early 1998, Kabila had Tshisekedi arrested and sent into internal exile. Kabila's regime set out to ban party and political activities in an attempt to consolidate its hold on power.

Domestically, one of the results of Kabila's victory was the collapse of the informal civil society networks that had kept Zaire operating under Mobutu's regime. After years of surviving Mobutu's corruption by exploiting it, the networks suddenly collapsed as Mobutu's corrupt military and political leaders were replaced by virtual unknowns.[32] Not only were local Congolese unsure of how to deal with the new regime, but they were also unsure who the new regime was. Kabila distanced himself from the established opposition parties in Kinshasa because he assumed (sometimes correctly) that their proximity to Mobutu made them suspect. Instead, he chose to fill his new government with returning exiles. This created a deep rift between the government and the governed, as the local population felt distanced from the new government, while the new returnees were unfamiliar with and suspicious of the establish domestic opposition.[33] For example, the new minister of justice had spent his entire career in Belgium, the new minister of cooperation in the UK, and the new minister of the interior in the United States.

Kabila's lack of political skills, inexperience, and monopolization of power are often cited as the reasons for his failure to capture popular support during his first twelve months in office. Kabila's strategy of rule relied heavily upon the informal issuance of "law decrees" without any fixed legal point of reference.[34] In November 1997, public opinion polls in Kinshasa found that less than 20 percent of the voters would support Kabila if elections were held at that time.[35] Many began to equate Kabila with Mobutu. One of the country's newspapers, Le Phare, ran a headline proclaiming: "L. D. Kabila = J. D. Mobutu." Such negative views were exacerbated by Kabila himself, who did little to apologize for his heavy-handed consolidation of power or his contempt for the established local political scene. Kabila was unable to communicate directly to the masses because he did not speak Lingala, the language of the army and of Kinshasa. He referred to Lingala as a "dirty" language and preferred to deliver his speeches in Swahili, using an interpreter.[36]

According to local human rights groups, the human rights situation in Kinshasa worsened in the first year of Kabila's rule.[37] Within that first year, the pace of political repression increased with each passing month. Moreover, popular opinion continued to view Kabila as a puppet installed by the Rwandans and Congolese Tutsi. The continuing presence of Rwandans and Angolans strengthened the view that he had sold out Congo to outsiders. Because his survival initially relied on external backing, Kabila surrounded himself almost entirely with Rwandan and Congolese Tutsi soldiers and advisers. Rwandans (or at least Congolese Tutsi) held key positions in the army. Given the longstanding anti-Tutsi rhetoric in Congo, exacerbated and exploited by the Mobutu regime, anti-Tutsi prejudice remained high among the Congolese. Therefore, all Tutsi presence in Kabila's government was regarded as evidence of Rwandan influence and control. Such sentiment was not helped by Paul Kagame's Washington Post interview, in which he claimed credit for waging and winning the anti-Mobutu rebellion.

Changing Strategies

By late 1997, however, Kabila began to change the strategies he employed for survival. There had been a clear tension between his reliance on external backers and
the lack of domestic support that dependency caused. Kabila began to take steps to
distance himself from several of his key external backers—both regionally and internationally. With each step, he was able to increase his own domestic support. Yet, the
key to his survival continued to be his reliance on external support. By 1998, the
main difference was in the friends he chose to keep.

At the international level, Kabila's relations with the United States began to
sour at the end of 1997. A clear sign of this occurred in December, when Secretary
of State Madeleine Albright held a peace conference with Kabila to draw attention
to Africa's "new leaders." Continuing the new U.S. tradition of protecting Kabila,
Albright spent much of her time deftly deflecting questions away from Kabila's
stonewalling of the UN investigation and reports of growing political repression
in Congo. Yet, as one observer commented, Kabila "refused to behave."[38] De-
nouncing the political opposition and threatening further crackdowns, Kabila
turned to Albright, smiled and proclaimed "Vive la démocratie." When President
Clinton visited Africa in late March 1998, Congo was not on the itinerary and relations had frosted over.

With regards to his Rwandan and Ugandan allies, Kabila did not act to address
the issue of Tutsi marginalization in Congo or the question of Banyamulenge citizenship. Since these were the issues that sparked the initial rebellion, Kabila was
sending his backers a strong message of rebuke. Even more troubling for his eastern
allies was the fact that he failed to provide Uganda and Rwanda with safe and secure
borders. Rather, the attacks by Ugandan and Rwandan rebel groups operating in the
east of the country—the primary reason each country initiated the original rebellion—continued after Kabila's accession to power. In a move that strengthened his
domestic support, Kabila began to reduce the Tutsi influence in his government, replacing several key ministers with candidates from Katanga. In effect, Kabila began
creating a new cabinet and regional governments that ran counter to the team that
put him in power. Yet, Rwanda and Uganda soon proved that they were not going to
sit idly by while the man they helped elevate to power slowly shut them out.

STAGE TWO: DEFENDING KABILA FROM HIS FORMER FRIENDS

Throughout 1998, Kabila had increasingly demonstrated his lack of gratitude to his
mentors. Responding largely to growing popular resentment in Kinshasa of the foreigners and the view that he was a puppet of these powers, Kabila unilaterally announced the end of the "military cooperation" with Rwanda and Uganda. He
publicly thanked them for their "assistance," and then asked them to withdraw their
troops immediately. While this move was greeted with enthusiasm at home, it
strengthened Rwandan and Ugandan resolve to once again intervene in Congolese
affairs. Putting together another group of disenfranchised Congolese (some of
whom had ties or were members of Mobutu's former regime), Rwanda and Uganda
orchestrated another rebellion in eastern Congo—this time with the goal of deposing the man they had imposed a year earlier.

By early August 1998, the rebels quickly seized Goma, Bukavu, Uvira, and Kisan-gani in the east. Leaping across the country in a captured aircraft, rebels moved into the west, initially capturing Kitona, Matadi, and the Inga Dam hydroelectric com-plex, and threatening the eastern suburbs of Kinshasa. Publicly, the rebels pro-claimed that Kabila had become worse than Mobutu and had to be removed. On 5 August 1998, from Goma, Bizima Karaha, ex-Kabila foreign minister and one of the rebel leaders, stated: "Kabila has failed to govern. In his one year in power he has done more political damage than Mobutu ever did in thirty-two years. This is a countrywide revolution. People are disillusioned and angry."[39] In particular, Kabila was attacked for nepotism and failing to appoint a government of national unity. Singled out were Kabila's cousin, Interior Minister Gaetan Kakudji; his nephew, Jus-tice Minister Mwenze Kongolo; and son, Army Chief of Staff Joseph Kabila.

Kabila's regime responded by painting the rebellion as a Rwandan/Tutsi invasion. Kabila's nephew, Justice Minister Mwenze Kongolo, stated on BBC radio: "This is a Rwanda invasion and Rwanda and Uganda are spearheading the invasion of the Congo." Kabila's spokesman Didier Mumengi added: "Rwanda and Uganda are criminal states that have meddled in foreign affairs while drawing on a feeling of pity from the international community after the 1994 Rwandan genocide."[40] Indeed, it was becoming increasingly clear that the various "rebel" movements involved in the DRC war were plagued by a lack of credibility, internal contradictions and conflicts, and dubious linkages with outside actors and interest groups. Today, despite the fact they remain incredibly unpopular among the populace they have "liberated," these armed groups and their foreign backers continue to threaten the (new) government in Kinshasa.

With the initiation of the second rebellion, Kabila's strategies for survival altered. While he continued to rely heavily on external friends, the make-up of his friend-ship circle changed significantly. Kabila was also forced to become more active in his diplomacy. "Stage two" of his survival was also characterized by an increased empha-sis on garnering domestic support for the regime.

Reformulating the Regional Strategy: Out with the Old, In with the New

The new rebellion was extremely successful in its initial stages, as town after town fell in the east and rebels in the west put the squeeze on Kinshasa. By 20 August, Ka-bila's regime was at the edge of the precipice. It was at this moment that Kabila en-gaged in a flurry of diplomatic activity. Within the first stage of his regime, Kabila's diplomatic skills were limited at best, as was evidenced by his display at the press conference with U.S. Secretary of State Albright. But within the first few weeks of the second rebellion, Kabila had managed to convince Zimbabwe, Namibia, and An-gola to send troops to his rescue.

Kabila's primary strategy for survival—reliance on external backers—remained the same. Kabila had relied on Rwanda and Uganda to put him in power and main-tain his position during the first year of his rule. In stage two of his survival, his break with Kagame's and Museveni's regimes required that he turn elsewhere. Kabila was able to build a new coalition through rapid diplomatic activities with Robert Mu-gabe, Sam Nujoma, and José Eduardo Dos Santos. Kabila was also successful in per-suading the Central African Republic, which shares a large border with the DRC, to open its territory to Kabila's troops in an effort to create a new front against the rebels in the north of the country.

Kabila's immediate salvation in the face of the rebellion proved to be the external intervention of Zimbabwe and Angola. Angolan government troops quickly responded to the rebel's threat in the west, all but annexing Kitoni, Matadi, and the Inga Dam hydroelectric power plant. This has proven to be fortuitous for the Angolan government, as it has helped the country's crippled economy and given them de facto control over the Congo River basin. Zimbabwean commandos retook control of Kinshasa's Njili airport and moved to halt the rebels' advance across the country. These interventions occurred under the guise of SADC solidarity, but, as various chapters in this collection illustrate, each state was motivated by its own individual interests and agendas.

Robert Mugabe quickly emerged as Kabila's primary champion and defender. Not only did his regime and associates benefit materially from the intervention, but Mugabe's status as regional statesman and power-broker increased. Yet, Mugabe's intervention was met with criticism both at home and abroad. Responding to critical comments from South Africa's Nelson Mandela, Mugabe stated: "Those who want to keep out, fine. Let them keep out, but let them be silent about those who want to help."[41] Yet, in the months that followed, it became clear that Zimbabwe had the most at stake of the numerous countries involved in the DRC. As *African Business* reported in January 1999, "The Zimbabwe dollar lost 60 percent of its value in 12 months, tobacco exports are down 37 percent, commercial lending rates rose above 40 percent and a budget deficit of Z$3bn is exacerbated by President Mugabe's U.S.$2m dollar a day Congo adventure."[42]

The situations in both Angola and Zimbabwe illustrate the fact that, to a certain extent, the DRC war has become a necessity for most of the combatants. With their domestic economies in trouble, they are relying on the spoils of war for their financial salvation. As the new backers drain Congo of its resources, the country's new friends may yet prove to be more expensive and burdening than the previous Rwandan partnership. However, it should be noted that the profits from plundering operations on both sides of the war are mostly going to individuals in the Zimbabwean, Angolan, Ugandan, and Rwandan regimes, rather than to state treasuries.

These situations had important ramifications for Kabila's survival strategies. Namely, Kabila established economic ties with his new allies in order to accumulate wealth for himself and his associates. On 23 September 1999, for example, Zimbabwean defense minister Moven Mahachi announced that Zimbabwe and Congolese defense forces had set up a joint diamond and gold marketing venture to help finance the war in the DRC. The venture associated Osleg, a company "owned" by the Zimbabwean army, with the Congolese company Comiex, reportedly representing the interest of the Congolese army. The venture was reportedly established to help cover the cost of the 13,000 Zimbabwean troops in the DRC.[43]

It appears, however, that Osleg was in fact owned by private military interests, including Zimbabwean general Zvinavashe. Zvinavashe also owned a private trucking company, Zvinavashe Transport, that supplied Zimbabwe's troops in the DRC. Moreover, Comiex was reportedly a creation of President Kabila, with his fellow ministers as private shareholders. This venture illustrated Kabila's own willingness to cash in on the DRC conflict, as well as the Zimbabwean elites' need to find new ways to exploit their country's intervention in the DRC. The war in Congo has not turned out to be the cash cow many originally expected. It was earlier thought that the appointment of Zimbabwean CEO Billy Rautenbach as the head of the Gecamines copper and cobalt parastatal might benefit Zimbabwe. This hope was furthered when a contract was signed between Gecamines and Rautenbach's Ridgepointe Overseas Ltd. for an 80 percent interest in Gecamines' Central Group operations. However, Gecamines is going through the worst crisis of its history, with its cobalt output 40 percent below that of 1998.[44]

Further evidence that Kabila was "selling off" Congo to Zimbabwe to pay for his survival came in the announcement that Zimbabwe's Agricultural and Rural Development Authority parastatal had been given 500,000 hectares of land for farming and livestock in the Mitwala and Muhila areas of Katanga.[45] Such an act illustrated the path taken by Kabila to ensure his survival. In stage two of his regime, Kabila's regional dependence became increasingly characterized by resource extraction by his erstwhile allies. Kabila himself became an active participant in the emerging "spoils of war" system. This creation of a conflict political economy[46] ensured Kabila's immediate survival while simultaneously transforming the DRC into an "economic colony" of the numerous intervening forces, from Rwanda and Uganda to Angola and Zimbabwe.

Surviving at the Global Level: United States, France, and Multinational Corporations

Kabila's relationship with the United States had turned frosty before the second rebellion. Interestingly, U.S. Special Forces maintained a visible presence in both Rwanda and Uganda at the outbreak of the second rebellion, which gave many the impression that it occurred with at least tacit approval from Washington, D.C. Such assumptions were seemingly confirmed when the Pentagon's spokesperson, Colonel Nancy Burt, reported on 6 August 1998 that a twenty-man U.S. military "assessment team" had been at the Rwandan border crossing near Goma at the time the Rwandan troops were crossing into the DRC.[47]

Such a move was not surprising given that Washington's initial support for Kabila was a result of (and subordinated to) its friendly relationships with Rwanda and Uganda. As Thomas Turner notes, "In 1998, the United States apparently accepted the assurances of its allies that Kabila could be overthrown quickly and easily."[48] Given U.S. backing of the Museveni and Kagame regimes, many central Africans believe that the United States either initiated or encouraged the rebellion against Kabila. The U.S. actions behind the scenes of the Lusaka ceasefire agreement illustrate its support for Museveni and Kagame. They favor a regional solution, particularly one that benefits Uganda and Rwanda. Moreover, the involvement of Sudan and Libya on behalf of Kabila has been a major source of concern for the United States.[49]

Interestingly, France has used the collapse of the "Anglophone" alliance as an opportunity to reintroduce its influence in the region. Reportedly, Kabila was open to Paris's overtures. It has been suggested that Chad and the Central African Republic's involvement on behalf of Kabila is due in part to France's attempt to regain influence in Kinshasa.[50]

Yet, Kabila's global survival strategies primarily concerned his relations with external economic interests. On the one hand, Kabila mortgaged what little was left of the copper and diamond industry to Zimbabwe in order to prevent his overthrow.

This meant that many of the Western speculative corporations were short-shrifted by the Kabila regime. For example, Banro Resources Corporation, operator of the nationalized Twangiza mining concession in Shaba, had its shares suspended on the Ottawa Stock Exchange on 1 August 1998; in response they filed a U.S.$100 million claim against the Kabila government in U.S. courts. At the same time, Kabila increasingly sought to lure foreign investors in order to bankroll the war. Part of his strategy involved the inflation of diamond sales figures to attract foreign investment interest. In June 1999, for example, Kabila claimed that the Congolese diamond mining company MIBA's (Minière de Bakwanga) total export sales were up by 38 percent with 1.67 million carats sold for a total of U.S.$22.9 million. Yet, most analysts viewed the accuracy of these figures with suspicion.[51] On 22 July 1999, Kabila announced the formation of the Lubumbashi Metal Exchange. This venture, like many of Kabila's initiatives, was purely rhetorical and was never realized. The goal of this action was reflective of Kabila's general strategy: to attract foreign investors in order to access up-front capital, much as he had done during his original rebellion against Mobutu.

Unfortunately for Kabila, the strategy was not successful. In fact, Congo's economy remains in serious straits. Before his assassination, tax revenues had been dropping steadily. Tax revenue collected by OFIDA, the Congolese customs and excise authority, totaled around U.S.$33.2 million for the January–March 1999 quarter, down from the U.S.$60.5 million collected during the same period in 1998. By mid-1999, Gecamines reportedly had longterm debts of U.S.$1 billion and trade liabilities of U.S.$50 million.[52] MIBA (which is 80 percent owned by the state and 20 percent owned by the Belgian corporation Sibeka) still appears to be in serious trouble. By most accounts, its problems are related to the fact that Kabila's regime was milking it dry. *African Business* reported that Kabila wasted no time helping himself to the company's coffers. In April 1997, the company was ordered to transfer U.S.$3.5 million from MIBA's account to Comiex, whose main shareholder was Kabila himself. Other "voluntary" contributions followed. On 23 February 2000, MIBA was ordered by the Kabila government to hand over its Tshibwe kimberlitic concessions to a company named Sengamines. Sengamines was created the month before and is controlled by Kabila's Comiex, Zimbabwean general Zvinavashe's Osleg, and a Cayman Islands-registered company called Oryx Zimcon Ltd.[53] Again, this illustrated Kabila's strategy of "selling off" the DRC's resources to his external protectors while simultaneously enriching himself. As Erik Kennes has argued, Kabila's regime was not able to link up with recent changes in the global economy.[54] Most of the world's mining companies have bypassed the DRC and have engaged in more profitable regions in Africa. Since the beginning of the anti-Kabila war, the real economic actors have been traders, small fraudulent companies, and those involved in military commercialism, all of whom operate under the logic of predation.

Playing the Ethnicity Card for Domestic Support

In the early stages of the war, Kabila enjoyed a tremendous upsurge in his domestic popularity, despite the country's economic collapse and the fact that half of the country was effectively in the hands of foreign-backed rebels and the other half was occupied by resource-extracting "allies." When the second rebellion occurred, Kabila was quick to portray it as a foreign invasion and called on Congolese to defend their homeland. For the previous few months, Kabila had been distancing himself from his Rwandan, Ugandan, and Congolese Tutsi backers. He had replaced Tutsi members of his original government with people from his own Northern Katangan region. Kabila's distancing move was popular with the citizens in Kinshasa. These earlier moves, however, lacked the racial and ethnic vindictiveness that soon characterized Kabila's call to arms in the face of the second rebellion.

Kabila's nationalistic rhetoric garnered him huge support in Kinshasa. Much of Kabila's rhetoric on radio and television was racial, aimed at turning public opinion against the Tutsi supposedly behind the rebellion. Echoing the radio broadcast in Rwanda that preceded the 1994 genocide, it was reported in the Western press that Kabila urged listeners to use "a machete, a spear, an arrow, a hoe, spades, rakes, nails, truncheons, electric irons, barbed wire . . . to kill the Rwandan Tutsi."[55] The result was a brief witch-hunt against all eastern Congolese and perceived foreigners, often judged exclusively by facial appearances.[56] Some were caught and killed by Kabila's troops or by the enraged populace, and thousands were rounded up and imprisoned "for their own safety."[57] Thus, Kabila's construction of a "Congolese" identity shifted away from a pluralistic, anti-Mobutu foundation to one of shared ethnic hostilities.

In the rest of the country, the presence of Rwandan and Ugandan troops supporting the rebels turned many Congolese toward Kabila. This was especially the case in rebel-held areas where the local population resented the presence of Rwandan and Ugandan soldiers and their reported brutality. Many also resented the hijacking of the local economy.[58] Both countries continue today to engage in strategies of harassing local farmers and businessmen in order to establish monopolistic control of the trade in their occupied zones. The gold, cobalt, timber, palm oil, coffee, and elephant tusks that they extract from eastern DRC have become a major source of foreign exchange and help bankroll their continued involvement in the conflict.

In an interesting rhetorical maneuver, Kabila blamed Uganda and Rwanda's invasion for the failure of his regime to democratize and develop. In an interview with *Jeune Afrique Economie*, Kabila claimed: "When we came to power, we said that we would organize general elections in two years' time. We launched the consultation process and the establishment of a constitutional assembly, but all these processes were stopped by this war of aggression. In the same way, we launched a three-year reconstruction program which the same war of aggression blocked."[59] This position ignored the history of repression and antidemocratic actions that preceded the second rebellion. Yet, it illustrated Kabila's ability to exploit anti-Tutsi/Rwandan sentiment for his own survival. Before his assassination, Kabila's waning domestic support rested almost exclusively on his self-portrayal as a defender of Congolese sovereignty against foreign invaders. This move was ironic given that his own rise to power was achieved by the intervention of those exact same invaders.

At the domestic level, therefore, Kabila's strategy for survival was to portray the rebellion as a foreign invasion and to construct a response steeped in nationalistic/xenophobic rhetoric. The underlying key to this strategy involved a question of legitimacy. Portraying all the rebels as foreigners and foreign puppets denied their legitimacy, as well as the authenticity of their complaints. Despite his own foreign installation, Kabila was increasingly able to portray himself as the legitimate representative of Congo. Yet, frustration with the high cost of the war continued to grow, both at home and among his backers. These pressures led Kabila to sign the Lusaka Accords on 10 July 1999. The agreement was aimed at establishing a ceasefire and the withdrawal of combatants from the front lines.[60] After signing the accord, however, it became clear that Kabila had little interest in abiding by it.

The Failure of Laurent Kabila's Survival Strategies

The Lusaka Accords were the most substantial of the numerous attempts to end the conflict in the DRC. One of the reasons that peace has been so elusive in the DRC was that, for most of the time, few of the combatants actually wanted peace to thrive. They had too much invested in the war, and their own economies were linked to the draining of Congo's resources. As *The Economist* so eloquently quipped: "Political and military big wigs are growing fat on the carcass of what was once a potentially rich country."[61]

Prior to his death, however, there were signs that Laurent Kabila's main allies—Zimbabwe, Angola, and Namibia—had reached the point where the benefits of intervention appeared to be far less than expected and the costs much greater. Increasingly, his allies pressured him to achieve a peaceful resolution and abandon his hopes for a military victory. Yet, Kabila refused to give up on the war.

For several months, Kabila and his government had used ceasefires as a chance to re-equip and reorganize their forces. Although Kabila signed the Lusaka agreements in 1999, he quickly announced that the deal was flawed and unacceptable. At first, Kabila rejected the mediator agreed upon at the Lusaka accord, Ketumile Masire, former president of Botswana. He began backtracking after signing the accords and demanded that the whole agreement be renegotiated.

Kabila's intransigence increasingly put him at odds with his backers. As *The Economist* noted: "Mr. Kabila has not just upset would-be peacemakers. He is also snubbing the allies who rode to his rescue two years ago and whose troops still prop him up."[62] In fact, Mugabe publicly hinted that Kabila should straighten up and listen to his peers. As his allies pressured him to accept further negotiations and ceasefires, it appeared that Kabila had not given up on his desire for a full military victory. As such, it appeared that the Kabila regime was moving toward a new stage—one in which Kabila would ignore his regional backers in an attempt to defeat the rebels on the battleground.

Just as Kabila was embarking on this third stage, a lone bodyguard shot him on 16 January 2001, almost forty years to the day that his hero Patrice Lumumba had been murdered. At the time of this writing, the details surrounding the assassination and its motivations still remain unclear. Two popular rumors on the streets of Kinshasa blame either deep disgruntlement within the army or Angolan involvement, because Angola's rulers were unhappy with the way Kabila was approaching the peace process.[63] While both rumors are suspect, they illustrate growing resentment of the continuation of the war and of Kabila's final strategy for survival. It is possible that Kabila was assassinated because of his desire to continue the war in face of growing internal and external pressure.

The Uganda and Rwanda-backed rebel organization, Congolese Rally for Democracy (RCD), continues today to move steadily westward, despite the ceasefire. Rwanda is seemingly satisfied with a military stalemate that gives it de facto control over almost half the country. Uganda is also reasonably satisfied, especially since it controls the northern section of Congo and is reaping the benefits of exporting Congolese diamonds, gold, timber, and coffee. For the anti-government combatants, a political economy of conflict has set in, where victory on the battlefield has become a secondary concern. More primary is the desire to perpetuate the fighting for the institutionalization of violence for profit.

THE FUTURE: LESSONS OF THE FATHER, PASSED DOWN TO THE SON

Whether or not Kabila's son and successor, Joseph Kabila, and the other combatants will eventually succeed in establishing peace remains to be seen. However, the first months of Joseph Kabila's reign seemed to offer more than a glimmer of hope. On the day he assumed office, Joseph Kabila gave his first address to the nation. In this speech, he promised to relaunch the Lusaka peace accord, establish an inter-Congolese dialogue, liberalize the economy, and open up the political system for the realization of democracy. In May, he lifted the ban established by his father and announced that political parties would be allowed to organize and take part in future peace talks.[64]

Hardly a week after his inauguration, he traveled to France, the United States, and Belgium. These trips had the immediate effect of increasing his legitimacy and status at home and abroad. While visiting Western leaders, he repeated his dedication to revising the peace process and also promised economic reforms that were clearly aimed at making his audiences happy. In July 2000, his father had granted a monopoly on diamond marketing to the Israeli company IDI Diamonds, which blocked many Western companies out and dealt a near-fatal blow to that sector.[65] While in the United States, Joseph Kabila promised that he would reverse the monopoly and take steps to further stabilize Congo's economy. (The Israeli firm responded by threatening prosecution if Congo canceled its contract.) The European Union, IMF, and World Bank all welcomed the announced reforms, seeing them as positive developments by the new Kabila government.[66]

In addition to improving the country's foreign relations and lifting the ban on political parties, Joseph Kabila's biggest break from his father's legacy was his resuscitation of the Lusaka peace accords. On 15 February 2001, Joseph Kabila announced his intention of cooperating with Masire to establish an "inter-Congolese dialogue" and to allow the deployment of the UN observer force. These were the two primary stumbling blocks his father had utilized to thwart the peace agreements. Joseph Kabila's reversal of his father's position breathed new life into the peace plan. By the end of March 2001, the first UN observers were in place. Yet, several months later, only sixty-two four-man teams of UN military observers were actually deployed across the entire country.[67] In what was seen as a display of good faith, Uganda announced a troop reduction and the Rwandan forces and their rebel allies pulled back not just the required 9 miles, but 125 miles. However, there are claims that the Rwandans have also increased the number of their troops in Congo. In response, Kabila appears to have sent many of the *Interahamwe* from government-held areas to the east.[68]

While these actions seem to signal that Joseph Kabila will not follow the path marked out by his father, it is also clear that the younger Kabila has learned valuable lessons from his father's earlier survival strategies. In fact, upon inauguration, Joseph Kabila's position was more precarious than his father's had ever been. The young Kabila's support system was frightfully small. On the one hand,

Kabila inherited a domestic power base that had shrunk during the final months of his father's reign. Laurent Kabila had increasingly relied on a small group of intimates, mostly Katangans and family members. When his son came to power, that group had split into two factions: those who supported a revived peace plan and those who were opposed to it (many of the latter were cabinet ministers whom Joseph Kabila eventually removed in a later restructuring of his administration).[69]

On the other hand, Joseph Kabila could not rely heavily on his own army, despite being army commander under his father. This was mostly due to the poor state of the DRC army, which continued to be plagued by desertion and dissent.[70] The 60,000-strong army has increasingly relied on child soldiers and on Rwandan and Burundian Hutus fighting alongside the trained Congolese soldiers. In fact, the Hutu fighters constitute the most important element of Congo's military, which makes the disarmament of these forces (which Rwandan leader Paul Kagame has made a prerequisite for Rwandan withdrawal from Congo) an extremely difficult problem for Kabila. The ineffectiveness and marginalization of the DRC army was illustrated immediately after the assassination of Laurent Kabila, when Congolese troops were confined to their barracks and disarmed while Angolan and Zimbabwean troops policed Kinshasa.[71]

Unable to rely too heavily upon the army or a domestic political power base, Joseph Kabila is extremely reliant on his Angolan and Zimbabwean backers. Militarily, it was Angolan and Zimbabwean troops who had held the front and coordinated logistics, while the Hutu fighters launched offensives.[72] Perhaps Laurent Kabila's biggest mistake was to turn his back on his regional allies. It appears that his son has learned from that mistake and is far more willing to follow the advice of his Zimbabwean and Angolan backers than his father had been at the end of his life. This is no doubt tied to the fact that Joseph Kabila's survival is clearly in the hands of these external patrons.

Yet, Joseph Kabila also shows signs of having learned the lessons of external reliance even better than his father. While Laurent Kabila's number of external supporters shrank over time, Joseph Kabila seems aware of the need to build a broad base of support. While aware that his ascendancy and survival so far have rested on the shoulders of his Angolan, Zimbabwean, and Namibian allies, Joseph Kabila has shrewdly sought to extend his circle of friends to include the Western powers his father had snubbed, particularly the United States and Belgium. These overtures seem to have earned him valuable points in Western capitals. In fact, *The Guardian* (Manchester) has dubbed Kabila the "new young darling of the West."[73] While such a label bodes well for Western economic interests in Congo, it does little to ensure that Joseph Kabila will not construct strategies for survival at the expense of Congolese well-being.

While it is still too early to forecast Joseph Kabila's future, a few points about his father's legacy are already obvious. Laurent Kabila's strategies of survival cost Congo and the region dearly. His reliance on external backers—first Rwanda and Uganda, then Zimbabwe, Namibia, and Angola—meant that Congo's sovereignty has been sorely compromised. The DRC has now become an economic colony for most of the combatants, with its resources being drained to the east and south. The institutionalization of violence for profit has enriched many of the region's elite but has devastated an already fragile economic situation. Local systems of survival, established under Mobutu's decades-long dictatorship, have been fundamentally restructured for the enrichment of armed forces, rather than local populations. The suffering of the population of Congo has not abated but continues as the country is torn apart by predatory forces. Moreover, Laurent Kabila's decision to play the race card further heightened ethnic distrust and hatred in an already volatile section of the world. Constructing a pluralistic "Congolese" community—a vital necessity for the region's development—will be a project that may take generations to achieve. Moreover, Laurent Kabila's regime failed to establish new networks of domestic power in the post-Mobutu Congo. Unlike Mobutu's elaborate redistribution system, the money garnered by the Kabila regime was often exported abroad. It will be a monumental task for Joseph Kabila's administration to fair any better.

Clearly, Laurent Kabila is not solely to blame for the disastrous effects of the war. Far from it. As Erik Kennes has acutely observed, the failure to achieve a peaceful, productive post-Mobutu order is "not only a failure of an individual (or a result of the foreign occupation of the country) but also the failure of an undigested political past."[74] Given such a situation, it is doubtful that Laurent Kabila (or anyone else) could have proven to be the political messiah many had hoped for. However, the strategies Laurent Kabila employed to ensure his survival had the unfortunate effect of making a bad situation even more tragic. As one observer put it, Kabila "left a poisonous political and economic legacy for his country and for his son."[75] It remains to be seen if the son can escape the sins of the father.

NOTES

---

1 The author would like to thank Edouard Bustin, John Clark, Erik Kennes, and Michael Nest for providing valuable assistance, constructive criticism, and insightful suggestions to earlier drafts of this work.

2. Carole J. L. Collins, "The Congo Is Back!" *Review of African Political Economy*, no.72 (1997): 277–278.

3. Carole J. L. Collins, "Reconstructing the Congo," *Review of African Political Economy*, no.74 (1997): 592.

4. For a discussion of Africa's "New leaders," see Dan Connell and Frank Smyth, "Africa's New Bloc," *Foreign Affairs* 7, no.2 (March/April 1998): 80–94.

5. William Gálvez, *Che in Africa: Che Guevara's Congo Diary* (Melbourne/New York: Ocean Press, 1999).

6. For good discussions of Kabila's life and his early career as a rebel leader, see Erik Kennes, *Essai biographique sur Laurent Désiré Kabila* (Brussels: Cahiers Africains, 1999), and Wilungula B. Cosma, *Fizi 1967–1986: Le Maquis Kabila* (Brussels: CEDAF, 1997).

7. Gérard Prunier, "The Great Lakes Crisis," *Current History* 96, no.610 (May 1997): 195.

8. For in-depth discussions of the 1994 Rwandan genocide, see Timothy Longman, "Rwanda: Chaos from Above," in Leonardo Villalón and Phillip Huxtable, eds., *The African State at a Critical Juncture: Between Disintegration and Reconfiguration* (Boulder, CO: Lynne Rienner, 1998), and Philip Gourevitch, *We Wish to Inform You that Tomorrow We Will Be Killed with Our Families: Stories from Rwanda* (New York: Farrar Strauss and Giroux, 1998).

9. Michael G. Schatzberg, "Beyond Mobutu: Kabila and the Congo," *Journal of Democracy* 8, no.4 (1997): 80; Peter Rosenblum, "Endgame in Zaire," *Current History* 96, no.610 (May 1997): 201.

10. Thomas Turner, "The Kabilas' Congo," *Current History* 100, no.645 (May 2001): 215; Frank J. Parker, "From Mobutu to Kabila: An Improvement?" *America* 177, no.8 (Nov. 1997).

11. Peter Rosenblum, "Kabila's Congo," *Current History* 97, no.619 (May 1998): 194.

12. John Pomfret, "Rwanda Led Revolt in Congo," *Washington Post,* 9 July 1997.

13. Rosenblum, "Kabila's Congo," 194.

14. Pomfret, "Rwanda Led Revolt in Congo."

15. François Ngolet, "African and American Connivance in Congo-Zaire," *Africa Today* 47, no.1 (2000): 70.

16. David Aronson, "Mobutu Redux?" *Dissent* 45, no. 2 (spring 1998): 21.

17. Quoted in ibid., 24.

18. David Aronson, "The Dead Help No One Living," *World Policy Journal* 14, no.4 (1997).

19. Aronson, "Mobutu Redux?" 24.

20. Jean-Claude Willame, "The 'Friends of the Congo' and the Kabila System," *Issue: A Journal of Opinion* 26, no.1 (1998); Ngolet, "African and American Connivance in Congo-Zaire."

21. Mel McNulty, "The collapse of Zaïre: implosion, revolution or external sabotage?" *Journal of Modern African Studies* 37, no. 1 (1999): 73.

22. Florence Aubenas, "Dans Goma Libéré, la Rebellion Impose sa Loi," *Libération,* 14 March 1997; *Le Monde,* "Triple faillite française," 19 March 1997.

23. Peter J. Schraeder, "Cold War to Cold Peace: Explaining U.S.-French Competition in Francophone Africa," *Political Science Quarterly* 115, no.3 (2000).

24. *Wall Street Journal,* 13 May 1997.

25. Ngolet, "African and American Connivance," 70–71; Parker, "From Mobutu to Kabila," 21.

26. For a more in-depth discussion and analysis of the mining sector, see Erik Kennes, "Le secteur minier au Congo: 'Déconnexion' et descente aux enfers," in Filip Reyntjens and Stefaan Marysse, eds., *L'Afrique des Grands Lacs. Annuaire 1999–2000* (Paris: L'Harmattan, 2000).

27. "Kabila sends a message to the world: 'Buzz Off,'" *The Economist,* 27 Sept. 1997, 47.

28. Tom Cohen, "Kabila Sworn In, Assuming Sweeping Powers to Rule Congo," Associated Press, 29 May 1997, accessed through http://www.ap.org.

29. Rosenblum, "Kabila's Congo," 195.

30. Edouard Bustin, "The Collapse of 'Congo/Zaire' and Its Regional Impact," in Daniel Bach, ed., *Regionalisation in Africa: Integration and Disintegration* (Oxford/ Bloomington: James Currey/Indiana University Press, 1999), 88.

31. Quoted in Parker, "From Mobutu to Kabila," 20.

32. Rosenblum, "Kabila's Congo," 196.

33. Ibid.

34. Kennes, *Essai biographique sur Laurent Désiré Kabila.*

35. Stefan Lovgren, "Mobutuism without Mobutu," *U.S. News and World Report* 123, 24 November 1997, 50.

36. Ibid.

37. Aronson, "The Dead Help No One Living."

38. Rosenblum, "Kabila's Congo," 199.

39. Quoted in Milan Vesely, "Carving up the Congo," *African Business* (October 1998): 12.

40. Ibid.

41. Ibid.

42. Milan Vesely, "Congo: Profit and Loss Account," *African Business* (January 1999): 37.

43. François Misser, "The Carpet-Bag Generals," *African Business* (December 1999): 31.

44. Ibid., 31–32.

45. Ibid.

46. See Mats Berdal and David M. Malone, eds., *Greed and Grievance: Economic Agendas in Civil Wars* (Boulder, CO: Lynne Rienner, 2000).

47. Quoted in Vesely, "Carving up the Congo," 12.

48. Thomas Turner, "War in the Congo," *Foreign Policy in Focus: Columbia International Affairs Online* 4, no.5 (1999).
49. Mwayila Tshiyemba, "Ambitions rivales dans l'Afrique des grands lacs," *Le Monde Diplomatique*, January 1999.
50. Ngolet, "African and American Connivance in Congo-Zaire," 79.
51. Milan Vesely, "Supping with the Devil?" *African Business* (September 1999): 36.
52. Ibid., 37.
53. François Misser, "Kabila Turns Diamonds to Dust." *African Business* (Jul./Aug. 2000): 31–32.
54. Kennes, "Le Secteur Minier au Congo."
55. Michela Wong, "Fear of Genocide Powers Rwanda's Regional Ambitions," *Financial Times*, 1 September 1998; Victoria Brittain, "Africa Heads Towards New Genocide," *The Guardian*, 31 August 1998.
56. Mel McNulty, "The Collapse of Zaïre: Implosion, Revolution or External Sabotage?" 55; Jerzy Bednarek, "La 'Marionette' Kabila Rebondit sur L'Ogre Rwandais," *Africa International* (December/January 1999): 38–41; Frederic Fritscher, "Un Régime Impopulaire qui s'efforce de Jouer sur la Fibre Nationaliste," *Le Monde*, 6 August 1998, 2; Frederic Fritscher, "Le Congo-Kinshasa rend le Rwanda responsable de la crise qu'il traverse," 7 August 1998, 4; and Remy Ourdan, "A l'Est, la Population Vit dans la Peur des Bombardements," *Le Monde*, 28 August 1998.
57. "The Cost of Kabila," *The Economist*, 3 October 1998, 48. It is unclear to what extent ethnic hatred against the Tutsi has been exaggerated by the Western media. In a personal correspondence, Erik Kennes has argued that during this initial "witch-hunt" no Tutsi were killed and those arrested were imprisoned under relatively humane conditions, compared to ordinary conditions of Congolese prisons.
58. Musifiky Mwanasali, "The View from Below," in Berdal and Malone, eds., *Greed and Grievance: Economic Agendas in Civil Wars* (Boulder, CO: Lynne Rienner, 2000).
59. "Interview with Laurent Kabila," *Jeune Afrique Economie*, no. 286, 3–16 May 1999, 15–31.
60. The Lusaka peace agreement has two parts: military and political. In addition to the ceasefire and troop withdrawal, the military part provides for the deployment of a UN force and the neutralization of the rebel groups. The political part calls for the establishment of an "inter-Congolese" dialogue, the transition to a democratic government, and the re-establishment of state authority throughout the entire national territory. See Filip Reyntjens, "Briefing: The Democratic Republic of Congo, from Kabila to Kabila," *African Affairs*, no.100 (2001): 313.
61. "War and Peace in Congo," *The Economist*, 29 April 2000, 41.
62. "A Snub from Kabila," *The Economist*, 19 August 2000, 39.
63. BBC World Service, 22 January 2001. One of the most thorough inquiries to date suggests that the assassin, Rachidi Kasereka, was motivated by disenchantment among the military, particularly former "child soldiers" from the eastern part of the country (Stephen Smith, "Ces Enfants-Soldats Qui Ont Tué Kabila," *Le Monde*, 10 February 2001). However, many questions remain unanswered, especially with regards to the possible involvement of participants from the south of the country and the possible involvement of Angola (Turner, "The Kabilas' Congo"). A full and complete explanation is unlikely to ever emerge.
64. Norimitsu Onishi, "Congo: Ban Ends on Political Parties," *New York Times*, 18 May 2001, 6.
65. Reyntjens, "Briefing," 314.
66. François Misser, "Lessons in Statecraft," *African Business* (April 2001).
67. Robin Denselow, "Quiet Spoken: UN Fears Cyprus-Style Division in Congo," *The Guardian* (Manchester), 28 June 2001, 1.
68. Ibid.

69. Turner, "The Kabilas' Congo," 217.
70. Danna Harman, "The Calm in the Eye of Congo," *Christian Science Monitor,* 7 May 2001, 1.
71. Reyntjens, "Briefing," 315.
72. Turner, "The Kabilas'Congo," 218.
73. Denselow, "Quiet spoken," 1.
74. Kennes, *Essai biographique sur Laurent Désiré Kabila.*
75. Turner, "The Kabilas' Congo," 218.

CHAPTER 5

Angola's Role in the Congo War

Thomas Turner

INTRODUCTION

ngola is participating in the current Congo war for the same reason that it
joined in the war of 1996–97, namely to defend itself against Jonas Savimbi's
National Union for the Total Independence of Angola (UNITA). Although
Angola sided with Laurent-Désiré Kabila on both occasions, sympathy for Kabila
and his regime was at best a secondary factor. This appeared to receive confirmation,
early in 2001, when Angola probably ordered, or at least welcomed, the assassination of Kabila.

In the first war, Angola contributed decisively to the overthrow of Mobutu Sese
Seko by Kabila. Similarly, the intervention of Angola and the other southern African
allies, Zimbabwe and Namibia, was decisive in preventing the second war from ending in a rapid overthrow of Kabila. Since its rescue of Kabila in 1998, Angola has
maintained a small military presence in Congo, mainly in oil-rich Bas-Congo. In the
aftermath of the defeat of Kabila's forces, including Zimbabwean troops, at Pweto
(Katanga), it was reported that Angola had sent troops to participate in a counterattack.[1] Following the murder of Kabila, Angolan forces in the capital, Kinshasa,
were reinforced.

Angola's strategy for "prevailing" in the war has comprised several elements: (1)
to pursue the fight against Savimbi, especially by interdicting his supplies; (2) to protect the oil installations that finance its own war effort; (3) to maintain a favorable
or compliant regime in Kinshasa. This third element could mean either supporting
the regime in power, or replacing it with a more suitable one.

As a second front in the war against UNITA, the Congo war has been fairly successful, as the rebel movement was weakened. The Angolan regime was, however,
dissatisfied with Laurent Kabila on at least two counts. First, he was incapable of
winning the war despite considerable aid from his allies. Indeed, as the Pweto battle
suggested, he was quite capable of losing the war to a pro-UNITA coalition. Second, he was obstructive as regards a negotiated end to the war, once the Angolans
had decided that that was what they wanted.

If one is searching for a parsimonious explanation, Angola's motivation is clear.
The Movimento Popular de Libertação de Angola (Popular Movement for the Liberation of Angola—MPLA) regime in Luanda is pursuing the reasonable aim of

regime survival, as most regimes do, most of the time.[2] Accordingly, I shall focus on the question of how a series of choices presented itself to Angola's decisionmakers. Characteristics of the MPLA regime and the geopolitical linkages between Angola and Congo will be introduced as needed.

As regards causes and motives, three alternative questions or approaches will be considered: (1) What has been "the weight of history" (Patrick Chabal's terminology) in Angola's choices?[3] (2) Are the Congo and Angola conflicts caused by "economic opportunities" rather than by "grievances," as suggested by Paul Collier of the World Bank?[4] (3) Do sentimental factors (ideological affinities, moral obligations etc.), evoked by Colette Braeckman among others, play a major part?[5] I begin by sketching the geopolitical context of Angola's decisions.

THE GEOPOLITICAL FRAMEWORK OF ANGOLA'S DECISIONS

The Angola-Congo border both separates and links the two Central African states. Angola comprises two blocs of territory on the Atlantic coast. By far the larger lies south of the Congo River and Democratic Republic of Congo (DRC). The Cabinda enclave, a small wedge of territory, lies north of the mouth of the Congo River and is separated from Angola proper by territory of the DRC.

Two major cultural zones straddle the Angola-Congo border: the Kongo zone in the West and the Lunda zone farther east. Kongo speakers are found in northwestern Angola, western Congo-Kinshasa (Bas-Congo Region), Cabinda, and Congo-Brazzaville. The Lunda zone is divided between DR Congo (Katanga and Bandundu Regions), Angola, and Zambia.

The Congo-Angola border has defined several transnational communities, notably the "Katanga gendarmes" (Lunda and others) who figure prominently in the recent Congo wars. When the Katanga secession ended in 1963, former prime minister Moïse Tshombe, a Lunda, sent a major portion of his gendarmerie (army) across the border into Portuguese Angola. When Tshombe became Congo prime minister in 1964, he used these fighters to help suppress the Lumumbist insurgency. Katangans mutinied in 1966 and 1967, after which many were massacred on the orders of President Mobutu Sese Seko. Others regrouped in Angola. In 1975, Katangans helped the MPLA defeat the Frente Nacional de Libertação de Angola (National Front for the Liberation of Angola—FNLA) and Mobutu's troops, near Luanda. In 1977 and 1978, Katangan Tigers from Angola invaded their home province. These "Katanga gendarmes" reappear in Congo in the 1990s, although few could have been involved in the secession.[6]

The "front line" between black-ruled and white-ruled Africa influenced Zaire-Angola relations for years and is invoked to justify current alliances. Being a "frontline state" was not a matter simply of being contiguous to white-ruled territory but to being engaged in the liberation struggle. Mobutu's Zaire, "staunchly pro-Western," was never a front line state.[7] Angola, on the other hand, was perpetually involved with war with South Africa until the signing of the Angola-Namibia Peace Accords of 1988, and was at the forefront of resistance to South African aggression.

As Zartman suggests, the independence of Angola led to a situation of "mutual encirclement" between Angola and Zaire: "Zaire's encirclement is a product of the radical states on half of its borders since 1975, when Angola joined the Congo Re-

public and Tanzania in independence; there has been enough active cooperation between the two Atlantic radicals and between Angola and Tanzania as front-line
states to give credence to the perception." Similarly, Angola saw itself surrounded,
with Zaire and Zambia as "conservative regimes tied by their extractive industry to
a world structure that includes South Africa [and its quasi-colony South West
Africa/Namibia]."[8]

Both in Angola and in Congo, minerals dominate the economy. Two extractive
industries provide most of Angola's revenues and are targets of fighting in the civil
war. There are major oil deposits along the coast of Cabinda and northwestern Angola, as well as along the 40 km (25 miles) of Congolese coastline separating the two
pieces of Angolan territory. Diamonds are found in large quantities, especially on
the Lunda plateau of northeastern Angola. Oil and diamonds finance the military
efforts of the government and UNITA, respectively.

Since 1998, a similar situation has emerged in Congo. The Kabila government
controls a strip of territory running from the coastal oilfields to the Katanga copper
belt and including the major diamond field at Mbuji-Mayi. The rebel zones—in the
east, northeast, and northwest—each include diamonds, gold, or other minerals.
Laurent Kabila gave his Zimbabwean, Namibian, and Angolan allies a share in
Congo's wealth. These interventions are "self-financing," in Braeckman's words,[9] although that does not mean that the profits from Congo go into the state coffers.
Likewise, Uganda and Rwanda profit from the resources in the zones they control.[10]

A REGIME SHAPED BY WAR

To understand the sources of Angolan participation in the current Congo war more
deeply, one must delve in the origins and evolution of the MPLA regime. The
MPLA has gone through several incarnations: liberation movement, Leninist party-
state, and now post-communist state supposedly committed to democracy and free
enterprise. Little by little, however, forty years of armed struggle have shaped a
"parastate," that is, a politicomilitary apparatus ill-suited to civilian politics,[11] or perhaps a "warlord" regime, which fights to control resources with which it finances its
fighting.[12]

Some of the MPLA's problems are due to the fact that Angola's nationalist movement was fractured from the beginning. The MPLA and its rival, the FNLA, both
claimed to be struggling for the independence of the entire colony, but both remained marked by their regional origins. The MPLA was founded by black and
mixed-race intellectuals in the capital and won support among the Umbundu of Luanda's hinterland, whereas the FNLA was founded by Kongo from the north. The
FNLA moved beyond its origins by recruiting Savimbi, of Ovimbundu origins, but
his defection and subsequent founding of UNITA left the FNLA a largely Kongo
party.[13] Cabinda was separate from the start; in 1963, a group of Cabindans met at
Pointe Noire, Congo-Brazzaville, and formed the Front for the Liberation of the
Enclave of Cabinda (FLEC).[14]

The opposed identities, grievances, and interests of the various ethnic groups are
products of Angola's two-fold colonial experience (informal empire and slave trade,
from the fifteenth to nineteenth centuries, and formal colonialism, during the nineteenth and twentieth centuries).[15] Luanda's mixed-race elite derives in part from the

commercial and administrative Creole elite, Portuguese-speaking and Catholic. That elite's connections with the interior had been limited to trade, mainly the slave trade, until the nineteenth century. Under twentieth century colonial rule, the Creoles suffered a drastic loss of status. They became mere adjuncts to the Portuguese. New elites, both Mestiço and black, challenged Creole supremacy.

Under twentieth century colonialism, Africans were legally compelled to work, but this requirement had markedly different consequences for different groups. Many Ovimbundu of the central highlands had to seek employment on coffee plantations in the Kongo area, since their agricultural economy could not sustain their large population. Those Kongo who did not work as agricultural laborers often were associated with business and trade in the Belgian Congo. Some of them became substantial businessmen, even plantation owners.

For the MPLA, armed struggle began in February 1961, when members attacked the São Paulo fortress and police headquarters in Luanda, attempting to free leaders of their party. About the same time, in northern Angola, attacks on Portuguese coffee planters led to a broad-based anticolonial revolt, led by an organization known first as the Union of Populations of Northern Angola (UPNA). Under Holden Roberto, the UPNA eventually became the FNLA.[16]

The Cold War fostered disunity among the liberation groups. FNLA operated from bases in Congo-Kinshasa, while the MPLA, excluded from Congo-Kinshasa, operated from Congo-Brazzaville and later from Zambia. The MPLA won the Angolan civil war of 1975--76 thanks to Soviet and Cuban backing and went on to establish a Leninist-style single-party regime. Yet there is a chicken-and-egg problem in explaining the orientation of the party and of its rivals. As Blum explains, "Although MPLA may have been somewhat more genuine in its leftist convictions than FNLA or UNITA, there was little to distinguish any of the three groups from each other ideologically. . . . Each of the groups spoke of socialism and employed Marxist rhetoric when the occasion called for it, and genuflected to other gods when it did not. In the 1960s, each of them was perfectly willing to accept support from any country willing to give it without excessive strings attached."[17]

Westad emphasizes the perceptions of outsiders, arguing that early contacts had shown the Soviets that the MPLA was a "possible adherent to Soviet ideas of state and society," even though it was far from being a communist party. As late as 1974, Soviet reports described the MPLA as a loose coalition of trade unionists, progressive intellectuals, Christian groups, and large segments of the petty bourgeoisie. The Soviet leaders consistently overestimated their ability to impose their views on foreign leftists. In this case, the Angolans and Cubans were able to shape Moscow's actions. In 1975, Fidel Castro initiated Cuban armed support for the MPLA without Moscow's knowledge, calculating correctly that he could force Moscow's hand.[18]

Although the Soviet Union had provided some aid to the FNLA in the early 1960s, they had switched to the MPLA in 1964, arguing that Roberto had curtailed his guerrilla operations in Angola under pressure from Washington. The amounts of aid, first to the FNLA, then to the MPLA, were very small.

In 1970, however, the Soviets saw an opportunity to gain clients in the region, as southern Africa nationalists felt that their efforts to gain American aid had failed. They also saw a danger that China, then targeting countries and movements that already received Soviet aid, might control large parts of Africa in a loose coalition with the United States. The Soviets offered the MPLA substantial military hardware, logistical support, and political training. But they found it difficult to work with the MPLA, due to its poor organization and widespread factionalism. In early 1974, Soviet diplomats spent much time trying to reunify the MPLA factions and create an alliance between the MPLA and Roberto's FNLA. The Soviet ambassador in Brazzaville reported that the MPLA had practically ceased to function. The only bright spot was a few pro-Moscow "progressively oriented activists."[19]

Following the Portuguese coup of 1974, which opened the door to Angolan independence, Moscow decided to strengthen the MPLA under Agostinho Neto and make the movement the dominant partner in a postcolonial coalition government. Soviet embassies in Brazzaville, Lusaka, and Dar-es-Salaam were instructed to "repair" the damaged liberation movement, but Neto and his supporters refused to cooperate.

As the Soviet Union, China, and the United States reinforced their respective clients, Angola headed for full-scale civil war. Late in 1974, the MPLA established itself in Luanda and other cities and took control of most of the Cabinda enclave. The Soviet Union was aware of increased American support for the FNLA starting in January 1975 and concluded that Roberto would make an all-out bid for power very soon. The Soviets could do little to help the MPLA resist the initial FNLA attacks, but they hoped that an alliance with UNITA could rescue their Angolan allies. By July 1975, as the MPLA was successfully counterattacking, Moscow still expected that the rival movements, or at least UNITA, would join an MPLA-led coalition government. Moscow did not believe that the United States or South Africa would intervene on a large scale.

In August, the tide turned again, thanks to major American aid to anti-MPLA forces and the intervention of South African and Zairian troops in Angola. When Brazzaville refused to permit increased aid to the MPLA through Congolese territory, Moscow asked Castro to intercede with Brazzaville. However, Castro used the occasion to promote his own plan to send Cuban forces to Angola, with the aid of Soviet transport and Soviet staff officers, to help direct military operations. Worried that such aid before independence would upset the United States and most African countries, Moscow refused. Castro then sent troops on his own.

The intervention of South Africa, unacceptable in African opinion, saved the MPLA. Seeing the new anti-MPLA operations as a joint United States--South African effort, Moscow decided to start assisting the Cuban operation in Angola immediately after independence day, 11 November 1975. As Neto declared the independence of the People's Republic of Angola, Cuban artillerymen with Soviet-supplied rocket launchers routed the FNLA-Zairian attackers just north of Luanda. Then, the Soviet General Staff took direct control of transporting additional Cuban troops to Africa, as well as providing advanced military equipment. By the end of November the Cubans had stopped the South African-led UNITA advance on Luanda. After two defeats south of the Cuanza River in December and the U.S. Senate vote against funding for covert operations in Angola, South Africa decided to withdraw. By March 1976, Roberto had given up the fight, whereas Savimbi had retreated to rural southeastern Angola with about 2,000 guerillas and their U.S. and South African advisers.

After the war, a struggle took place to define the MPLA. The MPLA, in Soviet opinion, had been saved from its own follies by advice and assistance from Moscow, which not only helped it win the war but also laid the foundation for the building of a Soviet-style "vanguard party." The Soviets backed "internationalists"—men like Nito Alves—who understood that the MPLA was part of an international revolutionary movement led by Moscow and that it therefore depended on Soviet support. By taking the lead in reorganizing the MPLA the internationalists would also be the future leaders of the Marxist-Leninist party in Angola.[20]

Neto, however, considered himself a major Marxist theorist and was encouraged in this assessment by Cuba's Castro. Neto asked for Cuban assistance in building a Marxist-Leninist party, and Castro spoke of Angola, Cuba, and Vietnam as "the main anti-imperialist core" of the world. The tensions in the Moscow-Havana-Luanda relationship were revealed in May 1977, when Cuban tanks blocked the coup attempt of Soviet favorite Nito Alves.

Following the attempted coup and a sweeping purge of MPLA members, the MPLA turned itself into a Marxist-Leninist party. MPLA attempts to collectivize agriculture, combined with attacks by South Africa and UNITA, disrupted production in the rural economy. The state came to depend almost entirely on the petroleum industry. Western companies, notably Gulf Oil (later Chevron), operated under Cuban protection against UNITA attacks.

In retrospect, it is clear that a crucial event occurred in 1979, when the longtime leader, Neto, died and was succeeded by Planning Minister José Eduardo dos Santos. Dos Santos had been trained in the Soviet Union in petroleum engineering, then in communications, and had been the first foreign minister of independent Angola. Despite this background, he would lead the transformation of Angola's party-state.

Until the late 1980s, Angola was ravaged by a combination of civil war, liberation struggle in neighboring Namibia, and Cold War proxy warfare. Then, in 1988, South Africa finally agreed to grant independence to Namibia and to stop supporting UNITA; in return the Cubans agreed to withdraw their troops. The MPLA's initial response to the South African withdrawal was to attack UNITA bases. The failure of this campaign, increasingly effective UNITA attacks on oil installations, and the collapse of communism in Eastern Europe combined to produce a transformation of the regime.

In mid-1990 the MPLA Central Committee decided to abandon Marxism-Leninism and the one-party state. UNITA and the government agreed in May 1991 on a ceasefire and a new constitution guaranteeing human and political rights. The two armies would be merged and multiparty elections would be held in 1992. The elections were supervised by the United Nations, which certified them as free and fair. The MPLA received the most votes, but not enough to avoid a runoff with UNITA. Savimbi, who must have expected to win, rejected the results, and civil war resumed.

Since 1993, the war has raged, off and on, despite an international environment favorable to the MPLA. In 1993, the Clinton administration recognized Angola, while the UN Security Council imposed an arms and fuel embargo on UNITA. In 1994, the UN brokered a peace agreement between UNITA and the government (the Lusaka Protocol), and in February 1995, the Security Council decided to send 7,000 UN troops to verify the ceasefire. The following month, fighting resumed nonetheless. The Angolan parliament amended the constitution in July 1995, creating two vice presidencies, one of them reserved for Savimbi. However, UNITA supposedly refused to allow him to accept the post. In December, fighting again resumed in northern towns controlled by UNITA.

Savimbi built up a "secret army" of perhaps 15,000 soldiers and numerous arms depots in Zaire. A large quantity of arms and munitions reportedly was stored in Mobutu's presidential domain at Gbadolite, then transferred to Gabon on the eve of the victory of the Alliance des forces démocratiques pour la libération du Congo-Zaire (Alliance of democratic forces for the liberation of Congo-Zaire—ADFL).[21] As part of this ongoing struggle against Savimbi, Angola decided to join the Rwanda/Uganda/ADFL effort to overthrow Mobutu.

ANGOLA AND THE FIRST CONGO WAR (1996 TO 1997)

Angola coolly calculated the pros and cons before intervening in the first Congo war, that against Mobutu. As Braeckman explains, Angola intervened for its own reasons: to destroy Savimbi's "secret army" and to break up the networks by which he disposed of diamonds.[22] Angolan authorities also hoped that the followup regime to Mobutu would be less inclined to allow UNITA such ready access to its territory.

Once Rwanda and Uganda had established a security zone along their western borders, Uganda hesitated to go farther into Congo/Zaire. Angola apparently made a last attempt to negotiate its differences with Kinshasa, before deciding to intervene. Once Angola entered, however, the war clearly would be won by Kinshasa. Even a "security zone" would have extended from Katanga to the Atlantic. When the "rebellion" began in October 1996, relations between Zaire and Angola appeared normal.[23] The Angolan leaders observed the beginning of the war in Kivu but prudently decided "not to decide."[24]

The Zairian foreign minister visited Luanda at the end of November; about the same time, an Angolan security official visited Mobutu at his home on the French Riviera. Early in December, Angolan president Dos Santos and Zairian prime minister Kengo wa Dondo met in Brazzaville and reportedly agreed to respect one another's security concerns. Angola would prevent the Tigers (alias Katanga gendarmes) from crossing its border with Zaire. In return, Zaire would prevent UNITA from using Zaire territory to export diamonds and receive arms, and would dismantle UNITA bases on its territory.[25]

However, Angola apparently decided that Kengo could not deliver on his promises. A number of close associates of Mobutu, including Generals Likulia Bolongo, Nzimbi Ngbale, and Kpama Baramoto, as well as civilians N'Gbanda Nzambo and Seti Yale, were selling hundreds of tons of arms and munitions to UNITA. Not only did this handicap the Zairian armed forces in their struggle against Kabila and the rebels, but it probably also caused Angola to enter the war.[26]

In place of Kengo's inability to deliver on his promise, as a reason for Angolan entry into the war, Braeckman cites a visit to Luanda by one of Mobutu's sons, who promised to abandon UNITA in exchange for Luanda's neutrality in the war. This promise was not kept. She quotes MPLA secretary-general Lopo do Nascimiento as saying "We had the proof that it was not so, that they were tricking us one more time."[27] The "proof" may well have concerned the arms sales.

Reyntjens reports that Angola decided in December 1996 to enter the war and insisted that Kabila must continue his campaign to Kinshasa. Braeckman's version is more convincing. She has Dos Santos sending his security advisor, General Manuel Helder Dias (alias Kopelipa), to Bukavu to observe the ADFL. Dias concluded that

Kabila was determined to capture Kinshasa and overthrow Mobutu. Dias and Lopo do Nascimiento also noticed that Mobutu's army was refusing to fight. The only troops offering any resistance were Rwandans and Angolans [ex- Forces Armées Rwandaises (Rwandan Armed Forces—FAR) and UNITA], 6,000 of whom supposedly had defended Bunia and Kisangani. This led the Angolan government to conclude, according to Braeckman, that they could kill two birds with one stone: They could smash Savimbi's "secret army" and punish Mobutu for twenty years of warfare.[28]

Angola intervened by sending the Katanga Tigers into Congo/Zaire to combat Mobutu. In mid-February 1997, several battalions (2,000 to 3,000 troops) were flown to Kigali, then sent by road toward Goma and Bukavu. The capture of eastern Kivu by the ADFL, or at least in the name of the ADFL, and the public identification of many officials as Tutsis, some Congolese and others Rwandan, had aroused a hostile reaction on the part of the local population. In this context, the arrival of so-called "Katangans" tempered somewhat the anti-Tutsi reaction. Katangans were seen as Congolese, not foreigners. "At last we are going to be defended by our people," it was said when the Katangans arrived.

Ironically, the "Katangans" who arrived were a mixed bag, and included many foreigners. Some of those who arrived in February were Congolese from provinces other than Katanga, while others were Angolans. A journalist reports observing them at Camp Sayo, in Bukavu, "speaking Lingala but also Portuguese."[29] These young men had been recruited in Angola, and included refugees from all over southern Zaire: Katanga, Kasai, Bandundu, and Bas-Zaire. They had been used in fighting against UNITA. Most of their officers and NCOs were Angolan. Their equipment—trucks, armored cars, etc.—was impressive by local standards.

These units took the name "Tigers" to recall the two attacks that their predecessors of the FLNC, commanded by "General" Nathaniel Mbumba, had made against Shaba/Katanga in 1977 and 1978. There was some continuity at the command level, in that some of the "generals" had participated in the capture of Kolwezi in 1978.[30] The "Katangans" played an important role in capturing Kisangani. Other Tigers headed toward their home province, first to Kalemie and then on to Kamina. But their success was due to the leadership and equipment of the Angolans.[31]

Angola reinforced its participation in April 1997, after the fall of Mbuji-Mayi and Lubumbashi, and a few weeks before the fall of Kinshasa. Additional Katangan and Angolan troops entered Zaire directly from Angola and seized Tshikapa on 23 April. This force then captured Kikwit and participated in the battle of Kenge, the last major battle of the war. There, the Katangans and Angolans defeated a combined force of Zairians (including elements of Mobutu's Special Presidential Division) and Angolans of UNITA.[32] In contrast, the Angolan soldiers did not take part in the capture of Kinshasa. It was out of the question, according to Bender, to lose any Angolan lives in what was expected to be a bloody battle. After all, Luanda's main objective was not to put Kabila in power but to cut off aid to UNITA.[33]

As Angola became more active in support of Kabila, observers noted a "displacement of the political center of gravity," in Reyntjens's words.[34] Whereas Kabila previously had made many trips to Kigali and Kampala to meet his external backers, Luanda now became the preferred site of such meetings. Later, the Angolan capital hosted the unsuccessful efforts of South Africa, the United States, and the United Nations to promote a negotiated solution to the war. The timetable of the war confirms the importance of Angola's intervention, as Reyntjens points out.[35] It took four months (October 1996–January 1997) for the "rebels" to occupy less than one-twentieth of Congo-Zaire, whereas the rest of the huge country fell in the three months following the arrival of the Katangans. It also seems true, as Braeckman notes, that Angolan support gave some breathing room to Kabila, hitherto entirely dependent on Rwanda and Uganda.[36]

Braeckman further claims that the Angolans hesitated to tie themselves too closely to the Rwandans, whose methods they found distasteful. She refers specifically to the killing of UNITA prisoners and of Rwandan Hutu civilians. "This malaise helps to explain why, later on, Angola would find itself in a camp opposed to its former Rwandan and Ugandan allies."[37] On this point, we should remain skeptical; some Angolans may have been shocked, but in any case, the Angolan authorities joined the other camp to pursue the fight against UNITA.

More interesting is Braeckman's claim that Angolan participation in the first Congo war was financed in part by France's Elf-Aquitaine oil company. Part of Elf's royalties went to a Franco-Russian company dealing directly with General Kopelipa, in order to help the general to buy arms and military equipment in Russia.[38] If this charge is true, it foreshadows another collaboration between Elf and the Angolans in the war of Congo-Brazzaville in October 1997.

Angolan participation in the first war was only partly successful. When Angola agreed to join, its objectives were limited: it hoped that the fall of Mobutu would bring an end to destabilization efforts launched from the territory of Congo/Zaire, and it intended to clean out the rear bases of Savimbi's army. In May and June 1997, immediately following the fall of Kinshasa, the Angolan army carried out its own offensives in Congo, attempting to locate and destroy UNITA bases. In particular, it tried to clean out Kamina base, in Katanga. Several thousand of Savimbi's fighters managed to escape, however. UNITA hung onto some of its bastions in Congo and kept the support of its local allies, despite the effort to create a "zone interdite" several kilometers wide along the Congo-Angola border.[39]

The Angolans also wished to see the DRC become relatively stable and soon came to regret their failure to impose political conditions on their ally, Kabila. They would have liked him to form a government of national unity, including members of the internal opposition, even before the fall of Kinshasa. In particular, they did not approve of the exclusion of Étienne Tshisekedi, the long-time leader of the anti-Mobutu opposition. For the most part, of course, Angola was not focused on Congo's problems but on its own war against Savimbi.

ANGOLA IN THE CONGO-BRAZZAVILLE WAR

If Angola did not pay much attention to the activities of Kabila during the first weeks following the fall of Kinshasa (though whether Angola could have shaped Kabila's choices is another matter), it was because Angola's attention was focused on events across the river in Brazzaville. Angola had joined in the war to oust Mobutu in order to pursue its own campaign against Savimbi, but it discovered that it would have to continue that pursuit across another state border. Many UNITA fighters had retreated to Congo-Brazzaville, and others had retreated to Angola's Cabinda enclave, between the two Congos.[40]

Pascal Lissouba, the recently elected president of Congo-Brazzaville, had committed the fatal error of welcoming UNITA and adding its fighters to his own militia, the Zulus.[41] In return for this favor, UNITA reportedly received arms shipments by air from Pointe Noire, a city controlled by Lissouba. The error was fatal in that in befriending UNITA, Lissouba quasi-automatically acquired an enemy in the form of the Angolan government. Angola intervened on the side of ex-president Denis Sassou-Nguesso, who thus was able to oust Lissouba.[42] As Braeckman points out, this had the paradoxical effect of placing Angola on the side of the "amis de la France," whereas earlier it had participated in the anti-Mobutu campaign alongside Uganda and Rwanda, which enjoyed American support.

From Cabinda, Angolan troops seized Pointe Noire, ensuring the victory of Sassou-Nguesso and preventing the destruction of the port, to the great satisfaction of the oil companies, notably Elf. In so doing, the Angolans broke the long stalemate in the Congolese civil war in favor of the French-backed Sassou. Angolan forces remained in the country under a special bilateral agreement through the end of 2001.

ANGOLA STICKS WITH KABILA: THE SECOND CONGO WAR

In August 1998, Angola, Zimbabwe, and Namibia foiled an attempt to overthrow Kabila, marking the opening chapter of the second Congo war. Angola's action should have surprised no one; like its earlier interventions in Congo-Kinshasa and Congo-Brazzaville, this intervention aimed to protect Angola's oil and to fight Savimbi. Although Angola had tried to work with Rwanda and Uganda to find a cooperative approach to the "problem" of Kabila, Rwanda eventually broke off further discussions and launched a bid to overthrow the Congolese leader.

The war began on 2 August, with a mutiny at Goma. Ten days later, "Congolese patriots and democrats" announced formation of the Rassemblement Congolais pour la Démocratie (Congolese Rally for Democracy—RCD), which supposedly had happened on 1 August, also in Goma.[43] The RCD listed a series of grievances against Kabila, including corruption and tribalism. As Nzongola-Ntalaja argues, however, the war was "above all a manifestation of the desire of his former allies to substitute for Kabila a new leadership team, much more competent and better able to do the dirty work of the Rwandan and Ugandan authorities vis-à-vis the armed groups fighting them from Congo territory."[44]

By 26 August, Congolese troops were guarding Kinshasa's Ndjili airport, while rebels (and their Rwandan allies) hid in surrounding houses. Across the river at Brazzaville, 7,000 former members of Mobutu's Special Presidential Division awaited their hour of revenge. That hour did not arrive, however. Instead, Zimbabwean troops disembarked at the airport, took up position around the periphery, and began bombarding the rebel positions.[45] At this point, Angola already had entered Congo three days earlier. Its troops moved from the Cabinda enclave into Congo's coastal towns of Banana, Moanda, and Boma. This was in response to "rebel" occupation (actually, Rwandan troops) of Matadi, Congo's main port, and of the hydroelectric complex at Inga.

Rwanda's original plan had called for a lightning offensive against Kinshasa, the rapid overthrow of Kabila, and his replacement by a new team that would immediately benefit from international recognition. The rebels and their backers, however, made multiple errors: They underestimated Congolese nationalism, they underestimated Kabila, and they failed to take into consideration the security interests of other states in the region, notably Angola.

Within the capital, the Kabila government mobilized people's self-defense committees to attack the rebels and anyone suspected of being a rebel or a Tutsi. "People's self-defense" clearly had a genocidal aspect, but so, too, did the rebel acts of cutting off electricity and running water to the city of six million people.

Kabila himself was busy lining up regional support. During the first three weeks of August, when rumor had him organizing a new Katanga secession or even fleeing to Cuba, he made contact with friendly chiefs of state to the south: Sam Nujoma of Namibia, Robert Mugabe of Zimbabwe, and Dos Santos of Angola. Congo had just joined the Southern African Development Community (SADC), perhaps at the urging of Zimbabwe. Mugabe chaired the SADC Organ on Politics, Defence, and Security.

Braeckman suggests that three factors, or bundles of factors—ideology, economics, and security—explain the decision of the three SADC member states to support the Kabila government. But as regards Angola, she adds a debt going back to 1975: "If Angola came to the rescue of Kabila and his people, it is also in remembrance of the heroic hours of November 1975 when the intervention of the Katangan soldiers modified the destiny of Angola and, thereby, the destiny of all of southern Africa."[46] On the eve of Angolan independence, the Katangans had stood alongside the MPLA troops to bar the route to the South Africans and to Mobutu's troops, who were supporting the rival movements (FNLA, UNITA) with the aid of the CIA. The effort of the Katangans apparently had enabled the MPLA to hang on until the arrival of the Cubans. And if the Angolans did not remember this debt, then Victor Mpoyo, state minister under Kabila, a Katangan, reminded them of it.[47]

Whatever the weight of this sentimental factor, Angola had other, more substantive reasons to break with its former allies and support Kabila. For one, UNITA vice president Antonio Dembo had just been received in Kigali, and Savimbi had just visited Uganda. For another, Uganda and Rwanda had sent their troops to the Bas-Congo—Angola's backyard—without consulting their ally, Angola. These two reasons justified, in Angola's opinion, its action in attacking the rebels from the rear and forcing them to withdraw.

This second war thus led to a reversal of alliances. Kabila's Congo signed a mutual defense pact with Zimbabwe, Namibia, and Angola[48] and received assistance from Chad and Sudan. Uganda and Rwanda became the allies of Savimbi's UNITA. Angola intervened to save Kabila's regime and, afraid of the vacuum that might result from his fall, to guarantee that no support would be forthcoming from Kinshasa to the UNITA rebels. It suspected that Rwanda and Uganda had close ties to UNITA. Both Entebbe and Kigali airports were thought to be important hubs in the gunrunning and diamond business of the Angolan rebels. At the time, UNITA was in the final stages of a major rearmament that guaranteed an imminent clash. In these circumstances, Luanda felt that an effort to break UNITA's supply lines in the DRC was an essential strategic objective.

In the months leading up to the second Congo war, UNITA had become increasingly powerful. The rebel movement had used the brief interlude of peace to rebuild its army. The glut of former Warsaw Pact weaponry for sale at this time benefited UNITA arms purchasers. Using false end-user certificates supplied by

Mobutu and others, and (in the words of the International Crisis Group) "the services of a number of shady arms dealers," they bought tanks, armored personnel carriers, artillery, antitank and antiaircraft weapons, and small arms.[49]

By mid 1998, it was essential for the Angolan army to cut UNITA's supply lines and deny it the use of Congo's ports and airfields. The rebels' perennial shortage of fuel was their critical weakness. They also would need spare parts, weapons and munitions in the coming clash. There were nonetheless risks associated with Luanda's decision to send thousands of its best troops to Congo when a major rebel offensive loomed. Angola was also faced with an external debt burden of U.S.$11 billion and depressed world oil prices at that time.

Since saving Kabila from defeat at the hands of the Rwandan army in August 1998, Angolan heavy artillery support and air power played a key role in defending the government-held towns of Mbuji Mayi and Mbandaka. Laurent Kabila depended heavily upon the support of his foreign allies: Angola and Zimbabwe to hold the front and coordinate logistics, and Burundian rebels, *Interahamwe,* and ex-FAR to launch offensives. The proceeds of diamond and cobalt sales—perhaps U.S.$1 billion a year—enabled him to purchase weapons and otherwise finance the war. However, to pay for the presence of the foreign forces, Kabila mortgaged the economic resources of government-held territory.[50]

UNITA attacks picked up almost immediately as the rebels moved to recapture those territories they had earlier surrendered to the government. The long-awaited UNITA offensive began in earnest in December 1998, with large-scale armor- and artillery-supported assaults on the towns of Huambo and Cuito in the central highlands. To repulse these attacks, the FAA was forced to fly in reinforcements from its forces in the DRC. Fighting raged through the spring, in the central region and in the north along the Congo border.

Both sides in the Congo war apparently joined in the Angola fighting. Rwandans, Ugandans, and Congolese rebels reportedly fought alongside UNITA. In March 1999, UNITA reportedly captured the border city of Maquelo do Zombo with the help of Congolese rebels. To recapture the town, the presidents of Angola, Namibia, Zimbabwe, and the DRC agreed to mount a joint operation. And indeed, on 28 April 1999 it was reported that UNITA had been driven back into Uige by FAA troops operating out of the DRC.

In September 1999, after the signing of the Lusaka Agreement on Congo, the Angolan government counterattacked. Its forces rapidly lifted the siege of Cuito and Huambo. Under the pressure, UNITA crumbled, in part because of a fuel shortage. Within months, the conventional military capacity that it had built up since 1994 was destroyed. FAA captured UNITA's fortified headquarters at Jambo on 24 December 1999. The last provincial capital in UNITA hands, Cazombo on the Zambian border, fell on 19 September, along with its strategically important airstrip.

In military terms, Angola's intervention in the DRC was a success. In 2000, UNITA was defeated as a conventional military force. This was due in large part to the presence of FAA troops in the DRC, which frustrated UNITA efforts to find fuel, munitions, and spare parts. Nevertheless, the rebel movement retains its nationwide organization and is capable of continuing its guerilla war. Already, in the midst of the government victories, there has been a rise in ambushes, hit-and-run attacks, standoff bombardments, and mine-laying actions across the country. Government control outside the towns is tenuous.

In Cabinda, rebels of the FLEC took three Portuguese construction workers hostage at the beginning of 2001. The Angolan army launched search operations to find the men, supposedly being held inside Cabinda. The rebels said they were not seeking any financial ransom for the hostages but instead would release them only when Portugal agreed to support self-determination for the territory. This bold move did earn FLEC a few headlines. But it was suggested that this increase in activity may well signal the beginning of the end for the rebel movement. The strength of the Angolan army was one factor in FLEC's declining prospects. Equally important was the close cooperation between Luanda and the governments of the two Congos.[51] In the past, the Cabindans had profited from bad relations between Angola and one or both of the two Congos.

Angola's commitment in the DRC war has been modest. After its initial intervention, its forces numbered no more than 5,000, and by the end of 2000, this had sunk to a force of 2,500. Its troops now limit themselves to protecting strategic points such as the Kamina airbase in Katanga and, in Bas-Congo, the port of Matadi and the Inga hydroelectric dam that feeds the Angolan grid. Angolan planes and helicopter gunships do remain ready, however, to intervene in the DRC if needed.

The economic spoils of the DRC war have been distributed by Dos Santos himself and help to cement his hold on power. The presidency controls Sonangol (National Angolan Fuel Company), which, in return for Angolan army assistance, gained control of DRC's petroleum distribution and production networks. The International Crisis Group claims that Angola thus gained control of a 1,000 km (620 miles) stretch of Atlantic seaboard, including DRC, Congo-Brazzaville, and its own Cabinda enclave, which could translate into further gains in the oil industry.[52] Angolan generals had already gained footholds in Congo's diamond industry soon after the intervention (continuing a practice begun in Angola itself).

Having restricted the ability of UNITA to wage conventional warfare, the MPLA regime may well have concluded that what remained to do was make a deal or series of deals designed to cut off the rebel movement's remaining ability to exchange diamonds for arms. The international campaign against "blood diamonds" might accomplish that, but it has taken a long time to take effect. In the meantime, or as a complement to that campaign, deals with Rwanda and Uganda could make it much more difficult for Savimbi to obtain arms. But such deals would depend on an end to the war that pitted Angola against the two Great Lakes states.

ANGOLA AND THE ASSASSINATION

There is a fairly strong circumstantial case that Angola had Laurent Kabila killed, or at least allowed it to happen. First, it was well known from mid-2000 on that Angola wanted the war to end but that Kabila was resisting. The International Crisis Group published a report in December 2000, one month before the assassination, outlining Angola's position. The section on Angola was entitled "The Godfather"![53] This is not proof in itself; Zimbabwe also had called for negotiations to end the war, as had the United States.

The second point is that Angola, more than any other outsider, had the means to translate its wish into action. Angolan forces were heavily involved in providing security in Kinshasa. In addition, several Lunda from Katanga, individuals considered to be close to Angola, held key positions in the military security sphere. These included Colonel Edy Kapend, aide de camp to President Kabila, and General Yav Nawej, commander of the Kinshasa military region. Although little is known of Yav's background, Kapend has had a very interesting career. Reportedly, he was one of a number of schoolboys from Kapanga, in Lunda country, who accompanied the Tigers of the FLNC on their retreat to Angola after the Shaba II invasion in 1978.[54] Following normalization of relations between Zaire and Angola later that year, he returned to Katanga and resumed his secondary studies.[55] He later studied philosophy at the University of Lubumbashi.

In the early 1990s, in the era of multiparty competition, Kapend apparently was active both in the predominantly Katanga political party, the Union of Independent Federalists and Republicans (Union des Fédéralistes et Républicains Indépendants—UFERI) led by Nguza Karl-I-Bond and in the Katangan militia called the Tigers. He then served in the "Katangan" force that accompanied Kabila on his march from Kivu to Kinshasa. In the aftermath of the ADFL victory, the self-proclaimed president moved to bring the "Katangans" under his personal control. Naming Kapend as his military advisor was one element of this project. Kabila's success was demonstrated in 1998, when Dr. Emile Ilunga, supposed civilian leader of the Katanga Tigers, joined the RDC rebellion; few of the Tigers troops followed him.

Laurent Kabila was killed on 16 January 2001, and a few days later, army commander Joseph Kabila was announced as his father's successor. One of his first actions was to name a commission to investigate the assassination; it was headed by a Zimbabwean officer. No official report has been made public, though President Joseph Kabila may have received a confidential version. The official position is that Kabila was killed by Kasereka Rachidi, a member of the presidential bodyguard, and that Kasereka himself was killed immediately thereafter. Kasereka, twenty-six years old, was from North Kivu. Beyond that, we have several contradictory versions of the events.

One explanation, or cluster of explanations, focuses on rivalries within the ADFL created under Rwandan sponsorship. The ADFL brought together four anti-Mobutu groups. In addition to Kabila's Parti de la Révolution Populaire (People's Revolutionary Party—PRP), which hardly existed at that point, other groups in the ADFL were: the Conseil de Résistance Nationale pour la Démocratie (National Council of Resistance for Democracy—CRND), led by André Ngandu Kasesse, who had broken away from one of the splinter groups of the Mouvement National Congolais-Lumumba (Congolese National Movement—MNC-L); the Alliance Démocratique Populaire (People's Democratic Alliance—ADP), led by Déogratias Bugera; and the Mouvement Révolutionnaire pour la Libération du Zaire (Revolutionary Movement for the Liberation of Zaire—MRLZ), led by Anselme Masasu Nindaga.

The alliance began to break up almost as soon as it was founded. Ngandu was eliminated only a month later. The ADFL put out the story that Ngandu—whose CNRD was the only one of the four movements to be engaged in armed struggle against the Mobutu regime—was killed in a Zaire army ambush. Few believed the story. Some blamed Kabila, who feared Ngandu as a dangerous rival. Others saw the hand of Rwanda or the Congolese Tutsi and said that Ngandu was killed because of his persistent questioning of Tutsi domination of the ADFL military.

Bugera, a Tutsi from Masisi Zone, North Kivu, became secretary general of the ADFL. He was widely regarded as Rwanda's man in the inner circle around Kabila, or one of several, along with Foreign Minister Bizima Karaha. After serving in the important post of state minister to the presidency, Bugera escaped Kinshasa shortly after Kabila's order that all foreign troops should leave and joined the "rebellion" against Kabila at the start of the current war.

Masasu Nindaga was named general and chief of staff of the new Congolese army, which meant that he commanded mainly the "kadogo," the very young Congolese who joined the ADFL on its march to Kinshasa. (Rwandans, Ugandans, and Angolans had their own commanders.)

Masasu was arrested in 1998, along with several Tutsi officers, and accused of preparing a "plot" against Kabila. Kabila released him in March 2000, apparently as a gesture of goodwill toward Kigali. But Masasu was arrested again, toward the end of 2000, along with a number of military men from North and South Kivu. Again, a coup plot was alleged. Masasu was transferred to Katanga, where he was executed. Thus, one cluster of arguments as to who killed Laurent Kabila focuses on revenge for the elimination of his rivals Ngandu and Masasu. These arguments should not be excluded, but they are not complete.

In February 2001, *Le Monde* (Paris) published a long report that was based on interviews with self-identified participants in the assassination and on a document in which the participants outlined their coup plot. According to this version, Kasereka was a minor figure in the plot. Organizers included other former child soldiers, Congolese who had begun their military careers as teenagers or even younger in Uganda or Rwanda. They had been with Kabila since 1996 but felt betrayed by him. There was no foreign involvement in the killing, *Le Monde* concluded.

However, *Le Monde*'s version fails to answer a number of key questions. In particular: Why were Congolese soldiers disarmed and confined to their barracks at Kinshasa's main military bases, Camps Tshatshi and Kokolo, on the eve of the assassination (apparently on orders from General Yav)? And why was Kasereka killed on the spot (apparently by Colonel Kapend), rather than captured and interrogated?

Kapend reappears in several other interesting episodes. Eleven Lebanese were arrested in the aftermath of the assassination and later killed. It was claimed, implausibly, that a list of the eleven names had been found on the person of the assassin Kasereka. This story was later modified to say that the name of one of the Lebanese had been found in Kasereka's address book. The arrests were rumored to have been ordered by Colonel Kapend. He appears again in one of the few accounts of the succession to the late Kabila. Supposedly, Interior Minister Gaëtan Kakudji suggested that he was best qualified to serve as interim president. Kapend then said that Joseph Kabila should be chosen, and Justice Minister Mwenze Kongolo agreed.[56]

In the eyes of Kinshasa and Lingala-speaking western Congo, Kabila's regime was based on the Swahili-speaking east. Within the regime, however, a split had emerged between people from Kivu (the provinces of North Kivu, South Kivu, and perhaps Maniema) and those from Katanga. The official story laid the blame on an unspecified North Kivu man.

The finger of suspicion soon shifted. Many leading regime figures were arrested on suspicion of involvement in the assassination, including Kapend, Yav, and several other Lunda. These arrests brought to the surface the rivalry between the Lunda and the Luba-Katanga, the two leading ethnic groups in Katanga. Laurent Kabila had bridged the ethnic gap, since he was a Luba by his father and a Lunda by his mother.

Beyond the ethnic rivalries loomed the prospect of a split between Congo's two main allies. The danger was that Zimbabwe—which had sent troops to back Kabila in 1998—might side with the Luba-Katanga faction, splitting the pro-Kinshasa coalition. In the first week of March, there were reports from Kinshasa of shooting between Namibian and Angolan troops, the latter siding with Lunda deserters. Namibia was a minor player, however a similar clash between Angola and Zimbabwe would endanger the unfolding peace process.

All of this leaves Angola with a big problem. If (hypothetically) the Angolans, through their Congolese allies Kapend and Yav, arranged the death of Laurent Kabila and his replacement by his son Joseph, did their policy succeed? Laurent Kabila was killed, his son took his place, and the Kinshasa government took a more cooperative stance toward the peace process. To that point, one can say that the Angolans succeeded. But their policy went farther. They favored replacement of Kabila by a new regime in which they would maintain considerable influence, and an ending of the war in which their economic and security interests would be protected.

Even if Kapend and Yav were not acting under instructions from Luanda, Angola remains only partly satisfied. The new president is moving toward an end to the war, a policy presumably favored by Luanda. But the Luba-Lunda split, the detention of Kapend, Yav, and other Lunda personalities, and the desertion of Lunda from the Congolese army all mean that Angola's influence over Joseph Kabila has been reduced.

CONCLUSION

The Congo war has been a domestic political issue for three of the five major foreign participants. In Uganda, the press has discussed the war for some time, often criticizing the government. Unsuccessful presidential candidate Dr. Kizza Besigye attempted to mobilize antiwar sentiment as part of his challenge to President Museveni. Since Besigye's campaign suffered from harassment and perhaps vote rigging, the 69 percent of the vote attributed to Museveni probably does not reflect the degree of support for an unpopular war. In Zimbabwe, the Movement for Democratic Change (MDC) has attempted to exploit antiwar sentiment in its campaign against President Mugabe. Namibia's participation in the war and the diamond mine it supposedly received as compensation have been debated.

Angola and Rwanda are both countries where the Congo war is not publicly discussed. The Rwanda government persists in the increasingly implausible position that it has no economic activities or interests in Congo. This position, contested by opposition forces outside the country, is not debated within Rwanda. Nonetheless, in Angola, there is increasing criticism of the continuing war in Angola itself. Church groups and other elements of civil society have called for peace. UNITA factions that have split from Savimbi have called for peace talks only to be accused of treasonable sentiments by MPLA hardliners. But all this debate focuses on the war in Angola. I have seen no Angolan discussion of the war in Congo, which for the Angolans, progovernment or otherwise, is only a sideshow.

Achieving peace will continue to be the primary public policy question in Angola, since peace is a prerequisite for other crucial questions including economic recovery, the fight against corruption, and the struggle for democracy. Yet peace in the neighboring DRC appears to be a precondition for peace in Angola. In that sense, Angolans have a major interest in the Congo peace process, even if they cannot influence Congolese choices as much as they might wish.

NOTES

1. Associated Press, "Congolese Government Masses Soldiers to Retake Key Towns," CNN World News, 12 January 2001.
2. On this point, see John F. Clark, "Foreign Policy Making in Central Africa: The Imperative of Regime Security in a New Context," in Gilbert M. Khadiagala and Terrence Lyons, eds., *African Foreign Policies: Power and Process* (Boulder, CO: Lynne Rienner, 2001).
3. Patrick Chabal, "Angola and Mozambique: The Weight of History," in *Working Paper* (1998) available at www.kcl.ac.uk/depsta/humanities/pobrst/pcpapers.htm.
4. Paul Collier, *Economic Causes of Civil Conflict and Their Implications for Policy* (Washington: World Bank, 2000).
5. Colette Braeckman, *L'enjeu congolais: l'Afrique centrale après Mobutu* (Paris: Fayard, 1999), 266.
6. Jean-Claude Willame, "Contribution à l'étude des Mouvements d'Opposition au Zaïre: Le FLNC," *Cahiers du CEDAF*, no. 6 (1980); Jean-Claude Willame, *L'odyssée Kabila: Trajectoire pour un Congo nouveau?* (Paris: Karthala, 2000).
7. Chester A. Crocker, *High Noon in Southern Africa. Making Peace in a Rough Neighborhood* (New York: W. W. Norton & Company, 1992), 31.
8. I. William Zartman, *Ripe for Resolution: Conflict and Intervention in Africa*, rev. ed. (New York: Oxford University Press for the Council on Foreign Relations, 1989), 143.
9. Braeckman, *L'Enjeu Congolais*, 407.
10. See chapters 8, 9, and 12 in this volume.
11. Misha Glenny, "The Age of the Parastate," *New Yorker* (8 May 1995): 45–53.
12. William Reno, *Warlord Politics and African States* (Boulder, CO: Lynne Rienner Publishers, 1998), and William Reno, "The Real (War) Economy of Angola," in Jakkie Cilliers and Christian Dietrich, eds., *Angola's War Economy* (Pretoria: Institute for Security Studies, 2000), 219–235.
13. Chabal, "Angola and Mozambique: The Weight of History."
14. Elizabeth M. Jamilah Koné, "The Right of Self-Determination in the Angolan Enclave of Cabinda" (paper presented at the Sixth Annual African Studies Consortium Workshop, Temple University School of Law, Philadelphia, 1998).
15. Chabal, "Angola and Mozambique."
16. On the origins of all the major anticolonial groups in Angola, see John A. Marcum, *The Angolan Revolution*, vol. 1 (Cambridge, MA: MIT Press, 1969).
17. William Blum, *Killing Hope: U.S. Military and CIA Interventions since World War II* (Monroe, ME: Common Courage Press, 1995).
18. Odd Arne Westad, "Moscow and the Angolan Crisis, 1974–1976: A New Pattern of Intervention," in *Cold War International History Project Electronic Bulletin*, no. 8–9 (winter 1996/1997), and no. 8–9 (1997) and Piero Gleijeses, "Havana's Policy in Africa, 1959–76: New Evidence from Cuban Archives," in *Cold War International History Project Electronic Bulletin*, no. 8–9 (1997).
19. Westad, "Moscow and the Angolan Crisis, 1974–1976."
20. Ibid.
21. Braeckman, *L'Enjeu Congolais*, 261.
22. Ibid., 264.
23. Filip Reyntjens, *La Guerre des Grands Lacs* (Paris: L'Harmattan, 1999), 70.
24. Braeckman, *L'Enjeu Congolais*, 264.
25. Reyntjens, *La Guerre des Grands Lacs*, 70, citing François Misser and Olivier Vallée, *Les gemmocraties. L'économie politique du diamant africain* (Paris: Desclée de Brouwer, 1997), 123–24.

26. Reyntjens, *La Guerre des Grands Lacs,* 70, citing J. Rupert, "Zaire Reportedly Selling Arms to Angolan Ex-Rebels," *The Washington Post,* 21 March 1997.

27. Braeckman, *L'Enjeu Congolais,* 265.

28. Ibid.

29. Ibid.

30. On the 1977 and 1978 invasions of Katanga, see Crawford Young, "Zaire: The Unending Crisis," *Foreign Affairs* 57 (fall 1978), 169–85.

31. Filip Reyntjens, *La Guerre des Grands Lacs,* 72, and Gerald J. Bender, "Relations between Angola and Zaïre/DRC, From Lumumba to Kabila," (New York: UN Secretary General's Resource Group on the Democratic Republic of Congo, 1998).

32. Reyntjens, *La Guerre des Grands Lacs,* 73.

33. Willame, *L'odyssée Kabila,* and Bender, "Relations between Angola and Zaïre/DRC, From Lumumba to Kabila."

34. Reyntjens, *La Guerre des Grands Lacs,* 74.

35. Ibid.

36. Braeckman, *L'Enjeu Congolais,* 266, and Reyntjens, *La Guerre des Grands Lacs,* 73–74.

37. Braeckman, *L'Enjeu Congolais,* 266.

38. Ibid.; as of this writing, the "Angolagate" story continues to unfold.

39. Ibid., 266–67.

40. Ibid., 267–68.

41. Élisabeth Dorier-Apprill, "Jeunesse et ethnicités citadines à Brazzaville," *Politique Africaine,* no. 64 (1996): 73–88.

42. See John F. Clark, "International Aspects of the Civil War in Congo-Brazzaville," *Issue* 26, no.1 (1998), 31–36.

43. RCD/CRD, "Political Declaration of the Congolese Rally for Democracy (RCD/CRD), Goma, August 12, 1998," *Association of Concerned Africa Scholars, Special Bulletin,* October 1998. Also see Afoaku, chapter 7 in this volume.

44. Georges Nzongola-Ntalaja, "Position du Professeur Georges Nzongola-Ntalaja sur la Crise en République Démocratique du Congo, Washington, August 13,1998," *Association of Concerned Africa Scholars, Special Bulletin,* October 1998.

45. Braeckman, *L'Enjeu Congolais,* 355.

46. Braeckman, 361, citing her interview with Mpoyo, published in *Le Soir,* 29 August 1998.

47. Ibid.

48. Braeckman, 393.

49. International Crisis Group [ICG], "Scramble for the Congo," in *Anatomy of an Ugly War,* ICG Africa Report, no. 26 (Nairobi/Brussels: 2000).

50. Ibid. Also see Koyame and Clark, chapter 12, in this volume.

51. "ANGOLA: Cabinda Rebels Under Pressure," IRIN, Johannesburg, 15 February 2001, citing US intelligence-gathering firm Stratfor.

52. ICG, "Scramble for the Congo."

53. Ibid.

54. Shaba was the new name given to Katanga province after Mobutu's renaming efforts throughout Congo in the early 1970s. In 1978 and 1979 exiled fighters from Shaba invaded their former home province from Angolan territory hoping to spur a general uprising against Mobutu. In both cases the rebels enjoyed the support of the Angolan government. For other details of these two invasions, see Crawford Young, "Zaire: The Unending Crisis."

55. Zartman, *Ripe for Resolution,* 159–60.

56. Karl Vick, "Congo's Strangely Smooth Transition," *Washington Post,* 27 January 2001, A13.

CHAPTER 6

A Political and Military Review of Zimbabwe's Involvement in the Second Congo War

MARTIN R. RUPIYA

T he middle of March 2001 witnessed the long awaited physical disengagement of the belligerents fighting in the Democratic Republic of Congo (DRC) as envisioned in the Lusaka Agreement. This in turn allowed the deployment of half of the promised 5,537 peacekeeping forces organized as the Mission d'Organisation Nations Unis au Congo (United Nations Mission to the Congo—MONUC). The deployment of the MONUC forces followed a tortuous wait by the belligerent African countries, who that had to sign a ceasefire twice in order to persuade an extremely reluctant UN to intervene.[1] These developments were taking place against the backdrop of the assassination of President Laurent Désiré Kabila on 16 January 2001 in Kinshasa, whereupon his son, Joseph, succeeded him. Joseph Kabila's approach to international relations had clearly breathed new life into the process.[2] In February 2001, the African belligerent states met at the United Nations, signaling their renewed desire for peace, and practically begged the UN Security Council to authorize the deployment of peacekeepers.

This paid dividends as, soon afterward, Uganda began withdrawing some 10,000 soldiers and Rwanda, after much procrastination, followed suit, announcing that it "expected to withdraw over 15,000."[3] The departure of Rwandan and Ugandan forces, as well as the arrival of the MONUC, has always been publicly stated as the precondition for the exit of Zimbabwe's military forces from the DRC. Until such time as the current UN initiative takes hold and brings about peace in the DRC, however, Zimbabwe remains locked in a conflict that has so far undermined its domestic political stability, eroded its economic well-being (due to the unprecedented unbudgeted expenditure on security), and, finally, stunted its already tenuous military capacity.[4] It has, however, now been widely acknowledged that the military intervention by the Southern African Development Community (SADC) allies, made up of units from Angola, Namibia, and Zimbabwe, did contribute significantly to the survival of the beleaguered Laurent Kabila regime.

Against the background of the current developments at a national level in Zimbabwe, the country's political and military intervention appears to have followed a legitimate course. A different picture emerges, however, if one takes a closer look at events as they have evolved in the DRC. In order to shed light on this situation, this paper undertakes a political and military review of Zimbabwe's involvement there. It begins with an analysis of the purposes of Zimbabwe's initial intervention in Congo. It then explores Zimbabwe's evolving strategy in the war. And finally, it accesses the impact of the war on Zimbabwe's domestic political, economic, and military structures. The hope is that this may inform policy in current operations or in the future.

The momentous decision by Zimbabwe to deploy a contingent of 600 Zimbabwean forces[5] under Operation Restore Sovereignty was made at the eleventh hour in August 1998. The fast-moving events at the time did not allow for prior public consultation or debate regarding the decision to deploy the country's armed forces. When the deployment was effected, given the impression that the force threatening Kinshasa was only a rag-tag dissident group, it was widely assumed that this would be a temporary military expedition, lasting no more than three weeks. More than thirty months later, the Zimbabwean force has ballooned to over 16,000, with no end to its role in sight unless the current UN initiative holds. In light of the history of past military deployments of confident states, the conservatism shown in the initial deployment and the actual lengthy period of stay, coupled with the astronomical increase in manpower, is not surprising. While on the one hand it reveals a failure by the intelligence arm to accurately predict the situation in Kinshasa, it also confirms the traditional inclination of military planners to err on the side of conservatism.

THE POLITICAL MOTIVATION AND
DECISION TO INTERVENE MILITARILY IN THE DRC

The political decision for Zimbabwe's involvement emerged from at least three important parallel developments. Before turning to these developments, however, it must be acknowledged that Zimbabwean officials had some inkling of what is now common knowledge. That is, they knew of the designs of Burundi, Rwanda, and Uganda to carve out territories of security influence in the regions of Congo that share contiguous borders with those states. President Mobutu Sese Seko's departure had been gradual and predictable, but he had left no obvious successor. This presented neighboring states with an opportunity to plot and attempt to "manage" their relations with their large but poorly organized and defended neighbor. Laurent Kabila and his Alliance for the Democratic Liberation of the Congo (Alliance des forces démocratiques pour la libération du Congo-Zaire—ADFL)[6] had been deliberately chosen as the successor to Mobutu by Rwanda and Uganda in the first Congo war of 1996--97. A deal had been secretly struck with Kabila at the small town of Lemera near the shores of Lake Tanganyika. Part of the general understanding of the pact appeared to relate to the internal security of Burundi, Rwanda, and Uganda vis-à-vis contending rebel groups that had enjoyed sanctuary in Mobutu 's Zaire. When Kabila embarked on his march on Kinshasa in October 1996, he had, as his vanguard, Burundian, Rwandan, and Ugandan forces under his nominal command.[7] Paul Omach, a Ugandan scholar, has described their coming together as an example of a "non-institutionalized, informal alliance ... [based on] neighboring states, which felt the security of their regimes threatened by the late Mobutu. . . ."[8] Uganda, for example, claimed that the towns of Bunia, Buta, Gemena, Gbadolite, and Kisingani are areas from which one of its enemies, the Allied Democratic Forces (ADF), has operated. The ADF is definitely known to have bases in the Ruwenzori Mountains, along the Uganda/Congo border; from there it carries out operations that threaten the security of Uganda.

Many other African states and the international community at large were aware of this "special arrangement" among Burundi, Rwanda, Uganda, and Kabila's ADFL in 1996--97. All were anxious to see the back of the discredited and corrupt Mobutu regime. Angola, Eritrea, Tanzania, Rwanda, Uganda, and Zimbabwe, among others, practically assisted in the forced removal of Mobutu from office in 1996--97. But many were not privy to the secret agreement to which we have alluded and were therefore to react in various ways when the new crisis erupted in 1998.

In the drive for Kinshasa, Kabila's forces made swift progress, as those of Mobutu did not offer any tangible resistance to the invasion. After occupying a large portion of the Congolese territory, Rwanda and Uganda sent urgent instructions for Kabila to halt his advance. To their chagrin, however, Kabila's march had gained its own momentum and continued. On arrival in Kinshasa, Kabila arrived at the presidential residence and was pleasantly surprised to find that the door was already ajar. In retrospect, the plan of Rwanda and Uganda must have been to occupy part of the country and install a weak leader in Kinshasa who would be unable to reverse the de facto balkanization of the Congo. This incident represents a strategic hiatus in the plan to realize the objectives of the "allies" who were ranged against Mobutu.

On 17 May 1997, Kabila declared himself president and soon appeared to have begun taking a line independent of Rwanda and Uganda, a move that effectively stopped the first attempt to dismember Congo. Being miffed at his rather independent line, the Rwandan and Ugandan presidents subsequently boycotted the first anniversary celebrations of Kabila's victory in May 1998.[9] Zimbabwean officials serving as part of the Rwandan UN Observer Mission at the time were perplexed at this turn of events but must have drawn conclusions that subsequently informed policy in August 1998. When the second "invasion" of Congo, this time against Kabila, was intimated in June and July 1998,[10] the real reasons, for those with their ear on the ground, were clear. The invasion itself was preceded by a very public fallout between former allies when Kabila ordered Rwanda and Ugandan troops to return to their countries on 28 July 1998.[11]

Returning to the reasons for Zimbabwe's involvement in the DRC war, the first development was, ironically, the appeal to intervene in the conflict made to President Robert Mugabe by Ugandan president Yoweri Museveni in Windhoek. Subsequently, a meeting was organized for all belligerents at Victoria Falls following an appeal from the "international community," led by the Organization of African Unity (OAU) and SADC.[12] Following an impasse in the discussions, the delegates decided to dispatch a committee made up of foreign ministers to verify the allegations and counterallegations on the ground. The committee, led by Zimbabwean foreign minister Dr. Stan Mudenge, would then report back to the summit of heads of states and government.

Upon arrival in the Great Lakes, Museveni surprised the delegation by brazenly asserting that he had deployed Ugandan forces in support of the "rebels" in the DRC. The "rebels" continued to march on Kinshasa even as the committee made its lightning tour of central Africa. From this incident, one may conclude, it was the revealing contact from Museveni, in a way, that determined Zimbabwe's subsequent foreign policy response. Parallel public claims by Commander Jean-Pierre Ondakane, "a prominent rebel leader, speaking at a lakeside villa in Goma on 28 July 1998, also pointed toward the desire for a short war."[13] Taking both of these statements into account, it was therefore clear that a military option was being employed in order to present a fait accompli when the summit reconvened. This contradiction presented a vexing problem to the Zimbabwean leadership, which saw Mugabe as embodying the role of African elder statesman and defender of Pan Africanism. The findings of the foreign ministerial delegation confirmed the view that only a superior military response would deter the intentions of rebels and their supporters. The seemingly unethical behavior of the leaders of the Great Lakes states in the view of Zimbabwe provoked the angst and commitment needed to thwart the designs of Burundi, Rwanda, and Uganda.[14]

The second development leading to the decision to intervene stemmed from the formal request made to SADC by a member state, namely, the DRC itself.[15] This was brought up for consideration by member states in the meeting of the Inter-State Defence and Security Committee (ISDSC) held in Harare in July 1998.[16] Zimbabwe, as chair of the Organ on Politics, Defence, and Security, and imbued with the spirit of the former Front Line States, felt that it could not shirk its responsibilities to a neighbor under threat from "imperialism." Given the perceived involvement of some Western participants with the key belligerent interveners, as is now common knowledge, nothing could hold back the Zimbabwean leadership participation in this perceived Pan Africanist venture.[17]

The third development was not an "active cause" but a "permissive condition," namely, that Zimbabwe had adequate military force at its disposal to undertake the mission. Zimbabwe's government had built up this force to support the foreign policy objective subsumed in its Pan Africanist ambitions, referred to above. Since attaining independence in early 1980, Zimbabwe embarked upon a major force integration that brought together elements of the former Rhodesian Security Forces and the armed elements of the two major political parties, the Zimbabwe African National Liberation Army (ZANLA) and the Zimbabwe People's Revolutionary Army (ZIPRA). Manpower training and availability of equipment soon benefited from a wide range of military assistance from Britain, China, Tanzania, Pakistan, and North Korea.[18] Subsequent battlefield experience was soon gained from operations mounted both at home,[19] and in neighboring Mozambique from the early 1980s until 1992.[20] The key component to emerge from all this was the ability of the Zimbabwe Defence Forces (ZDF) to put into the field a brigade-sized combat unit, involving air power, tanks, and special infantry forces. In the intervening period until 1998, the ZDF also enjoyed operational experience under various UN peacekeeping missions on the African continent.[21]

Given that the states intervening in Congo against Kabila seemed to be in clear violation of international law, and given the sanction of the SADC for the mission, Zimbabwe felt completely justified in its counterintervention. The logic of Namibia's participation in the war was quite similar, while that of Angola combined these legal and political imperatives with those of security.[22] In my view, whatever economic interests Zimbabwe subsequently acquired in Congo were not part of its initial calculus of intervention.

ZIMBABWE'S STRATEGY IN THE CONGO WAR

Politics always establish the purposes and means of war, and in this case, Zimbabwe's political stake in the DRC served to determine the strategic objectives that in turn decided the military strategy. The political situation of the Kabila regime in the DRC in August of 1998 reflected a highly polarized and regionally divided society. The previous conflict had resulted in the division of the country into spheres of factional control in the north, east, central and southwest. Following a July decree ordering the immediate expulsion of Rwandan and Ugandan forces, an orchestrated uprising ensued in the regions. The towns of Bukavu, Goma, Kisingani, and Kalemie were immediately wrested from government control. This did not necessarily determine the political control of the DRC, however. After the initial seizures of regional centers, it was clear that similar action had to be mounted against the capital Kinshasa in order for the rebellion to be recognized by the international community. In other words, Kinshasa *was* the DRC, and the political control of this capital was imperative.

Within Kinshasa, the rebels initially infiltrated the various suburbs of Kimbanseke, Masina, Kingasani, and Mikonga. They also gained control of part of the international airport of Ndjili, resulting in the very public cancellation of international flights into and out of Kinshasa. Furthermore, the hydroelectric facility at the huge Inga Dam near Kinshasa was seized, threatening the capital's energy and water supply. The lifeline city of Matadi, located near the mouth of the Congo River and serving as the seaport as well as road and rail route for daily supplies of foodstuffs and fuel to the capital, was also threatened. The tactical strategy was to starve the population of Kinshasa and forcibly hound Kabila from the state house, or even assassinate him. The British Broadcasting Corporation (BBC) confirmed this reality during September. At the time, the BBC indicated that Kinshasa was "four days from starvation."[23]

The impact of the rebel march on Kinshasa was immediate. Laurent Kabila, previously protected by forces from the neighboring states of Rwanda and Uganda, had at that point become unreliable to them, and, for fear of assassination, immediately went into hiding. By so doing, he partly surrendered overt political control of the DRC for a time. Foreign governments from the developed world reacted to this "situation of insecurity" by ordering the evacuation of their nationals from Kinshasa. Belgium, Britain, France, and the United States mounted airlifts to locations across the river in Congo-Brazzaville or Libreville, Gabon, in preparation for repatriation to home countries.[24] This action added further pressure, seeming to confirm the lack of an effective government in the DRC.

Zimbabwe's military strategy therefore took its cue from the early political and military maneuvering of the rebel force, which had established several important patterns. First, the operation would be a joint operation. It was, however, evident that the incoming forces would *not* be linking up with a local force, at least in the initial stages, since the forces available within the host country were untrustworthy. This was not a new phenomenon to the Zimbabwean forces, as they had had similar experiences with Resistencia Naçional Moçambicana (Mozambican National Resistance—RENAMO) forces, who disguised themselves as Frente de Libertação de Mozambique (Liberation Front of Mozambique—FRELIMO) troops during the 1980s Mozambique war. However, this development meant that the Zimbabwean forces and their allies would have to physically protect the person of Laurent Kabila. The latter embodied the legal and sovereign government of the DRC in strategic terms. Second, it was also evident that other international forces were already at play in the conflict in the DRC, and there was therefore a need to make a symbolic gesture of defiance to these actors. In short, a message demonstrating a very overt and heightened sense of military preparedness was required in order to force underground the shadowy and irregular forces on both sides of the divide in the DRC. A publicly mandated SADC operation was one way of criminalizing some of the forces already competing for power without revealing themselves in the war. Third, there was also an urgent need to win the support of the ordinary people in Kinshasa in the battle for the political capital.

The challenge was therefore to safeguard Kabila, mount relief operations to key occupied towns, and drive the rebels away from Kinshasa. This latter task presented the real prospect of fighting in built-up areas, a prospect for which none of the belligerents was adequately prepared. This realization culminated in Zimbabwe marshaling and deploying a unit of tanks and Cascavel armored vehicles, apart from the helicopters and fighter ground attack aircraft that were confirmed by the servicemen themselves.[25] The tactical challenge was to launch a lightning-style operation, based on mobile warfare doctrines, in a coordinated way with Angolan and Namibian units. This would primarily focus on relieving Kinshasa of immediate threat from the Rwandan forces. This objective would provide the political trump card of ensuring some semblance of political order and continuity in the DRC.

The manner of the initial military deployment had been coordinated with the Angolan and Namibian defense forces. Key elements among the forces detached from the allied countries were the tank and air power squadron formations. These provided rapid advance and decisive engagement with the "targets" as represented by the forces deployed from Rwanda and Uganda. These had adopted well-prepared defensive positions that, significantly, had not taken into account an adversary who would exercise complete dominance and superiority of the skies in and around Kinshasa, Matadi, and the Inga dam wall area.

The Zimbabwean combat unit deployed in Kinshasa was equipped with various types of aircraft, tanks, and armored vehicles, and supported by contingents of special forces from the parachute and commando brigades. According to the public reports, the latter special units had been placed on standby in case the initial force required beefing up. This was fortuitous as the "rebels" were merely a screen operating in front of well-equipped regular forces from Rwanda and Uganda. The SADC allies immediately reinforced their tiny expeditionary units. Since their adversaries were fighting far from their own borders, however, they exercised considerable caution in their initial engagements with the SADC forces.

The actual fighting with strategic significance in the DRC war occurred in three phases. The first phase was from August to September 1998 when, after the initial assaults, it became clear that the "rebels" were only a superficial cover for well-organized Rwandan and Ugandan regular units.[26] Success during this phase was assisted by the spontaneous involvement of the local people. Previous atrocities carried out by mainly Rwandan Tutsi soldiers had left the population deeply embittered toward occupiers. However, once the tables were turned, Kinshasa residents unleashed themselves with a vengeance on the Tutsi soldiers, forcing many of them to flee into the forests. This was an important dimension of the success in the initial phase that has thus far received little acknowledgement.

The initial impact of the deployment by SADC allies was positive, given the strategic objectives identified above. First, beleaguered President Laurent Kabila did escape with his life, though barely, from the suspect troops.[27] Second, important secondary cities and infrastructure networks in the vicinity of the capital were secured. Electricity was restored to Kinshasa with the assistance of Zimbabwean engineers "nearly a month after it was cut by rebels who had taken control of a hydroelectric plant."[28] Third, the capital Kinshasa and its suburbs were soon rid of "invading" troops, and, much more significantly, the Ndjili international airport was reopened for commercial and normal business operations. This relayed an important signal of political control by the incumbent regime to the interveners and the outside world.

This immediately changed the nature of the war into the first conventional war among states on the African continent. During this second phase, six national armed forces, grouped into two camps, confronted each other on Congolese territory. Covert action was quickly abandoned as both sides upped the ante and openly deployed their national military assets. These included fighter planes, helicopters, tanks, artillery pieces, and rockets employed by all branches of the armed forces, including air forces, infantry, and naval units. The next six-week period of the war witnessed intense fighting, during which the belligerent states threw everything they had at each other. A number of developments emerged from this activity. While forces from Burundi, Rwanda, and Uganda had been routed from the environs of Kinshasa, engagements that occurred further afield, and nearer their own borders, resulted in the dissipation of the initial advantage enjoyed by the SADC allied forces. Soon, the increased military hardware brought into play by all sides led to a stalemate, with Angola, Rwanda, and Uganda tending to dominate the areas of geographic contiguity. During this phase, the challengers lost valuable equipment and manpower and were therefore forced to withdraw. The Lusaka Agreement attests to this. It orders a ceasefire and divides control of territory into four main areas of east, northern, central and west Congo. At that time, Burundi, Rwanda, and Uganda controlled the former two areas, while the SADC allies dominated the latter.

This stalemate on the battlefield soon influenced the political dialogue that was to culminate in the signing of the Lusaka Peace Settlement on 10 July 1999. Curiously, within a month of this agreement, fierce fighting broke out in Kisingani between Ugandan and Rwanda forces.[29] After the third strategic phase began, Zimbabwe's strategy shifted almost entirely to the diplomatic front. On the ground in the DRC, Zimbabwe mainly worked with the Congolese government forces to secure the control of the major cities of the central and western areas and to repulse attacks from rebel and interventionist forces. Rather than pursue the war further east, the Zimbabwean leadership determined that a political solution was the next step in the resolution of the war.

IMPACT ON ZIMBABWE'S POLITICAL, ECONOMIC, AND MILITARY STRUCTURES

The decision by Zimbabwe to intervene in the DRC has led to generally adverse socioeconomic trends in the country. Meanwhile, the war has also delivered a blow to the political standing of the Mugabe regime, both at home and abroad. This discussion, however, will focus mainly on the internal consequences of the war for the current regime and for the Zimbabwean population.

First, the stakes of the war in the DRC go well beyond the interests of the parties now vying for control in Kinshasa, and even beyond the interests of the intervening powers. The major Western powers, international lending institutions, and media have interests in the war, as well. While Zimbabwe deployed its military in an effort to influence what appeared to have been regional and localized political differences, the adverse response from the international media has been astounding. Both the major networks of CNN and BBC, soon after the conflict moved into the second stalemate phase, decided to deliberately ignore the war. Meanwhile, the regional dominant media, based in South Africa, mounted an unrelenting campaign, portraying the involvement as "illegitimate," ill-advised, and based on personal quests for enrichment from the gold and diamonds in the DRC.

The International Financial Institutions (IFIs) (i.e., the International Monetary Fund and the World Bank) chimed in with incessant economic arguments, calling for the abandonment of the country's intervention in the DRC on grounds of the need for fiscal discipline. This was in direct contrast to the public messages that the same institutions were issuing to Rwanda and Uganda, for instance. This strategy of the IFIs successfully diverted important public opinion from the real core issues at stake. It also partly succeeded in delegitimizing the sterling efforts of the SADC allies to uphold the principles of sovereignty and territorial integrity illustrated through their military deployment. As a result of the orchestrated international media war against the SADC allies, who were in the midst of fending off a determined and coordinated military thrust, Angola, Zimbabwe, and Namibia were forced to defend themselves against those distortions within SADC, the OAU, and the UN.

The powerful information tool of foreign media deployed in the "battle for the hearts and minds" succeeded in influencing the opinions of the ordinary people in Zimbabwe. Government attempts at explaining the war locally have not been as robust as the increased level of deployment demanded. Consequently, Zimbabwean society has been divided at a crucial time, with its forces engaged in a foreign war. The war controversy was to exacerbate a nascent political schism that has come to dominate politics in the country during the 1998--99 period, and has had an important impact on the Zimbabwean domestic front in political terms.[30] Before the war, there had been no meaningful opposition party to talk about. The political divide over the DRC war reached unfortunate levels when President Joseph Kabila paid a state visit to Zimbabwe in March 2001 and was given the privilege of addressing parliament. All the opposition members of parliament boycotted the proceedings.[31]

The second area of controversy, closely related to that above, concerned the increased and unbudgeted military expenditure that the country was forced to make in support of its operation in the DRC. The costs of the war for Zimbabwe are exacerbated by the country's distance from the theaters of deployment. The country's two main air bases, at Harare and Gweru, are over 5,000 km (3,100 miles) from Kinshasa, the main staging point for operations in the DRC. Transportation costs alone therefore imposed a huge burden on the military and its budget. Zimbabwe's military involvement in the DRC conflict required a steady increase in the number of troops involved. While a contingent of some 6,000 troops initially went into Congo, this gradually swelled by nearly 300 percent to some 16,000 following the assassination of Laurent Kabila in January 2001.[32] Even with the stalemate in place, simply maintaining the status quo of controlling the designated areas defined by the Lusaka Accord required over 10,000 forces to be deployed.

Another aspect is that the costs of the war have had to be paid largely in U.S. dollars, while the value of the Zimbabwean dollar has been rapidly falling against the U.S. dollar. Following the practice inherited from UN peacekeeping missions, ZDF troops have been given monthly allowances in U.S. dollars to supplement their meager pay and to reward them for the direct risks to which they have been exposed.[33] Furthermore, the hiring of East European transport planes and fighter helicopters further "dollarized" the war, increasing defense expenditures from Zimbabwe's slender budget. The costs of the Congo war have been a matter of great dispute in Zimbabwe, and some estimates range as high as U.S.$30 million per month. In August 2000, the minister of finance, Dr. Simba Makoni, admitted that the country had already spent over Z$10 billion on the war to that time and warned that this level of expenditure was unsustainable.[34] Before the war, the government had crafted an estimated budget of Z$5.4 billion for 1997–98, expecting this to fall to Z$5.2 billion in the 1999 fiscal year. This budget had been criticized by an adverse parliamentary report, presented in March of 1998, that had called for increased spending on the condition of service, buildings, and maintenance on the defense forces.[35] Clearly, it was hoped that the DRC regime would, in the weeks following Zimbabwe's deployment, begin assisting with the payment of some of the military costs. The fact that this has not been realized has further strained the finances of Zimbabwe.

Furthermore, almost incrementally, the government began to give credence to the argument that Zimbabwe should realize an economic gain from its participation in the war. The government had been previously criticized for failing to exploit its military commitment to the Mozambican government during the war of the 1980s. Instead, it effectively helped to create the environment for South Africa to then enter into the Mozambican market and reap the profits of commerce in that country after 1992. Thus, a number of state-sponsored "business familiarization visits" of Zimbabwean companies to the DRC were arranged, and have continued to be encouraged as the two countries try to forge even more integrated linkages. According to scholar Michael Nest, this process was also facilitated by the economic collapse within the DRC following the departure of Mobutu. At that time, the DRC was forced to look toward southern Africa for imports previously obtained from Western Europe.[36]

Adding to the frustration of the DRC war are the long-standing calls within the Zimbabwean society to reduce military expenditure and demobilize excess forces, calls that have not been addressed since the mid-1980s. The events in the DRC obviously resulted in a failure to achieve progress on this issue since 1998. In the previous year, the Zimbabwean government had announced in parliament that it was going to reduce the approximately 40,000 armed forces to 25,000. Given the stalemate and demands on the battlefield, however, the military actually had to take on additional manpower.

Untoward and unbudgeted military expenditure has, not surprisingly, strained relations within the country. Expenditure on public sector investment, welfare, and production has clearly suffered as a result of the unprecedented spending on defense. Shortages of essentials such as fuel and other commodities, as well as foreign exchange, have characterized the Zimbabwean trade and economic environment.

For the first time in the history of independent Zimbabwe, food riots occurred, and they continued to take place with an alarming frequency during 2000 and 2001. The government was forced at one point to deploy armed forces on the streets in a bid to maintain law and order. Sadly, this had implications for civil-military relations, which have also become strained.

Even as social stability seemed to be unraveling at home, a further development hitherto not associated with the ZDF was becoming manifest within Congo; this was the capture of troops in battle as well as the abandonment of military positions as a result of the superiority of hostile forces on the front lines in the DRC. The incident at the small town of Pweto, north of the Zambian border, illustrated this phenomenon. Following the ferocious attack in December 2000 by a superior Rwandan force, deployed thousands of kilometers from Kigali, over 300 ZDF forces, together with their DRC colleagues, were forced to abandon their positions and seek succor in a refugee camp across the border in Zambia. This phenomenon had been heretofore unheard of in the short history of the ZDF since 1980, and one may assume that this caused untold damage to the morale of the ZDF troops. Certainly, in the highly contested local media, where civil-military relations were already at low ebb, cartoonists began to mock the ZDF's alleged military prowess.

Finally, the military effort in Congo has served to squander all of the military investment that had been acquired before August 1998. It is now doubtful that the ZDF could raise, within 72 hours, a fully equipped, multitask military unit including air cover, armored cars, tanks, and special infantry forces with one or two motorized units, organized as a combat brigade. The high rate of equipment wear in the harsh terrain of the DRC has exacted a heavy price on the serviceability of military assets. This has led to a high rate of operational losses and the abandonment of heavy equipment as a consequence of unserviceability for combat.[37] Replacement values and sources have also become prohibitively more expensive given the inexplicable sanctions imposed on the SADC allies by the U.K. and U.S. governments.[38] The development of the stalemate on the battlefield attests to the fact that both sides have lost so much equipment that a modern conventional war is no longer possible. With the military instrument now revealing its limitations, only political negotiations can bring about peace.

CONCLUSION

The striking of the Lusaka Agreement, through which limited involvement of the UN in the form of the MONUC force was worked out, is an important development for Zimbabwe in military, political, and economic terms. This was further enhanced by the Disengagement and Redeployment Plan by the defense chiefs of all the belligerent countries signed in Harare on 6 December 2000, and subsequent negotiations undertaken since the assassination of Laurent Kabila. These have required the belligerent troops to withdraw to a distance of 15 kilometers (9.3 miles) from each other as of 15 April 2001 in order to remove the possibility of employing major weapon systems (as at such a distance they all would be out of range). Second, the agreement by the defense chiefs, in line with the political guidelines of the Lusaka Agreement, also envisaged the complete withdrawal of all foreign forces from the DRC by September 2001.[39] At the moment of this writing, according to the UN monitoring and verification groups in the DRC, all belligerents, with the exception of the Ugandan-backed group of Jean-Pierre Bemba (Mouvement pour la Libération du Congo—MLC), have complied with the requests.

Even more encouraging, in August 2001, the long awaited Inter-Congolese dialogue, under the chairmanship of the Botswana former president, Sir Ketumile Masire, also met in Gaborone. The highest level representatives of all the factions and government of the DRC attended this gathering. Civil society, churches, and other interested groups representing some 3,500 entities were also in attendance. A further meeting has been scheduled for 15 October in Addis Ababa, at the OAU. The political entity created by the Lusaka Accord is, therefore, working through the auspices of the continental and international community as the peace process unfolds. This reflects the broadening of the political dialogue and participation platform in the DRC conflict that has so far been absent. This space, previously monopolized by men and women with guns, is now becoming the domain of a wide cross-section of the Congolese society, which is the only route to bring about lasting peace in that troubled land.

This development has largely vindicated Zimbabwe's public posture and foreign policy statements in support of Operation Restore Sovereignty since August 1998. This choice for a political settlement has validated the SADC, the OAU Organ on Conflict Prevention Mechanism, and Zimbabwean positions on the DRC conflict. Its arrival has been timely, however, for beleaguered political, economic, and military relations in Zimbabwe. On balance, the country appears to have made a huge sacrifice for its involvement in the war, which has left it scarred, impoverished, and politically divided. It is unfortunate that there has been no national rejoicing or relief following the momentous decision in which the Inter-Congolese dialogue was given the opportunity to flourish and influence the future politics of that great country.

Notes

1. The Lusaka Peace Settlement or Agreement was first signed in July 1999 by all belligerent states as well as nonstate actors involved and was later submitted for the signatures of other belligerents in April 2000.

2. He has, for example, accepted the mediation efforts of former president Sir Ketumile Masire of Botswana. This was a major sticking point with his father. He has also very publicly engaged the West in a development that appears to have undercut the close relations previously enjoyed by the country's main detractors, Rwanda and Uganda.

3. This has since been called into question as President Paul Kagame announced an unequivocal decision to remain in the DRC for security reasons at the April 2001 commemoration of the genocide event. See, "Rwanda Threatens Not to Withdraw from DRC," *The Daily News* (Harare), 9 April 2001.

4. *The 1998 Third Report of the Departmental Committee on Security Ministries,* presented to the Zimbabwe 3rd Session of the 4th Parliament on 24 March (SC2–1998), painted a grim picture of the state of the armed forces, accommodation, and equipment as well as the deplorable conditions of service. There are also unconfirmed reports of the peace initiative possibly coming unstuck as a result of differences between the SADC allies, not mentioning differences that have emerged between Rwanda and Uganda. Political succession differences were reported by Silvia Aloisi, "Split Weakens Kabila Allies," *Daily Nation* (Nairobi daily), 22 March 2001, 11.

5. "Zim. Sends Two More Battalions to Congo," *Electronic Mail & Guardian,* Johannesburg, South Africa (SA), August 28, 1998, accessed at http://www.mg.co.za/mg/news/98aug2/28aug-zim_congo2.html (5 February 2001).
6. The ADFL launched an offensive against Mobutu Sese Seko in October 1996.
7. Mahmood Mamdani, "Rwanda Rebels Aren't Going to Win this Time," quoted in *Electronic Mail & Guardian,* Johannesburg, SA, August 14, 1998, accessed at http://www.mg.co.za/mg/news/98aug1/14aug-congo.html (8 February 2001).
8. Paul Omach, "The African Crisis Response Initiative: Domestic Politics and Convergence of National Interests," *African Affairs* 99 (2000): 81.
9. A BBC Africa correspondent, Laurent Ndayahurume, quoting diplomats referring to the relationship between Rwanda and Congo, in "World: Africa: the Rwanda Connection," broadcast 4 August 1998, GMT 18:54.
10. Statement by Commander Jean Pierre Ondakane. See "The Mystery Man in Charge of Congo's Rebels," in *Electronic Mail & Guardian,* Johannesburg, SA, 18 August 1999, 1, accessed at http://www.mg.co.za/mg/news/99aug18-congo.html (5 February 2001).
11. "We'll Be in Kinshasa in a Week, Say Rebels Own Correspondent," *Electronic Mail & Guardian,* Johannesburg, 17 August 1998, 2, accessed at http://www.mg.co.za/mg/news/98aug-congo.html. (5 February 2001).
12. Mamhood Mamdani, "Rwandan Rebels Aren't Going to Win This Time," *Human Rights Watch,* "Democratic Republic of Congo: Casualties of War," 11, no.1 (A) (February 1999): 3, accessed at http://www.hrw.org/hrw/reports/1999/congo/Congoweb.htm.
13. "The Mystery Man in Charge of Congo's rebels."
14. Many analysts on the DRC tend to overlook the central role played by Burundi as part of the Rwanda-Uganda axis.
15. Article 4 of the Declaration of the Treaty of SADC (1992) provides for military assistance or obligations to member states. See also Michael Nest, "Ambitions, Profits and Loss: Zimbabwean Economic Involvement in the Democratic Republic of the Congo," in *African Affairs,* 100 (July 2001): 470–73.
16. This is a body, operating below the Summit of Heads of States and Government, made up of foreign, defense, and security ministers as well as army chiefs of all the SADC member states.
17. See the controversial convergence of U.S. and Uganda policies on the African continent in the well-argued piece by Omach, "The African Crisis Response Initiative," 73–95.
18. As a result of the military relations, Hawk Aircraft—later to be used extensively in the DRC war—were acquired from Britain, artillery and tanks from Korea, and Cascavel Armoured Cars from Brazil. Sadly, relations of the ZDF with the British Military Advisory Training Team (BMATT), were terminated—as at the end of March 2001—in the midst of political recriminations between Zimbabwe and Britain.
19. This was during the dissident era and subsequent deployments in Matebeleland.
20. Against RENAMO and South African Defence Forces Units deployed in Mozambique at the time.
21. The forces participated in Somalia, Angola, and Rwanda.
22. On Angola's goals and stakes in the conflict, see chapter 5 in this volume.
23. BBC World News, 9 September 1998, published at GMT 11:56, accessed at http://news.bbc.co.uk/hi/english/world/africa/newsid 167000/167635.stm (5 February 2001).
24. *Electronic Mail & Guardian,* Johannesburg, SA, 17 August 1998, 1, accessed at http://www.mg.co.za/mg/news/98aug2/17aug-congo2.html (2 February 2001).
25. "Zim. Sends Two More Battalions to Congo." Also see Group Captain Chingono, "Air Power Superiority in the DRC Conflict," in *The Air Force Magazine* 2, no.1 (May 2000),

8–9; and Flight Lieutenant Charles Mazorodze, "Initial Technical Operational Experience in the DRC," in *The Air Force Magazine* 2, no.1 (May 2000), 10.

26. While Uganda quickly acknowledged the involvement of its armed forces, it took Rwanda until November to confirm what had by then become common knowledge. During this phase, SADC allied forces benefited from their overt deployment and tactical operations against the furtive and poorly concealed activities of Rwanda and Uganda. It was only in November 1998 that Rwanda finally admitted to its presence in the DRC, and after that, the gloves were off. After November, the regular forces of the six belligerent armies were involved.

27. The fact that elements of his own forces were a major threat to his security is testified to by his assassination on 16 January 2001.

28. "World: Africa: Kinshasa Four Days From Starvation," BBC News, 9 September 1998, published GMT 11: 56, accessed at http://news.bbc.co.uk/hi/english/world/africa/newsid_167000/167635.stm (5 February 2001).

29. This is generally referred to as "Kisingani I" in Kampala. Before March 2001, there were to be two subsequent battles, called "Kisingani II" and "Kisangani III," pitting the two "allies" fighting inside the DRC against one another.

30. In September 1999, a predominantly urban-based labor-supported opposition party, the Movement for Democratic Change (MDC) was established. Within a year this clinched fifty-seven seats against the ruling party's sixty-two seats in parliamentary elections held in June 2000.

31. This development was unfortunate in our view. The main reason for the country's involvement in the DRC is the noble cause of Pan Africanism, and this should have informed crossparty behavior to result in the solid support of Joseph Kabila and his efforts to bring about peace in the DRC.

32. Already by 28 August 1998, "Zimbabwe Had Sent in Two More Battalions to Congo" as reported in *Electronic Mail & Guardian*, Johannesburg, SA., accessed at http://www.mg.co.za/mg/news/98aug-zim_congo2.html (21 February 2001). According to this report, the two battalions were drawn from the Kwekwe-based Fifth Brigade and a unit of Cascavel armored vehicles flown from Manyame airbase by Angola's Russian-made troop carriers.

33. Current U.S. dollar denominated field allowances are being paid in a Z dollar equivalent as the country has exhausted its foreign currency reserves.

34. Constantine Chimakure, "Zimbabwe Out of DRC by May," *The Zimbabwe Mirror* (Harare weekly) 6–12 April 2001, 3. At that time, U.S.$1 equaled approximately Z$55. Thus, the minister was acknowledging an expenditure of over U.S.$182 million.

35. *3rd Session of the 4th Parliament of Zimbabwe, Third Report of the Departmental Committee on Security Ministries*, presented to the House on 24 March 1998 (SC2–1998).

36. Michael Nest, "Ambitions, Profits and Loss," 470.

37. Anecdotal evidence suggests that new Landrovers and Toyota Landcruisers deployed in the DRC became completely worn out within two months of deployment on average as a result of the harsh operational terrain in the DRC. These weapons are the popular machine-gun platform and close support vehicles for armored cars in the urban areas used in many conflicts in Africa and elsewhere. Interviews of the author with returning soldiers, Harare, Zimbabwe, 1999.

38. Unconfirmed reports assert that in attempting to keep British-purchased Hawk aircraft airworthy, Zimbabwe has had to approach middlemen in Kenya in order to circumvent the sanctions imposed by the U.K. This is likely to further increase the costs.

39. Editorial, *The Namibian Defence Force Journal* 12, no. 10 (May–July 2001): 1.

PART III

The Contestants of the Kabila Regimes

CHAPTER 7

Congo's Rebels

THEIR ORIGINS, MOTIVATIONS, AND STRATEGIES

OSITA AFOAKU

INTRODUCTION

On 2 August 1998, barely fourteen months after the conclusion of the war initiated by the anti-Mobutu coalition, the emergence of a new armed movement heralded the beginning of a second war of liberation in the Democratic Republic of Congo (DRC), this time against the regime of Laurent Kabila. The conflict arose out of differences between the founder members of the Alliance des Forces Démocratiques pour la Libération du Congo-Zaire (Alliance of Democratic Forces for the Liberation of the Congo—ADFL), the coalition that installed Kabila at the head of Congo in May 1997. Military victory against Mobutu's army offered only temporary healing to the dissension that plagued the movement from its inception. Kabila's decision in July 1998 to dismiss the Rwandan contingent of the Forces Armées Congolaises (Congolese Armed Forces—FAC) thus served as a catalyst to a crisis that was already underway.

The anti-Kabila rebellion was largely the creation of Ugandan and Rwandan governments whose hostility toward Kabila was fueled by a dubious notion of national interest. But the emergence of the rebel opposition was also a function of the failure of the ADFL regime to construct a broad domestic constituency by opening the political space to civil society groups and NGOs. Not only did Kabila impose autocratic rule on Congo, but his government also failed to take a principled stance on the Banyamulenge nationality question, as well as on the security concerns of his principal allies. Essentially, Kabila pursued a contentious foreign policy without the benefits of a supportive domestic political base. Not surprisingly, his fledgling regime was ill-equipped to handle pressures from overbearing allies (and their Western patrons) who had an important stake in a friendly and stable Congo. Significantly, more than two years after the rebels embarked on what turned out to be "Africa's first world war,"[1] they were unable to achieve their stated objectives of replacing the Kabila dictatorship with a transitional government of national unity, restoring popular confidence in the Congolese state, and jump-starting the process of national reconciliation and state reconstruction.

This chapter attempts to shed light on the failure of Congo's "second rebellion" by examining the rebels' motivations and strategies. It argues that not only were there serious discrepancies among the stated motivations of the various anti-Kabila rebel groups, but that they lacked the politically cost-effective strategy needed to attain their objectives. Specifically, the rebels committed a serious political blunder by entering into an alliance with Rwanda and Uganda, Kabila's erstwhile allies who were deeply resented by many Congolese for exerting undue influence on their national affairs. This relationship made it difficult to separate the rebels' so-called "emancipatory" agenda from the economic and security interests of their allies. Further, Kabila's opponents relied heavily on an ill-conceived strategy of overthrowing the government through a lightning military defeat of the FAC (or what was left of the latter after significant desertions by disloyal soldiers). Unfortunately, following the decision by Angola and Zimbabwe to come to Kabila's rescue and the resulting shift in the balance of power, Congo became the theater of a protracted and intensely brutal conflict. The rebels ignored Kabila's proven capacity for rallying domestic support by exploiting the growing anti-Tutsi/Rwanda sentiment in the country. Similarly, by equating Kabila with Mobutu they could not foresee the government's success in manipulating the ambiguous notions of state sovereignty and territorial integrity to its advantage. As evidenced by the nonviolent stance of the civil opposition, the rebels grossly underestimated the people's intolerance for the use of force to resolve political differences. Finally, not only was the anti-Kabila movement fragmented from its inception, but rebel forces further alienated the Congolese masses by engaging in human rights violations, financial corruption, destruction, looting, and similar practices that made them look like an army of occupation.

BACKGROUND TO THE ANTI-KABILA "REBELLION"

Events related to the 1994 genocide in Rwanda—the influx of about a million Rwandan Hutu into eastern Congo; the UN decision to shelter Hutu refugees still organized in political and military structures, and personnel responsible for the genocide, in UN High Commission for Refugees (UNHCR) camps close to the Rwandan border; and Mobutu's complicity in the atrocities committed by Hutu extremists—culminated in Kabila's ascent to power in May 1997.[2] Apparently, there was a consensus among Congo rebels about the deficits of the Kabila regime, and the rebellion was intended to correct and forestall the recurrence of those deficits. Since the rebels were important actors in the events that led up to Congo's second war, what follows is a preliminary effort to shed light on their motivations and strategies by determining the extent to which they made a systematic attempt to apply the critical lessons offered by Kabila's misrule.

Unlike Etienne Tshisekedi and the other opposition leaders, whose credibility was tainted as a result of their involvement in the Mobutu system, Kabila initially enjoyed the political advantage of being perceived as a faithful disciple of Patrice Lumumba, Congo's slain nationalist and first premier, and an unwavering opponent of Mobutu. He was thus well positioned to tap the widespread anger in Congo at the monumental corruption and waste attributed to the old political order. Following their success in overthrowing the Mobutu regime in May 1997, Kabila and his supporters gained wide recognition abroad as important actors in Congolese politics. At home, they were hailed by the people as "*libérateurs*" and forerunners of a new political era.[3] Sadly, against the backdrop of Kabila's rapid ascent to power, the country began a dramatic slide toward its dismal past. This state of affairs has been attributed to the "easy victory" secured over Mobutu and the understated "contradictions" that would haunt Kabila and his supporters:

· First, the alliance that removed Mobutu was essentially military and regional. Congolese people did not liberate themselves, but rather were liberated. Very soon liberators began to be perceived as occupiers. The masses of the people were onlookers in their own destiny.
· Second, while there was consensus around removing Mobutu, there was no wide-ranging program that addressed both the internal and regional issues for a sustainable post-Mobutu government.
· Third, the new leader of the ADFL was casually agreed upon as the leader without consultations with the Congolese he would rule.
· Fourth, the new leadership entered Kinshasa as conquerors with little understanding of and much contempt for all the unarmed civil and political forces inside the country. These unarmed forces were either seen as cowards or collaborators.
· Fifth, Kabila had a free hand to do as he pleased politically, and he immediately embarked with a "winner take all" attitude. Very early in the regime it was clear that the transition from warlordism to statesman was not going to be easy for this particular president. When alarm bells were sounded by Congolese patriots and opposition forces, they were drawn out by an almost universal apologia that "the man must be given a chance."
· Six, the regional consensus soon gave way to interstate rivalries by the various states for personal influence with the "big man." Consequently the tail began to wag the dog as he got enormous room to play one state or group of states against another.[4]

A specific lesson of the Kabila regime is related to its failure to undertake a comprehensive reform of the new national army. Instead of creatively integrating former Mobutu soldiers into a new FAC, the government alienated the rank and file of the old FAC by subjecting them to a mandatory dehumanizing re-education program. Consequently, it missed an opportunity to develop an essential tool for national reconstruction.[5] As discussed later, when they most needed it, neither the government nor the rebels could count on the discipline of FAC units that fought on their side. Notably, the perception that the military under Kabila was run by noncitizens raised the scepter of foreign domination among many Congolese. For instance, about 15,000 young soldiers patrolling Kinshasa in the wake of Kabila's rule did not speak French or Lingala, the two major languages spoken in the capital city, and were regarded as strangers, as were many unidentified soldiers working for state security services.

In addition, there were public misgivings about strategic posts that Kabila's allies held in the central government. Lt. Col. James Kabarebe, Kabila's first army chief of staff, was the head of the Rwandan Republican Guard before he led the forces that overthrew Mobutu. Jackson Nzinza, a Ugandan Tutsi who became Congo's chief of national security, was the head of Rwanda's Internal Security Organization before his participation in the ADFL invasion. It is believed that Nzinza had taken part in numerous political murders, an activity he allegedly continued to practice in Congo. Bizimi Karaha, Kabila's foreign minister, was another Rwandan Tutsi; his uncle was a legislator. Col. Ibingira, who later became commander of north Kivu, allegedly played a major part in the massacre of Hutu refugees.[6]

Kabila's autocratic style could potentially offer useful (negative) lessons about what would be the acceptable mode of relationship between rebel groups and the people. While liberation from Mobutu gave Kabila and the ADFL some credit and popularity, the system of governance that they sought to impose on the Congolese public was rapidly rejected. As evidenced by a poll conducted in Kinshasa in August 1997, the Congolese people wanted a symbiotic relationship between the armed and nonviolent oppositions against Mobutu; 86 percent of respondents wanted a meeting between Kabila and the leaders of the nonviolent opposition. During his first six months in office, Kabila consistently polled lower than Tshisekedi, the leader of the largest of the nonviolent opposition groups, the Union pour la Démocratie et le Progrès Social (Union for Democracy and Social Progress—UDPS).

Kabila, however, had no interest in sharing power.[7] His predilection toward political centralization was apparent while the revolt against Mobutu was still underway. He promoted himself from spokesperson to uncontested leader of the ADFL early in the rebellion. The January 1997 death of fellow ADFL co-leader Kasase Ngandu, reportedly killed under mysterious circumstances, cleared the way for Kabila to take total control of the coalition. At the end of the revolt, he proclaimed himself transitional president of Congo without serious consultation with political leaders and organizations involved in the rebellion. At Kabila's insistence, it was agreed that "anything that the president of the movement says had the force of law."[8] By October, he had unilaterally suspended all the committees charged with facilitating the transition process. Dissension inside the ADFL was suppressed with the threat of arrest, detention, and other extrajudicial measures. Political leaders and organizations that were part of the Sovereign National Conference and the prodemocracy movement before the ADFL rebellion tried in vain to secure Kabila's commitment to political reform.[9] There were also concerns that the country was retreating into the decadent era of patrimonial politics when access to top political and military appointments was determined by the degree to which individuals demonstrated unquestioning loyalty to the head of state and commander in chief.[10]

The Kabila regime alienated its supporters at home as well as Western governments and NGOs. In June 1997, a USAID team arrived in Congo to assess its assistance needs, especially with regard to meeting the government's April 1999 target of holding democratic elections. However, during his visit to Washington the following month, Kabila's foreign minister, Bizima Karaha, did little to allay the Clinton administration's misgivings about Kabila's stance on democratic transition when he referred to the government's deadline as merely "a goal" in light of the continuing instability in the country. Karaha further alarmed his American hosts when he categorically ruled out any participation in the new government by opposition leader Etienne Tshisekedi. Ignoring the fact that the United States was among the few countries that recognized Tshisekedi's short-lived appointment as transitional prime minister in the turbulent early 1990s, Karaha described the UDPS leader as a "provocateur" who "wants to create anarchy and chaos. . . . an enemy of the people and of the government."[11] Kabila's foot-dragging on democratic reform, coupled with his refusal to cooperate with international investigators concerned with the alleged massacre of Hutu refugees by his troops, contributed in large measure to the erosion of his government's image abroad.[12] Although Karaha presumably represented the government of Congo at the UN discussions on these massacres, his pronouncements were unambiguously reflective of Rwanda's long-standing interest in keeping the government of Congo in friendly hands. It is not surprising that Kigali would be so uncomfortable with Tshisekedi, who would likely have become Kabila's most formidable rival in an open electoral contest. Notably, Tshisekedi and his nonviolent coalition could not be co-opted into the armed rebellion that toppled the Mobutu regime.[13] Indeed, throughout the Rwanda/Ugandan-backed revolt against the Kabila regime, his coalition did not shy away from condemning the use of force to resolve political differences.[14]

Kabila maintained a narrow base of domestic support that consisted of three constituencies. First, there were the Tutsi soldiers, including the Banyamulenge people of eastern Congo, who rapidly came to be resented by the Congolese as foreigners. (Early in the rebellion, little distinction was made between Rwandan and Congolese Tutsis.) Second, there were the Katangans who would continue to support Kabila in spite of intra-Katangan conflicts. Third, there were the "kadogos," the young men and boys who were recruited by the ADFL army in the course of its march from the east to Kinshasa. Kabila's inner circle of supporters, as well as Kabila himself, was without its own political base. Many of them had returned from exile, and this made them totally dependent on Kabila since they lacked an internal constituent base.[15]

While Kabila's relationship with his external allies was his most critical asset, it was also the main source of his political problems. Less than one year after the anti-Mobutu revolt, the alliance began to show signs of strain as a result of Kabila's inability to eliminate insurgency movements that were carrying out crossborder raids against Rwanda and Uganda from Congolese territory. Specifically, these security concerns brought into sharp focus Rwandan president Kagame's long-term objective of sponsoring the anti-Mobutu revolt—to make Congo safe for his country by replacing Mobutu with a friendly leader. The choice of Kabila, who did not have a solid political base inside Congo, to lead the rebellion against Mobutu seemed most appropriate. To guarantee Kabila's continuing good intentions after the May 1997 victory, he was expected to retain a number of Tutsis in key positions in the government and the army. He was further expected to allow a Rwandan zone of influence in north and south Kivu, to be controlled by Rwandan troops and Congolese Tutsi or Banyamulenge auxiliaries trained in Rwanda. Despite this arrangement, Kabila incurred the wrath of his allies as they grew increasingly impatient over continued incursions into Rwanda by Hutu rebels operating from eastern Congo. At the same time, the Kagame regime stepped up its support of the Banyamulenge Tutsi in their demand for political autonomy in south Kivu. The credibility of Kabila's government plummeted as many Congolese came to the conclusion that the Rwandan mission in their country had changed from liberation to colonial occupation.[16]

By the end of 1997, Kabila was under increasing pressure to abandon what had evidently become a difficult relationship with his protectors. A decision to terminate the alliance seemed all the more inevitable as a result of rumors of an impending palace coup against Kabila. For instance, it is believed that as early as January 1998, the intelligence chiefs of Angola, Rwanda, and Uganda held discussions regarding the desirability of finding an alternative leader for Congo.[17] It was also apparent that a coup against Kabila would be welcome in certain international circles. This scenario was floated in a summer 1998 issue of *World Policy Review* that demonized President Kabila for his lack of commitment to democracy and human rights. Calling Kabila a "thug," the author of the article, Frank Smythe, stated that "Voices from all quarters say that the Kabila regime is corrupt. Even his former allies in Rwanda, Uganda, and Eritrea have begun asking whether they should have recruited another Zairian to lead operations in eastern Zaire." At the same time, it was reported that, "shiny new military hardware was appearing at Kigali airport in Rwanda."[18]

Other incidents that occurred in June--July 1998 also indicated that relations between Kabila and his allies had reached a boiling point. Some of the president's collaborators had strong suspicions that a Rwandan officer was about to assassinate Kabila during the Independence Day festivities on June 30. James Kabarebe was personally suspected, and Kabila's guards allowed the chief of staff to enter the president's office only after he had been bodily searched and disarmed. A few days later, Kabila replaced Kabarebe with his own brother-in-law, Celestin Kifwa. In this atmosphere of mutual suspicion and acrimony, Tutsi families in Kinshasa began to feel insecure and started to leave. Kabila himself did a lot of traveling during these crucial days. He visited Namibia and Cuba, presumably seeking support, given the momentous divorce that was taking place.[19] In an effort to counter the growing threat to his regime, Kabila yielded to the rising anti-Tutsi sentiment in Kinshasa. On 27 July 1998, he announced the dismissal of all foreigners from the Congolese army.[20] As argued by Herbert Weiss, "one may wonder whether, after being in power for one year, Kabila had the military and organizational strength to do much about" the security situation that predated his government, considering the fact that "in the east, the Rwandans and Ugandans were themselves active on both sides of the border attempting to deal with this problem, but with limited success." Thus, as the author rightly concluded, Kabila's decision to embrace insurgency groups such as the *Interahamwe* and the government of Sudan, which was known to be backing anti-Museveni insurrectionists, "was the most important cause of the divorce" with Rwanda and Uganda.[21]

Unfortunately, the timing of this decision did little to improve Kabila's political fortunes as a significant segment of the elite had become disillusioned with his leadership. However, Congo's second war was primarily the result of strategic calculations by Rwanda and Uganda to attain security objectives that had previously motivated them to instigate the anti-Mobutu revolt. As evidenced by their role in Congo since 1996, Rwanda and Uganda were likely to support any "friendly" government in Congo. Owing to their narrow fixation on security, they did not actively encourage the Kabila regime to implement democratic reform. Nor can either government boast strong democratic credentials. The approval they have received from Western governments and multilateral NGOs is primarily a function of their commitment to free market economic reform and their ability to maintain internal stability.[22] It is thus puzzling that the rebels would enlist the support of these governments in their quest to correct the ills of the Kabila regime.

THE MOTIVATIONS OF THE ANTI-KABILA REBELS

As noted earlier, Kabila's erstwhile allies viewed him as an impediment to peace and stability in their countries. This concern fueled a quiet effort at military preparation calculated to overwhelm the Congolese armed forces with tactical surprise along the lines of the 1996 invasion that removed Mobutu from power. Armed rebellion against the government was initiated only six days after Kabila ordered Rwandan officials out of Congo. Although some rebel troops were involved in the initial stages of the war against the Kabila government—mostly Congolese Tutsi and former Mobutu officers—there is much evidence that Rwandan and Ugandan soldiers formed the major portion of the invading forces.[23] Interestingly, the opposition had no clear objectives, aside from removing Kabila from power, during the first two weeks of armed conflict with government forces. In fact, the political wing of the rebel coalition was nonexistent during this period. In his September 1998 report, Rassemblement Congolaise pour la Démocratie (Rally for Congolese Democracy—RCD) secretary Jacques Depelchin indicated that many politicians had become thoroughly disillusioned with Kabila's leadership before the outbreak of conflict; however, "When you are in that kind of situation, how you break . . . it's not easy to figure out." In contrast, "The military side was better prepared [for the rebellion], because military intelligence had actually plotted the way in which Kabila had been moving steadily away from the objectives that we all had."[24] In other words, the anti-Kabila rebels were essentially the creation of external actors. This is confirmed by the following chronology of events that dramatically changed the history of Congo and central Africa:

- 2 August: The commander of the Armée Nationale Congolaise (Congolese National Army—ANC) 10th brigade—one of the best units in the new Congolese army—stationed in Goma, declares his desertion from President Kabila. He is soon joined by the 12th brigade in Bukavu. Rwandan army units are reported to be crossing the frontier in force. In Kinshasa, a firefight begins between Congolese Tutsi soldiers who refuse to be disarmed and other FAC, largely Katangan, soldiers. The Tutsi are routed and most are killed, although some manage to escape into the bush west of Kinshasa. A pogrom, encouraged by the Kabila regime, is soon launched against all Tutsi in Kinshasa and other cities.

- 4 August: In a spectacular cross-continent airlift, a plane full of Rwandan and Ugandan soldiers (according to some accounts also Congolese) led by James Kabarebe lands at Kitona army base located in the Lower Congo near Cabinda. The base holds some 10,000 to 15, 000 former Forces Armées Zaïroises (Zairian Armed Forces—FAZ) soldiers who are being "re-educated." Kabarebe and his approximately 150 soldiers manage to mobilize these troops to join the uprising against Kabila. Later, more troops from the east join this enterprise. Within days, they capture a number of towns and, most importantly, the Inga hydroelectric dam, where they are able to cut off electricity supplies to Kinshasa as well as Katanga. At that point, the capital is threatened both by starvation and military occupation. Kabila calls on the city's population to arm itself and to defend the capital.

- 20 August: A group of Congolese politicians—for a wide variety of reasons and coming from very different political backgrounds—unite in Goma to form the political wing of the anti-Kabila movement, the Rassemblement Congolais pour la Démocratie (Congolese Rally for Democracy—RCD).

- 23 August: Angola attacks the Rwanda-Uganda-RCD positions in the Lower Congo from its bases in Cabinda. The anti-Kabila forces are surrounded. Some of their troops reach the outskirts of Kinshasa, where they are attacked by the population and massacred. The cross-continent maneuver has failed, but in the east there are virtually no pro-Kabila forces and the "rebellion" achieves military control.

· 26 August: Zimbabwe sends a military expedition to Kinshasa to support the Kabila regime. Later, Namibia and Chad also send troops that take up positions supporting Kabila. Some reports also speak of Sudanese involvement on Kabila's side.[25]

That the military wing of the anti-Kabila rebellion preceded the political wing is further evidenced by the fact that rebel military commanders, some of them Rwandans, acted as spokespersons for the opposition before and while the political wing was still in the formative stage. On August 15, Bizimi Karaha, who had fled Kinshasa to join the rebellion, explained to reporters that the Kabila government was deliberately targeting Banyamulenge Tutsi in the eastern province of Kivu. He dismissed as useless any political initiative by the Organization of African Unity (OAU) and regional heads of governments to end the war unless they "come and talk to us."[26] Congolese politicians eventually convened at the eastern city of Goma on August 16 to initiate the process of establishing the Congolese Democratic Coalition—later renamed RCD—to act as "a government-in-waiting."[27] Significantly, the emergence of the political wing of the movement could not mask the external sources of the violence that eventually engulfed Congo and regional actors. Although what the anti-Kabila revolt needed was a revolutionary movement with credibility among the Congolese people, and especially among those in the east who were under its control, many of the more than 100 political parties and the hundreds of civic organizations formed during the anti-Mobutu movement in the early 1990s remained cool toward the anti-Kabila opposition. Their perception, like that of the population in general, was that the rebellion was a front for Rwandan and Ugandan forces. The need to broaden the opposition prompted RCD president Ernest Wamba dia Wamba to invite "all principal parties fighting against Kabila's dictatorship" to join the rebel coalition after his appointment.[28] Commenting on the politicians before a crowd of Congolese citizens in the eastern town of Bunia, rebel military commander Jean-Pierre Ondekane underscored the subordinate status of the political wing when he warned that "I told them I will personally shoot them one by one if they isolate themselves from the people."[29]

At their inaugural convention in mid-August 1998, members of the main rebel coalition decried the growing "crisis in state institutions,"[30] with its attendant plethora of political and economic woes, including corruption, nepotism, vote-catching, arbitrary rule, growing impoverishment of the population, mismanagement of public funds by Kabila and his entourage, and the government's inability to restore peace, security, and unity at the national and regional levels. They further accused the government of repressing democratic forces through wholesale massacres, political assassinations and imprisonment, discrimination and human rights violations, and the incitement of ethnic hatred. According to a communiqué issued by the RCD leadership, other concerns that compelled civil society groups to enter into a politico-military coalition against the government included "Kabila's new management practice," which worsened "the evil causes at the root of the ruin of our country": his predilection to usurp the people's sovereignty through autocratic rule and personalization of state institutions, namely the army, the government, the parliament, justice, and the central bank. Finally, they condemned Kabila for abusing the draft constitution, depriving the people of their right to a say in the management of national resources, stalling the democratization process, and "placing our territory at the disposal of military-fascist groupings for their acts of destabilization throughout the sub-region."[31] Against this backdrop, the rebels pledged their commitment to the following objectives at the domestic level:

· Bring to an end any form of dictatorship by establishing the rule of law and good governance.
· Build a united, democratic, and prosperous state by safeguarding national sovereignty, territorial integrity, and equal rights to citizenship.
· Encourage the process of national reconciliation, democratization, and reconstruction.
· Fight tribalism, nepotism, corruption, misappropriation of public funds, the arbitrary, widespread impunity [sic].
· Encourage peasants, workers, women, and youth to self-organize so that they are able to defend their material and moral interests.
· Promote the Congolese people's social welfare through specific measures, most particularly in the areas of health, education, and employment.
· Build an integrated economy through a rigorous and responsible management, starting with priority sectors, in order to lay a foundation for the country's economic development.

At the subregional and international levels, they pledged their commitment to the following objectives:

· Safeguard security by striving for peace and stability in the subregion and in Africa as a whole.
· Undertake to never allowing the Congolese territory to be used as a base to destabilize neighboring countries.
· Promote subregional and regional integration and solidarity through economic development.
· Champion the development of the African renaissance.
· Strive for equitable international cooperation with all due respect for mutual interests.[32]

RCD president Wamba Dia Wamba summed up the motivations of his rebel coalition when he declared that "I have been an exponent of what I call emancipatory politics that emphasize a notion that all people think, and that one has to start from that premise. People must be empowered so that they can participate in improving their own lives, but also making sure that the institutions that are put in place reflect these aspirations"[33] Commenting on the war, Horace Campbell suggested that the "modest objectives" outlined by the rebels were consistent with Cheikh Anta Diop's proposal in the 1950s pertaining to Congo's pivotal role in the political and economic development of eastern and central Africa. Although he described the RCD as "a pan-African organization with objectives for peace and renewal" whose leadership had "a long history of involvement in the struggles for democratic participation and expression," Campbell was keenly aware of the dangers of inferring the motivations of Kabila's opponents solely from their declarations. He thus cautioned that "The test is whether within the structure of the leadership there is transparency, accountability and democratic politics."[34]

The task of implementing the Goma declarations was complicated by the lack of cohesion among rebel groups, which was indicative of the diverse motives and interests that sparked the hostility toward the Kabila regime. The politicians and intellectuals who came together to form the RCD originated from very different, even conflicting, backgrounds. Essentially, the rebel movement was a collection of strange bedfellows; the members were loosely held together by a common objective of overthrowing a government they detested for different reasons. Somewhat after the RCD was formed, another anti-Kabila movement, the Mouvement pour la Libération du Congo (Movement for the Liberation of Congo—MLC), was formed in the northern part of Congo. The MLC was headed by Jean-Pierre Bemba, the son of a wealthy businessman and former Mobutu associate who became one of Kabila's ministers. Not only were the two rebel organizations located in different regions, but Bemba's political background and experience differed significantly from that of Wamba dia Wamba, who was a college professor and longtime opponent of the Mobutu regime.[35]

THE DILEMMAS OF A FRACTURED OPPOSITION

The anti-Kabila alliance was plagued from its inception by divisions and infighting. The duration of the war exposed the various forces that made up the alliance and their diverse and competing motives. In August 1999, only a month after the signing of the Lusaka ceasefire agreement, a new dynamic of conflict emerged within the alliance. A major battle took place between the Ugandan People's Defense Forces (UPDF) and the Rwandan Patriotic Army (RPA), resulting in the death of over 600 troops and civilians. This incident brought to light "persistent and serious differences between the longtime allies over the objectives and strategies of the war in the DRC."[36] While Uganda showed some interest in encouraging the Congolese people to develop an alternative leadership, the Rwandan government was particularly interested in overthrowing Kabila, who was arming the radical Hutu enemy. The Rwandans were also more skeptical about the capacity of the Congolese people to work out an internal political settlement. The Rwandans' first priority was to establish a secure border with the DRC. Although the immediate crisis was managed, with the leaders of both countries agreeing on a ceasefire and removing their commanders from Kisangani, relations between the two countries remained cool.

The differences between Rwanda and Uganda were reflected in conflicts and shifting alliances within the rebel movement. The result was a perennial difficulty in unifying rebel factions behind a common agenda. After the advent of Bemba's group, the rebel movement was further divided between the MLC and RCD, with their headquarters in Gbadolite and Goma, respectively. The MLC enjoyed a major advantage over the main rebel organization in that its leadership originated from the northern area, where it was active. Its support was largely regionally homogeneous, and it was the only rebel group that could not be linked to any Tutsi connection. Considering Bemba's background, however, the MLC can potentially be linked to

Mobutuism, since Bemba's father was an important baron of the Mobutu regime.[37] It is also unclear to what extent Bemba may be pursuing regional goals for Équateur, rather than national ones.

Early in the war, the RCD was split into two rival factions, the supporters of Wamba dia Wamba forming one faction and the militarist core of the coalition that comprised Banyamulenge Tutsi, FAC officers, and former Mobutists another. Wamba's faction was supported by Uganda and eventually moved to Kisangani; the other faction was based in Goma and supported by Rwanda. While Wamba and his faction stressed the need to legitimize the rebellion by broadening its popular base, the militarist faction defined the objective of the rebellion narrowly in terms of physical removal of Kabila from office. The two groups also disagreed over political and administrative control and resource exploitation in RCD-controlled territory. As a result of conflicts of interest between the two rebel factions, Wamba and his supporters were forced to relocate to the northeast, where they established a separate headquarters in May 1999 as RCD-Kisangani;[38] following the Rwanda-Uganda clashes in Kisangani, the group later moved its headquarters to Bunia. This branch of the RCD also refers to itself as the RCD-Mouvement de Libération (RCD-ML).

Subsequent to the Goma split, Wamba dia Wamba and his associates maintained that Wamba was still the target of "putsches, conspiracies, mutinies carried out [within RCD-Kisangani] with the help of Ugandan officers and authorities." Wamba's major political foes this time were Mbusi Nyamwisi and Tibasima Ateenyi, respectively General Commissar and Deputy General Commissar of RCD-Kisangani. The two allegedly recruited tribal militias from their ethnic groups with the aim of forcing Wamba to relinquish his position as president of RCD/Kisangani. At the same time, Ugandan soldiers were accused of taking sides with the Hema community in a land dispute with their Lendu rivals. The Ugandans' apparent partiality came to light when UPDF's Col. Muzora named a Hema as interim head of Ituri province and placed under arrest the governor who was favored by RCD-ML. Following a decision by Ugandan officials to "deport" the deposed governor to Kampala, a bloody conflict ensued between the Hema and Lendu.[39]

In this climate of mutual hostility and mutual mistrust, Uganda's effort in January 2001 to merge the RCD-ML, MLC, and the little-known RCD-National (another splinter faction) had only a slim chance of success. The proposed merger was intended to forge a unified rebel front in the Upper Congo, but Kampala's credibility as a broker had been compromised. Furthermore, in another display of allied paternalism, Ugandan officials appointed MLC president Jean-Pierre Bemba to head the new coalition, the Front de Libération du Congo (Congolese Liberation Front—FLC). But Bemba had close ties to Wamba's foes in the Nyarnwisi-Ateenyi faction of RCD-Kisangani, and they were in favor of the merger. On the other hand, while the Wamba faction sided with the Lendu in their conflict with the Hema, the Ugandans were supporting the Hema, and one of the leaders of the FLC was a prominent Hema. Not surprisingly, Wamba and his supporters balked at the merger as a ploy by the Museveni regime to impose a pro-Uganda leadership in an area controlled by RCD-Kisangani.[40]

The dilemma arising from the fracturing of the rebel movement can be understood as a function of the need to "finance" the war effort. Congo had been carved up into virtual fiefdoms and, like the government, rebel leaders exploited agricultural and mineral resources under their control to finance the war. Also, like the government, they granted commercial rights to their allies, who were contributing human and material resources toward the war effort. Inevitably, this mutual quest to "make the war pay for itself," led to the formation of informal and quasiformal patron-client networks involving allied officials, rebel leaders, and local politicians in rebel-controlled territories. In this context, it is appropriate to say that there were two different, but related, wars: Simultaneously, there was the war to overthrow Kabila, and there were intra-opposition struggles for political and administrative control of rebel-held territories that were fueled by economic motives.

For the rebel leaders and local politicians, winning the internal war was very important, as it was expected pay off in the context of postrebellion political contests. For the Rwandans and Ugandan allies, it was necessary to act as mediators in intrarebel conflicts to ensure favorable outcomes in terms of their immediate and future security and economic interests. Unfortunately, it became increasingly difficult to delineate the boundaries of authority, privileges, and rights in rebel-controlled territories as the war progressed. Rebel groups and local communities faced the threat of losing their autonomy as a result of the self-appointed king-making role of allied officials and soldiers, who frequently interfered in intrarebel and community affairs. Paradoxically, to the extent that the allies made authoritative decisions that undercut the prerogatives of their hosts, their actions were detrimental to the cause of democracy and human rights in Congo. Ultimately, as the war progressed it became increasingly difficult to legitimize the rebellion as a result of intrarebel conflicts and divisions, which further aroused public misgivings about the motivations of the rebel movement.

THE REBELS' BLITZKRIEG STRATEGY

The decision to overthrow the Kabila regime was initiated by a small circle of Congolese militants and allied officials who favored the use of violence to effect a change of government in Kinshasa. Specifically, the military emphasis in the rebel strategy was due to the configuration of forces in the rebel movement. The main rebel coalition that initiated the war against the government was dominated at its inception by the Banyamulenge Tutsi and ex-Mobutuists, who represented the core of the militarist tendency in the rebellion.[41] Further, given the success of the armed revolt against Mobutu, it was considered rational to replicate a method that had worked in the past. A "quick victory" strategy seemed feasible, considering that the best units of the FAC had joined the rebellion. Optimism about a *blitzkrieg* seemed well founded at the beginning of the conflict as rebel forces claimed to be in control of both the Kivu provinces and portions of Orientale and Bas-Congo provinces, representing approximately 15 million inhabitants in total. Rebel forces initially encountered little resistance since several FAC units were deserting the government, thus raising the expectation that they could "reach Kinshasa" in a matter "of few days."[42]

Three weeks after the rebels initiated attacks on government positions, liberation looked increasingly unlikely and earlier predictions of success were rapidly replaced by fears that the war would pull the rest of Congo, and indeed all of central Africa, into a complex and longterm conflagration. Contrary to preliminary assessments of the balance of power, the logistical capacities of the rebel forces and their external allies turned out to be more limited than was the case in 1996, when a similar military coalition made its way from the east to Kinshasa. Notably, the foreign armies that had played a crucial role in bringing down the Mobutu regime were now divided, with Angola supporting Kabila. In addition, Kabila received military support from Chad, Namibia, Zimbabwe, and probably the Sudan. In the third week rebel troops were forced to retreat from Kitona, Matadi, and Inga when they came under intense pressure from the added military power of Kabila's new allies.[43]

While this development was portrayed in the press as a big victory for the government, the RCD insisted that the withdrawal of its forces from Kinshasa was a strategic move to minimize destruction of important infrastructures. At the same time, the idea of a short war was kept alive in rebel circles through a curious attempt to dismiss the strategic implications of Kabila's success in acquiring new allies. According to rebel propagandists, neither Zimbabwe nor Angola could afford to bear the political and economic costs of a protracted military presence in Congo. The deployment of Angolan troops in Matadi, Inga, and Kitona was considered a defensive action to create a rear base from which they could more effectively confront the military expansion of the União Nacional para a Independência Total de Angola (National Union for the Total Independence of Angola—UNITA) in the northern regions of Angola. The incursion into Congo by Angolan troops was more of a front for Angola's internal war than a sign of support for Kabila.[44] Similarly, it was suggested that, considering Zimbabwe's limited military capability and the depreciation of its dollar, the Mugabe regime would be hard-pressed to remain in Congo should the war continue for more than six months. Namibia's decision to send up to 500 infantry troops to help repel the rebel advance toward Kinshasa was dismissed as "symbolic deployment to support the claim of Mugabe in the SADC discussion that they are supporting a legitimate government" in Congo.[45] Sudan's role in the war did not seem to raise serious concerns since the Khartoum regime was presumably using Congo as a staging ground to attack the military headquarters of the Sudanese People's Liberation Army (SPLA) at Maridi. The possibility of a prolonged involvement in Congo by Sudan would only "create a further complication for Zimbabwe," which "has been one of the main supporters" of the SPLA.[46]

Although the decision by Angola and Zimbabwe to come to Kabila's rescue did not definitively tip the balance of power in the government's favor, it forced both sides into a stalemate, with the rebels controlling the eastern half of the country. The rebels' hope for a quick victory was stillborn because of other factors that differentiate the anti-Kabila war from the previous war. The notion that the 1996–97 war was a revolution, coupled with generalized antagonism toward the Mobutu regime, resulted in a considerable amount of support for the ADFL inside the country and abroad. In the second war, Kabila was able to rally public support for the government by tapping into the rising anti-Tutsi/Rwandan/Ugandan sentiment in the country, and most Congolese were convinced that Congo was being invaded by foreign armies. The consequence was two-fold; there was very little popular support for the anti-Kabila forces, and there were more Congolese fighting on both sides in the second war than in the first. This paradox is best illustrated by the actions of Mai-Mai guerrillas, who emerged during the 1997–98 phase of the Kabila regime to challenge the FAC, at that time closely allied to the Rwandans. Since they were essentially dedicated to expelling non-Kivu forces and people from what they considered as their territory, the Mai-Mai turned against the anti-Kabila rebels because of their Tutsi-Rwandan-Ugandan connection.[47]

Kabila was certainly not admired outside Congo, but he was successful in rallying international opinion against the rebels by invoking the OAU charter. Early in the conflict, UN Secretary-General Kofi Anan expressed concern about possible violation of the territorial integrity of Congo.[48] Until his assassination in January 2001, Kabila was accorded international recognition in the OAU, the United Nations, and the European Union as the legitimate head of the government of Congo. Even though the legal basis for Kabila's tenure in office was scanty at best, it was sufficient to shield Angola and Zimbabwe from the wrath of the international community. Kabila's allies were able to parade themselves as guarantors of Congolese sovereignty. In contrast, Rwanda and Uganda were forced to shroud their activity in Congo in secrecy.[49] Despite Rwanda's and Uganda's stated security and humanitarian reasons for embarking on a second successive war in Congo, the Kabila regime effectively portrayed them as uninvited aggressors. Ironically, Rwanda and Uganda were the prime targets of UN investigations for illegal exploitation of Congo's natural resources, though Angola and Zimbabwe were equally guilty of turning their military involvement in Congo into an economic venture. Despite the absurd application of international law to the Congolese crisis, both the government and rebel leaders were guilty of mortgaging the country's resources in order to prevail in the war. The war created opportunities for the elites on both sides to enrich themselves through bogus contracts and other fraudulent commercial and financial practices.[50]

WAR CATASTROPHE, HUMAN SUFFERING, AND ALIENATION

The Lusaka Ceasefire Agreement of 1999 epitomized the dilemma faced by the Kabila regime and, particularly, the rebels. Both sides were reluctant signatories to the agreement, and there were violations by both sides as well. These resulted not only from the limitations of the agreement but because all parties needed to recoup something for the investment of human lives and resources they were squandering in Congo. The belligerents persisted with their military adventurism precisely because neither side was able to accomplish its objectives.[51]

Unfortunately, as a result of their persistence, the war became more intense; it then dragged on for two and half years and caused staggering destruction of infrastructure, human life, and the environment. According to a survey conducted by the New York-based International Rescue Committee (IRC), the death toll approached 3 million by April 2001. Significantly, the survey, which focused only on rebel-held territories, attributed a relatively small proportion of the deaths—a few hundred thousands—to the battles waged by the warring armies. The vast majority of deaths resulted from starvation, disease, and deprivation.[52] For instance, it is estimated that of the first 1.7 million war deaths recorded in Congo by 2000, only 200,000 were by violence. Even as a ceasefire held on the front lines after the Lusaka agreement, massacres continued behind rebel lines, where militias and rebel armies terrorized some of Congo's more densely populated districts. Frequently, villages were attacked on the suspicion that inhabitants were helping the other side. In addition, the so-called negative forces, such as Kabila's Hutu allies, were simply homicidal as they conducted night raids on Congolese villagers, maiming or slashing to death their victims and plundering their belongings. According to an aid worker for Pharmacists Without Borders, who took part in humanitarian assessment in the

Kasai region, "People are dying of nothing, everything." Starving villagers in the diamond-rich region sarcastically referred to peanuts as "red gems."[53] Around Kalima in Maniema province, the British medical aid group Merlin documented two-and-a-half times more deaths than births in a population that was growing at an annual rate of 3 percent before the war. The children were particularly vulnerable to war-related diseases and starvation in Congo, where they perished at an extraordinary rate. Around Moba, in the province of Katanga, nearly half of the infants died before reaching their first birthday in 2000. By March 2001, infant mortality has worsened in the province, with three out of four children dying before age two in the district of Kalemie.[54]

It is estimated that 40 percent of wartime deaths in Congo could have been avoided by access to basic health care, which was becoming scarce even before the successive crises that have defined the country since mid-1996. By August 1998, when the anti-Kabila movement was initiated, only two of eleven provincial health inspectors had working vehicles.[55] The challenge of providing help for war victims was exacerbated by Congo's dismal economic situation. Sadly, despite promises by NGOs and UN member states to commit more resources to humanitarian disasters in Africa, international response to the devastation caused by the anti-Kabila war proved to be as slow and inadequate as in previous cases such as Somalia, Rwanda, and Sierra Leone. Journalist Carl Vick summed up the plight of Congo's war victims as follows:

> As assessments of Congo's devastation accumulate, help has been very slow in coming. A January plea from the World Food Program to more than double its Congo food aid to $110 million has been barely one-third funded by rich countries. UNICEF has received just a tenth of the $15 million needed for essential drugs and therapeutic feeding centers. And despite vows of action from Washington that greeted the IRC's first survey, U.S. disaster relief to Congo remains at just $13 million. Halfway through the fiscal year, that sum is already exhausted.[56]

On the night of Thursday, 18 January 2001, Communications Minister Dominique Sakombi confirmed Kabila's death in a statement broadcast on the state-run television, ending two days of rumors and speculations that began when the president was gunned down by one of his guards at his marble palace.[57] The next day, Sakombi announced that Joseph Kabila, the president's thirty-year-old son, who had been named interim head of government a day after his father was fatally shot, would assume "the permanent responsibilities as head of the government and the army."[58] Kabila's death epitomized the senseless devastation caused by the war as well as the cynicism and alienation that characterized public attitudes toward the state in the post-Mobutu era in Congo.

While diplomats and African leaders pondered the implications of the power vacuum left by the assassination, most Kinshasa residents could not disguise their indifference. A 10:00 P.M. curfew imposed by the authorities was widely ignored by residents who wanted to have a drink or dance at the city's bustling nightclubs. "What are they going to do to us that is worse than what we've lived through already?" was the nonchalant response from one of the partygoers who was approached by a reporter.[59] Exploited and abandoned by the elites who hijacked the state in postcolonial Congo for the purpose of material accumulation and self-aggrandizement, the Congolese masses have routinely relied on the informal networks of the underground economy to meet their basic needs. Many were too preoccupied with the game of survival to worry about the ramifications of the latest episode in the politics of self-destruction that have been the scourge of Congo since independence. A female hotel employee captured this pervasive climate of disengagement when she said; "No, the people are too hungry to mourn. We are tired. We want just to eat and for our children to eat and go to school and to dance. Just those simple things are a struggle. So, Mobutu, Kabila, another Kabila—we don't care."[60]

In Goma, one of the rebel-held towns in eastern Congo, residents seemed more concerned about whether Kabila's death would bring peace or a worse war than they had already endured. But there was no question that they despised the rebels, not only because of their ties to the Tutsi and Rwandans but also because of war weariness, flagrant human rights abuses by rebel soldiers, and a general belief that the rebellion had destroyed the economy. Ironically, although the people in this part of Congo conceded that Kabila was not a democrat, many regarded him as the lesser of two evils, and they made no secret of their willingness to support his son, too. Essentially, they mourned Kabila's death in defiance of the rebels.[61]

The pattern of public reaction to Kabila's death also underscored the extent to which the war resulted in the fragmentation of the Congolese polity. While reports of the assassination were met with relative indifference in Kinshasa, thousands of mourners jammed the streets of Lubumbashi, the capital of Kabila's native Katanga province.[62] Kabila consolidated his rule by offering strategic appointments to close relatives and members of his ethnic homeland. Although his rule did not improve the lot of ordinary Katangans, as evidenced by their share of war-related afflictions, he was consistently assured of their loyalty. Having adhered to the patrimonial tradition that was fully entrenched in Congo when he captured power in 1997, his death elicited a degree of public sorrow among his people that was befitting to "a great son of the soil." Significantly, the president's cronies seemed more preoccupied with the business of preserving the status quo than with the dire ramifications of his demise. Commenting on one of the most absurd rituals of presidential succession in postcolonial Africa, Justice Minister Mwenze Kongolo, one of Kabila's ministers, offered the lame assurance that "I want the public to understand that we didn't want the idea of a monarchy."[63]

CONCLUSION

The political catastrophe and human suffering caused by the abortive armed rebellion against the government of Laurent Kabila have demonstrated the limitations of violence as a way of resolving political problems. Against this background, there is an urgent need to refocus national attention on political dialogue within the framework of an inclusive national sovereign conference or other similar forum. However, the prospects for a national dialogue will remain bleak until the new Congolese regime and rebel groups unequivocally abandon armed conflict in keeping with the Lusaka ceasefire agreement. A national conference would pave the way for the construction of a democratic constitution that would reflect the people's aspiration for an inclusive system of governance and material welfare. The key to producing such a constitution is the determination of Congolese leaders and civil society groups to invest the time and resources necessary to ensure the participation of all relevant constituencies in the process. Among other things, this approach will give the Congolese people the opportunity to define the nature and scope of military involvement in national life, as well as establish legal safeguards against coups. To restore popular confidence in the state, there must be a mandatory requirement that coup plotters like Mobutu be tried and punished, even long after they are forced from power. Further, the new constitution ought to include a strong provision for specialized human rights courts with powers to award compensation to victims. There ought to be a constitutional requirement for mandatory representation of historically marginalized groups, such as women and ethnic minorities, at all levels of government.

Unfortunately, although Kabila's sudden death has forced the warring parties to return to diplomatic solutions, there are many challenges facing the Lusaka ceasefire signatories and the wider international community in implementing the Congolese peace agreement. The most important limitation of the Lusaka peace agreement is that it focused on the major warring parties without dealing with the more complex issue of disarming non-Congolese armed groups destabilizing the region from their bases in Congo. The largest of these groups are the forces associated with the former Rwandan army (the ex-FAR) and *Interahamwe* militias that carried out the 1994 Rwandan genocide. While they are not the root cause of Congo's problems, they provide a rationale for neighboring governments to conduct counterinsurgency operations and continue the occupation of Congolese territory, which has had had terrible humanitarian and human rights impacts so far. The response of the international community to the problem of the armed groups has been disastrously negligent. Ultimately, in order for this strategy to succeed, it must be linked to the development of political institutions and the formation of a national army and police in Congo that will inhibit the re-emergence of domestic armed groups and foreign intervention. In this regard, the success of an inter-Congolese dialogue, particularly in integrating and rationalizing the armed forces, will be critical. It is also linked to prospects for political change and dialogue in the neighboring countries, which have been exporting their civil wars to Congo.[64]

While it is the primary responsibility of the people of Congo and their leaders to devise longterm solutions to their political and economic problems, the international community can support their efforts in some basic ways. For instance, UN member states must embrace the fact that lasting peace in Congo and the rest of central Africa will rest largely on an effective program of disarmament, demobilization, reintegration, or resettlement. This calls for upgrading of the current Mission d'Organisation des Nations Unis au Congo (United Nations Mission to the Congo—MONUC) from phase II (disengagement of forces) to phase III (withdrawal and disarmament), which in turn calls for the commitment of more UN troops and resources. Western governments and financial institutions must collaborate with Congolese officials in devising ways to recover public money stolen by Mobutu and his cronies and discourage future leaders from hiding such money abroad. Similarly, they can support the processes of liberalization and national reconstruction in Congo by writing off a portion of the country's foreign debt. Finally, the global community can help reduce senseless bloodshed and human rights abuses in Congo and neighboring countries by imposing an arms embargo on governments and rival political groups that engage in the brutalization of local opponents and/or unnecessary wars.

1. "Arms Ravage a Rich Land, Creating Africa's 'First World War,'" *The New York Times International* at http://www.nytimes.com/library/world/africa/020600africa-congo.html, February 6, 2000.

2. Philip Gourevitch, *We Wish to Inform You that Tomorrow We Will Be Killed with Our Familes: Stories from Rwanda* (New York: Picador, 1998), 242–353.

3. Osita Afoaku, "The Politics of Democratic Transition in Congo (Zaire): Implications of the Kabila 'Revolution,'" *The Journal of Conflict Studies* 19, no. 2 (1999): 72–92; René Lemarchand, "The Fire in the Great Lakes," *Current History* 98, no. 628 (May 1999): 195–201.

4. Tajudeen Abdul-Raheen, "An Agenda for Peace in the DRC and the Great Lakes Region: More Pan-Africansim Is the Answer, Not Less," in *The 1998 Rebellion in the Democratic Republic of the Congo,* Association of Concerned Africanists, Special Bulletin, nos. 53–54, October 1998, 66–67.

5. Herbert Weiss, "War and Peace in the Democratic Republic of the Congo," *Current African Issues,* Nordiska Afrikainstitutet, No. 22 (2000), 7. [Monograph.]

6. Ellen Ray, "U.S. Military and Corporate Recolonization of Congo," *CovertAction,* no. 69 (spring–summer 2000), 7.

7. Weiss, "War and Peace in the Democratic Republic of the Congo," 6.

8. Jacques Depelchin, "Crisis in the Congo," excerpts from remarks by Dr. Jacques Depelchin, Rapporteur of the Bureau of the Assembly for the Rassemblement Congolais pour la Démocratie (RCD), Columbia University, September 30, 1998, available at http://www.congorcd.org/statements/ja.htm.

9. On political reform in Zaire before the advent of the ADFL rebellion, see Thomas Turner, "Zaire: Flying High above the Toads: Mobutu and Stalemated Democracy," in John F. Clark and David E. Gardinier, eds., *Political Reform in Francophone Africa* (Boulder, CO: Westview, 1997), 246–61.

10. Jacques Depelchin, "Crisis in the Congo;" for a comprehensive critique of Kabila's policies, see "The 1998 Rebellion in the Democratic Republic of the Congo," Association of Concerned Africanists.

11. Ray, "U.S. Military and Corporate Recolonization of Congo," 7.

12. Ray, "U.S. Military and Corporate Recolonization of Congo," 7–8.

13. Weiss, "War and Peace in the Democratic Republic of the Congo," 3–4; also see Weiss's chapter, "Zaire, Collapsed State, Surviving State, Future Policy," in I. William Zartman, ed., *Collapsed States: The Disintegration and Restoration of Legitimate Authority* (Boulder, CO: Lynne Rienner, 1995), 157–170.

14. Etienne Tshisekedi, Union for Democratic and Social Progress (UDPS), Memorandum of the Democratic Opposition Forces, in *The 1998 Rebellion in the Democratic Republic of the Congo,* Association of Concerned Africanists, 30–34.

15. Weiss, "War and Peace in the Democratic Republic of the Congo," 6.

16. Lemarchand, "The Fire in the Great Lakes," 199–200.

17. Weiss, "War and Peace in the Democratic Republic of the Congo," 13.

18. Ray, "U.S. Military and Corporate Recolonization of Congo," 9–10.

19. Weiss, "War and Peace in the Democratic Republic of the Congo," 13.

20. Lemarchand, "The Fire in the Great Lakes," 199–200.

21. Weiss, "War and Peace in the Democratic Republic of the Congo," 9–10.

22. Musveni and Kageme are among the so-called "new generation" of African leaders who have been applauded for their discipline and commitment to progress even as they are being criticized for not doing enough in regard to democracy and human rights. See, for instance, Keith Richburg, "Africa's New Leaders: Reasons for Worry," *Current History*

(November 1997): 29. For a less pessimistic perspective on the domestic policies of these leaders, see Marina Ottawa's critique of these regimes in "Africa's 'New Leaders': African Solution or African Problem?" *Current History* 97, no. 619 (May 1998): 209–213.

23. Ray, "U.S. Military and Corporate Recolonization of Congo," 10.

24. Depelchin, *Crisis in the Congo*.

25. Weiss, "War and Peace in the Democratic Republic of the Congo," 9–10; for primary sources detailing the unfolding of events in the Congo between 2 August and 26 August 1998, see the following: "Congo Summit Ends Amid Increased Fighting," *CNN.com*, 8 August 1998; "Rebels Reportedly Cut Electrical Power to Kinshasa," *CNN.com*, 13 August 1998; "Evacuations Begin from Congo as Fighting Rages On," *CNN.com*, 15 August 1998; "Kabila Searches for Support as Congo Rebels Consolidate," *CNN.com*, 17 August 1998; "Angola Enters Congo War," *CNN.com*, 22 August 1998.

26. Bizima Karaha quoted in "Evacuations Begin from Congo as Fighting Rages On."

27. "Kabila Searches for Support as Congo Rebels Consolidate Control."

28. Wamba dia Wamba quoted in "Kabila Returns to Congo Capital, Vows to Defeat Rebels," *CNN.com*, 16 August 1998.

29. Jean-Pierre Ondekane quoted in "Kabila Searches for Support as Congo Rebels Consolidate Control."

30. "Political Declaration of the Congolese Rally for Democracy (RCD/CRD)," Goma, August 12, 1998, in *The 1998 Rebellion in the Democratic Republic of the Congo*, Association of Concerned Africanists, 3–5.

31. "The Removal of Kabila and the Alternative: The Position of the Rassemblement Congolais pour la Democratie (RCD)," RCD Headquarters, Goma, 17 August 1998, in *The 1998 Rebellion in the Democratic Republic of the Congo*, Association of Concerned Africanists, 6–8.

32. "Political Declaration of the Congolese Rally for Democracy (RCD/CRD)."

33. Wamba dia Wamba cited in Campbell, "Notes on the Pace of the Struggle for a New Mode of Politics in the Congo," in *The 1998 Rebellion in the Democratic Republic of the Congo*, Association of Concerned Africanists, 48; For detailed discussion on Wamba's concept of new mode of politics, see Wamba dia Wamba and Mahmood Mandani, eds., *In Search of a New Mode of Politics in Africa* (London: James Curry, Ltd., 1994).

34. Campbell, "Notes on the Pace of the Struggle for a New Mode of Politics in the Congo," 48.

35. Weiss, "War and Peace in the Democratic Republic of the Congo," 18.

36. "Uganda and Rwanda: Friends or Enemies?" *The International Crisis Group*, available at: http://www.crisisweb.org/projects/showreport.cfm?reportid=37, May 4, 2000.

37. Weiss, "War and Peace in the Democratic Republic of the Congo," 18.

38. Jacques Depelchin, *Statements: What You Need to Know about RCD/Kisangani*, available at http://www.congorcd.org/statements/whatyouneedtoknow.htm.

39. Ibid.

40. Ibid.; "Rebels Merge," *New Vision*, Kampala, Uganda, 17 January 2001, available at http://www.newvision.co.ug/detail.php?story=3082; *Statements: RCD-K/ML Regrets the Imposed Merger with MLC*, Republique Democratique du Congo, Rassemblement Congolais pour la Democratie, Quartier General/Bunia, Bureau du President, Kampala, 17 January 17 2001, available at http://www.congorcd.org/statements/rejectionofmerger.htm.

41. Mahmood Mandani, "Why Foreign Invaders Can't Help Congo," *Electronic Mail & Guardian*, Johannesburg, South Africa, 2 November 1998.

42. "The Removal of Kabila and the Alternative: The Position of the Rassemblement Congolais pour la Démocratie (RCD)," RCD Headquarters, Goma, 17 August 1998, in *The 1998 Rebellion in the Democratic Republic of the Congo*, Association of Concerned Africanists, 6.

43. Campbell, "Notes on the Pace of the Struggle for a New Mode of Politics in the Congo," in *The 1998 Rebellion in the Democratic Republic of the Congo,* Association of Concerned Africanists, 54–57.

44. See Thomas Turner's chapter 5, in this volume.

45. Campbell, "Notes on the Pace of the Struggle for a New Mode of Politics in the Congo."

46. Ibid.

47. Weiss, "War and Peace in the Democratic Republic of the Congo," 9–10.

48. U.N. Secretary-General Kofi Anan quoted in "Rebels, Government Troops Claim Battle Gains in Congo," *CNN.com,* 12 August1998.

49. Rwanda initially denied military involvement in the second war; see "Congo Launches Counterattack, Says Rebels Retreating," *CNN.com,* 10 August 1998; in addition to its longstanding security concerns, Kigali claimed the Kabila regime was responsible for lynching Tutsi and Rwandan women and children; see "Rebels, Government Troops Claim Battle Gains in Congo."

50. For criticisms against Rwanda and Uganda for illegal exploitation of Congo's resources, see Christopher Wren, "Security Council Demands that Rwanda and Uganda Leave Congo," *The New York Times International,* on the Web at: http://www.nytimes.com/library/world/africa/061700congo-un.html, June 17, 2000; Nicole Winfield, "U.N Council Wants Congo Details," available at http://www.washingtonpost.com/wp-srv/aponline/200110122/aponline21437000.htm.

51. "Scramble for the Congo: Anatomy of an Ugly War," *The International Crisis Group,* available at http://www.crisisweb.org/projects/showreport.cfm?reportid=130, December 20, 2000; for the full text of the Lusaka Agreement, see Peace Agreements Digital Collection: Democratic Republic of Congo, United States Institute of Peace, 1200 17th Street NW, Suite 200, Washington, DC, 20036–3011.

52. Karl Vick, "Death Toll in Congo War May Approach 3 Million: Conflict Leaves Trail of Starvation, Disease and Carnage," *Washington Post Foreign Service,* 30 April 2001, A01.

53. Ibid.

54. Barbara Crossette, "War Adds 1.7 Million Deaths in Eastern Congo, Study Finds," *The New York Times International,* on the Web at: http://wwwnytimes.com/library/world/africa/060900un-congo.html, 9 June 2000.

55. Vick, "Death Toll in Congo War May Approach 3 Million;" Crossette, "War Adds 1.7 Million Deaths in Eastern Congo, Study Finds."

56. Vick, "Death Toll in Congo War May Approach 3 Million."

57. Arnaud Zajtman, "Congo President Laurent Kabila Dead," available online at: http://www.washingtonpost.com/wp-srv/aponline/20010118/aponline144952_000.htm, 18 January 2001.

58. Arnaud Zajtman, "Kabila's Son to Be Sworn In Soon," available online at: http://www.washingtonpost.com/wp-srv/aponline/20010119/aponline062550_000.htm, 19 January 2001.

59. Jon Jeter, "Congolese People Grieve Little Over Slain President," *Washington Post Foreign Service,* 20 January 2001, A21.

60. Ibid.

61. Ian Fisher, "In New Kabila, Anxious Congo City Thinks It Has the Least of Current Evils," *The New York Times International,* on the Web at: http://www.nytimes.com/2001/01/20/world/20CONG.htmlprint?page=yes, 20 January 2001.

62. Carl Vick, "Congolese Leaders Offer Rationale for Presidential Choice," *Washington Post Foreign Service,* 21 January 2001, A29.

63. Mwenze Kongolo quoted in ibid.

64. "Disarmament in the Congo: Investing in Conflict," *International Crisis Group,* available online at: http://www.crisisweb.org/projects/showreport.cfm?reportid=312, undated.

CHAPTER 8

The Complex Reasons for Rwanda's Engagement in Congo

Timothy Longman

W hen war broke out in Eastern Congo in August 1998, many observers noted the similarities between the new rebellion and the war that had toppled the regime of Mobutu Sese Sekou only fourteen months earlier.[1] Like the first war, the second began with ethnic Congolese Tutsi taking up arms to defend themselves against scapegoating and attacks by government supporters. Both wars began along the Congolese border with Rwanda, in Uvira, Bukavu, and Goma, and quickly spread along two fronts—up the Congo River and along Congo's northern border and to the south into the mineral-rich provinces of Katanga and Kasai. In both wars, after initially denying involvement in the fighting, the Rwandan government eventually admitted to participation, justifying its intervention on humanitarian and defensive grounds, and, as before, Uganda threw its support behind the rebellion as well.

Yet if highlighting the similarities between the two rebellions was meant to imply that the Rassemblement Congolaise pour la Démocratie (Rally for Congolese Democracy—RCD) would follow the example of the Alliance des Forces Démocratique pour La Liberation du Congo/Zaire (Alliance for the Democratic Liberation of the Congo-Zaire—ADFL) to quick victory—as the organizers of the second rebellion apparently intended—the contrasts between the two rebellions soon proved the limits of the comparison. While many Congolese discontented with the Mobutu regime welcomed the ADFL advance across the country, few Congolese, even among Kabila's enemies, embraced the RCD. Instead, they denounced the rebellion as an invention of foreign governments hostile to the interests of the Congolese population. The reaction of the international community was also markedly different. While the world's major powers (especially the United States and Britain) had been sympathetic to Rwanda's security concerns and professed humanitarian intent in the wake of the 1994 genocide in Rwanda, continuing human rights abuses in Rwanda and a less clear security threat dampened international support for the second rebellion.[2] More significantly, other African states were not united in their opposition to Kabila as they had been to Mobutu. The intervention of Angola, Namibia, and Zimbabwe on Kabila's behalf put a halt to the RCD's rapid advance. The lack of a persuasive justification for intervention ultimately contributed to divisions within the RCD and a breakdown of the alliance between Rwanda and Uganda.

Given the hostility with which the Congolese population has greeted the Rwandan intervention and the problems that the war has caused for the Rwandan government, both within Africa and in the broader international community, the reasons for Rwanda's involvement in the war are not self-evident. In fact, Rwanda's leaders seem to have been motivated by a wide range of objectives that have shifted over time. Their stated justifications for intervention—to eliminate continuing threats to Rwandan security posed by Hutu rebels based in Congo, to protect Congolese Tutsi, and to promote democracy—did play a role, but the war seems also to have been inspired by other motives less defensible in international circles: the need to quell domestic unrest, opportunities for personal and national enrichment, and the desire to be a regional power. The increasing importance of these unstated reasons for intervention helps to explain Rwanda's reluctance to withdraw from Congo even after its stated goals have been largely accomplished.

HUMANITARIAN INTERESTS AND ETHNIC SOLIDARITY

Rwandan troops were involved in the fighting in Congo from the beginning, as news agencies reported their presence in Bukavu and elsewhere, but as in the first Congolese war, the government of Rwanda initially denied any involvement in the second war. For several weeks after the fighting began in Eastern Congo on 2 August 1998, Rwanda's leaders claimed that the war was an internal Congolese dispute. Rwandan president Pasteur Bizimungu, army spokesman Major Emmanuel Ndahiro, and Foreign Minister Anastase Gasana, among others, disavowed any Rwandan involvement, with Gasana claiming, "Rwanda has its own problems that it is trying to solve, it cannot go fighting wars in Congo. This is purely Congo's internal affair."[3] Leaders of the RCD at first also denied Rwandan involvement.[4]

Rwandan leaders apparently felt that they could not admit an extraterritorial intervention so clearly in violation of international law until they had prepared the international community to accept it. Hence, during the first weeks of the war, Rwandan officials denied involvement yet affirmed the RCD's justifications for taking up arms. The RCD's perspective is well expressed by Jacques Depelchin, one of several prominent academics who joined the RCD. In a speech given at Columbia University in September 1998, he gave two basic reasons for the rebellion: Kabila's corrupt and authoritarian tendencies and his move toward genocide, the same reasons used to justify war against Mobutu. According to Depelchin, "The war is a continuation of the first war because the objectives for which we were fighting, Kabila turned his back on them. We wanted to move away from all of Mobutu's practices: using the bank like his personal kitty, concentration of power in the hands of one ethnic group, corruption, refusing to open the democratic process, refusing to allow other political forces to participate. All those things for which we had fought for were not happening."[5]

Like Depelchin and other RCD leaders, Rwandan officials mentioned their concern over Kabila's corruption and hostility to democracy, but their main justification for "possible" intervention (in reality an explanation for the intervention they had already undertaken) was the threat of genocide against Congolese Tutsi. In late August, for example, Rwandan minister of state Patrick Mazimhaka accused Kabila of launching a genocide against Congolese Tutsi and warned that Rwanda could be "drawn into the war in neighboring Congo if the killing of Tutsis is not stopped."[6]

Many foreign observers, as well as some Rwandans, accept the Rwandan Patriotic Army's (RPA) claims of humanitarian motives. This perspective is founded on a specific understanding of the RPA's relationship to the 1990--94 war in Rwanda and particularly to the 1994 genocide there. According to this understanding, the RPA invaded Rwanda in 1990 on purely—or primarily—humanitarian grounds, and they began fighting again in April 1994 to put a halt to the genocide of their Tutsi relatives. This view perceives the Tutsi in the RPA as having a strong sense of ethnic connection to Tutsi elsewhere and as having been deeply touched by the cold-blooded murder of their parents, brothers, and sisters in the genocide.[7] If they have occasionally stepped outside the bounds of international law, as in their treatment of Rwanda's Hutu population or, in this case, their extraterritorial intervention in Congo, it is understandable, because of the terrible tragedy they have experienced.[8] The humanitarian defense of Rwanda's misbehavior is generally accompanied by a reminder of the international community's failure to intervene in the 1994 genocide, implying that the RPA has a right to assume that no one else will defend the Tutsi population and that extraordinary circumstances justify extraordinary measures.[9] The title of one article sets this perspective out clearly: "At the source of Congo's war—a shrine of human bones" left from the 1994 genocide.[10]

Given the Rwandan Patriotic Front's (RPF) own authoritarian rule in Rwanda, few people take seriously its professed concern for democracy in Congo, and even those who do doubt that the current war can succeed at bringing about democracy. As Mahmood Mamdani writes, "Foreign invasion cannot give us democracy as a turnkey project. This was true of Uganda in 1979 and of Congo in 1997. And it remains true of Congo in 1998."[11] Another author suggests that the real goal of the Rwandans was less to bring about democracy than merely to topple Kabila and replace him with a more compliant puppet. "The military tactics of the 'rebels' were based on the erroneous assumption that popular uprisings would greet their insurrection. They, and their puppet masters, however, underestimated the level and intensity of Congolese nationalism. For the Banyamulenge at much less than one percent of a population of fifty million to challenge the rest of the country to a fight is flying in the face of disaster."[12]

While Rwanda's interest in democracy is questionable, the concern for Congo's Tutsi was real, and the interest in defending Congo's Tutsi was probably, at least initially, more than a mere "pretext" or "fig leaf"[13] to justify intervention. Many in the RPA have strong connections to the Tutsi community in Congo. The RPA's leadership is comprised almost entirely of Tutsi who grew up as refugees outside Rwanda, and while the most powerful RPA officials come from Uganda, the Tutsi refugee community in Congo was large and contributed many troops to the RPA. The Rwandan Tutsi refugees became well integrated with the native Congolese Tutsi community in Eastern Congo,[14] and many Congolese Tutsi (as well as some Congolese Hutu) actually joined the RPA during its 1990--94 war with Rwanda, though most of these returned to Congo during the 1996--97 war. The RPA's involvement in the first war increased the bonds between Rwandan and Congolese Tutsi, and the RPF retained a presence in Congo until just before the beginning of the second war. Hence, violence against Tutsi in Congo directly affected the RPA. As early as September 1997, the move to install non-Tutsi troops in North and South Kivu led to violence in that region, some of which targeted Tutsi.[15] In early 1998, violence broke out in South Kivu between Banyamulenge troops and Mai-Mai militia, former allies in the ADFL, after the government moved to increase the level of ethnic integration in the Forces Armées Congolaises (Congolese Armed Forces—FAC).[16] When Kabila began to exclude Tutsi from his government and from leadership positions in the FAC in late 1997, he targeted not only Banyamulenge and other Congolese Tutsi[17] but also some RPA officials who remained in powerful positions in the FAC. Denunciations of Tutsi that Kabila reportedly made on Congolese radio in late August and the subsequent attacks on Tutsi civilians in Kinshasa and elsewhere after the beginning of the war must surely have affected Rwandan government and RPA officials, just as they claimed.[18]

The problem with the humanitarian justification for intervention in Congo is the same problem posed by the RPA's relationship to the genocide in Rwanda: Attacking a country increases the vulnerability of scapegoated groups and makes genocide more likely. While this in no way justifies genocide, nor makes it less heinous a crime against humanity, the knowledge that the context of war is a major causal factor in explaining genocide does place a burden of caution on those who would wage war. The ideology of genocide generally portrays the dominant group as vulnerable, so that genocide becomes a defensive action in the minds of its perpetrators. Attacking a country with a well-developed genocidal ideology lends credence to the argument that the dominant group is in fact threatened and needs to defend itself by eliminating internal enemies.[19] It should not be surprising, thus, that violence against ethnic Albanians *increased* after NATO began bombing Serbia, since the war augmented the Serbian sense of vulnerability. Similarly, some observers of the Rwandan genocide have pointed out the paradoxical nature of the RPA's intervention in Rwanda. On the one hand, the RPA put a halt to the genocide of Tutsi in regions they captured, but on the other, their invasion of Rwanda was a primary reason why genocide was possible, because it made the Hutu population feel vulnerable.

While the RPA invasion of Eastern Congo has certainly prevented massacres of Congolese Tutsi for the time being, research that I conducted in Goma and Bukavu in March 2000 made it abundantly clear that in the longterm, the second war has *heightened* the vulnerability of Congolese Tutsi. The war is massively unpopular with the population of North and South Kivu, which deeply resents the RPA presence. Although Congolese from many ethnic groups are involved in the RCD administration, most people see Tutsi, both Congolese and Rwandan, as the primary powers in the RCD. Many Congolese with whom I spoke questioned the national loyalties of the Congolese Tutsi. They claimed that the Tutsi had been demanding citizenship rights in Congo, but once the RPF came to power in Rwanda, many left to live in Rwanda. Now, according to Congolese perceptions, Congolese Tutsi have invited a foreign army to occupy their country. This perception of Tutsi as having greater loyalties to Rwanda than Congo is widely held, even among otherwise progressive elements in civil society, while anti-Tutsi hatred is even more virulent in other sectors of society. While the presence of RPA troops protects the Tutsi for the moment, Tutsi will clearly be vulnerable in Congo if the RPA troops depart. Making up a comparatively small portion of the population, even in their areas of greatest concentration in North Kivu, the Tutsi will find their dominant political and military position difficult to protect.[20]

Hence, the RPA's presence poses a paradox from the perspective of protection of Tutsi. The RPA clearly does prevent anti-Tutsi violence. Yet their own actions, particularly attacks on civilians and other human rights abuses,[21] increase public resentment and hatred of Tutsi, thus heightening the need for protection of Tutsi. The RPA, thus, is simultaneously increasing the threat to Tutsi and offering them protection.

SECURITY CONCERNS

Security Threats from Congo

The second motive for involvement in Congo that Rwandan officials will publicly admit is the continuing threat to security in Rwanda posed by elements of the former Rwandan army and the *Interahamwe* militia operating out of Congo. When RPF leader Paul Kagame ultimately admitted RPF involvement in the first Congo war, he justified it primarily as a defensive action.[22] RPA spokesman Claude Dusaidi claimed that Rwanda invaded because the government had gained information about a threatened invasion by the former Rwandan army based in the Congolese refugee camps.[23] Many in the international community had long been aware of the problem that the presence of armed elements in the Hutu refugee camps posed for Rwanda. Since international actors were not themselves willing to intervene to separate armed elements from legitimate refugees, "When the ADFL used force to disperse the camps and to require unwilling Rwandans to return home, governments and international agencies applauded."[24] Given the security threat posed for Rwanda by the *Interahamwe* and ex-FAR present in the camps, many diplomats, journalists, and scholars regarded the RPF's decision to intervene as understandable. Many were also willing to overlook the fact that the RPF attacked Hutu without discriminating between combatants and unarmed civilians, in clear violation of international humanitarian law.[25] The idea that Rwanda had a legitimate defensive interest in intervening in Congo legitimated their involvement in the war long after they had closed the refugee camps and routed the remnants of the Hutu army, as Mobutu himself was ultimately defined as a security threat.

Given the diplomatic success of the defensive justification for intervention in the first war, it should not be surprising that the RPF turned to security concerns to justify its intervention in the second war. An escalation of attacks in Rwanda by armed Hutu elements in late 1997 and early 1998 raised clear concerns within the RPF over its ability to maintain control over the majority Hutu population in Rwanda. The most serious attacks occurred in the northwestern prefectures of Gisenyi and Ruhengeri, on the border with Congo, where attacks by Hutu militia and counterattacks by the RPA escalated into a virtual civil war by early 1998.[26] Numerous killings of genocide survivors were reported, as well as attacks on camps of Congolese Tutsi refugees, and attacks reached even into the heartland of the country, Gitarama, where a December 1997 raid on the Gitarama prison freed 500 Hutu accused of involvement in the genocide.[27] A new organization, the Rwanda Liberation Army, took credit for the attacks and gained a degree of international attention in 1998.[28]

The Rwandan government did, thus, have legitimate security concerns, and its claim that the insurgents were using Congo as a base of operations seems to have been well founded. Whether Kabila actually formed an alliance with armed Hutu elements in Eastern Congo, as RCD and Rwandan critics have claimed,[29] is difficult to know, but Rwandan Hutu rebels clearly did use Eastern Congo as a base of operation. Following the RPA's intervention in Congo in 1998, violence within Rwanda dropped off precipitously.[30] Many in the international community have seemed willing to accept security concerns as a reasonable justification for this RPF intervention, as they did with the first war.

There are, however, some clear difficulties with security as a justification. First, while controlling Hutu rebel activity could justify invasion of North and South Kivu, it cannot explain why the RPF carried the rebellion into Katanga, Kasai, and Orientale, where there was no evidence of Hutu militia activity. While moving beyond Eastern Congo was justified in the first war by the perception that security would not be established in the region until Mobutu was removed, no similar consensus about Kabila as a security threat existed, as demonstrated by the willingness of Angola and other African states to intervene on his behalf.

Second, as with the humanitarian justification, Rwanda's continuing presence in Eastern Congo and in particular its violent treatment of the Congolese population has exacerbated anti-Rwandan and anti-Tutsi sentiments in Congo. Local militias, now known almost universally as Mai-Mai,[31] were allies with the Banyamulenge and RPA in the first war, but they broke with Kabila's government because of their frustration at the continuing RPA presence in Eastern Congo and the disproportionate power of Banyamulenge and other Congolese Tutsi. Kabila's attempt to reach out to the ethnic groups they represented was a major source of conflict with Rwanda, and when the second war began, Mai-Mai groups fled into the forests, from which they have since mounted resistance. As the war has continued, more and more Congolese have joined Mai-Mai groups, and in some cases, they have allied themselves with Hutu militia groups (now generally called *Interahamwe*). Thus, rather than wiping out Congo-based militia as a threat to Rwanda, the RPF may have increased both popular support for militia and the numbers of militia members. In any peace settlement, these militia groups, who have apparently received support from the Kabila regime, represent a difficult problem to confront.

Domestic Security Concerns

The idea that nothing serves to unify a divided country like an external threat—and nothing so well as a war—is so widely repeated as to have become a truism. Yet Rwanda's intervention in Congo seems an unlikely candidate for rallying patriotic unity. The vast majority of Rwanda's population is Hutu, while the minority Tutsi ethnic group is widely perceived to dominate the government. Since the RPF took power in July 1994, the government has been comprised of diverse political parties and Hutu have served in prominent positions, but the RPF has been the real power behind the scenes. As Reyntjens observes, although fourteen of twenty-seven cabinet ministers in 1999 were Hutu, in all but two cases, the general secretary of their ministries was a Tutsi from the RPF.[32] At the top level, the greatest power lay not with the Hutu president, Pasteur Bizimungu, but with Paul Kagame, the vice president and minister of defense. This impression was confirmed when Bizimungu resigned in 2000 and Kagame became the new president. Most Hutu perceive the government as a "Tutsi" government, and they see the human rights abuses carried out by the RPA and police since 1994 as in part ethnically motivated.[33] Many Hutu complain that the RPF acts more like a colonizing force than a legitimate government. Hence, a war in Congo initiated by the RPF in order to ensure its own security against a perceived threat from Hutu rebels is not likely to appeal to the Hutu masses.

Nevertheless, the war in Congo could help to create internal Rwandan unity in several ways. Most importantly, it could unify a divided Tutsi population. An important division exists between the survivors of the genocide and the Tutsi who have returned to Rwanda from exile. The RPF is composed predominantly of returned exiles, while survivors, many of whom are women and orphans, have little representation in the government and very little power. As early as 1995, I heard survivors complain about their relative marginalization within the RPF.[34] Resentments of the RPF have increased among survivors, "who find that the current government fails to satisfy their demands for justice and assistance. These Tutsi deplore the lack of progress in prosecutions for genocide as well as the prosperity of government officials grown rich from corruption while many survivors . . . struggle in abject poverty."[35]

Some of these survivors have thrown their support behind a multiethnic movement calling for the return to Rwanda of King Kigeli V Ndahindurwa, who was driven into exile in 1961 by a Hutu uprising. Although the monarchy had lost popular legitimacy among the Hutu by the end of the colonial era, the king was historically believed to represent all Rwandans, regardless of their ethnicity. The revival of the idea of the monarch as a figure who could unite Rwandans across ethnic lines has created support for the return of the king, even among Hutu in regions that once strongly supported the 1959 revolution. Further, since the king cannot be tainted by association with the genocide, he could challenge the RPF in a way that Hutu leaders could not.[36] The RPF clearly views this multiethnic monarchist movement as a major threat, and RPF leaders may have hoped that the engagement in Congo would regain Tutsi support around the common Hutu threat and serve to divide Hutu and Tutsi united in the monarchist movement.

Important divisions also exist within the RPF and the community of returned exiles between exiles from the francophone countries of Burundi and Congo and those from Uganda and other anglophone countries. Power within the RPF is clearly dominated by Tutsi, who, like Kagame, were exiles in Uganda. While some Tutsi returned from Burundi and Congo are in prominent government positions, the most powerful positions are held almost entirely by Ugandan returnees. Within the civilian community, Tutsi returned from Uganda have enjoyed the greatest economic opportunities while other returnees have been left behind. Hence, some francophone returnees have also been attracted to the monarchist movement.[37] Some RPF leaders may have hoped that the invasion of Congo would appeal to returnees from Congo, since it was justified as a defense of Congolese Tutsi.

Finally, the war has offered at least some opportunities to enlist the support of Hutu. Immediately after taking power, the RPF began to arrest Hutu that they suspected of participation in the genocide, but the number of suspects far exceeded the capacity of the Rwandan legal system to evaluate the validity of accusations, press formal charges, and hold trials. With the closure of refugee camps in Congo driving Hutu back into Rwanda in 1996, thousands more suspects were arrested, creating a prison population of over 120,000 people. This huge population of Hutu, only a small portion of whom will ever have a day in court, has been a source of problems for the government with both the international community and the Hutu population, most of whom have relatives in prison. With the war in Congo creating a need for additional soldiers, the RPF has turned to the prisons as a source of recruits. Captured members of the Hutu militia groups or Hutu accused of lesser offenses have apparently been offered an opportunity to join the RPF in Congo rather than wait indefinitely in prison. Witnesses interviewed in South Kivu in March 2000 reported that they recognized among recently arrived RPF soldiers Hutu who had formerly been in their communities as refugees.[38] The recruits are evidently put through "solidarity camps," where they are given pro-RPF indoctrination and taught RPA military discipline before being sent to join RPA units in Congo.[39] While witnesses I interviewed in Congo questioned the degree to which these Hutu soldiers were actually willing to fire on Hutu militia, their presence in the ranks of the military clearly does present the RPF with an opportunity to influence them and integrate them into their cause. Furthermore, it removes a portion of a potentially restive population from Rwanda and offers them an opportunity for limited freedom in exchange for a change in loyalties. While I do not claim that this is a major factor influencing the RPF's involvement in the war, it has served as a way of soliciting support from an otherwise hostile Hutu population.

ECONOMIC INTERESTS

Although humanitarian and security concerns may have been important initial motivations for Rwandan involvement in the second war, these concerns do not fully explain Rwanda's continued engagement in Congo. Instead, other, less internationally acceptable reasons appear to have had a strong influence, despite denials by the RPF. The most obvious of these is the opportunity for both national and personal enrichment. Rwanda is a small, overpopulated country with almost no natural resources. In contrast, Congo is extremely rich in natural resources and has abundant land. Congo exports diamonds, gold, uranium, copper, and other minerals, as well as coffee, tea, and other export crops. Congo's wealth helped to prop up the Mobutu regime long after it had lost public support. Kabila was able to support the ADFL as it advanced across Congo in the 1996--97 war, in part through giving concessions of Congo's minerals to international corporations.[40]

Strong evidence suggests that Rwanda has profited substantially from its involvement in Congo. Rwanda and Uganda have both become transit points for diamonds and other minerals extracted from Congo and generally smuggled out of the country illegally.[41] Rwanda's former protegé, Wamba dia Wamba, now head of the RCD-Bunia (the branch supported by Uganda), has accused both Rwanda and Uganda of looting Congo's minerals. According to Wamba, "In the case of Rwanda it is a state policy."[42] This perspective was supported by numerous witnesses with whom I spoke. Witnesses from Walikale, a region where Mai-Mai militias have been active, reported that in some communities the population had been driven into regroupment camps where they were required to mine coltan, a mineral used in microchips and cellular phones and traded at a very high price on international markets.[43] According to one report, Rwanda has been exporting as much as U.S.$20 million of coltan per month. Rwanda's diamond exports increased from 166 carats in 1998 to 30,500 carats in 2000.[44] The fighting that broke out between Rwandan and Ugandan troops in

Kisangani in mid-1999 was apparently fueled in large part by competition over the diamonds that are transported through this major commercial center.[45]

According to people whom I interviewed from various parts of North and South Kivu, the plunder of Congo is not limited to extraction of mineral wealth but includes looting goods. Various witnesses reported that when RPA troops attacked a village they suspected of harboring militia groups, they commonly sacked the town, taking whatever valuable items they could transport. This occurred even far from the Rwanda border, where transportation of goods is relatively easy. For example, witnesses I interviewed from Shabunda reported that after RPF troops chased Mai-Mai out of town in January 2000, they looted goods from the community, loaded them in a plane, and shipped them back to Rwanda.[46]

The exact extent to which Rwanda is profiting from its intervention in Congo is difficult to determine, but the evidence of the economic benefits taken from Congo is clearly visible in the current level of prosperity in Kigali. Economic activity in Rwanda today goes far beyond what either the Rwandan economy alone or the current level of international investment could support. The elevated number of commercial flights into and out of Kigali alone suggests exceptional economic activity, not to mention a construction boom that has occurred over the last several years and the proliferation of restaurants, nightclubs, and commercial ventures. This prosperity comes despite the high cost of sustaining the war, which one can reasonably assume is being financed by Congo itself. Hence, extraction of resources and goods from Congo seems to benefit not only the Rwandan government and army but also individuals engaged in smuggling and other forms of trade, including RPA officers and others.

POLITICAL TRIUMPHALISM AND THE MYTH OF A "TUTSI CONSPIRACY"

The final motivation for military engagement in Congo is a bit more subtle, but it ranks among the most important explanations for why Rwanda has remained engaged in Congo: political triumphalism. The RPF has been an extremely successful movement, and this success has bred a sense of entitlement among RPF leaders. Fred Rwigyema and Paul Kagame, subsequently founders of the RPF, were Rwandan Tutsi refugees who were among the original members of the National Resistance Army (NRA), a rebel movement led by current Ugandan president Yoweri Museveni. The NRA's successful conquest of Uganda against great odds helped convince the many Tutsi in the NRA that the conquest of Rwanda could be possible as well. Like the NRA, the RPF began as a bush rebellion, but it too gradually expanded, captured land, and ultimately swept to power in Kigali. The odds of the RPF's victory were even longer, since unlike the NRA, which had a substantial base of support among several large ethnic groups in Southern Uganda, the RPF's base of support, the Tutsi, constituted less than 15 percent of Rwanda's population.[47]

Hence, the RPF came to power with a degree of triumphalism, with a sense that they were a victorious army that could not be defeated. (In fact, the Kinyarwanda nickname that RPF soldiers took for themselves was *inkotanyi,* "the indefatigable ones.") The RPF's perception of themselves as having put an end to the genocide of their people also shapes their perspective, imparting a sense of moral rectitude. The failure of the international community to stop the genocide and later to confront the security problems posed by armed Hutu groups in the refugee camps in Congo and the spread of violence to Congolese Tutsi convinced the RPF that no one else was willing to defend the interests of the Tutsi people.[48] The RPF's sense of responsibility, feeling of moral certainty, and confidence—verging on arrogance—in its own military capacity all influenced its intervention in the first Congo war. The fact that it and its Ugandan allies were able to create a rebel force that was able to surprise the world by sweeping to victory across the vast country of Congo in only eight months contributed to the RPA's sense of invincibility.

These attitudes of moral entitlement and military dominance shaped Rwandan relations with the Kabila regime. While Kabila had been a longtime opponent of Mobutu, he had disappeared entirely from public view when Kagame and Museveni brought him in as head of the ADFL several weeks into the rebellion. They continued to regard Kabila as a junior partner, even after he became president of a country much larger and wealthier than theirs. According to veteran Great Lakes analyst Jean-Claude Willame, the RPF viewed the rebellion as its own initiative and the ouster of Mobutu as something that the Congolese alone could not have accomplished. "For Kagame, thus, the 'Congolese rebels' play only a supporting role in a process directed from blow to blow by Rwanda."[49] As the ADFL advanced across Congo, the RPF sought to exercise its influence in captured territories much as it had in Rwanda, by installing Congolese from diverse ethnic groups in titular positions but placing real power in the hands of Banyamulenge and RPF officers in nominally inferior positions. While RPF dominance was possible in Rwanda, where Tutsi constitute over 10 percent of the population and the RPF had justified claims to Rwandan citizenship, Tutsi constitute far less than 1 percent of Congo's population. Although many Congolese were thankful for the assistance that they received from neighboring countries in ousting Mobutu, they deeply resented Rwanda's attempt to wield power in their country after the war, particularly given the strong anti-Tutsi sentiment within Congo.

Kabila's ties with Rwanda and the continuing presence of Rwandan officers in the army and government were, thus, a severe political liability for Congo's new president, yet the RPF leadership proved incredibly insensitive to Kabila's predicament. Kagame's July 1997 boast in a *Washington Post* interview that Rwanda had been key to the ADFL victory put Kabila in an awkward position and inspired his first attempts to move Rwandans and Banyamulenge out of key positions.[50] The RPF treated Kabila's attempt to exercise independent power and his replacement of Tutsi in the government as the act of an anti-Tutsi extremist, tantamount to the genocidal behavior of the Rwandan Hutu leadership in the 1994 genocide. Yet even at the beginning of the second rebellion, Tutsi held political power in Congo far out of proportion to their presence in the population, including positions as foreign minister and minister of state.[51] The RPF leadership seemed to believe themselves entitled to wielding power in Congo in a way that the other sponsors of the ADFL did not, and they treated Kabila's attempts to act independently as a personal betrayal. Ultimately, the replacement in mid-July 1998 of James Kabari, a Rwandan Tutsi, as chief of staff of the FAC seems to have been the spark that drove Rwanda to act, despite the degree to which such a move was understandable within the context of Congolese politics.[52]

In discussing the political arrogance of the RPF leadership, I do not mean in any way to support the idea of a "Tutsi conspiracy" that some critics of the Rwandan and

Ugandan governments promote. According to this theory, Ugandan president Yoweri Museveni is actually a Tutsi, not a Muhima of the Banyankole, and he and the Tutsi leaders of the RPF have conspired over the past two decades to create a massive Tutsi kingdom in the Great Lakes region, beginning with Uganda, then spreading to Rwanda, Burundi, and, finally, into Congo. This theory is backed with racist depictions of the Tutsi as greedy, dishonest, and power-hungry and with claims that they are a Nilotic group with no right to live in a Bantu area, the same type of language used to justify the Rwandan genocide.[53]

In fact, Rwandan actions in Congo have not been carefully planned out within a well-developed "conspiracy." Instead, the RPF leadership has been driven in a more haphazard fashion by a sense of entitlement and invincibility based more on its military might than its ethnic affiliation. This triumphalism has blinded the RPF leadership to the impact that RPF actions have on how Tutsi are perceived. Tragically, actions motivated by RPF arrogance have exacerbated anti-Tutsi sentiments, creating a difficult situation for thousands of Congolese Tutsi—as well as for other Congolese who have supported the two rebellions. This arrogance of power also contributed to the eventual break between Rwanda and Uganda, as ultimately RPF leaders could not tolerate Uganda usurping the role of puppet master that they rightfully saw as their own.

RWANDAN STRATEGIES IN THE SECOND CONGO WAR

Rwanda's intervention in Congo has been militarily quite successful but has faltered largely because of political constraints and miscalculations. The RPF sought to mimic its successes in the first Congo war by following the same patterns of assault. Initial attacks began along the Rwandan and Burundian borders with combined RPF and Congolese forces—primarily Tutsi and Banyamulenge members of the RCD, but also some former soldiers from Mobutu's army who had previously been the targets of the RPF's attacks. After quickly securing the border regions of North and South Kivu, the RPF and RCD forces moved west along two fronts, toward the mineral regions of Katanga in the south and Orientale in the north. Capturing the diamond and gold mines in these two regions provided a revenue base to support the war while at the same time denying Kabila's government and the FAC sources of revenue they needed to defend themselves. This path of assault was exactly the path that the ADFL had taken two years earlier to great success.

The major departure from the military strategy used in the first Congo war was a daring assault on the strategic area at the mouth of the Congo River in the far western part of Congo. Just days after launching the attack along Rwanda's borders, the rebel soldiers hijacked a Congo Air jumbo jet and used it to fly Rwandan and RCD soldiers to an airbase at Kitona in the Bas-Congo region. After quickly taking control of the airbase, they began to ferry in hundreds of reinforcements, using large Russian-built troop transport planes. The Rwandan and RCD troops quickly captured the vital Atlantic ports of Boma and Matadi and the power plants and power lines along the Congo River, then began marching on the capital, Kinshasa. By the second week of August, RPF and RCD troops were less than twenty miles outside of Kinshasa.[54]

The RPF and RCD assaults in both the east and west of Congo ultimately foundered not because of military failings but because of political miscalculations. In the first war, the RPF was highly successful at gaining popular support for its presence in Congo by creating the ADFL as an anti-Mobutu movement. As the ADFL advanced across Congo, they received support not only from local residents, who believed that the rebels were freeing them from thirty-one years of authoritarian rule, but also from many of Mobutu's own troops, who switched sides because of their own frustrations with Mobutu and in hopes that the ADFL could bring about a better future for Congo. In the second war, the Rwandans tried to repeat this strategy, creating a Congolese movement that could gain popular support from people disenchanted with Kabila, but the RCD was from the beginning an awkward coalition of former ADFL soldiers (particularly Banyamulenge); former Mobutu associates and Forces Armées Zairoises (Zairian Armed Forces—FAZ) soldiers driven out of power by Kabila; civil society activists, such as human rights activists Maitre Emungu and Joseph Mudumbi; and intellectuals such as Depelchin and Wamba dia Wamba. The motivation for the rebellion clearly came from the Banyamulenge and from Rwanda, but Rwandan leaders were sufficiently conscious of the unpopularity of the Tutsi to realize that they needed to give an impression of broad popular support. It is not fully clear why prominent individuals like Mudumbi and Wamba would be drawn into the RCD, since Rwanda's avowed interest in democracy seems to have had little basis in action, but the RCD officials clearly failed to bring along a substantial constituency, as the RPF had apparently hoped. Most Congolese were quick to denounce RCD leaders as mere puppets seeking personal fortune, and indeed the humble, poorly guarded offices of RCD officials in Goma suggest immediately their limited real authority.

The divergent motivations of the RPF and its Congolese allies have led to conflicts and ultimately divisions in the RCD, as Rwanda has moved leaders in and out of power. Wamba dia Wamba received support from Uganda to form an alternate RCD branch after Rwanda pushed him out as chairman of the movement, and more recently, Rwanda orchestrated the replacement of Emile Ilunga as head of the RCD-Goma by Adolphe Onusumba. The regular rotation of leaders has done nothing to improve the image of the RCD-Goma as more than a mere front for Rwandan ambitions. In contrast to the Mouvement pour la Libération du Congo (Movement for the Liberation of Congo—MLC), which controls much of Équateur province and is led by a leader who has a degree of local popular appeal, the RCD-Goma still almost entirely lacks popular support. Over time, even many Banyamulenge have become critical of the RCD, because its arrogance and abusive behavior have increased the precariousness of the Banyamulenge position within Congo.[55]

The failure to gain popular support has been a major handicap for the RPF and the rebel movement it supported.[56] Not only did this lack of popularity contribute to the fracturing of the rebels into three movements, but it inspired resistance from local populations. Whereas in the first war local militia groups such as the Mai-Mai joined forces with the rebels against Mobutu, in the second war, they have taken up arms against the rebels. The popular impression that Rwanda invaded Congo substantially enhanced Laurent Kabila's popularity. He was able to portray himself as the defender of Congolese interests against the foreign invaders from Rwanda and Uganda. Although the RCD tried to rally popular support by accusing Kabila of nepotism, corruption, and incompetence, he had at that point not been in office long enough for the general population to grow weary of him, and the fact that Rwanda had originally supported him undermined their arguments that he was a bad leader.

Given this context, the invasion from the west of Kinshasa, although a brilliant military move, was a terrible political miscalculation. The airlift of troops into Kitona reinforced the impression from the beginning that the second war was not a rebellion but a foreign invasion. Given an apparent choice between a mediocre Congolese leader and a foreign Tutsi occupation, most Congolese were quick to choose Kabila over the RPF. Furthermore, the rapid move on Kinshasa, clearly against the popular will, inspired other African countries to intervene on Kabila's behalf. Angola sent in troops that quickly crushed the invasion force approaching Kinshasa.[57] Namibia and Zimbabwe also sent troops that were able to slow the advances in eastern Congo. Confronted with both the FAC and well-armed foreign troops along the front, a hostile population and armed militia attacks within the territory ostensibly under its control, a splintering of the rebel movement, and a break with its chief ally, Uganda, the RPF found itself in an uncomfortable position. For the first time in its history, the RPF found its sense of manifest destiny challenged. Without any realistic hope of achieving its goal of once again marching to victory in Kinshasa, the RPF has been forced to enter into negotiations that may finally bring an end to the conflict.

CONCLUSIONS

As I have attempted to demonstrate, Rwanda's intervention in Congo since 1998 has been inspired by complex motives that have sometimes conflicted. The desires to eliminate security threats and to protect Congolese Tutsi have been undermined by the desire for enrichment and the arrogance with which the RPF has acted in Congo. In the longterm, the cost of maintaining the war in terms of resources and personnel, as well as international support, may inspire the RPF to expand the withdrawal it began in early 2001. But the actions of the RPF—in particular, the failure to build a Congolese base of support for their movement, the engagement in extensive human rights abuses, and the exploitation of Congo's resources—have meant that in the end, the war will have accomplished very little for Rwanda. Security threats are likely to remain, both for Rwanda and for Congolese Tutsi, because of the expansion of anti-Rwandan hatred, and the expense of the war may in the end outweigh the profits taken. Unless some true regional settlement can be reached, the risks of future war remain high.

NOTES

1. Cf., Jacques Depelchin, "Crisis in the Congo," lecture given at Columbia University, New York, NY, September 30, 1998 (mimeograph). Louise Turnbridge, "Revolt Threatens Kabila Regime in Congo: Tutsis Seem Intent on Separation," *The Ottawa Citizen*, 5 August 1998. Reuters reported on 4 August 1998, for example, that "Army rebels have risen up against President Laurent Kabila in the east of the Democratic Republic of the Congo in a revolt *that mirrors the uprising that brought him to power just over a year ago*." (italics added).

2. The Clinton White House gave mixed signals to the warring parties. While State Department spokesperson James P. Rubin said just after the start of the rebellion "I'm not prepared to comment on whether we would like to see a change in the Government

there . . ." (Steven Erlanger, "U.S. Sees Rwandan Role in Congo Revolt," *New York Times*, 5 August 1998), just a few days later another State Department spokesperson, James Foley, said "We urge all countries in the region to respect the territorial integrity of the Congo, refrain from becoming involved in the conflict and respect international law" ("More Congo Fighting, Rwanda Denies any Blame for Rebellion," Deutsche Presse-Agentur, 6 August 1998).

3. "More Congo Fighting."

4. The first leader of the RCD, Arthur Ngoma, argued that the revolt had no ethnic motive and had no Rwandan involvement. "This is a struggle of the Congolese people," he claimed ("Congo's Foreign Minister Defects to Rebels, Fighting Spreads to City in Jungle," *Toronto Star*, 6 August 1998.

5. Depelchin, "Crisis in the Congo."

6. "Foreign Troops in Congo Fighting, Rwanda Levels Genocide Charges," Deutsche Presse-Agentur, 28 August 1998. The foreign minister of Uganda made a similar claim a month later: Ofwono-Opondo and Richard Mutumba, "Kabila and International Criminal, Says Kutesa," *New Vision*, Kampala, Uganda, 1 October 1998.

7. Philip Gourevich, *We Wish to Inform You that Tomorrow We Will Be Killed along with Our Families* (New York: Farrar Strauss and Giroux, 1998) is an excellent expression of this perspective of the RPF as heroes motivated only by the desire to save their families.

8. For example, respected historian Jean-Pierre Chrétien ["Le Rwanda piégé par son histoire," *Esprit* (August–September 2000) 170–189] writes: "On comprendra donc que je n'aie pas fais partie des bonnes âmes qui, dès lendemain du génocide, se sont précipitées pour exiger la perfection du nouveau régime établi à Kigali, d'autant que ce pays avait besoin d'un Nuremberg et d'un plan Marshall à sa mesure et qu'il n'a eu ne l'un ni l'autre." ("One will understand, thus, that I was not among those good souls who, from the day after the genocide, rushed to demand perfection of the new regime established in Kigali, all the more so since this country had need of a Nuremberg and a Marshall plan in its measure and that it got neither.")

9. Depelchin, "Crisis in the Congo," similarly justifies the RCD's rebellion by reminding his audience of the international community's failure to act in Rwanda and mentioning the "specter of genocide" in Congo.

10. "At the Source of Congo's war—A Shrine of Human Bones," *Mail and Guardian*, 27 August 1999.

11. Mahmood Mamdani, "A Foreign Invasion in Congo Can't Deliver Democracy," *Mail and Guardian*, 30 October 1998.

12. George Dash, "Understanding What Is Happening in the Congo," posting on Rwandanet, August 25, 1998.

13. Filip Reyntjens, "Briefing: the Second Congo War: More Than a Remake," *African Affairs* 98 (1999): 241–250.

14. For a discussion of the diverse origins of Congo's Tutsi and Hutu communities, see Timothy Longman, *Forced to Flee* (New York: Human Rights Watch, July 1996).

15. Cf., United Nations Department of Humanitarian Affairs, "Information Note on the Democratic Republic of the Congo," Nairobi, 26 September 1997.

16. Jean-Claude Willame, *L'Odyssée Kabila: Trajectoire pour un Congo nouveau?* (Paris: Karthala, 1999), 139–159; "Fighting Flares in Eastern Democratic Congo," Deutsche Presse-Agentur, 27 February 1998.

17. The term "Banyamulenge," literally "people from Mulenge," emerged as a label in the 1960s for a group of Kinyarwanda speakers from the South Kivu highlands above Uvira and Fizi who trace their migration to Congo back over a century to the periods of consolidation of rule in Rwanda and Burundi. Since the 1996–97 war, the term has increasingly been used to refer to all Congolese Tutsi.

18. Lara Santoro, "Congo Leader Urges Nazi-Style Tactics against Tutsi," *The Christian Science Monitor*, 2 September 1998; "Foreign Troops in Congo."

19. On the relationship between war and genocide, see Robert Melson, "Revolutionary Genocide: On the Causes of the Armenian Genocide of 1915 and the Holocaust," *Holocaust and Genocide Studies* 4, no. 2 (1989): 161–174.

20. See my report, Timothy Longman, *Eastern Congo Ravaged: Killing Civilians and Silencing Protest*, New York: Human Rights Watch Short Report, vol.12, no. 3 (A) (May 2000): 30.

21. Longman, *Eastern Congo Ravaged*.

22. "Rwandans Admit a 'Major Role' in Helping the Rebels in Congo," Agence France Presse, 11 July 1997.

23. According to the *New York Times*, "Mr. Dusaidi said Rwanda saw the war as a pre-emptive strike, an act of self-preservation. The first goal was to knock out the camps and rout the Hutu forces inside them. The second was to oust Mr. Mobutu, who had harbored them in the first place" (James McKinley, "Rwanda's War Role May Haunt Congolese," *The New York Times*, 12 July 1997.

24. Timothy Longman and Allison DesForges, *Zaire, Attacked by All Sides: Civilians and the War in Eastern Congo*, New York: Human Rights Watch Short Report, vol. 9, no. 1 (A) (March 1997): 13.

25. See ibid. for a discussion of attacks on refugees and other civilians.

26. Ann Simmons, "Rising Violence in Rwanda Stirs Fears of Ethnic War; Officials Insist Rebel Attacks Unconnected," *The Toronto Star*, 15 December 1997; Mseteka Buchizya, "Hutu Rebels Renew Fight in Rwanda, Burundi," *The Toronto Star*, 14 January 1998; Ronald Siegloff, "Murder and Vengeance Stalk Rwanda as War Rages Once More," Deutsche Presse-Agentur, 18 February 1998.

27. African Rights, *Rwanda: The Insurgency in the Northwest* (London: African Rights, September 1998); Stephen Handelman, "The Killing Fields of Africa Are Busy Again," *The Toronto Star*, 15 February 1998; Simmons, "Rising Violence."

28. Filip Reyntjens, *Talking or Fighting? Political Evolution in Rwanda and Burundi, 1998–1999*, Uppsala: Nordiska Afrikainstitutet, 1999, 11; African Rights, *Rwanda*.

29. Cf., Depelchin, "Crisis in the Congo."

30. Ian Fisher, "Rwanda's Huge Stake in Congo's War," *New York Times*, 27 December 1998; Reyntjens, *Talking or Fighting*, 11.

31. The term "Mai-Mai" was adopted by militia groups from a few ethnic groups in North Kivu, particularly Hunde and Nyanga. Other groups were known as Simba and Bangelima. While as late as 1996 local militias used a variety of names, during the 1996–97 war, the term "Mai-Mai" came to be used more generally to refer to non-Rwandan militia groups. Similarly, *Interahamwe*, a term that originally referred to the youth wing of Rwanda's ruling party, has come to refer to any Hutu rebel groups. Congolese Hutu, ex-FAR soldiers, and numerous others are all known as *Interahamwe*.

32. Reyntjens, *Talking or Fighting*, 5.

33. Rony Brauman, Stephen Smith, and Claudine Vidal, "Politique de terreur et privilège d'impunité au Rwanda," *Esprit* (August–September 2000): 147–16.

34. A complaint I heard several times was that one's rank in the RPF was based on length of time within the organization. Since Tutsi in Rwanda were not able to be active members, survivors who have joined the RPF, even many who supported its operations in some way prior to 1994, have been relegated to the lowest ranks. Several people complained to me of a university professor being ranked a private within the RPF despite his public prominence.

35. Human Rights Watch, *The Search for Security*, 4.

36. Ibid., 4–5.

37. Ibid., 5; Brauman, Smith, and Vidal, "Politique de terreur et privilège d'impunité au Rwanda," 151.

38. Interviews in Bukavu and Kavumu, 12–16 March 2000.

39. "Changing Sides in a Land of Terror: Former Rebels Join the Army in Rwanda, a Country Still at War with Itself Six Years after the Genocide Which Killed 800,000," *Manchester Guardian,* 22 November 2000.

40. Howard French, "The Curse of Riches: In Africa, Wealth Often Buys Only Trouble," *The New York Times,* 25 January 1998.

41. Cf., Bjorn Willum, "Civil War Finance by Diamonds and Donors: Struggle for the Treasure Below," *Aktuelt,* 18 January 2001.

42. Gunnar Willum, "Rebel Leader Confirms What Western Donors Deny: Uganda Plunders Congo," *Aktuelt,* 22 January 2001.

43. Interviews in Goma, March 6, 2000, and Mbarara, Uganda, March 3, 2000. Several news reports have since corroborated this finding.

44. Dena Montague and Frida Berrigan, "The Business of War in the Democratic Republic of Congo: Who Benefits?" *Dollars and Sense* (July 2001): 15–19.

45. "Uganda, Rwanda War in Congo Was Avoidable!" Africa News Service, 18 August 1999.

46. Interviews in Bukavu, March 13, 2000.

47. Gerard Prunier, *The Rwanda Crisis: History of a Genocide,* 2nd ed. (New York: Columbia University Press, 1997), provides excellent insight into the RPF. See especially 61–74, 356–389.

48. The Rwandan situation bears resemblance to Israel's relationship with its neighbors, since many Israeli politicians seem to have a sense that only Israel is willing to ensure the survival of the Jewish people, that the experience of the Holocaust gives a moral sanction to the actions of the state, and that no other power can compare to theirs.

49. Willame, *L'Odyssée Kabila,* 39. "Pour Kagame donc, les 'rebelles congolais' ne jouent qu'un rôle d'appoint à un processus mené de bout en bout par le Rwanda."

50. John Pomfret, "Rwandans Led Revolt in Congo," *The Washington Post,* 9 July 1997.

51. "Military and Tutsis in Mutiny against President Kabila," Deutsche Presse-Agentur, 3 August 1998.

52. Willame, *L'Odysée Kabila,* 203–230; Reyntjens, "The Second Congo War," 242–246.

53. On the anti-Tutsi propaganda in the Rwandan genocide, see Allison DesForges, *Leave None to Tell the Story: Genocide in Rwanda* (New York: Human Rights Watch, 1999), 65–95.

54. "Congo Accuses Rwanda of Attacking: Rebels Seize Two Towns Fear Ex-Ally's Border," Reuters, 5 August 1998; Howard French, "Two Sides Prepare to Battle over Congo's Capital," *New York Times,* 17 August 1998; "Kinshasa Is Dark After Rebels Seize Power Transformer; They Claim Victory, Cutting Off Power, Moving toward Capital," *Baltimore Sun,* 14 August 1998.

55. This is based on interviews with Banyamulenge and others in Bukavu in March 2000.

56. Ian Fisher, "Rebels Can't Conquer the Hearts of the Congolese," *New York Times,* 13 August 1999.

57. "Thousands of Angolan Troops Stream into Congo; Luanda Government Confirms Support for President Kabila," Reuters, 25 August 1998.

CHAPTER 9

Museveni's Adventure in the Congo War

UGANDA'S VIETNAM?

JOHN F. CLARK

To analyze foreign policy by way of historical analogy is certainly a method fraught with pitfalls, but one with advantages that are also not inconsiderable. When the historical analogue is well known to an audience, a convenient shorthand for comparison automatically exists. Moreover, when the lessons of history seem clear, the prescriptive power of past episodes can be quite strong and direct. The trick, it would seem, is to acknowledge the differences between analogous cases as well as the similarities. If due care is taken in this regard, the value of a historical analogy can be inestimable.

In this chapter it is argued that Uganda's intervention in the recent Congo war[1] is somewhat analogous to the United States' intervention in Vietnam beginning in the late 1950s. The evocation of this analogy is self-consciously intended to serve as a warning to the government of Uganda and is meant to be prescriptive. The United States entered the Vietnam conflict as a self-confident great power, secure in its purposes and values and economically vibrant; it withdrew, some fifteen years later, weakened, conflicted, self-doubting, and morally and financially diminished. The confidence of national populations crests and falls over the course of decades as public perceptions of governmental legitimacy and national strength rise or decline. The American population experienced a nadir in the national mood and outlook that coincided with the United States' deepest involvement in the Vietnam war. Likewise, Uganda began its involvement in Congo at a moment of national renewal and hope. The circumstances of its withdrawal remain to be seen.

With due regard for the caveat issued above, it is best to turn immediately to the differences between the two situations. First, Uganda shares a direct border with Congo, while Vietnam was thousands of miles away from American shores. This fact means that the stakes for Uganda in the Congo are necessarily greater, though the psychological stakes for U.S. success in Vietnam were hardly negligible. Second, of course, Uganda is a relatively small and weak African state, not a global superpower, though it did emerge as an important subregional actor in the mid-1990s. Third,

Uganda has intervened not only on behalf of a sitting (if illegitimate) government but on behalf of a constellation of rebel forces. In fact, it appears that the Ugandan and Rwandan governments virtually created them.[2] Finally, the ultimate outcome and impact of Uganda's intervention is not yet known. Although the initial net impact has been adverse, the Museveni regime may yet find a way to turn the Congo war to its popular advantage, or at least limit the damage caused by the war.

Nonetheless, the parallels between the two cases are striking. The Ugandan government entered the second Congo war without a full review of the interests involved. It has become incrementally more involved over time, and the stakes of the war for Uganda have increased with each passing month. Moreover, as one analytical report observed, "The Ugandan government would probably like at least partly to disengage from the DRC, but now finds itself too deeply involved to get out easily."[3] The Congo war is a quagmire from which the Museveni government cannot easily withdraw. Herein, too, lies the relevance of the Vietnam analogy, though the closest parallel in the two situations lies in the deleterious effects on the interveners.

This chapter discusses three aspects of Uganda's intervention in the Congo war: its motivations for intervening, its strategies of intervention, and the impact of the intervention. There is much debate about the first and third of these considerations, though little about the second. In general, this chapter argues that Uganda's motivations for intervening have been wrong-headed, its strategies in the intervention ill-conceived, and the outcomes of the intervention negative. Many of the same observations were made of U.S involvement in Vietnam. Finally, like the United States in Vietnam, the Ugandan government maintains a very different perception of the point of the war than those who are fighting it within the target country.

UGANDA'S MOTIVATIONS FOR RE-ENTERING CONGO AND FOR STAYING IN[4]

This section analyzes the debate over Uganda's motivations for participation in the second Congo war of the 1990s, that which began in August 1998. Uganda was of course deeply involved in the 1996--97 war that displaced Mobutu Sese Seko from power in Congo, and it is important to be aware of Uganda's role in the first war.[5] Nonetheless, the origins and motivations for participation in the second war are distinctive and should be analyzed separately.

The outbreak of the more recent Congolese civil war caught many outside observers by surprise. The first sign of the impending crisis for many was the failure of Rwandan vice president Kagame and Museveni in May 1998 to attend the first anniversary of Kabila's seizure of power. Later the same month, Kabila's minister of economy and oil, Pierre Victor Mpoyo, accused "top Ugandan officials" of smuggling timber, gold, and diamonds from the eastern parts of the DRC and accused "some counterparts" of Kabila in the Great Lakes of slandering the Congolese president.[6] The events leading directly to the war began with Laurent Kabila's decision, taken on 14 July 1998, to replace his Rwandan chief of staff, James Kabarebe, with a native Congolese officer. Two weeks later, on 27 July, Kabila announced that all Rwandan soldiers would have to leave the country and return home. The common perception at this time was that Kabila had come to fear a coup d'état against him carried out by Tutsi elements prominent in the Forces Armées Congolaises (Congolese Armed

Forces—FAC). Shortly thereafter, on 2 August, it was revealed that Congolese rebels had taken up arms against the Kabila regime in eastern regions of the country. Kabila immediately charged that his country was under attack by Rwanda and Uganda and that those countries had generated the rebellions.[7] At that moment, Uganda denied that it was involved in the Congo rebellions, and it did not admit the presence of its troops for nearly one month.[8]

Understanding Uganda's recent intervention is largely a matter of understanding the motives of the person, President Yoweri Museveni, who ordered the Ugandan People's Defence Forces (UPDF) into Congo. According to a number of highly placed sources, the decision to intervene was made by the president himself, after consultation with only a few close military advisers. Apparently, neither important civilian advisers nor the Parliament were consulted before the decision was taken.[9] There is little evidence that societal interest groups, bureaucratic constituencies, or even Museveni's own cabinet had much influence on the decision. Unlike in more institutionalized settings, the will of the president himself is indisputably the key to foreign policy decisionmaking in Uganda. However, one can never be completely confident about estimating Museveni's motivations, and even the president himself may not have been certain what they were.

Despite the difficulties of explanation, however, one can meaningfully sort through the various claims about the reasons for Uganda's latest foreign intervention. Two of the explanations circulate widely enough that they cannot be ignored, though they do not deserve sustained attention.[10] The first is that Museveni is seeking to build a Tutsi-Hima empire in the greater Great Lakes region of Africa. This "theory" stems first and foremost from the somewhat parallel relationships between the Hima and Bairu identity groups among the Banyankole people of Uganda and the Tutsi and Hutu groups of the Banyarwanda. The argument is superficially bolstered by the role that the Museveni regime played in helping the (Tutsi-dominated) Rwandan Patriotic Front gain power in Rwanda in 1994.[11] Yet, Museveni's alliance with Rwandan Tutsi in exile was much more a matter of convenience than it was one of primordial ethnic fealty. Moreover, other facts of Museveni's behavior belie this argument. Museveni has not sought to promote Tutsi or Banyamulenge politicians within the movements he sponsors in Congo.[12] Moreover, Museveni's base of support within Uganda is far wider than that of the Hima, or even the Banyankole in general, and it is unlikely that he would jeopardize this support in such a misguided course.

A second conspiracy theory is that Museveni is acting at the behest of Anglo-American interests in the Great Lakes to help realize a grand design of anglicizing the entire region and sidelining French as a language of intraregion communication.[13] Such a theory was evoked in Paris in some circles at the time of the campaign against the Habyarimana regime in Rwanda and the genocidal rump government that followed it.[14] More generally, some French statesmen have been suspicious of the motives of British and American diplomats in the region for many years. Both the evidence and ordinary logic undermine this argument, however. First, the United States has shown its genuine displeasure with Museveni's adventure in Congo by suspending all military aid. Second, the American diplomats worry that the Congo adventure will (a) stimulate political instability inside Uganda and (b) shake Uganda's growing but fragile economy. Since Uganda is currently a showpiece for the proponents of structural adjustment, such developments would undermine the American argument that cooperation with the IFIs can deliver real economic benefits. Finally, no motive of the Anglophone powers in urging Museveni to invade Congo can be demonstrated, and there is no reason to believe that Museveni would do the bidding of the "Anglo-Saxon" West if he were commanded to serve as a proxy.

Four other explanations for Uganda's intervention in the Congo war deserve more serious attention. First, there is the official argument that Uganda intervened in Congo because of severe threats to its security emanating from the border regions; second, there is the argument that Museveni was mainly motivated by ideological considerations; third, there is the argument that Uganda intervened in Congo because of its alliance with Rwanda; and fourth is the view that Uganda is in Congo mainly to reap the economic rewards of occupation. Each of these is considered in turn below.

The first (official) explanation of Uganda's decision to re-enter the Congo was that Kabila's government was not providing security along Uganda's western frontiers. Ugandan officials also added, for rhetorical effect, that its intervention was intended to stop the renewed "genocide" against the Banyamulenge.[15] The charge related to security stemmed from the fact that the Allied Democratic Forces (ADF) rebels based in Congo across the border from the Ugandan districts of Bundibugyo, Kabarole, Kasese, Bushenyi, Rukungiri, and Kisoro had been conducting raids into Ugandan national territory since 1996. These raids had also been cited to justify Uganda's support to the Alliance des Forces Démocratiques pour la libération du Congo-Zaire (Alliance of Democratic Forces for the Liberation of Congo-Zaire— ADFL) rebels who had overthrown Mobutu in 1997. These raids typically involved the theft of local property; the abduction of young men and women, who were forced to act as concubines, porters, or rebels themselves; and random killings, especially of those believed to be involved with the government.[16] Most outraging to Ugandan sensibilities was the ADF raid against the Kichwamba Technical School in Kasese district in June 1998, in which some eighty students were burned alive inside their locked dormitories.[17]

In Uganda's charge that Kabila failed to provide security along the border, it is unclear whether Uganda was accusing him of outright support for the ADF or merely incompetence in failing to prevent it from operating from Congolese territory.[18] Once Uganda had occupied large swathes of Congolese territory, however, it claimed to have found a "smoking gun" demonstrating Kabila's full knowledge and approval of ADF activities along the Ugandan border. Specifically, Ugandan military forces revealed in the local press evidence of a large-scale Sudanese presence in eastern Congo in support of the ADF, a claim accepted by knowledgeable observers.[19] The ADF allegedly received supplies and training from Sudanese officers in eastern Congo, using materials that were flown into the territory by the Sudanese army. Given their military occupation in eastern Congo, such claims cannot be independently verified. When asked what Kabila's motive was in allowing parts of his territory to be controlled by a foreign power, Ugandan officials aver that Kabila was desperate for allies from any quarter who would help him strengthen his own chaotic army.[20]

That Ugandan authorities, including President Museveni, were and are concerned about infiltrations along Uganda's western border is beyond argument. In pursuing ADF rebels on both sides of the Uganda-Congo frontier, the National Resistance Movement (NRM) government also responded to the genuine outrage of the Ugandan people, particularly those living in the western districts. Yet the nature of Uganda's intervention suggests that pursuit of the NRM was not President Museveni's main goal. As noted by Prunier, the fact that the UPDF is deployed "more than 1,000 kilometers from [the Congo-Uganda] frontier" is *prima facie* evidence that Museveni and his government have other goals.[21]

Indeed, in its support of the rebellion of Jean-Pierre Bemba's Mouvement pour la Libération du Congo (MLC), the UPDF is deployed far to the west of Kisangani in the Équateur region. Meanwhile, the ADF vigorously continues its activities along Uganda's border. For instance, on 10 December 1999 the ADF invaded the major town of Fort Portal, took over a prison, and abducted a large number of prisoners. The numerical strength of the UPDF in the area was insufficient for an immediate response, much to the consternation of local residents.[22] Another problem with the official explanation of Uganda's intervention in the DRC was that the UPDF was already allowed in Congolese territory under the terms of DRC-Uganda security agreements. According to the Ugandans, a "Memorandum of Understanding" signed between the DRC and Uganda shortly after Kabila's rise to power provided for joint operations of the UPDF and the FAC.[23] The UPDF could certainly have crossed the Congo-Uganda frontier in pursuit of rebels under the terms of this agreement without engaging in all-out war against Kabila.

Ugandan authorities respond to such arguments by contending that the only way to achieve real security along the border is to get to the root of the problem, that is, to remove from power the regime installed in May 1997.[24] Yet to believe that the removal of this regime would improve the security situation along Uganda's border with Congo, one would have to make two assumptions: first, that its successor regime would be friendly enough toward Uganda that it would desire to safeguard Uganda's security and, second, that it would have the capacity to do so. But such assumptions are unjustified. It is doubtful that any successor to the regime of the Kabilas would be able to exercise effective control over the country's eastern reaches. Necessarily, any new leader of Congo will worry about his own security in power and about the political sensibilities of the politically relevant Congolese public. This constituency can hardly tolerate the perception that the strings of leadership in Kinshasa are being pulled from Kampala or Kigali. Moreover, it is doubtful in the extreme that the current leaders of the NRM government, especially the savvy Museveni, could have suffered from such illusory assumptions. If Museveni was primarily concerned about the threat of crossborder attacks by the ADF, he would certainly have deployed his army immediately across the border.

The second (ideology) argument begins with the fact that many Ugandans of all classes perceive President Museveni to be a virtual savior of the country, a "founding legislator" à la Rousseau. Museveni's long struggle in the bush between 1981 and 1986, which led to his seizure of power in Kampala, is now legend in Uganda, having been lovingly documented by the president himself.[25] During the struggle, Museveni repeatedly demonstrated personal courage, self-sacrifice, and steely determination. More importantly, Museveni sought to sway people to his cause with a doctrine of national unity and local autonomy. As Prunier has put it, Museveni has long been a "revolutionary," and a "nationalist reformer," for whom "certain essential ideals" guide his action.[26] Despite the improprieties present in every election campaign of the NRM since 1986,[27] there is little doubt that Museveni and the movement would prevail in genuinely free and fair elections.

Another part of this argument depends on the view that Museveni has sought to spread this ideology beyond Uganda. In the mid-1990s, Museveni was characterized by some authors as the first of a "new breed" of African leaders devoted to fair governance and efficient state-building.[28] Museveni's aid to the Rwandan Patriotic Front (RPF) in 1990 and after, and the subsequent rise to power of Paul Kagame in Rwanda, provided *prima facie* evidence that Museveni was seeking to spread his ideology to neighboring states. In explaining Museveni's support for the rebels in the 1996--97 Congo war, Prunier insists that the Mobutu regime was virtually the "systematic opposite" of everything for which Museveni stands. Similarly, Prunier suggests, Museveni has sought the ouster of the Kabila regime for essentially the same reason: because its rule has relied so much on political oppression, corruption, and patronage and has accomplished so little in terms of national development in the process.[29]

There are quite a number of problems, however, with putting Museveni's ideology at the center of an explanation for Uganda's involvement in Congo, as Prunier does. First, the "ideology" of the Museveni regime is difficult to discern in the assemblage of the rhetoric and actions of the regime. Museveni claims to stand for national unity, "democracy," self-reliance, development, and intra-African cooperation and against corruption, tribalism, and dictatorship, but such platitudes hardly constitute a political program. Museveni initially presented himself as a Marxist while he was in the bush but quickly abandoned such "convictions" and warmly embraced the neoliberal strategies of the World Bank and IMF (the international financial institutions, or IFIs) upon assuming power.[30]

In practice, Museveni has famously rejected multipartyism as being inappropriate for Africa's fragmented polities and constructed a no-party "movement" system of government, which effectively functions like a one-party state.[31] While the Museveni regime may have performed much better than the rather dismal African average, its props are not so different from many other African regimes. At the center of power in Uganda one finds a very high concentration of Banyankole and a fair number of the family members of both President Museveni and his wife, Janet.[32] Generous patronage is paid out to supporters of the regime, particularly prominent multipartyists who "defect" to the movement. One observes a casual attitude toward the rule of law, as in Museveni's dispatch of the UPDF to Congo without an enabling law from the Parliament, as specified in the constitution.[33]

Second, if ideology is Museveni's main motive for external action, one may ask why he did not move against Mobutu at some earlier point. In fact, Museveni avoided confrontation with Mobutu, and found a *modus vivendi* with him between 1986 and 1996. It was not until Rwanda's Kagame engaged him in direct confrontation in 1996 that Museveni joined the fray. Moreover, the regime of Daniel arap Moi in Kenya is only marginally less corrupt, repressive, and arbitrary than that of Mobutu, and yet Museveni manages to get on quite well with President Moi. If Museveni is in fact a "revolutionary," he is generally cautious about attempting to stimulate parallel "revolutions" abroad.

Third, if President Museveni was originally motivated by ideology to overthrow Mobutu in Zaire, it seems that he would have insisted on putting someone more competent and national-minded in power than Laurent Kabila. Ugandan officials have protested that the Uganda government did not try to select Congo's leaders for them, that they only were supporting an indigenously generated revolutionary movement in 1996--97.[34] This may or may not be the case. Nonetheless, the fact that Museveni collaborated with Rwanda to help Laurent Kabila achieve power in Kinshasa contradicts the ideology thesis. It was widely appreciated in the Great Lakes region in 1996 that Laurent Kabila had a long history as a local warlord who relied primarily on violence, intimidation, and illegal mineral extraction.[35] Certainly, senior Ugandan officials must have been aware of Kabila's miserable prerulership record in 1996. There was no evidence to suggest that Kabila was destined to be an effective, principled, or statesmanlike leader at that time.

One arrives at the most plausible explanation for Uganda's participation in the Congo war by putting the Rwanda-Uganda alliance at the center of the argument. Specifically, a number of developments inside Congo and between Congo and Rwanda had put the regime of Paul Kagame at risk by late 1998. In turn, Museveni could not afford to see the Kagame regime fall from power at that time without suffering major security problems of its own.

To understand Museveni's dilemma in August 1998, then, one must start with the evolution of relations between his ally, Kagame, and Laurent Kabila in the previous year. Paul Kagame and the largely Tutsi leadership of the RPF regime in Kigali had good reasons for coming to fear Kabila during this time.[36] Naturally, Museveni would have been fully aware of the concerns of the Rwandan leadership about Kabila's leadership. According to Prunier, "Although it is very difficult to know what actually passed at that moment between Kigali and Kampala, it is probable that in the spring of 1998 Major General Kagame managed to convince his Ugandan ally of the impossibility of treating with Kabila and of the necessity of overthrowing him. It [only] remains to know how and when."[37]

In keeping with his preferred strategy, Kagame mounted his now-famous effort to seize Kinshasa in August 1998 by airlifting troops to Kitona airbase in Bas-Congo. These forces very nearly took Kinshasa and overthrew Kabila at the very start of the war, and would have done so if not for the intervention of Angola and Zimbabwe on Kabila's behalf. Rwanda's army was prominent in this invasion from the beginning, and it only later became evident that the UPDF was, as well. According to a prominent Ugandan journalist, the Ugandan leadership was not initially aware of Rwanda's plan, but once belatedly made aware of it, Museveni decided to provide some troops.[38] Kagame's plan might well have succeeded were it not for the unexpected intervention of Zimbabwe, and then Angola, on Kabila's behalf. By the end of August, however, Kagame's gamble had failed.

After Kagame failed to remove Kabila in his initial gambit, the Rwandan leader's regime was left in a highly vulnerable position. First, one should recall that the postgenocide Tutsi population inside of Rwanda, even with the impressive in-flow of Tutsi from neighboring countries since 1994, numbers only a few hundred thousand. In turn, the contemporary RPF relies overwhelmingly on Tutsi officers and troops, and thus the demographic basis for the RPF is quite small. Second, as of late August 1998, the RPF faced an impressive array of enemies: internal opponents, the Angolan and Zimbabwean expeditionary forces in Congo, the FAC itself, and the rump of Habyarimana's Forces Armées Rwandaises (Rwandan Armed Forces—FAR) and the *Interahamwe,* who had escaped into Congo in 1994.[39] Third, a large part of the Rwandan Patriotic Army's (RPA) strength in 1998 owed to the continual training and equipping of the army by sympathetic outside forces, notably the United States military.[40] This support was soon to be officially withdrawn when it was realized in Washington that Rwanda had engaged in a risky effort to overthrow a regime that Rwanda itself was largely responsible for installing in power. In short, in August 1998 it appeared very much as though Kagame had probably bitten off more than he could chew.

Museveni, however, could not afford to see his ally fall from power with equanimity. The Museveni regime itself faced certain vulnerabilities associated with rebels operating from across international frontiers. If it also faced a hostile regime in the south, which any successor regime to Kagame would likely be, then it would be rendered even more vulnerable. Moreover, Museveni would naturally be loath to suffer the *political* blow to his prestige that would accompany Kagame's fall from power. Finally, if Kagame were to fall from power, Museveni would likely face yet another influx of Tutsi refugees from Rwanda. As a result of such considerations, it is logical that Museveni would have continued to support Kagame, a man with whom he also had a personal bond of friendship and a history of cooperation. Thus, though Rwanda almost certainly initiated the war against Kabila for its own ends, Museveni felt obligated to support the effort for political and personal reasons.

Another set of putative motives for Uganda's second intervention in the DRC has to do with the exploitation of the country's material resources. The fact that the volume of highly valuable commodities now flowing out of Congo via Uganda has increased dramatically since late 1996 is quite beyond dispute, but the meaning of this fact hardly speaks for itself. Rather, Uganda's involvement in the market for Congo's natural resources only raises specific questions about the relationship between the original motivation for Uganda's intervention and the UPDF's continuing presence in Congo, about Uganda's ultimate purposes in Congo, and about the extent to which President Museveni is truly in control of the Ugandan national army.

There are three distinguishable arguments about Uganda's economic motives in Congo, but only two are relevant to the initial intervention. The first is that officials of the Ugandan government purposively planned and executed Uganda's invasion in order to further the economic interests of the state. As argued by William Reno, the invasion and occupation of eastern Congo could plausibly be part of a longterm, rational process of state-building.[41] Other theorists, seeking primarily to explain wars in the peripheral areas of the world, have also attributed such wars to the state-building process.[42] This theoretical approach would suggest that Museveni went into Congo with the idea of building up the national treasury.

Indeed, some empirical evidence also seems to support this idea. The extraction and export of Congolese natural resources, including timber, coffee, gold, diamonds, and other commodities, via Uganda has in some regards had a salutary effect on Uganda's national economy. Specifically, the revenues from such trade may have helped to ease the burden of Uganda's growing current accounts deficits. In 1997, for instance, gold and gold compounds were Uganda's second largest source of export earnings, after coffee, amounting to some U.S.$81 million, or 12 percent of all export revenues.[43] This is remarkable since Uganda produces extremely little gold domestically. Ugandan businessmen have also been able to increase the quantity of manufactures that they sell in Congo since the beginning of 1997. Ugandan trucks loaded with such products as soap, metal roof sheeting, plastic goods, and canned foods now ply the roads to Congo bearing the fruits of Ugandan light industry to be traded for local goods.

A closely related argument emphasizes Museveni's desire to integrate Uganda economically with the other states of east and central Africa. Museveni's enthusiasm for East African Cooperation,[44] including the integration treaty signed in late 1999, is apparent. Despite the challenge that Uganda's nascent industries will experience in the face of Kenyan competition, Museveni genuinely believes that integration serves Uganda's economic interests. Thus, the prominent Ugandan journalist Charles Onyango-Obbo averred that the unforgivable sin that Kabila committed against Museveni was making the decision to take Congo into the Southern African Development Community (SADC) regional trade bloc in early 1998.[45] According to Onyango-Obbo, this decision put Congo in the position of serving South African, rather than Ugandan and Kenyan, economic needs.

There are two major problems with this argument. First, it is far from clear from the evidence that Uganda is experiencing a net economic gain from its involvement in the DRC. There are considerable costs, as well as benefits, associated with Uganda's intervention in Congo. These are considered in more detail in the final section of this chapter. Second, it is highly problematic that Uganda's profits from Congo will increase because of the war. Despite the reality of much theft by rogue elements of the UPDF, the main economic gains of Uganda in Congo are achieved through quasilegitimate business. In other words, most of the Ugandan officers engaged in commerce in Congo are trading products for the commodities that they are receiving. Thus, the question is whether Uganda as a state would profit more from peacetime commerce with Congo or through war-induced economic disarray. The fact that Ugandan gold exports plummeted to only U.S.$19 million in 1998 from four times that level the previous year suggests that war may not, after all, be good for business or for Uganda's trade figures.[46] As for satisfying the IFIs with a positive economic performance generated by Congolese loot, they are now highly perturbed with the Ugandan government for damaging its national budget through increased military spending.

A second economic argument about Uganda's intervention in DRC is that Museveni ordered his army into Congo so that they could plunder for their own, personal benefit. Perhaps the most common (and accurate) observation about the practice of African politics is that rulers patronize their key supporters to gain support for their regimes. This argument shares with the previous one the assumption that the UPDF is acting with the blessing of President Museveni, but it suggests that the UPDF is actually engaged in criminal activity that does not benefit the Ugandan state or people at large. One illuminating analysis of the UPDF has described the army's officers as being "entrepreneurs of insecurity" who acquire gains from conflict both within Uganda and outside, in Congo.[47] The means of achieving such gains are variable. At the petty level, soldiers in Uganda's troubled regions often conspire with local rebels to steal money and property from local residents. On a grander scale, senior officers, most notoriously the president's own brother, Salim Saleh, profit by selling (often defective) arms to the government at inflated prices. Other senior officers are well known for stealing the pay of ordinary soldiers, who are often victims themselves of their own venal commanders.[48] This argument suggests that the loyalty of Museveni's key military supporters is rewarded and reinforced by the free hand that Museveni gives them to plunder.

This argument, however, is contradicted by some evidence that the UPDF was not initially enthusiastic about the war. According to the International Crisis Group, one senior Ugandan military official told them that Museveni actually had to convince a reluctant high command to go along with the invasion. They quote the officer as saying, "We felt that the Rwandese started the war and it was their duty to go ahead and finish the job, but our President took time and convinced us that we had a stake in what is going on in Congo."[49] This statement suggests that while certain Ugandan officers may be engaged in profitable business in Congo now, such opportunities were not necessarily on their minds in August 1998. Instead, they may have been considering their own lives, those of their men, and the damage to the UPDF's prestige that it would suffer in losing a war.

A third economic argument is that the officers of the UPDF only became interested in the economic potential of occupying Congo after their re-entry into the country in late 1998. This argument acknowledges that the UPDF is engaged in plunder as well as legitimate business in Congo but perceives the Ugandan army to be now only loosely under the control of its own commander. If this is the case, then President Museveni himself may not encourage or condone the commercial and criminal activities of the UPDF. This plausible scenario need not suppose, however, that President Museveni intended his troops to engage in such activities when he originally ordered them into Congo. Rather, officers of the UPDF likely began engaging in them spontaneously once they had begun their duties of occupation.

That Museveni could be unaware of the well-documented illegal business activities of his own brother, Salim Saleh, is beyond imagination. The only question is whether President Museveni encourages such activities or only tolerates them. It may even be the case that President Museveni "negotiates with," rather than commands his army in some instances, as some evidence suggests.[50] If this is the case, Museveni may not be able to extract his own forces from Congo now even if he wishes to do so. Certainly, commanders who are deeply engaged in profitable businesses would be loath to leave Congo, despite the evident military failure of the army to displace Kabila. Were President Museveni to order a withdrawal from Congo against the will of his commanders, he might well be inviting coup against himself.

This view would also explain the clashes between the UPDF and the RPA in Kisangani in August 1999 and again in March and April 2000. In neither case did Museveni or Kagame seem to have ordered their commanders to attack the forces of their ally.[51] Indeed, there is no reasonable security issue that could have led to the clashes between the RPA and UPDF in Kisangani. Rather, most of the media have concluded that the first clashes were generated by the rivalry over access to resources of commanders in the two armies, and the second by the desire for revenge by UPDF commanders, whose forces suffered far more in the first round of fighting. Such a conclusion is more logical than the notion that the UPDF and RPA went to battle with one another "due to persistent and serious differences over the objectives and strategies of the war in Congo."[52]

To return briefly to the Vietnam analogy, Uganda's motives, like the United States in Vietnam, are not altogether clear. Uganda does not seem to have re-entered for ideological reasons, as the United States did, but nor do its motivations seem to have much to do with national interest. If any states had an interest in seeing the Vietnamese revolution and reunification fail in the 1960s, it was other states in southeast Asia, not the United States. Likewise, in the second Congo war, it is Rwanda that has a direct interest in the outcome of the Congo war, and not Uganda. Another similarity in the two situations is that Uganda now finds it difficult to withdraw from the "quagmire" in which it finds itself.

UGANDA'S STRATEGIES IN THE CONGO WAR

In accord with the lack of coherence in Uganda's Congo policies, it is far better to speak of the country's "strategies" than its "strategy." Moreover, one's analysis of

Uganda's strategies depends directly on what one perceives to be the country's main goals in Congo. And, as we saw just above, its goals in the Congo war are far from clear and obvious. Accordingly, in this section, I analyze Uganda's goals in Congo with due regard to the range of its foreign policy goals in general, the fact that it had both minimal and maximal goals there, the fact that its goals changed over time, and the fact that different actors within Uganda may had specific goals different from those of the state in general.[53]

Uganda's evolving strategies in the Congo war must, first and foremost, be seen in the context of its broader foreign policy exigencies. The root purpose of Uganda's foreign policy, like that of other African states, is to keep its ruler in power over the medium term.[54] In this regard, Uganda's foreign policy can only be seen as an adjunct of Museveni's domestic goals, which serve the Museveni regime's fundamental goal most directly. While a variety of domestic strategies might have been pursued to stay in power, Museveni has chosen a relatively positive one that relies on economic growth and building state capacity, as well as suppression of the opposition under the cover of his "no-party" ideology.[55] The foreign policy component of this domestic strategy requires, above all, for Uganda to remain in the good graces of the IFIs and the Western donors. As a result, the Museveni regime, having staked its legitimacy on the delivery of economic growth to the population, is more dependent on the IFIs—and specifically the good will of the United States—than other African countries facing far more severe economic circumstances. Hence, a "negative goal" of Uganda in the Congo war has also been not to alienate itself from its main Western backers.

Fortuitously for Museveni, the regime of Laurent Kabila had fallen out of favor with the West in general and the United States in particular by the time of the August 1998 Rwanda-Uganda invasion of Congo. Kabila had of course come to power with the backing of Rwanda and Uganda as well as, indirectly, the United States and most other states in Africa and Europe. At the moment of Kabila's installation in power in Kinshasa in May 1997, only France seemed to be troubled by the turn of events. Yet Kabila had fallen out of favor with most of the international community by the end of his first year in power. Kabila's most important failings included his refusal to cooperate with the UN mission sent to investigate the massacre of Rwandan Hutu civilians during the liberation war and his utter failure to begin the arduous process of rebuilding the Congolese state and economy. His rule was nearly as kleptocratic as that of Mobutu, and with even less flair. Nor was he able to justify his dictatorship in terms of post-genocide guilt (as could Rwanda) or in terms of an illusory ideology of politico-economic development (as could Uganda). Accordingly, Museveni's need to keep the favor of the key Western donors did not prevent him for ordering the UPDF into Congo in 1998.

When the second Congo war began in August 1998, Uganda initially backed Rwanda in that country's risky gamble to overthrow Kabila by airlifting troops to Bas-Congo. Although Ugandan troops were not part of this effort, Museveni apparently knew of the move and did nothing to dissuade his ally from taking the risk. There was certainly no public denunciation of the move from Uganda, which was already secretly sending troops into eastern Congo.

Once Rwanda was defeated, thanks largely to the intervention of Zimbabwe and Angola, a high-profile disagreement between Rwanda and Uganda on the appropriate means for displacing Kabila from power soon emerged. It seems that each of the two allied rulers sought to replicate his own experience in coming to power in the Congo war to remove Kabila: Kagame wanted to send a professional, foreign-based army (with little popular support) to seize control of the capital, while Museveni wanted to assist disgruntled local segments of the population to engage in a slowly building rebellion against their own ruler. Some analysts even argued that this disagreement was a major reason why Uganda and Rwanda originally clashed in Kisangani in August 1999.[56]

The military aspect of Uganda's policy in Congo has been to recruit, train, and arm soldiers to fight in the two rebel groups that it supports [the Rassemblement Congolaise pour la Démocratie-Bunia (RCD-Bunia) and the Mouvement pour la Liberation du Congo (MLC) of Jean-Pierre Bemba].[57] Given Museveni's contention that the success of the Congo war ultimately depends on the initiative of local leaders and the political support that they can garner among ordinary Congolese citizens (as Museveni himself did between 1980 and 1986), this strategy accords well with his ideology and own experience. Uganda has generally deployed fewer of its own national troops into Congo than has Rwanda, and has tried harder to build up and train local forces. According to an April 2001 Security Council report, Uganda only had about 10,000 soldiers in Congo, compared to some 25,000 for Rwanda.[58]

One can discern an evolution in Uganda's strategies of support for the two rebel groups in Congo due to changing events. As long as the RCD was united and the Uganda-Rwanda alliance intact, Uganda focused its efforts on building up the RCD, headed by Wamba dia Wamba. The split of the RCD into a Goma faction headed by Emile Illunga and a Kisangani (now Bunia) faction headed by Uganda signaled the divergence of the two former allies, leading up to their first clash in Kisangani in August of 1999. Although Museveni initially favored Wamba as a like-minded ideological thinker, he finally came to recognize that Wamba lacked a strong domestic following in Congo, particularly in Orientale and North Kivu, and that his military organizational skills were limited. According to one source, the RCD-Bunia had only 2,500 troops after the split, while the RCD-Goma had 17,000 to 20,000.[59] Understanding Wamba's limitations as a guerilla leader, the Ugandan leadership, upon its entry into the Équateur region in late 1998, selected Jean-Pierre Bemba to lead a new rebel movement in that region. Bemba had a number of advantages over Wamba, including his local popularity, the wealth and connections of an established local businessman, and the organizational skills needed to train and equip a capable rebel force. Bemba's fighting force had grown from a mere 158 in December 1998 to between 6,500 and 9,000 in late 2000.[60] Due to his growing reputation for getting results, Uganda selected him to head the umbrella organization (the Front de Libération du Congo—FLC) that linked two factions of the RCD-Bunia and the MLC in early 2001. To some extent the military successes of the MLC in 2000 may have even revived Museveni's hopes for a rebel military victory in Congo.

Like Rwanda, Uganda also has employed strategies in the Congo that have to do with the nonstate, private goals of the main military officers, as well as with state-level goals. These strategies involved the extraction of economic wealth from Congo, and they served the purposes both of enriching individual UPDF officers and important civilian supporters of President Museveni, and of furnishing off-budget funding for Uganda's continuing occupation of northeastern Congo. Off-budget support for Ugandan military activities is particularly important because World Bank guidelines specify that Uganda should spend no more than 2 percent of its

GDP on its military and security efforts. According to many sources, including the UN Security Council report, Uganda has only been able to meet this goal by using off-budget funds to pay for military services in Congo.

According to the same Security Council report, the extraction of resource wealth from Congo by Uganda has preceded in two stages. In the first stage, between September 1998 and August 1999, the UPDF simply looted existed stockpiles of minerals, livestock, and agricultural and forest products. The report specifically charges that the overall Ugandan commander at the time, General James Kazini, looted timber from the Amex-bois company located in Bagboka in August 1998, and timber of another company, La Forestière, the following December.[61] In January 1999, Kazini reportedly conspired with MLC leader Bemba to seize some 200 tons of coffee beans from the SCIBE company in the Équateur region.[62] Similarly looted of their stocks during the same period were banks, mines, and factories. During the second, or "extraction" phase of Uganda's exploitation, UPDF commanders allegedly took over business concerns or organized their own companies to further exploit Congo's natural resources. For instance, a Ugandan-Thai company called DARA-Forest began harvesting timber and running a sawmill in Orientale Province in late 1998, with the active connivance of occupying Ugandan forces.[63] Meanwhile, President Museveni's brother, Salim Saleh, and Saleh's wife, Jovia Akandwanaho, took charge of the exploitation of diamonds in the portion of Congo controlled by Uganda. This couple also set up a private air transport company, Air Alexander, to transport both official supplies and commercial goods into Congo and illicit natural resources out.[64] Even Museveni's erstwhile protégé in Orientale, Wamba dia Wamba, recently condemned the UPDF for its plundering of Congo's natural resources.[65]

To complement its strategies of occupation, extraction, and local force-building, Uganda undertook a diplomatic strategy to help realize a range of goals in Congo. As noted by one astute Ugandan observer, Phillip Kasaija, "The Museveni government has been eager to sign [a variety of diplomatic] agreements, as it has become increasingly clear that the conflict cannot be won militarily. It has been the thinking of Kampala that it can achieve its national interest through diplomacy, which it had first thought it could achieve by military means."[66] Indeed, the Lusaka Agreement of July 1999 contains a clause that called upon the regime of Laurent Kabila to engage in a process of political consultation and reconciliation with opposition forces. Had Kabila taken this pledge seriously, it might well have meant the end of his regime in 1999 or 2000. Kasaija reminds us that diplomatic activity over the Congo war began almost simultaneously with the onset of the war itself. Before the Lusaka process got underway, there were a serious of meetings at Victoria Falls (Zimbabwe), Pretoria, Addis Ababa, and Grande Baie (Mauritius). After the Lusaka process had begun, parallel negotiations took place at other venues, under the auspices of the UN, the Organization of African Unity (OAU), and the French government.[67] The most important achievement of these pre-Lusaka negotiations was the Sirte Agreement, brokered by Murammar Gaddafi and signed by Kabila and Museveni, among others, in April 1999. Like the Lusaka Agreement that soon followed, this agreement called for a ceasefire, the placement of African peacekeeping troops in Congo, and the gradual withdrawal of all foreign forces. It also "encouraged" the DRC to initiate a national dialogue to resolve the internal political stand off. This agreement failed to become the basis for peace, however, when it was rejected by Rwanda, which had not participated in the negotiations.

Instead, the Lusaka Agreement, signed in July 1999, has become the basis for continued diplomatic efforts to resolve the DRC conflict. Like the Sirte Agreement, these accords acknowledged the security interests of Rwanda and Uganda in Congo and linked their withdrawal to the introduction of peacekeepers into the country and to the launching of a national dialogue. As Kasaija notes, "For Uganda, the accord legitimized the Uganda army's presence in the DRC. The parties to the agreement, Kabila inclusive, acknowledged the legitimate interests of Uganda in the DRC."[68] The legitimization of the UPDF in the DRC in Congo, in turn, served two larger purposes for Uganda. First, it gave a perfect cover for the looting activities of Ugandan military officers and Museveni's political cronies and family members in eastern Congo. Second, it diverted attention from the fact that the international community would normally view Uganda's invasion and occupation of parts of a neighboring country as a blatant violation of international law. Since Kabila agreed to a process of political dialogue that he never implemented, Uganda could justify its continued presence on grounds of nonfulfillment of the Lusaka Agreement. Accordingly, Uganda did not lose favor with its main Western allies or with the multilateral lending agencies.

Since Laurent Kabila's assassination in January 2001, Uganda's diplomatic strategy has been rendered more difficult. World opinion clearly shifted against Uganda and Rwanda and in favor of Joseph Kabila, who has shown signs of taking the Lusaka Agreement more seriously. Another major blow was the release in April 2001 of the UN Security Council report, which roundly condemns the economic activities of Rwanda and Uganda in Congo. Museveni's initial reaction was deny the UN allegations and announce both a withdrawal of troops from Congo and from the Lusaka diplomatic process. Whether or not Museveni makes good on the latter pledge remains to be seen, but actions have not followed his words to date.

Uganda's evolving strategies in the Congo war have traced its own evolving goals and the exigencies of events themselves. Given that the private goals of Museveni's cronies in Congo have come to overshadow his original purposes for intervention, the Museveni regime has increasingly sought to justify its presence in Eastern Congo while making fewer efforts to resolve the conflict or even win the war. Like the Johnson administration in the Vietnam War, the Museveni regime entered the war without a clear set of goals and strategies. It has supported a very weak ally that would not even exist were it not for Ugandan intervention. It entered the war with multiple and unclear goals, and its strategy has wavered in the face of events on the ground. Also like the U.S. involvement in Vietnam, domestic support for Museveni in the Congo war has been tepid at best. While the urban population has generally opposed it, rural constituencies have paid it less attention. Finally, Uganda's strategies in Congo do not accord well at all with its most important putative goal there. Uganda has deployed its troops deep into Congolese territory, rather than along the western frontier, where the ADF operates. As a result, relatively few Ugandans accept or understand their government's justifications for its involvement in Congo.

THE OUTCOMES OF UGANDA'S INTERVENTION IN CONGO

The overall outcomes of Uganda's participation in Congo cannot yet be determined since the intervention is ongoing, but the results seem to be mixed so far. In fact, the net effect of the war on Uganda's politics, economy, and society will never be determined with scientific certainty. For those interested in the issue, this will likely remain a matter of debate for years to come. At this point, only a very tentative assessment may be attempted.

One key area for debate will be the net effect of the Congo war on Uganda's economy. From the late 1980s through the mid-1990s, President Museveni had compiled an impressive record of economic achievement for his country. Using 1987 as a base year, Uganda's manufacturing index increased over five-fold in the period leading up to 1998.[69] Economic growth per annum averaged over 8 percent for the five years between 1994 and 1998, while consumer price increases did not exceed 10 percent per annum any year during the second half of the 1990s.[70] Some analysts have implied that the Congo war can be a source of continuing economic prosperity for Uganda. Indeed, there is no question that Uganda has plundered millions of dollars worth of natural resources from Congo, as revealed in the recent Security Council report. As noted above, Reno suggests that Ugandan plundering in Congo could be part of a strategy of state-building on the part of President Museveni.[71] In addition to building loyalty among a base of supporters in the military, the re-export of gold and diamonds, he argues, could help Uganda's balance of payments and keep Uganda in good standing with the IFIs.

While the final judgment cannot be made on this score, the preliminary evidence does not suggest that the war has generated an economic boom for Uganda. Reno noted that Uganda's gold exports, which are all in fact re-exports of Congolese gold, jumped to a value of U.S.$81 million in 1997, a year in which the UPDF spent much of its time in Congo. In 1998, during which the UPDF was occupying eastern Congo for five months, Ugandan gold exports were a mere U.S.$19 million.[72] This figure suggests that the rewards of looting in the Congo are likely to be fleeting. Moreover, Uganda's overall exports declined steadily from a peak of U.S.$639 million in 1996 through 1999, reaching a low of U.S.$463 million in the latter year.[73] Meanwhile, Uganda's current account deficit rose every year in the 1996 to 1999 period from U.S.-$252 million in 1996 to U.S.-$477 million in 1999.[74] Meanwhile, GDP growth cooled from 7.4 percent in the 1998--99 fiscal year to only 5.0 percent in the subsequent fiscal year, with growth predicted to be only about 6.0 percent in the 2000--01 year as of March 2001.[75] Although these results look impressive by the African standard, they represent a cooling rather than an acceleration in the Ugandan economy vis à vis the first half of the 1990s.

The most direct economic loss for Uganda is represented by increased defense costs. The overall defense budget for Uganda increased by some 91 billion Ug. shillings (to 209 billion Ug. shillings), or 89 percent, for the fiscal year ending 30 June 1999.[76] According to the IMF, military spending jumped from 14.8 percent of the overall budget to 19.8 percent between the two fiscal years.[77] In the 1999--2000 year, the military budget remained at a high level of 190 billion Ug. shillings.[78] The official Ugandan Ministry of Finance figures do not include significant off-budget expenditures of the UPDF, which many knowledgeable Ugandans, as well as UN Security Council officials, assume to exist.[79]

A number of very significant secondary economic costs have also accrued to Uganda due to its Congo war. These include the loss of productivity of soldiers serving abroad, increases in health costs for the longterm disabled, and the loss of revenues in Uganda's troubled regions due to increasing insecurity there. These losses will work their way imperceptibly through the Ugandan economy over the coming years.

The political consequences of the Congo war for the Museveni regime are even more difficult to estimate. While there has been strong criticism of Museveni's unilateral dispatch of the UPDF into Congo in the urban areas, rural opinion is much harder to judge. In general, however, one can easily observe an overall loss of public support for the Museveni regime in the results of recent election results. Museveni won approximately 74 percent of the vote in the 1996 elections, for which the turnout was 73 percent; hence, a strong 54 percent of the eligible voters endorsed Museveni in these elections. Museveni lost in only six of Uganda's forty-five districts, all of them in the north of the country. In the 2001 elections, Museveni's winning percentage declined to 69 percent in the recent elections with only 57 percent turnout of the voting population. Accordingly, Museveni gained the support of only 39 percent of the eligible voters in the recent poll. In the 2001 elections, Museveni lost nine districts, including the urban Kampala and Mukono districts in the south. Moreover, the amount of government fraud and coercion increased dramatically in the 2001 poll, though government intimidation was also salient in the 1996 vote. In the preparations for the 2001 elections, some 11.6 million citizens were registered to vote, although the Uganda Bureau of Statistics has estimated that only some 8.9 million citizens should be of voting age.[80] The 2001 campaign itself was marked by blatant government intimidation of opposition candidate Kizza Besigye and the other candidates.[81] Under Museveni's "no-party" system, opposition political parties are not allowed to organize, open offices, recruit members, or openly campaign for opposition candidates. Accordingly, the real decline in Museveni's popularity is difficult to measure, though apparent.

The regional erosion of support for Museveni inside Uganda is even more evident. Even before the outbreak of the Congo wars, the NRM government had failed to capture the imagination or win the support of large swathes of the population in the northern sections of the country. Notably, the northern Acholi, who once supported Obote during his two stints in power, have remained unreconciled to Museveni's rule. The inability of the NRM government and the UPDF to defeat the rebellion of the Lord's Resistance Army (LRA) in the north, active since the late 1980s, has left a significant portion of the population embittered toward the NRM regime.[82] This bitterness is increased by the abuses of the UPDF against the local population in the area. Since the outbreak of the Congo wars, moreover, UPDF forces have been relocated from northern Uganda to Congo, leaving the northern areas more open than ever to the predations of the LRA. As a result, Museveni's support has particularly eroded in these areas.

Since 1996, the NRM government has faced a new threat in the west, the rebellion of the ADF. In this region, too, frustration is growing among the civilian population due to the government's inability to staunch a destructive rebellion with little popular support. Ironically, though this rebellion has served as Uganda's main pretext for its Congo interventions, the ADF remains active in the area. It has repeatedly eluded the Ugandan army, which operates deep inside Congo. Since Museveni stakes his legitimacy largely on having re-established public order in the country, the insecurity in the north and west present a major challenge to his regime.

As the Museveni regime has gradually lost support, it has had to turn increasingly to repression to divert challenges to its legitimacy. Recently, Western human rights organizations have begun to emphasize the extent to which the state's repressive apparatus stifles dissent in Uganda.[83] Just as the regime recently manipulated the presidential elections, it stage-managed the 2000 referendum on political parties to ensure the result it wanted, namely, a public endorsement of the perpetuation of the "no-party" system.

Another consequence of the Congo war for Ugandan politics is rising levels of corruption, of which the Western world has recently begun to take note.[84] The fact that the president's brother and brother-in-law are allowed to openly plunder Congo's resources obviously sets a very poor example for other government officials. Given that hundreds of stolen Congolese vehicles are now in the hands of Ugandan military officers inside Uganda itself, it is impossible for the regime to hide any longer behind the facade of moral rectitude that deceived Westerners for so long. Indeed, rising levels of corruption may help explain why the Museveni regime is witnessing a slow erosion of public support.

Hardest of all to measure, but arguably most important, are the social consequences of the Congo war. In the early 1990s, Uganda began a program of demobilizing large numbers of soldiers who had been recruited to fight in Museveni's campaign to overthrow the dictatorship of the previous regimes. By the mid-1990s, this program was bearing some fruit, with Uganda slowly recovering from the social breakdown of a long and bitter civil war.[85] At that moment in its history, Uganda's future seemed to be bright, having an apparently efficient and vigorous government and improving economic fortunes. With the onset of the Congo wars, however, the ranks of the Ugandan army have again begun to swell as recruitment for the Congo war and for service against internal rebels rises. Those who are posted to the war zones will inevitably become imbued with a culture of violence and corruption, which civil war and occupation inevitably breed, instead of learning the economic skills of an honest civilian life. It is not at all difficult to imagine that such cadres of soldiers may evolve into a self-perpetuating class of rent-seekers, prospering at the expense of productive civilians whose security and well-being will be correspondingly reduced.

CONCLUSION

Like the United States in the Vietnam War, the Ugandan government has been diminished by its participation in the Congo war. Whatever ideological goals Museveni may have had in the Congo intervention, they certainly have not been realized by his adventure there. Rather, the levels of repression and corruption in his government have escalated, while Ugandan citizens have a diminished sense of their president's respect for the rule of law. Even the putative goal of improving the country's internal security situation has not been realized. Instead, the Ugandan forces in Congo have been caught up in the local conflicts, such as that between Hema and Lendu, and have sullied their previously good reputation as a result. Meanwhile, their officers have seemed more bent on profit and exploitation than military achievement. Finally, Museveni has alienated himself from his staunchest external allies and fallen into conflict with his closest regional supporter. All that remains is the inevitable withdrawal in defeat and the full manifestation of the negative consequences.

1. This chapter, like others in this volume, is primarily focused on the second Congo civil war of the 1990s, that which began in August 1998. This war has be distinguished both from the Congolese civil war that broke out at the moment of the country's independence, lasting until 1964, and the civil war of the 1990s that displaced Mobutu Sese Seko from power. The later war began in October 1996 and ended with Laurent Kabila's seizure of power in May 1997.

2. See chapter 7 in this volume.

3. Economist Intelligence Unit [EIU], "Country Report: Uganda," 1st quarter, (London: EIU, 2000), 8.

4. This subject is examined at greater length in John Clark, "Ugandan Intervention in the Congo War: Evidence and Explanations," *Journal of Modern African Studies* 39, no.2 (2001): 261–287, an article devoted entirely to this aspect of Uganda's involvement. The section is largely a summary of that work.

5. For a brief analysis of the first Congo war (of the 1990s), see Dunn, chapter 4 in this volume.

6. *The East African* (Nairobi weekly), 1–7 June 1998.

7. *New Vision* (Kampala daily), 7 August 1998.

8. *New Vision,* 26 August 1998.

9. Confidential interviews, Kampala, November and December 1999.

10. These two conspiracy theories are also brought up and immediately dismissed by Gérard Prunier in his examination of the Congo war; see Gérard Prunier, "L'Ouganda et les Guerres Congolaises," *Politique Africaine* 75 (1999): 43–44.

11. Gérard Prunier, *The Rwanda Crisis: History of a Genocide* (New York: Columbia University Press, 1995), 118–19.

12. For leadership of Congo, Museveni has supported (in turn) Laurent Kabila, Wamba dia Wamba, and, more recently, Jean Pierre Bemba, none of whom is a Munyamulenge or Tutsi.

13. Asteris Huliaras, "The 'Anglo-Saxon Conspiracy': French Perceptions of the Great Lakes Crisis," *Journal of Modern African Studies* 36, no.4 (December 1998): 593–609.

14. Prunier, *The Rwanda Crisis,* 104–06.

15. *New Vision,* 26 August 1998, and 28 August 1998.

16. Human Rights Watch, "The Movement System and Political Repression in Uganda," (New York: Human Rights Watch, 1999), 124; Ruddy Doom and Koen Vlassenroot, "Kony's Message: A New *Koine?* The Lord's Resistance Army in Northern Uganda," *African Affairs* 98, no.390 (1999): 5–36.

17. *East African* (Nairobi weekly), 15–21 June 1998.

18. Herbert Weiss, "War and Peace in the Democratic Republic of Congo," *Current African Issues,* no. 22 (Uppsala: Nordiska Afrikainstitutet, 2000), 10.

19. Ibid.

20. Confidential interviews, Kampala, Uganda, November and December 1999.

21. Prunier, "L'Ouganda et les Guerres Congolaises," 44.

22. *Monitor,* 10 December 1999.

23. *New Vision,* 13 September 1998. I wish to thank Mr. Phillip Kasaija for pointing out this detail to me.

24. Confidential interview, Kampala, Uganda, 8 November 1999.

25. Yoweri Museveni, *Sowing the Mustard Seed: The Struggle for Freedom and Democracy in Uganda* (London: Macmillan, 1997).

26. Prunier, "L'Ouganda et les Guerres Congolaises," 44.

27. On the 1989 elections, including NRM manipulation of events leading up to election day, see Nelson Kasfir, "'Movement' Democracy, Legitimacy and Power in Uganda," in Justus Mugaju and Joseph Oloka-Onyango, eds., *No-Party Democracy in Uganda: Myths and Realities* (Kampala: Fountain Publishers, 2000).

28. Dan Connell, Dan and Frank Smyth, "Africa's New Bloc," *Foreign Affairs* 77, no. 2 (March/April 1998): 80–94.

29. Prunier, "L'Ouganda et les Guerres Congolaises," 44.

30. J. Kiyaga-Nsubuga, "From 'Communists' to Neo-Liberals: The Transformation of the National Resistance Movement (NRM) Regime's Economic Policy 1986–1989," discussion paper no. 5, 1997/98, Department of Political Science and Public Administration, Makerere University (27 November 1997).

31. Kasfir, "'Movement' Democracy, Legitimacy and Power in Uganda."

32. These include the president's brother, Salim Saleh, and Janet Museveni's relatives, Brigadier James Kazini and former minister Sam Kutesa.

33. According to Article 210 of the constitution, "Parliament shall make laws regulating the Uganda People's Defence Forces, in particular, providing for . . . (d) the deployment of troops outside Uganda." No such law was in place at the time of the Congo deployment, and none has subsequently been passed.

    Many Ugandans also argue that it is actually the military High Command that takes real decisions related to security and not Museveni's cabinet. This point was driven home to me by prominent Ugandan journalists, students, and opposition politicians, and tacitly admitted by senior civilian officials in the regime. When one asks ordinary Ugandans who they think would become president in the event of Museveni's death, many name Eriya Kategaya, the first deputy prime minister, who is number two in the military command hierarchy. Very few believe Vice President Specioza Kazibwe, who is constitutionally entitled to the post, would become president. On the militarism of the regime, also see A. G. G. Pinycwa, "Uganda and Military Interventions: Reflections on Two Historic Roles Since 1979," (paper presented at the Conference on Regional Peacekeeping, National Demilitarization and Development in Africa, Bellagio, Italy, June 1999).

34. Confidential interview, Kampala, Uganda, February 2000. It should be recalled that Kabila and Museveni once shared both a Marxist ideology and exile in Tanzania, where the two were in sporadic contact.

35. Michael Schatzberg, "Beyond Mobutu: Kabila and the Congo," *Journal of Democracy* 8, no. 4 (October 1997): 70–84.

36. See Longman, chapter 8, in this volume.

37. Prunier, "L'Ouganda et les Guerres Congolaises," 53.

38. Robert Kabushenga, interview with the author, Kampala, April 2000.

39. Although these latter military forces were ravaged during the 1996–97 Congo war, they made up in hostility to Kagame and the Tutsi what they lacked in organization and arms.

40. *East African,* 20–26 July 1998.

41. Will Reno, "Stealing Like a Bandit, Stealing Like a State," (paper presented to the Department of Political Science, Makerere University, 14 April 2000).

42. Mohammed Ayoob, "Subaltern Realism: International Relations Meets the Third World," in Stephanie Neumann, ed., *International Relations Theory and the Third World* (New York: St. Martin's Press, 1998).

43. EIU, "Country Report: Uganda," 3rd quarter (London: EIU, 1999), 5.

44. East African Cooperation is the somewhat incongruous name for the institutions of economic integration created by Kenya, Tanzania, and Uganda to carry on the work of the long-defunct East African Community of the 1960s.

45. Interview with the author, Kampala, Uganda, 8 December 1999.

46. EIU, "Country Report: Uganda," 1st quarter, (London: EIU, 2000), 5.

47. See Sandrine Perrot, "Entrepreneurs de l'Insécurité: La face cachée de l'armée ougandaise," *Politique Africaine* 75 (October 1999).

48. Perrot, "Entrepreneurs," 66–67.

49. International Crisis Group [ICG], "Uganda and Rwanda: Friends or Enemies?" 4 May 2000, available at http://212.212.165.2/ICGold/projects/rwanda/reports/rw02emaina.htm (6 July 2001).

50. Apparently, some commanders in the army are virtual barons whose troops are personally loyal to them. It appears to be the case that some units and their commanders seek deployment in specific areas in order to be able to engage in corruption and local commercial activities. See Reno, "Stealing Like a Bandit, Stealing Like a State," 13. Most knowledgeable Ugandans flatly reject the notion that Museveni does not bring to book any commander who directly challenges his authority, however.

51. ICG, "Uganda and Rwanda: Friends or Enemies?"

52. Ibid.

53. On the complexity of foreign policy goals in general, see John F. Clark, "Evaluating the Efficacy of Foreign Policy: An Essay on the Complexity of Foreign Policy Goals," *Southeastern Political Review* 23, no. 4 (December 1995): 559–79.

54. John F. Clark, "Foreign Policy Making in Central Africa: The Imperative of Regime Security in a New Context," in Gilbert Khadigala and Terrence Lyons, eds., *African Foreign Policy: Power and Process* (Boulder, CO: Lynne Rienner 2001).

55. Kasfir, "'Movement' Democracy, Legitimacy and Power in Uganda."

56. See ICG, "Uganda and Rwanda: Friends or Enemies." It must be noted, however, that the logic of this argument is far from clear. That the leading officers of the two countries would have fought for control of Kisangani for economic reasons, on the other hand, has an obvious rationality.

57. On the origins and evolution of these groups, see Afoaku, chapter 7, in this volume.

58. United Nations Security Council [UNSC], "Report of the Panel of Experts on the Illegal Exploitation of Natural Resources and Other Forms of Wealth of the Democratic Republic of the Congo (S/2001/357)," 12 April 2001, para. 116.

59. ICG, "Scramble for the Congo: Anatomy of an Ugly War," 20 December 2000, available at http://www.intl-crisis-group.org/projects/showreport.cfm?reportid=130 (8 July 2001).

60. Ibid.

61. UNSC, "Report of the Panel of Experts," para. 34.

62. Ibid., para. 35.

63. Ibid., para. 47.

64. Ibid., para. 74.

65. *Monitor,* 18 February 2001, 29.

66. Phillip Kasaija, "Uganda's Diplomatic Strategy in the DRC Conflict," Makerere University, typescript, June 2000, 4.

67. Ibid., 5–9.

68. Ibid., 13.

69. EIU, "Country Report: Uganda" (1999), 5.

70. Ibid. and EIU, "Country Report: Uganda" (2000), 5.

71. See Reno, "Stealing Like a Bandit, Stealing Like a State."

72. EIU, "Country Report: Uganda" (2000), 5.

73. Ibid.

74. Ibid.

75. International Monetary Fund [IMF], "Real GDP Growth: Uganda," available at www.imf.org/external/np/prsp/2001/uga/01/020201.pd (20 July 2001).

76. Ugandan Ministry of Finance, Planning, and Economic Development, "Medium Term Expenditure Framework 1998/99–2001/2002," July 1999. The budget increase was some U.S.$61 million at 1999 exchange rates. The portion of spending for defense in the overall Ugandan national budget rose from 12.5 percent to 19 percent.

77. IMF, "Real GDP Growth."

78. Ugandan Ministry of Finance, Planning, and Economic Development, "Budget Speech: Delivered at the Meeting of the 5th Session of the 6th Parliament of Uganda at the International Conference Centre on Thursday, 15th June, 2000."

79. UNSC, "Report of the Panel of Experts," para. 115–117.

80. Human Rights Watch, "Uganda: Not a Level Playing Field: Government Violations in the Lead-Up to the Election," available at www.hrw.org/reports/2001/uganda (20 June 2001).

81. Ibid.

82. Heike Behrend, "War in Northern Uganda: The Holy Spirit Movements of Alice Lakwena, Severineo Lukoya and Joseph Kony (1986–1997)," in Christopher Clapham, ed., *African Guerrillas* (Oxford: James Currey, 1998), and Doom and Vlassenroot, "Kony's Message," 5–36.

83. Human Rights Watch, "Hostile to Democracy."

84. *Economist* (London), "The Shine Fades of Museveni's Uganda," 1 May 1998, 41.

85. Nat J. Colletta, Markus Kostner and Ingo Wiederhofer, "Case Studies in War-to-Peace Transition: The Demobilization and Reintegration of Ex-Combatants in Ethiopia, Namibia, and Uganda," World Bank discussion paper no. 331 (Washington, D.C.: The World Bank, June 1996).

PART IV

Ambivalent States, Early Outcomes, and Nonstate Phenomena

CHAPTER 10

The Impossible Neutrality?

SOUTH AFRICA'S POLICY IN THE CONGO WAR

CHRIS LANDSBERG

INTRODUCTION

In early 2002, the South African Department of Foreign Affairs (DFA) stated: "The current most important issues with regard to the Central African Region are conflict resolution, promotion of peace and stability and good governance and economic reconstruction and development. In this regard, the specific challenges facing South Africa are to assist in the resolution of the conflict in the Democratic Republic of the Congo (DRC) through the comprehensive implementation of the Lusaka Cease-fire Agreement." The DFA further asserted that other challenges in the DRC "... include the promotion of the values of democracy and good governance and the implementation of sound stable economic policies." It was upfront in recognizing that "the other main priorities for South Africa are the expansion of its trade and economic relations with the countries of the region."[1]

When considering a retrospective of South Africa's policy in the Congo war over the past half-decade or so, the policy pronouncements of the DFA clearly highlight that southern and central Africa form post-apartheid South Africa's sphere of influence and areas of economic comparative advantage in African and international affairs. Given its own socio-economic challenges of unparalleled inequities between blacks and whites, grotesque levels of poverty, and sluggish economic growth on the home front, it is the policy position of Pretoria that South Africa needs a stable environment in southern and central Africa. The policy holds that such a stable regional terrain is essential in order to facilitate trade on the continent. South Africa further wants to contain, and more ideally prevent, a spillover of such conflicts into its own territory. Specifically, South Africa would like to avoid refugee flows, as pockets among all races in the country's population are already highly xenophobic.

Thus, any assessment of the rationales behind South Africa's policy toward the conflict in the Democratic Republic of Congo (DRC) should focus not so much on exclusive, bilateral relations but on Pretoria's broader georegional policy and strategies. For South Africa the conflicts in central and southern Africa are inextricably intertwined, forming as they do an "arc of conflict." Thus, Pretoria's policy positions and options toward the late Laurent Kabila's embattled DRC must be located within the framework of South Africa's overall Africa policy. The context of the "Renaissance Africa"[2] is also helpful in probing its stance vis-à-vis the Congo war.

This context includes South African economic interests as well. For if South Africa's economic relations with the rest of the continent are to drive Africa's renewal, the South African corporate sector, especially its mining-industrial core, is expected to buy into the renaissance project. Anglo/DeBeers has historically had a major stake in the Southern African mining industry, reaching north into the Congo. Other South African private sector conglomerates include SASOL, ESKOM, and GENCOR. Hence, the African National Congress (ANC) government's politicodiplomatic interests in the stabilization and postconflict reconstruction of the DRC cannot be divorced from such interests. In fact, many captains of such industries have come out in favor of Mbeki's African Renaissance idea, and the New Partnership for Africa's Development (NEPAD), since a success in this regard would open market opportunities for them.

Pretoria has, since 1994, regarded peace in any regional country in conflict—Zimbabwe, Swaziland, Lesotho, Angola, and the DRC—as conducive to stability for the broader subregion and as beneficial to South Africa's national interest. Often South Africa even pursues a deliberate linkage strategy that seeks to link peace initiatives in two or more countries, as, for example, in Angola and the DRC. However, just as Pretoria's regional strategy at times seemed both opportune and prudent for conflict resolution, so regional contradictions and dilemmas pursued and faced by Pretoria, as well as contradictions in its regional policy, served to undermine stability. Indeed, South Africa's policy stance has been strongly influenced by regional dynamics.

Therefore, while South Africa's has frequently pursued policies of (thankless) peacemaking and diplomacy, its pursuit of these strategies has allowed its neutrality and sincerity as peacemaker to be questioned by some of the belligerents.[3] Furthermore, Pretoria has persistently faced two major predicaments in its diplomatic efforts. It is at once trying to mediate between two or more sides of the conflict and, at the same time, experiencing tensions between itself and (one of) those two camps. Between 1998 and 2000, Laurent Kabila and his allies, Zimbabwe, Angola, and Namibia, accused South Africa of siding with Congo's antigovernment rebels. These states have questioned Pretoria's alleged evenhandedness. Indeed, Congo's allies have also criticized what they saw as Pretoria's indulgence of their enemies.

Whether true or false, such charges have brought into sharp relief South Africa's ostensible leverage in the DRC conflict in particular, and Africa in general. Because its neutrality and credibility has often been questioned, it has proved itself to be a wary, ambivalent peacemaker. These dilemmas faced by South Africa have exacerbated divisions within the Southern African Development Community (SADC). By the time South African president Nelson Mandela left office in June 1999, SADC had become a highly balkanized organization with deep splits and cleavages. A main cause of the divisions were the stand-offs between South Africa and the three SADC member states who decided to intervene in the PRC on behalf of Laurent Kabila's government.

For example, fallout over the conflict in the DRC and divisions in SADC have been linked to differences between South Africa and Zimbabwe over the status of the SADC Organ on Politics, Defence, and Security.[4] These differences have been symptomatic of more deeply felt economic tensions between South Africa and its neighbors. Thus the question of South Africa's policy toward the DRC concerns more than simply the DRC itself—it also involves South African policy toward its regional neighbors and SADC as well.

THANKLESS DIPLOMACY AND "PARTIAL IMPARTIALITY" IN THE FIRST CONGO WAR

In September and October 1996, a massive rebellion of Banyamulenge Tutsis in eastern Zaire threatened the very existence of the ruling regime in Zaire. Soon after the onset of the rebellion, autocratic Zairian president Mobutu Sese Seko accused Burundi and Rwanda of provoking the conflict. Mobutu's deputy prime minister and minister of national defense claimed to possess evidence that Burundi and Rwanda had trained and armed the Banyamulenge. Both Burundi and Rwanda denied the charges. Rwanda countered the charges by claiming that Mobutu had harbored *Interahamwe*, ex-Forces Armées Rwandaises (FAR) soldiers, and members of the former Hutu government in refugee camps in Zaire. The Rwandan government even suggested that it would take advantage of the prevailing disorder in Zaire and clear its enemies from the Kivu region. In response, Mobutu Sese Seko declared a state of emergency in the Kivu region. He imposed military rule over the provinces in an attempt to "eliminate all subversive networks in the region."[5]

In spite of these threats, the Banyamalenge were on the verge of seizing a swathe of eastern Zaire. Mobutu's soldiers were reported to be hastily fleeing the area. In less than a fortnight of all-out fighting, the rebels had captured Bukavu and were advancing on the Goma airport. The entire area between Lake Tanganyika and Lake Kivu was soon said to be under rebel control.[6] The rebels had created what amounted to a *cordon sanitaire* between Rwanda and their enemies in Zaire.

Mobutu maintained that Rwanda was now actively supporting the Banyamalenge. In turn, Rwandan vice president Paul Kagame insisted that "people who want to exterminate us must be resisted."[7] He was emphatic in declaring that "If Zaire brings the war to us, we shall fight Zaire. . . . We are ready to fight even though we seek no war with Zaire."[8] The military situation was greatly complicated by the presence of some 300,000 to 400,000 Rwandan refuges in Zaire.

Meanwhile, South Africa, then under the leadership of President Nelson Mandela, decided to launch a diplomatic initiative to end the war. On 19 February 1997, Mandela announced that he had invited Kabila, chairman of the rebel Alliance des forces démocratiques pour la libération du Congo-Zaire (Alliance of Democratic Forces for the Liberation of Congo-Zaire—ADFL), to visit South Africa. Mandela further announced that Mobutu and Kabila had agreed to "discuss their problems."[9] One report claimed that Mandela had "blurted out" his announcement of the talks, implying a lack of international mediation experience by the new South African governing elite.[10] Nonetheless, on 26 February it was announced that Mandela had persuaded Kabila "to negotiate," and Mandela suggested that peace might be possible.[11]

But no sooner had Mandela made the announcement than war in Zaire escalated dramatically. Matters had deteriorated so much that the West began to disengage. The United States government was reported to have moved 1,200 marines into the area in order to evacuate its citizens. France, Britain, and Belgium had also moved military units to neighboring Congo-Brazzaville, in position to evacuate their citizens. These external powers were less concerned about trying to help to restore the peace than about the safety of their citizens.

While the rebel advance persisted, Mandela continued offering South Africa's good offices and diplomatic facilitation. He again invited Kabila to travel to South Africa from Lubumbashi, an invitation that the rebel leader accepted. During his stay in South Africa, Kabila held talks with both President Mandela and the influential deputy president, Thabo Mbeki. Both South African leaders impressed upon Kabila the need for "a negotiated settlement" to the conflict in Zaire.[12] Both South Africans pushed ahead with their preferred stance of the democratic peace and convinced Kabila of the need for an accommodating regime that would include Mobutu Sese Seko. The South African initiative was widely believed to enjoy U.S. backing behind the scenes. On 17 April 1997, President Mandela announced in Cape Town that a meeting between Kabila and Mobutu had been arranged and that both had accepted South Africa's mediation. It was also rumored that both Kabila and Mobutu had accepted South Africa's mediation credentials at the expense of a rival mediation bid from Nigeria.

But while the announcement of the mediation was a breakthrough, this was not reflected by a decrease in violence back in Zaire. By the later half of April 1997, the rebels were closing in on Kinshasa. At the same time, the French government, which had long propped up the Mobutu dictatorship through both military and diplomatic means, had effectively distanced itself from Mobutu. Paris came out endorsing South Africa's stance and called for the formation of a transitional government.

Pretoria's hand was now strengthened, and on 29 April 1997, President Mandela again announced in Cape Town that Mobutu and Kabila had both agreed to meet on a South African warship, the *Outeniqua,* in international waters off Pointe Noire, Congo-Brazzaville; where Mandela would be mediating.[13] Bill Richardson, U.S. representative at the UN, endorsed South Africa's role and cajoled Kabila and Mobutu to cooperate.[14] The meetings began as scheduled in international waters on 2 May 1997.

Pretoria's "ocean diplomacy" sought to promote peace through a political opening in Zaire. Pretoria's strategy was also to offer Mobutu Sese Seko a face-saving exit strategy while pushing Kabila to come to terms with other elements of the Zairian opposition. During the *Outeniqua* mediation process, however, Pretoria's limited leverage soon revealed itself. During Mandela's mediation effort, Mobutu apparently offered to step down "for health reasons" and offered to hand over power to the speaker of the council of the country's Transitional Parliament. However, this idea was rejected out of hand by Kabila, who seemed utterly determined to gain the Congolese presidency for himself. A final mediation session was scheduled for later in May, but when the time arrived, Kabila refused to board the South African warship to talk peace. Instead, Kabila insisted that Mobutu submit his resignation

In the interim, Kabila also rejected any idea of a ceasefire. He warned that: " . . . my forces will continue to advance on all fronts." Kabila insisted that Mobutu resign within eight days.[15] "If we make it to Kinshasa before eight days," he warned, "then too bad; we cannot sit while he makes up his mind."[16] This episode was a harbinger of things to come in future relations between Kinshasa and Pretoria.

The main problem with South Africa's mediation effort was that it was accompanied by a major rebel assault on the Congolese capital, Kinshasa. Amidst these dynamics, the talks collapsed. Just two weeks after South Africa's ocean diplomacy initiatives, Mobutu relinquished power, on 16 May 1997, thereby ending nearly thirty-two years of dictatorial rule. In the end, the mediation effort proved superfluous. Kinshasa fell to the ADFL with remarkably little killing, as Mobutu's forces hoisted the white flag and surrendered, with thousands of others fleeing the capital city. Following Mobutu's ignominious fall, the United States advised its citizens to leave immediately. France, the U.K., and other states also made evacuation plans. It was left to Africans to sort out the problem and try to stabilize a Zaire-Congo devastated by Mobutu's ruinous rule and a savage war of "liberation."

THE MANDELA GOVERNMENT AND
THE EMERGENCE OF THE AUTOCRAT KABILA

On 17 May 1997, Laurent Kabila declared himself head of state, rebaptizing the country the Democratic Republic of Congo. With the departure of Mobutu, the question on every mind was whether Kabila would prove more democratic, or whether he would turn out to be just as dictatorial as Mobutu had been. If anything, most powerful foreign actors gave a cautious welcome to Kabila's ouster of Mobutu. U.S. president Bill Clinton stated that the United States wanted to see "a transition to genuine democracy."[17] UN Secretary-general Kofi Annan urged Kabila to respect the "choice and voice of the people."[18] The Organization of African Unity (OAU) welcomed Kabila's victory.

Pretoria meanwhile moved hastily to push for the DRC's inclusion as the latest member of the SADC. The rationale was that Pretoria would have better control—and thus influence—over Kabila, and so be able to nudge him in the direction of democratization, or at least some form of liberalization, for the fragile state. South Africa, its government believed, would be able to apply inducement measures—including both carrots and sticks—more effectively with the DRC inside SADC than on the outside. Pretoria even offered Kabila some postconflict reconstruction aid in exchange for Kabila toeing the democratization line. Of course, postconflict reconstruction would also serve South Africa's economic interests. Thus, while Congo's entry into SADC was squarely in South Africa's economic interests, Pretoria seemed more preoccupied with the military and political dimensions of the postconflict situation.

Again, the limited leverage of Pretoria—the presumed giant—revealed itself. It soon emerged that the inclusion of the DRC in SADC had further disunited that organization, as Kabila began to accuse South Africa of arrogance. He suggested that it was trying to promote democratization "South Africa style"—a *Pax Pretoriana*—in the DRC in particular, and Africa in general. Indeed, by that time, South Africa had made the extension of democracy a central plank of its Africa policy. As we now know, however, Kabila had no interest in a genuine political opening in Congo.

Even before tensions arose with Kabila, South Africa's democratization goals had triggered divisions in SADC. South Africa was at loggerheads with Zimbabwe's Robert Mugabe and other SADC members over questions ranging from the SADC Organ on Politics, Defence, and Security, to failed trade negotiations, to its democratization policies.

THE ANTI-KABILA REBELLION AND PRETORIA'S MANEUVERS

Scarcely one year after Kabila had seized power, armed rebels from the ranks of the AFDL calling themselves the Congolese Rally for Democracy (RCD) suddenly turned on him in late July 1998. The rebels had not taken kindly to Kabila's erratic exercise of power, or to his indifference to the security interests of their backers, Uganda and Rwanda.[19] The rebels were inspired to act when Uganda and Rwanda turned against Kabila after having helped to install him in power. They found him to be an undependable ally who might even work actively against their security interests. Moreover, under Kabila's rule, Rwanda and Uganda were slowly being excluded from access to Congo's mineral wealth.[20]

South Africa's first mistake was its failure to condemn the rebellion, and in particular the incursions into the DRC of Rwanda and Uganda. This stance went against the grain of Pretoria's own doctrine of condemning coups d'état. It also infuriated Kabila, who came to believe that he could not depend on Pretoria in his greatest hour of need. Otherwise, Pretoria's response to the renewed rebellion seemed to indicate a bias toward Uganda and Rwanda as "African Renaissance"-motivated states on a similar wavelength to its own.

It was left to a new grouping of Kabila's friends—Zimbabwe, Namibia, and Angola—to intervene militarily in his defense. The important thing to note here is that Zimbabwe, Namibia, and Angola intervened under the auspices of the SADC Organ. As chairperson of SADC, and also because of its adherence to its doctrine of the "democratic peace," and a commitment to "the peaceful resolution of disputes," Pretoria refused to get involved militarily. Thus, the two camps in SADC were at loggerheads, both in terms of procedure and in terms of strategy.

But no sooner had three of SADC's principal members intervened in the DRC than another conflict flared up in yet another SADC country—Lesotho. The prospect of a coup d'état in the mountain kingdom was so real that Pretoria, which had denounced the military interventions by the three SADC states in the DRC, was forced to take the military option in Lesotho in September 1998. Thus, another contradiction in South Africa's foreign policy emerged, in that South Africa had intervened militarily in a neighboring country in order to roll back a coup attempt. This move was interpreted by the pro-Kabila alliance as a double standard, since South Africa had refused to intervene in the DRC on the side of the beleaguered Laurent Kabila.

Kabila, Mugabe, Angolan president Jose Dos Santos, and Namibian president Sam Nujoma soon accused South Africa of promoting "regional apartheid policies."[21] These leaders further accused South Africa of siding with Uganda, Rwanda, and the RDC rebels in efforts to topple Kabila. Indeed, it became a dominant strategy on the part of these states to challenge vehemently South Africa's neutrality. South Africa was also accused of harboring Congolese rebels. In November 1988, DRC foreign affairs minister Jean-Charles Okoto went as far as to suggest in Pretoria that, "[T]his is the place where the plot has started. South Africa is really the home of the so-called rebels. When you look around there is not any other African country where those rebels are receiving everything."[22] Okoto's statement apparently referred to South African arms sales to Uganda and Rwanda, as well as to alleged South Africa moral support for the anti-Kabila forces.

Kabila was even more blunt in his rhetorical attacks. He labeled South Africa "puppets of the aggressors."[23] On the arms front, these states seemed to have reason to doubt Pretoria's presumed even-handedness. Pretoria continued to sell arms to Uganda and Rwanda while blatantly refusing to sell weaponry to Kabila. To be sure, however, South Africa did sell arms to Kabila's allies, Namibia and Zimbabwe.

Pretoria reacted by bitterly rejecting Okoto's remarks. Former South African foreign minister Alfred Nzo angrily labeled the charges as being "most unfortunate because they were untrue."[24] As Nzo opined, "South Africa's neutrality in finding solutions to the current crisis in the DRC remains unquestioned."[25] Deputy Minister of Foreign Affairs Aziz Pahad joined in the debate, stating that South Africa's policies were geared toward ending "the real possibilities of war."[26]

Mandela meanwhile tried to restore South Africa's dented credibility and pride by redoubling his mediation efforts. He met with Rwandan strongman Kagame and pushed for "a negotiated settlement."[27] He also met with Ugandan president Yoweri Museveni and further promoted the notion of a "negotiated settlement and ceasefire."

Later, Pretoria continued to try vigorously to assert itself as an indispensable mediator in the DRC conflict. In October 1998, Nelson Mandela averred that, "where you have parties to a conflict, they themselves cannot supervise the implementation of the resolution."[28] He perceived South Africa as the best possible mediator for the crisis and tried to establish South Africa's diplomatic credentials by bringing the crisis to and end. South Africa officially supported the Chiluba/Zambia mediation efforts (that led to the Lusaka Agreement) as an official SADC- and OAU-sanctioned initiative, while simultaneously pursuing its own initiative as well.

In a further effort to placate his critics, Mandela opted for an ostensibly more even-handed approach. Instead of principally engaging the rebels and their key external backers, Uganda and Rwanda, Mandela reached out to one of the DRC alliance members, Namibian president Nujoma. He tried to impress upon Nujoma the need for a speedy solution to the conflict in the DRC. It was noteworthy that he failed to cajole Robert Mugabe and Dos Santos at the time. It should be remembered that relations between the latter two and Pretoria were at an all-time low by then.

REGIONAL ECONOMIC CONSERVATISM AND IMPLICATIONS FOR PRETORIA'S PEACE STRATEGY

The shortcomings and problems experienced by South Africa on the military and political front are linked to what can be described as a conservative conception by Pretoria of its interests in Africa. Pretoria has essentially behaved like a political revisionist power by making the promotion of democratization and "democratic peace" a core tenet of its Africa diplomacy while simultaneously preserving the economic status quo by pursuing largely self-interested trade policies vis-à-vis its neighbors.[29] There clearly appeared to be a disjuncture between South Africa's foreign policy and diplomatic objectives on the one hand and economic and trade relations on the other. Post-apartheid South Africa has long enjoyed a massive trade surplus with its neighbors by a six to one ratio in its favor.[30] While it sought to preserve its historically favorable economic relations with its neighbors, it deigned to recommend domestic political reform for the very same neighbors.

These have been among the factors at the heart of the growing tensions between South Africa and other major SADC actors, particularly Zimbabwe, but also Namibia and Angola. The Congo conflict served as a stage on which these tensions were being played out. Pretoria's economic conservatism was expressed in the priority it gave to pursuing an almost exclusively subregional posture focusing on SADC;

it would probably have been more beneficial for South Africa to have joined the Common Market for East and Southern African States (COMESA) as well as SADC.[31]

Given that most members of the SADC are also members of COMESA, such a move would have given Pretoria a chance to work toward harmonizing the two groupings. Such a move could also have expanded the scope of political and security cooperation in east and southern Africa and led to a more coordinated strategy on transitions in the DRC before and after the toppling of Mobutu. Yet COMESA has been marginalized, presumably because it is regarded as an unwieldy grouping of diverse states that are at varying levels of political and economic development and stability. But this is scarcely a reasonable excuse. This argument has also been contradicted by the way in which the SADC has been allowed to expand into the heart of what the Africa division of the South African DFA refers to as the continent's "equatorial zone," of which the DRC is a major part.[32] There is a view that suggests that the DRC's entry into SADC was the step that turned Museveni against Kabila; as such, entry could be seen as a big economic coup for South Africa.[33]

SADC has also made overtures to Uganda and Kenya, which suggests a selective expansion of the organization at the expense of the poorer and less stable members of COMESA. But now that potentially rich Congo has joined, the SADC organization is witnessing just how difficult it is to digest more, particularly unstable, members. In fact Congo's inclusion has been so difficult that it threatened the very viability of the SADC. An alternative policy position might have been for SADC's expansion to be pursued in the context of harmonizing the trade policies of SADC and COMESA. This would probably have left Pretoria less exposed than it is now, at loggerheads with the SADC's more important members states over the DRC and embroiled in a tussle over the status of the SADC Organ. Under a harmonized SADC/COMESA arrangement, Rwanda and Uganda would not have been excluded from the SADC summit in Mauritius, where the Congo issue was debated at an early stage. Their exclusion was apparently against the will of Pretoria, which was then maneuvered into a show of solidarity with Kabila—one made all the more compelling by the South African-led SADC intervention in Lesotho (regardless of the fact that the Lesotho and DRC scenarios are not comparable).

As stated above, a major flaw in South Africa's Africa policy has its origins in the tensions between South Africa and Zimbabwe. This soon spilled over into their rival approaches to the DRC and their differences over the SADC Organ. These tensions stemmed from South African foot-dragging in renewing the preferential trade agreement between itself and Zimbabwe shortly after the Mandela government assumed power, as well as Mandela's impatience with Mugabe's increasingly dictatorial rule.

Of course, there have been similar tensions between Pretoria and its partners in the Southern African Customs Union (SACU)—Namibia, Botswana, Lesotho, and Swaziland—over a new customs agreement. But these economic tensions extend to non-SADC states as well. Kenya, for example, feels threatened by South African northward economic penetration, while it is unable to gain access to South African markets in turn. While Pretoria is at pains not to be seen as a "bully" in political, diplomatic, and military terms, its self-perceived good will is undercut by foreign perceptions that it often acts like an economic "ruffian." To counter this, the South African foreign policy executive and DFA, along with the Department of Trade and Industry (DTI), need to engage business and labor interests in an effort to align

South Africa's regional economic policy with its geopolitical and security interest in southern Africa and beyond. Otherwise, South African economic forces will continue to complicate Pretoria's foreign policy interests and exacerbate tensions between South Africa and its neighbors.

Perhaps the time has come for different stakeholders in South Africa's foreign policy—the DFA, the DTI, the National Economic, Development and Labour Council (Nedlac), and the Congress of South African Trade Unions (COSATU)—to face up to the issue and consider some policy incentives that would begin to restore Pretoria's damaged credibility. The advantage of involving actors like Nedlac and COSATU is that they can undertake initiatives that Pretoria cannot afford to be involved in while dealing with its highly sensitive counterparts in the subregion. Such local agents should recognize that policy differences between Pretoria and Harare over the DRC may be symptomatic of deeper economic and trade tensions. The Zimbabwean business community has gone so far as to accuse South Africa of intending to deindustrialize Zimbabwe's economy. There is also the much-reported effort of Zimbabwe to regain the economic sphere of influence in Mozambique that it lost during the 1990s. Harare feels that it was pushed out of that country once the situation stabilized there and apartheid came to an end in South Africa—on top of resistance from Pretoria in renewing the bilateral preferential trade agreement. Perhaps accelerated progress in renegotiating the SACU agreement as well as ratifying and implementing the SADC trade protocol may mitigate South Africa's "bullying" image.

FROM TOUGH TO QUIET DIPLOMACY: THE ARRIVAL OF PRESIDENT THABO MBEKI

By the end of Mandela's term in office relations between him and Mugabe were frosty, and there was a virtual "cold war" between Pretoria and Harare. When Mbeki became president, he had to concede that South Africa's policy toward the DRC was in need of major overhaul. Mbeki announced that South Africa was singling out Zimbabwe's Robert Mugabe and Rwanda's Paul Kagame as the regional power brokers, and thus the key actors in achieving a settlement of the Congo war. This meant, inter alia, that Mbeki had to improve South Africa's relationship with Mugabe.

Mbeki invited President Mugabe to be his guest of honor at his presidential inauguration ceremony on 16 June 1999. He held talks with Mugabe on bilateral and multilateral affairs. He was also instrumental in getting the South African Football Association (SAFA) to host "an inauguration soccer spectacular" between South Africa and Zimbabwe.[34] South African ended up losing that match 1-0 in front of a capacity crowd at the First National Bank Stadium in South Africa. The inauguration match provided a platform and opportunity for Mbeki to send a powerful message to Africa, the world, and his detractors back home that he would take Africa seriously by engaging influential partners like Zimbabwe's Mugabe and Rwanda's Kagame and by investing a great deal of political capital in finding solutions to Africa's wars.

Mbeki's first day in office was spent with southern African counterparts, deliberating on efforts to end the war in the DRC. He impressed upon his counterparts the importance of successfully concluding the attempted Lusaka Agreement. With this and other moves, Mbeki wanted to shed South Africa's image as a "reluctant re-deemer." While South Africa supported the Chiluba/Zambia effort, it also embarked on its own mediation efforts through consultation with other regional partners. In real terms South Africa has more military muscle and political clout then Zambia, and it believed that these attributes placed it in a good position to assume the lead-ing peace-broker role.

Mbeki's new minister of foreign affairs, Nkosazana Dlamini-Zuma, announced soon after her appointment that securing peace in the DRC would rank as her top foreign policy priority.[35] No sooner had she been appointed than she traveled to the DRC and Rwanda to meet with leaders of those countries to stress the need for a "negotiated settlement" to the conflict, as well as the urgency of a ceasefire in the near term. Zuma made it clear to Kabila that she would be dealing with all sides to the conflict, including rebel leaders. In early July 1999, Mbeki held talks with Wamba dia Wamba and Etienne Tshisekedi and impressed upon them the impor-tance of all belligerents implementing the Lusaka Agreement. While this inclusive approach did not go down well with Kabila, the foreign minister insisted that South Africa would work "consistently and tirelessly to promote a ceasefire."[36] Dlamini-Zuma denied allegations that South Africa was arming the rebels and said that her country was "totally impartial."[37]

During the last half of 1999 and the first half of 2000, Mbeki continued to push for a peace plan for the DRC and urged all foreign forces to withdraw from the DRC. The 1999 Lusaka Peace Agreement on the Congo war was preceded by a South African ten-point plan to resolve the war. That plan called, inter alia, for the withdrawal of foreign forces from the DRC, the establishment of a UN peacekeeping force, the deployment of a Joint Military Council (JMC), and the beginning of an inter-Congolese dialogue that would lead to peace and reconcil-iation. South Africa stressed the need for the establishment of a broad-based gov-ernment of national unity in the DRC. Many of the ideas and suggestions contained in the South African ten-point plan were incorporated into the Lusaka Peace Agreement, but Pretoria refused to take open credit for the breakthroughs. Both Mbeki and his former director-general of foreign affairs, Jackie Selebi, were careful not to come across as smug, and instead referred to the breakthrough as a collective African one.

In a most dramatic foreign policy about-face, Mbeki then decided to adopt a stance in favor of South African participation in a peacekeeping mission for Congo. He has eventually conceded that South Africa cannot be seen to be making peace while showing a disinclination to keep the very peace that it so eagerly brokers. In keeping with this new approach, the Mbeki government was instrumental in urging the UN to establish a peacekeeping force for the DRC. It lobbied both the General Assembly and the Security Council for such a mission, and in January 2000, the UN decided to establish the UN Mission to the Congo (MONUC).[38]

Mbeki has committed South Africa to playing an active role in MONUC. This decision was a far cry from the cautious and ambivalent peacekeeping posture of Nelson Mandela. The Mandela administration was bent on playing a diplomatic, rather than a peacekeeping, role in Congo, the Lesotho peace-enforcement episode notwithstanding.

South Africa has budgeted an amount of R80--100 million (some U.S.$10--14 million) for the mission. It has also pledged R1 million (some U.S.$120,000) toward the JMC and is the only country to have pledged such an amount. In April 2001, South Africa dispatched the first contingent of military support staff to back up the MONUC forces. By the end of 2000, some 100 technical specialists of the South African National Defence Force had already been deployed in the DRC.[39] In addition, some eighty support staff have already left for Congo, though it remains to be seen whether South Africa will dispatch a full military battalion in due course.

While Pretoria was considering the merits and demerits of participation in the MONUC operation, it has responded to the post-Laurent Kabila environment by embarking on a two-pronged shift in strategy. One leg of the strategy was targeted at the new Joseph Kabila regime, whose speedy consolidation was hardly a democratic event. The other dimension was aimed at the rebel movements.

The new strategy for the first facet is to engage the young Kabila by providing him with support and encouragement for what seems to be his acceptable commitments to both the Lusaka Agreement and the inter-Congolese dialogue. In short, the Joseph Kabila regime seems to be cooperating with reasonable outside partners and moving in Pretoria's desired direction. An added advantage of Joseph Kabila's cooperative approach is that Mbeki can potentially delink his relationship with Mugabe from his relationship with the new Congolese leader. Mugabe has not been forthcoming in Mbeki's quiet diplomacy maneuvers to defuse and contain the flammable "land grab" debacle in Zimbabwe and almost seems determined to embarrass the South African leader. The dilemma Mbeki has faced since late-1999 has been that he needs to help calm the situation in Zimbabwe while at the same time engaging Mugabe, who has positioned himself as a very resolute and influential actor in the Congo conflict. As a result, every outside state that has sought to mediate in the Congo war has had to contend with Zimbabwe's formidable and resolute ruler.

Let us now briefly move to the second dimension and consider South Africa's engagement with the divided and disorganized rebel movements. Pretoria's consistent policy approach sought to cajole all the rebel movements to recommit themselves to both the Lusaka peace process and the inter-Congolese dialogue process. Pretoria opted to do this while staying in close contact with Rwanda and Uganda, seeking their cooperation and backing. In exchange, Pretoria offered to court the UN and persuade it not only to stick to its commitments and implement the MONUC mandate but even to augment that operation.

The inter-Congolese dialogue started in October 2001 in Addis Ababa, though the talks were soon suspended after only a few days. South Africa openly committed itself to supporting, and even offered to host, the inter-Congolese dialogue "where all the role-players in the DRC can negotiate a new political dispensation for their country."[40] All the parties agreed to relocate the talks to South Africa, a move viewed as a significant compromise on the part of Kinshasa, which had previously questioned South Africa's impartiality.[41] While the European Union pledged U.S.$1.8 million toward the inter-Congolese dialogue, the United States U.S.$1 million, Britain U.S.$500, 000, South Africa committed U.S.$107, 000.[42] The Mbeki government further offered to sponsor the full R50, 000 for the second round of talks that was held in February of 2002 at Sun City, South Africa. Apart from this, South Africa continued to play a behind-the-scenes, facilitating role and encouraged and cajoled all the players to engage in a dialogue that would lead to a pact spelling out a new power sharing mechanism for an interim government. South Africa also impressed upon Zimbabwe and Angola the need to proceed with troop withdrawals before the inter-Congolese dialogue started. Both governments committed themselves verbally without any guarantees to do so in practice.

CONCLUSION

Given these multiple dimensions of South Africa's policy, then, how do we assess its intervention in the recent and ongoing Congo conflicts? South Africa generally received high marks in the West and other international quarters for having injected itself diplomatically into the civil war that ended Mobutu's long dictatorship and brought Kabila to power. It was through that move that Pretoria decisively emerged as a regional power outside of the SADC area. Pretoria effectively upstaged the external great powers such as the United States, Russia, France, and the United Kingdom as the new regional power on the block. Even Nigeria, which was going through a highly capricious and difficult transition between 1998 and 1999, had to concede that post-apartheid South Africa was becoming a political force to be reckoned with in Africa. However, *regionally*, within SADC, the reviews on Pretoria's diplomacy were decidedly mixed. While some observers saw an emerging regional power, other witnessed an ambivalent regional power that did not know how to wield influence.

At the end of the day, it was not so much the endgame of the Mobutu regime, and South Africa's mediation efforts in it, but the military effort backed by Angola, Uganda, and Rwanda that brought Laurent Kabila to power. Even when the evidence was clear that Kabila was convincingly winning the armed struggle against Mobutu, South Africa still insisted on diplomacy and mediation. Pretoria was convinced that there could be no military solution to the conflict in Zaire-Congo. South Africa has been criticized in some quarters for not having participated in the military coalition of forces that brought about the transition in Congo in 1997. Such critics assume that Pretoria would have been in a position to exercise greater leverage over subsequent events in the Congo if it had intervened in this manner. In hindsight, given the DRC's current turmoil, one could say that events have proved Pretoria right: A negotiated political transition to a post-Mobutu dispensation, rather than the military defeat of Mobutu, might have spared the region the second round of military conflict that is now on-going.

A diplomatic solution to that conflict was scarcely guaranteed, of course. Nonetheless, Francis Kornegay and I have argued in our study, *From Dilemma to Détente: Pretoria's Policy Options in the DRC,*[43] that, under the circumstances at that time, and in the absence of a declared SADC consensus on intervening on Kabila's behalf against Mobutu, it is not clear how South Africa could have played a military role outside an internationally mandated peacekeeping initiative. Instead, South Africa opted for engaging the DRC diplomatically—something that subsequently became the dominant theme in South Africa's Africa policy. It attempted to elicit Kabila's cooperation by means of reconstruction and development incentives. By April 1997, however, a military victory for Kabila was in sight, and nothing was going to deter him from realizing that objective, not even the powerful presence of the saint-like Mandela. Could it have been that Pretoria's diplomacy might have benefited from some military leverage? Perhaps, but in our view, politics and diplomacy will ultimately settle the fate of the DRC.

Let us now assess Mandela's reactions and strategies with regard to Kabila's rise to power. South Africa, together with Namibia, was also instrumental in pushing for Congo's entry into the SADC immediately after Kabila's sudden ascendancy. Nonetheless, despite South Africa's commitment to help the Kabila government with postconflict reconstruction, relations between Pretoria and Kinshasa never seemed to gain any mutually beneficial momentum. Good relations had broken down and were never restored fully, while Kabila preferred to rely on his military backers. Kabila seemed set on keeping Pretoria at arms length, while his relations with his former principal backers, Uganda and Rwanda, were becoming increasingly strained. To be sure, Pretoria itself exercise some curious policy options. A major flaw in the South African approach at the time of its diplomatic intervention in the transition from Mobutu to Kabila was the absence of a broader regional policy on the Great Lakes, as well as on the East African subregion, linked as it was to both the SADC and COMESA.

This flaw was not just a shortcoming on South Africa's part. It was shared by other states as well, all of which appeared to have their own vested interest in supporting the rebellion led by Kabila. There was a notable absence of diplomatic and political coordination linked to the larger objectives of stabilizing Congo and the broader Great Lakes region, and that region's incorporation into broader east and southern African cooperation and integration processes. In short, while the effort to back Kabila was an expression of African agency, it was hardly an example of pan-African cooperation.

Before concluding, three main facets of South Africa's stake in the Congo war need highlighting. First, South Africa wanted Congo to join SADC not only to gain influence over the political process, and nudge Kabila in its desired directions, but also because of the commercial stakes of the Congo, including future mutual investment opportunities. This might have inadvertently triggered grievances on the part of Museveni and Kagame, just as Mugabe, Dos Santos, Nujoma, and their client, Laurent Kabila, had their grievances with Pretoria. Second, the relationship between South Africa's mediation efforts, and those of Chiluba, was interesting. Since it has more military muscle, South Africa assumed the role of the real guarantor of agreements, while giving official support to the SADC- and OAU-backed processes, which put Zambia in the leading role. Third, and overall, South Africa's commercial interests, and especially perceptions of South Africa's presumed imperialist tendencies, (unintentionally) frustrated some of its diplomatic ambitions.

In conclusion, then, South Africa improvised throughout its intercession in the Congo conflicts and genuinely tried to put into place the building blocks of a Pan-Africanist cooperation. Several factors served to complicate and even derail its efforts, however, as we saw above. With South Africa having decided to take the plunge in favor of peacekeeping and to come out in support of the efforts of the new Joseph Kabila regime, backed up by support for the Masire-led inter-Congolese dialogue process, the jury is still out on whether it will be successful in these efforts. And while we are awaiting the jury's verdict, one interim lesson for Pretoria is worth pondering: it is almost impossible to pursue a mediation option in a volatile arena such as the DRC and the Great Lakes region of Africa. Perhaps the solution lies in the option of constructing alliances with like-minded and reliable partners.

Whether many such partners can reliably be found beyond Botswana, Tanzania, Mozambique, Malawi, and of course Nigeria, is an open question. The dominant lesson from South Africa's policy toward Congo over the past five years or so is that, unless it is absolutely compelled to, South Africa will not go it alone.

1. South African Department of Foreign Affairs, West and Central Africa, http://www.dfa.gov.za/events/afraeq.html/21January2002.
2. The "African Renaissance" can be regarded as an ambitious bid for continental renewal as reflected in a series of political and economic initiatives involving such continental powers as South Africa, Nigeria, Algeria, Tanzania, Senegal, the OAU, and other partners. The objectives of the African Renaissance are to promote political democratization and stability in Africa and the continent's reintegration into the global economy. The African Renaissance should therefore be considered as an effort by Africa's leaders to take responsibility for the continent's destiny. Such efforts are embodied in the Millennium African Recovery/Renaissance Plan (MAP) and the merging of this particular plan with Senegal president Wade's "Omega Plan," which now forms the New Africa Initiative. For a discussion of the African Renaissance, see Francis Kornegay, Chris Landsberg, and Steve McDonald, "Participate in the African Renaissance," *The Washington Quarterly* 24, no. 3 (summer 2001).
3. See Francis Kornegay and Chris Landsberg, "From Dilemma to Détente: Pretoria's Policy Options on the DRC and Great Lakes," Centre for Policy Studies: Johannesburg, Policy Brief 11, April 1999.
4. The SADC Organ on Politics, Defence, and Security was established in 1996 to institutionalize cooperative security in the region. The idea was to integrate further military and human security and promote democratization. While South Africa's president Nelson Mandela served as chairperson of SADC, Zimbabwe's president Robert Mugabe was elected the chair of the organ. All this was an attempt to balance power in the region. The two leaders have long disagreed on the purpose, function, and operation of the organ. Mandela even threatened to resign over the schism. For a discussion, see Willie Breytenbach, "The Failure of Security Co-Operation in SADC: The Suspension of the Organ for Politics, Defence and Security," *South African Journal of International Affairs* 7, no. 1 (summer 2000). Also see Chris Landsberg and Mwesiga Baregu, eds., *From Cape to Congo: Southern Africa's Evolving Security Architecture* (Boulder, CO: Lynne Reinner Publishers, 2002), forthcoming.
5. "Keesings Record of World Events," *Monthly News Digest,* Bethesda, Maryland, October 1996.
6. Ibid.
7. Ibid.
8. Ibid.
9. "Keesings Record of World Events," February 1997.
10. Ibid.
11. Ibid.
12. "Keesings Record of World Events," April 1997.
13. "Keesings Record of World Events," May 1997.
14. Ibid.
15. Ibid.
16. Ibid.

17. Quoted in Reuben Phathela, "South Africa's Peacemaking Roles during the First and Second Zaire/Democratic Republic of Congo Rebellions, 1996–2000," unpublished master's thesis, University of the Witwatersrand, Johannesburg, November 2001, p. 56.
18. Ibid., p. 72.
19. See chapter 7, in this volume.
20. For the motivations of Rwanda and Uganda in sponsoring the rebellions, see chapters 8 and 9, in this volume.
21. See Steven Friedman, Claude Kabemba, Chris Landsberg, Maxine Reitzes, and Zondi Masiza, "State of Anxiety? Reconstructing the State, Democratization, and Economic Growth in Southern Africa" (unpublished paper, Centre for Policy Studies, Johannesburg, April 1999), 14.
22. *The Citizen*, 17 November 1998.
23. *The Citizen*, 10 December 1998.
24. *The Star*, 18 November 1998.
25. Ibid.
26. Ibid. For a further official view of this strategy, see Deputy Minister of Foreign Affairs Aziz Pahad, "South Africa and Conflict Resolution in Africa" [Address delivered at the conference on the launch of the South African chapter of the African Renaissance (SACAR), Kempton Park, 7–9 April 2000].
27. *The Citizen*, 24 October 1998.
28. *The Citizen*, 29 October 1998.
29. Francis Kornegay, "Recasting South Africa's Regional and Global Role for the 21st Century" (unpublished paper prepared for the United Nations Development Programme in South Africa, July 1999), 3.
30. Kornegay and Landsberg, "From Dilemma to Détente."
31. Francis A. Kornegay and Chris Landsberg, "Mayivuke iAfrika: Can South Africa lead an African Renaissance?" Centre for Policy Studies: Johannesburg, Policy Issues ad Actors (PIA) 11, no. 1 (January 1998): 36.
32. Kornegay and Landsberg, "Mayivuke iAfrika: Can South Africa lead an African Renaissance?"
33. On this point, see chapter 9, note 45, in this volume.
34. Centre for Policy Studies, Johannesburg, *Socio-Political Monitor* (unpublished internal publication, June 1999).
35. N. Dlamini-Zuma, Minister of Foreign Affairs of South Africa, Foreign Affairs Budget Vote Speech (National Assembly, Cape Town, 14 March 2000).
36. ZA (South Africa) Now, *Mail and Guardian*, 25 July 25 1999. www.mg.co.za/mg/za/news.html.
37. ZA (South Africa) Now, *Mail and Guardian*, 28 January 2000. www.mg.co.za/mg/za/news.html.
38. ZA (South Africa) Now, *Mail and Guardian*, 25 January 2000. www.mg.co.za/mg/za/news.html.
39. For this information, see the Department of Foreign Affairs' internet source: http://www.dfa.go.za/events/afraeq.html/21January2002.
40. Ibid.
41. Claude Kabemba, "Central Africa: A Review," *Central Africa: A Review, South African Yearbook of International Affairs, 2001–02* (Braamfontein: South African Institute of International Affairs, 2002), 273.
42. This information was shared with the author by Sagaren Naidu, Senior Researcher, Institute for Global Dialogue (IGD), Braamfontein, South Africa.
43. For full information, see note #2, above.

CHAPTER 11

Arms Proliferation and the Congo War

AUGUSTA MUCHAI

There have been numerous efforts to find a diplomatic solution to the Congolese crisis, which has severe regional ramifications. Frederick Chiluba, Zambia's president, has been shuttling around the region trying to find a peace formula, while at the other end of the continent Libya's Muammar Gaddafi has launched his own initiative. But none of these diplomatic efforts has so far shown any signs of making progress.[1]

INTRODUCTION

The nature and magnitude of the protracted conflict and war in the Democratic Republic of Congo (DRC) has been a cause of concern both for all the states in the region and for the world community at large. Leading a long list of concerns is the issue of proliferation of arms. This chapter discusses the local events and international factors that have favored arms proliferation in the Congo war. A historical perspective of events is outlined to lay the ground for analyzing the extent of the problem. The mode of arms transfer is examined only from the general perspective; that is, sources and avenues of entry. Acknowledging that the arms employed in the war are supplied from foreign states not in the war, the "foreign hand" in the arms proliferation is also discussed.

Several peace initiatives have been made in an effort to end the wars in Congo that have been raging for over five years. Some of these initiatives will be analyzed in order to evaluate to what extent they incorporate the means to address the problem of arms proliferation. It seems that the problem is not well articulated in the peace initiatives and processes, since those involved are mainly preoccupied by the need for a cease-fire and not the problem of arms proliferation. Arms proliferation is a complicated issue because arms are very difficult to control even where there is a will to do so. It is only through concerted efforts that some reasonable amount of success can be achieved in managing the menace.

In theory, there are codified rules and procedures meant to control and regulate the movement of arms in the international system. A brief discussion is made in this chapter on the international arms protocol created under the auspices of the United Nations. The extent of arms proliferation in the Congo indicates that there is a problem with the regime, which should control arms acquisition by states and nonstate groups. This will be discussed and the weaknesses in the regime will be identified.

In the course of the war, several states have been drawn in, either in support of the government or the rebels or as "mediators." Among the states intervening in the crises, some have been interested in a diplomatic or political resolution, and others inclined to a military resolution. Still other states have been involved as manufacturers and suppliers of the arms utilized in the war. Indeed, the perpetual fighting has led to proliferation of arms in the Great Lakes region. This is evident in the states involved on either side: Angola, Namibia, Zimbabwe, Libya, and Chad on the side of the government troops and Rwanda, Uganda, and Burundi in support of the rebels. Zambia and South Africa have sporadically sought to serve as mediators, though South Africa has also been an arms supplier to both its SADC partners (Zimbabwe, Angola, and Namibia) and to the anti-Kabila interveners (Uganda and Rwanda).

By necessity, the scope and extent of arms proliferation in the Congo war is examined from a very general point of view. This is because of the limited nature of facts and information available and accessible in view of the discreet nature of arms transactions. The general term "arms" will also be employed because of the thin line between legal and illicit arms. There is much evidence that even legally acquired arms have ended up being utilized in an illegal way. An example is when the regime of Zairian president Mobutu Sese Seko disintegrated in 1997 and its disgruntled soldiers ended up misusing or selling their guns for personal gain. Also, the manufacturers, exporters, and suppliers of arms have little say or influence on the ultimate use of arms by the end user. The arms keep changing hands, and it would be difficult to keep track of their ultimate destination or ownership.

In the Congo war as well as in other conflicts and war-ridden parts of the region, the most commonly used arms are those usually referred to as "small arms" and "light weapons." Even though the term "arms" is used here in a very general way, it would be important for the sake of clarity to make some important distinctions. Small arms and light weapons deserve particular attention because they are easily available, modest in price, and hard to detect when transferred clandestinely. Small arms, also known as "personal weapons" in military terms, are those that can be carried and operated by one person, while "light weapons," in military terms, are those that can be carried and operated by a crew of two or three people.[2] As the United Nations further specifies, "Small arms comprise revolvers, and self-loading pistols, rifles, and carbines, submachine guns, hand-held under barrel and mounted grenade launchers, portable anti-aircraft guns, portable launchers of Anti-Aircraft Missiles systems and light mortals of less than 100mm caliber."[3]

The nature of small arms and light weapons contributes heavily to the problem of arms proliferation. They are especially suited to irregular warfare due to their easy concealment, cheapness, ease of use, wide availability, and durability.[4] Moreover, they require low maintenance and training to operate. This makes them the weapon of choice for rebel groups, criminals, and poorly organized combatants in protracted war and conflict situations, as in the DRC. These distinctions do not comprehensibly define light arms, and even the UN definition may also be open to debate. Nonetheless, they serve to provide some common understanding on the general application of the term "arms" as used in this chapter. It should be noted that heavy conventional weapons have also played a significant part in the DRC as well as other conflict situations in the region. They tend to be used to back up military or paramilitary forces using light weapons, even though their use in the Great Lakes appears to have been less significant.[5]

ARMS PROLIFERATION AND THE COMPLEX OF WARS IN THE GREAT LAKES REGION

The Congo war has been described as Africa's "most African" war in the entire postcolonial era.[6] This observation springs from the fact that the states of the Great Lakes and of central Africa have been embroiled in interminable interstate and intrastate wars throughout the 1990s. There seems to be a very contagious political and military terrain, as a sneeze in one country sends the nearby states shivering with a cold.[7] This is manifested in the spillover effects of unresolved internal conflicts, which, over a period of time, extend to the neighboring states. Widespread arms proliferation has been a part of these processes in virtually every instance.

The current crisis evolved out of internal conflicts within Rwanda, Burundi, and the former Zaire, fed by refugee and armed exile groups based in neighboring states. The country of Rwanda has a long history of hostilities between its main identity groups, the Hutu and Tutsi, as well as political instability. The recent civil war in Rwanda began in 1990 with an invasion of Tutsi rebels from Uganda, after the armed Tutsi had organized themselves into the Rwandan Patriotic Front (RPF). In this war, RPF received support from the Ugondon president Yoweri Museveni in appreciation of the support he had received during Uganda's civil war of 1981--86. Museveni launched the process of arms proliferation in the region in the 1990s when he allowed the RPF to take stocks of arms from the Ugandan People's Defence Forces for their war against the regime of Juvénal Habyarimana in Rwanda. According to Prunier, "The invading forces had taken with them a fair amount of equipment including heavy machine-guns, mortars, BM-21 multiple rocket-launchers, recoilless rifles and Russian ZUG light automatic cannons. Some of President Museveni's own bodyguard even stole the presidential staff radio communication vehicles, a feat they later recalled with a mixture of childish glee and embarrassment."[8]

Meanwhile, France and neighboring Zaire, then still under Mobutu, militarily aided the Habyrimana regime.[9] At the height of ethnic hostilities in Rwanda, plans were put into effect to import and distribute thousands of machetes and small arms and to train Hutu men to eliminate Tutsis in certain regions.[10] These arms would later find their way into Zaire in the hands of the Hutu refugees and militiamen who fled their country at the climax of the 1994 RPF invasion that finally ended the Rwandan genocide. No mechanism was put on the ground to disarm the refugees, *Interahamwe,* and the defeated Rwandan soldiers. They crossed the border with their arms and freely mingled with the local communities in former Zaire, increasing tension in an already volatile country facing ethnic and political strife. The arms were added to the numbers already in circulation in the host country in the time up to the country's civil and international war.

In Burundi, similar ethnic hostilities were taking place. As with the Rwanda civil conflict, the intercommunal strife in Burundi has a long history. The current round of conflict dates back in 1993, when the Tutsi-led army staged an attempted coup against a freely elected Hutu president.[11] Even though the coup was not successful, it triggered a series of retaliatory armed conflicts that naturally increased the demand and supply for arms in Burundi. The attacks on the Hutu government advanced from radical Tutsi militia to the Tutsi-led army and Hutu militia and rebels, which all served to multiply the numbers of arms in circulation. If the activities of the rebels could have been contained within Burundi's boundaries, perhaps the problem would be less complex. But since 1998, the rebels have reportedly coordinated their actions with Hutu forces in Rwanda and the Eastern of DRC, thus importing arms into these countries. Worse still, the Burundi Hutu rebels fought alongside the army of Laurent Kabila after he came to power in the DRC.[12]

The mingling of the Rwanda and Burundi rebel groups with disgruntled communities in the DRC served as an impetus for the consolidation of a general rebellion to oust Mobutu.. The rebellion that broke out in 1996 led by Zairian Tutsi was joined by dissidents intent on deposing the regime in Kinshasa, further compounding the problem of arms proliferation. The conflict finally developed into a national rebellion aimed at the overthrow of the central government. The culmination of these events was the triumphant entry, in May of 1997, of Kabila's Alliance des Forces Démocratiques pour la libération du Congo-Zaire (Alliance of Democratic Forces for the Liberation of Congo/Zaire—ADFL) into Kinshasa, shortly after Mobutu fled the country.[13]

The forces involved in helping Kabila oust Mobutu compounded the problem of arms proliferation. Between July 1996 and May 1997, Kabila's ADFL received support from the unhappy soldiers deserting from Mobutu's army, as well as from Rwanda, Uganda, Burundi, and Angola.[14] The military support offered by these countries served well to increase the arms supply in the Congo war. Rwanda and Uganda in particular got involved in the war because they were interested in removing rebels opposed to their governments from bases in eastern DRC. When this important objective was not achieved through the assistance given to Kabila's ADFL, relations grew sour.

In 1998, a new rebellion started in eastern Congo that soon developed into a major international war: the second Congo war. Kabila gained support from Zimbabwe, Angola, and Chad, which sent troops to support the Congo national army, as well as from Sudan and Namibia. The rebels received support from Rwanda and Uganda. The involvement of these countries in the second Congo war led to an intensification of local conflicts and general proliferation of arms, causing far-reaching effects. It was, for instance, a great surprise that Jonas Savimbi's União Nacional para a Independência Total de Angola (National Union for the Total Independence of Angola—UNITA) actually accumulated military equipment and strength as the Congo war intensified. In Uganda, the Allied Democratic Forces (ADF) also gained momentum after Museveni got heavily involved in Congo.[15] Although Museveni had putatively intervened in Congo specifically to halt the ADF's activities,[16] the latter actually profited from the general proliferation of arms in the area. Closely following the trend were the rebels in Burundi who also took advantage of the situation in Congo. Burundi is also said to have assisted the anti-Kabila rebels, while the militias from Hutu Rwanda lent a helping hand to Kabila.[17]

The polarization of the various national armies and rebel forces into two camps contributed to arms proliferation as each ally sought to acquire combative gear. This process could possibly be compared to the arms race during the Cold War, albeit not on the same scale. The idea and practice of forming military alliances heightened the demand and supply for arms in Congo and the broader region. While lobbying and the formation of new alliances were an ongoing process in the political arena, there were unexpected developments on the battlefields. In August 1999, the key allies in the war against Kabila, Rwanda and Uganda, turned their guns against one another and fought it out at Kisangani. The implication of the threat of military imbalance between the two allies also contributed to arms proliferation in the Congo war.

THE SOURCES OF ARMS IN THE CONGO WAR

A large percentage of the arms in circulation in the Congo war were not acquired in the past decade. In addition to those acquired through the protracted conflicts involving the Tutsi formerly living in Uganda, and the conflicts in Rwanda, Burundi, and the DRC, other arms that had been in circulation much earlier. The historical perspective on arms proliferation in Congo can be traced back through the Cold War era to the late colonial period. The officers of Congo's colonial-era Force Publique were taught in the best military academies of the United States, France, Belgium, and Israel, and trained by experts from Germany, Egypt, China, and South Korea. They were supplied with some of the most sophisticated equipment ever seen in Africa, including a batch of Mirage jets supplied by France.[18] There are no records indicating how, when, or if the arms provided by the colonial states were ever collected or even destroyed. Some were eventually absorbed into nonstate groups within Congo, and they have not been accounted for since. Congo's vicious civil wars of the 1960s ensured that many of these arms found their way into the hands of various rebel groups and militia during the period. Although some of the weapons were rendered obsolete by technology, the numbers circulating increased the demand for continual supplies of new arms and bred a culture of armed conflict.

In the subsequent era, the United States and the Soviet Union supplied large stocks of light weapons to Cold War client states, including many in Africa.[19] Zaire, among other developing countries, acquired weapons, partly to impress or cow the population and as a source of illegal money for corrupt officials. As a key African Cold War ally of the United States, Zaire was one among several states that benefited directly from United States policies. The former Zaire was certainly one of the most significant arms importers in the Great Lakes region before 1990.[20] The former Zaire was also used by the United States as a conduit to supply arms to the UNITA rebels in Angola under the Reagan Doctrine in the 1980s.[21] During the period, Mobutu's government is said to have "skimmed off" millions of dollars worth of weapons meant for UNITA for their own forces.[22] It was through his military domination that Mobutu managed to sustain himself as a dictator for three decades, and he needed adequate military influence to wield power over his subjects and opponents.

Following the end of the Cold War, and in the era of the Congo wars, the sources of arms proliferated. The sources now include Eastern Europe, the West, and some parts of Africa, among others. To start with sources in Eastern Europe, some of the largest suppliers included Russia, Romania, and Slovakia. Others, whose sales are less publicized, include Belarus, Brazil, North Korea, and Bulgaria.[23] Albania and Israel have been mentioned as conduits.[24] Most of the arms coming from Eastern Europe are surplus arms accumulated during the Cold War. States were willing to sell weapons for profit, as opposed to their earlier, more political considerations.[25] The ex-communist states needed to get rid of their old stocks in favor of new technology. Belarus, which gained independence from Russia in 1991, has been a key source of arms for Africa.[26] With a more than adequate supply of weapons available to the Mobutu regime, the Zairian president continued to build up his arms arsenals. The stocks acquired by the Mobutu regime were subsequently spread to a variety of groups via army defectors. These arms were available for use when the time was ripe for the ADFL to oust Mobutu.

The sources from Western Europe are mainly the former colonizers. The key states often mentioned in connection with the Great Lakes region, and in particular the DRC, are France and Belgium. France copiously supplied various heavy and light weapons to the Rwanda government, especially after the October 1990 RPF invasion from Uganda. Over U.S.$6 million worth of arms were transferred to the Rwandan government between 1991 and 1992. French military support also took the form of military training and deployment of troops to protect French citizens in Rwanda.[27] These arms found their way into the hands of *Interahamwe* fighters, who used them first in the Rwandan genocide of 1994 and then in the Congo war.

Arms deployed in the Congo war have also been obtained directly or indirectly from African countries. Egypt and South Africa have been particularly noted as sources of arms to the countries of the Great Lakes region.[28] These two states have domestic arms manufacturing industries that they have used to supply belligerents in the current Congo war, and the wars preceding it. The Ugandan National Resistance Army (NRA) supplied the RPF with small arms and light weapons following the defection of NRA soldiers and officers of Rwandan origin to the RPF.[29] Even though Uganda is not known to be one of the states in Africa manufacturing arms, its military policies in the region have served to create an indirect supply. Its supply to the RPF and its involvement in the Congo war have contributed heavily to arms proliferation in the DRC. The late Kabila is reported to have bought Scud missiles from Iran, a move aimed at intimidating the rebels and their Rwandan and Ugandan backers at the time of their attempt to capture Kinshasa.[30] The military might deployed by the Ugandan and Rwandan forces during the Congo War, and their insistence on having forces on the ground to protect their interests, has continued to serve as justification for each state to continue acquiring superior weapons.

The worlds of the manufacturers and the end users in Congo are far apart. The many parties involved in a single weapons purchase bridge the distance. The purchase of a single weapon can involve several nations, corporations, or brokers[31] who are involved at various levels: purchasing, brokering, transporting, and delivering at the actual points of reception. The modes of transportation to the entry points include air, ground, and sea, depending on the scale of transaction. Some of the more frequently used African airfields for flights into eastern Congo-Kinshasa include Entebbe (Uganda), Kigali (Rwanda), Luanda (Angola), and even Juba (southern Sudan).[32] The African seaports include Asab (Eritrea), Beira and Nacala (Mozambique), Conakry (Guinea), Dar es Salaam (Tanzania), Djibouti, Durban (South Africa), Luanda (Angola), Merca (Somalia), Mombasa (Kenya), and Monrovia (Liberia). On arrival, the arms are forwarded to their destinations by road, rail, air, or ferry, often via interior distribution centers, such as Port Bell (Uganda), Ouagadougou (Burkina Faso), and Juba.[33]

Many governments in Africa have served as conduits in the arms transfers. The decision of a government to allow its air space, land, or high seas to be exploited by the transporters is often based on sympathy for one of the parties involved in the Congo war. For example, the Tanzanian government is reported to have allowed its territory to be used to facilitate the movement of arms and ammunition to the anti-Kabila rebels and their supporters.[34] Although Tanzania may have acted mainly with an eye to its bilateral relations with Uganda, the fact that the arms and ammunition would end up in Congo should have made it desist, if it wanted to respect international norms. African governments need to reexamine their positions on arms sales, which contribute to the problem of arms proliferation. They should be identifying sustainable resolutions to conflict and collecting illegal arms for destruction as steps toward peace building.

The natural resources in the Congo have contributed to prolonging the war and promoting the arms trade on both sides. Both Kabila's allies and those opposing him have reportedly benefited from the exploitation of Congo's resources. Its mineral wealth has been used to finance the war and purchase arms, as well as to secure his allies' loyalty. The Congolese government has depended upon the diamond mines of Mbuji-Mayi above all, getting a minimum of U.S.$100 million a year from the city's riches at the height of the fighting.[35] One diamond-mining village close to Mbuji-Mayi was simply turned over to Zimbabweans to reward them for joining the fight.[36] Armed rebels also benefit from the sale of the diamonds and utilize the proceeds to finance the war. Trade and business interests rather than any desire to liberate the Congolese have played a major role in the current conflict in Congo.[37]

It is not only those directly involved in the conflict who exploit the resources but also the merchants of war who sell arms to both sides. The longer the war lasts, the better for arms and diamond dealers who are involved in the lucrative trade. It is doubtless true that Western Europe and the United States view the untapped resources of Congo and the rest of Africa as being important for their economic future, as some observers insist.[38] They stand to gain little, however, as long as the resources are controlled by local warlords who only seek to buy East European small arms, rather than capital equipment from Europe and the United States The availability of resources to the warlords encourages more arms transfers, which ends up enriching the militarists and the armaments industries. The prolongation of the war is an assurance of a ready market for arms. The proceeds from the sale of the natural resources have therefore played a role in arms proliferation in the Congo war.

PEACE INITIATIVES AND ARMS PROLIFERATION

This section explores the relationship between the various peace initiatives undertaken to resolve the Congo war and the problem of arms proliferation. Since August 1998, a number of diplomatic meetings have been held at different times to resolve the conflict in the DRC.[39] As the crisis was escalating in August 1998, Southern African Development Community (SADC) leaders first met in Victoria Falls, Zimbabwe, to settle the conflict. Differences soon emerged in this meeting as some members supported military action and others were opposed to it. Notably, South Africa was opposed, but Angola, Namibia, and Zimbabwe went ahead and deployed forces in the DRC in support of Kabila. What was meant to be a diplomatic effort ended up being a military undertaking that contributed directly to arms proliferation. A

second Victoria summit was held on 18 August 1998, and again the meeting ended in
disarray as the rebels demanded to have direct talks with Kabila. This was the first
meeting to which the rebels were invited, and it would have been a prime opportunity to discuss the problem of arms proliferation with all the parties. Subsequent talks
were held on 22 August 1998 in Pretoria, South Africa. During the meeting, President Nelson Mandela called for a ceasefire and reversed his initial opposition to military intervention in the DRC. However, the ceasefire was not honored in the wake
of continued fighting.

The search for a resolution was then taken up at the Organization of African
Unity (OAU) level, in Addis Ababa, when the organization sponsored three days of
peace talks on the DRC.[40] Like the previous meetings, this one ended in stalemate,
and, as in previous meetings, the problem of arms was not addressed. Several other
meetings followed toward the end of 1998, and a series of others were held in 1999.
In spite of the many diplomatic efforts, the determination of all sides to prevail militarily continued to plague the peace initiatives. The debate then centered on the urgent need for a ceasefire and the immediate withdrawal of foreign troops from
Congo. A meeting held in Sirte, Libya on 19 April 1999 called for a ceasefire, the
withdrawal of all foreign troops, and the deployment of African peacekeepers. Alas,
no action was taken to implement the resolutions made on paper.

The Lusaka Agreement signed on 27 August 1999 represented the culmination
of remarkable diplomatic efforts made by president Chiluba under the umbrella of
SADC.[41] The agreement provided for the establishment of a joint military commission made of African countries to monitor the implementation of the agreement
and the disarmament of the armed groups. It also endorsed the deployment of a UN
peacekeeping force in the DRC, UN Mission in the Democratic Republic of Congo
(Mission d'Organisation Nations Unis au Congo—MONUC). The mandate of
MONUC is to monitor the disengagement of forces from confrontation lines.[42] If
it is to achieve any meaningful success, MONUC must not only concentrate on in-
hibiting belligerents from pursuing conventional warfare on the front lines, but also
must prevent guerilla warfare at the grassroots and ethnic conflict in many parts of
the DRC. A well-integrated approach toward a halt in arms proliferation is the only
means to sustainable peace in the DRC.

All of these initiatives were indeed commendable, but they were also incomplete.
This is because the initiatives centered on diplomatic, political, or even military resolutions, without addressing the very pertinent issue of arms proliferation. The
problem of arms proliferation will continue to be a major obstacle to the efforts to
reach a peaceful resolution to the war. The free circulation of arms hampers the
ceasefire initiatives: For instance, rogue elements can use their arms without the
sanction of political representatives. In the real sense, arms proliferation has inhibited diplomatic efforts and conflict resolution in favor of continued fighting, and the
result has been the escalation of ongoing conflicts.

THE EMERGENT ARMS CONTROL REGIME:
A FRAMEWORK FOR FUTURE PROGRESS

Despite the failure to control the proliferation of small arms in the Great Lakes, some
recent efforts have been made to address the problem there. These generally have

built on earlier initiatives. If the problems of small arms proliferation is to be dealt with over the medium term, it is likely to be through the mechanisms discussed here.

The notion of limiting conflicts through arms control dates back to the early nineteenth century, but those ideas were not realized leading up to World War I, in the interwar period, or after World War II. During the Cold War, the bipolar political system did exert some control over the transfer of arms, though not to Cold War client states. With the disintegration of the bipolar political system, surplus weapons flooded the world market uncontrollably. Although the Cold War era had posed a great threat to peace and security, the problem of uncontrolled arms proliferation grew worse in the 1990s. On the African continent, uncontrolled arms flows have been a thorn in the side of peace, as arms exacerbate both intra and interstate conflicts. Recently, however, significant arms control initiatives have again emerged.

To achieve the fundamental objective of arms control, these initiatives and agreements must cut across the subregional, regional, and international levels. Elements that must be included are domestic legislation and international implementation, enforcement, and monitoring. In recent years, the initiatives undertaken at the regional and subregional levels have been more impressive than those at the global level. The Americas have been credited by the Small Arms Survey for having played a pioneering role in the fight against small arms proliferation.[43] The Organization of American States's (OAS) Fire Arms Instruments, adopted over 1997 and 1998, represents the first step taken at the regional level to combat the illicit arms trade and improve controls over the movement of small arms.[44] The West African moratorium is another remarkable arms control regime. The idea of a West African moratorium on small arms grew out the conflict resolution efforts of northern Mali in the 1990s, and a 1996 proposal of Malian president Alpha Oumar Konare.[45] The Economic Community of West African States (ECOWAS) endorsed the concept, and the heads of state of all sixteen ECOWAS members signed the "Declaration of a Moratorium on Importation, Exportation and Manufacture of Light Weapons in West Africa" on 31 October 1998 at their twenty-first summit in Abuja, Nigeria.[46] The moratorium has faced problems at the implementation level,[47] but it demonstrates the political willingness of the ECOWAS heads of state to confront the problem.

Recent initiatives in the Great Lakes and Horn of Africa regions are further demonstrations that national leaders are recognizing that the problem of arms proliferation requires a multinational effort. These initiatives also acknowledge the fact that many states are involved in both the legal and illicit trade in arms. Unlike initiatives in other regions, those in Great Lakes and Horn of Africa are different in that they have been initiated by nonstate actors as well as by states.[48] The subregional initiative's main objective is to identify national and regional priorities for implementing the Nairobi Declaration and the draft subregional action program. The Nairobi Declaration was made by the ministers of foreign affairs of ten countries in the Great Lakes and the Horn of Africa who met in Nairobi on 15 March 2000 to deliberate on the problem of arms proliferation.[49] The meeting was also a subregional preparation for the July 2001 UN Conference on the Illicit Trade in Small Arms and Light Weapons. One of the fundamental objectives of the Nairobi Declaration is the formation of "national focal points" that would be instrumental in implementing the Coordinated Agenda for Action on the arms problem in the Great Lakes and the Horn of Africa.[50] Some of the issues of concern in the Coordinated Agenda include regional cooperation, legislative measures, control, seizure, forfeiture, collection, destruction, information exchange, record keeping, and public awareness. Operational and capacity building proposals in the Coordinated Agenda aim at developing or improving national training programs to enhance the capacity of law enforcement agencies to fulfill their roles in the implementation of this agenda for action. The initiative's implementation procedures are still under discussion, but the parties have demonstrated some inclination to address the problem. It is still early to judge the tangible results of the initiative, but the progress so far is somewhat encouraging.

Apart from the subregional initiatives, all African states came together recently for the first time to forge a common approach to the problem under the auspices of the OAU. The OAU convened a ministerial preparatory conference in July 1999 in preparation for the July 2001 UN arms conference.[51] A follow-up meeting, held in Bamako, Mali, on 30 November and 1 December 2000, served both to consolidate an African common position for the UN conference and to articulate, for the first time, a continent-wide strategy for tackling the small arms problem. The resulting Bamako Declaration stresses both the need for action on the part of supplier countries and the need to curve demand for small arms. The importance of prevention is recognized, together with control and reduction.[52] The European Union Program on Illicit Trafficking demonstrates a similar spirit of regional action. The program reflects the member states' desire to take concrete measures to curb the illicit trafficking and use of conventional arms.[53]

At the global level, it is only recently that the UN has focused a concerted effort on the problem of arms proliferation. Former UN Secretary-General, Boutros-Ghali helped direct attention to the issue and challenged the international community to find effective solutions to the problem, which was vividly illustrated by the conflicts the UN was grappling with at the time. The UN made a number of efforts between 1995 and 1999 to survey the magnitude of the problem and to identify possible enforcement measures.[54]

Negotiations for the Protocol against the Illicit Manufacturing of, and Trafficking in, Firearms, their Parts and Components and Ammunition (typically referred to as the "Firearms Protocol") have been in underway since 1999.[55] The purpose of the Protocol is to promote and facilitate cooperation among states to combat, and eventually eradicate, the illicit manufacturing of and trafficking in firearms, their parts, and ammunition.[56] With all due preparations, the long awaited UN arms conference was finally held in July 2001. It was an historical juncture, for the first time bringing together all states of the world to address this issue of common concern. The conference provided an opportunity to the member states to develop and refine a powerful firearms protocol that would thereafter govern the manufacture, transfer, enforcement, and other aspects of arms trade. Even though the event was marked with diverse debates and some disagreements, it represented a major step forward in addressing the problem.

Although the United States has sometimes been credited for taking the lead in the fight against arms proliferation, its position at the conference generated acrimony when U.S. representatives argued that America does not see global action as the way forward. Rather, the United States argued that it is up to individual states to take action. Further, the United States did not recognize the need for a follow-up conference, arguing that states are not accountable to the UN or the international community, but to their own laws.[57] This radical stance against concerted efforts and in favor of individual state action suggests that there will be strict limitations on achieving the stated goals and implementing the agreed-upon program of action. Already, the Protocol seems to be stymied by the very problem it was meant to address, namely the harmonization of national laws across the regions. The United States, for instance, requested that Section 11, Paragraph 20, which refers to restrictions on the civilian possession of arms, be eliminated from the program of action.[58] It would be ironic to allow civilians to arm themselves while simultaneously undertaking effort to collect arms already in circulation among civilians in an attempt to enhance security. Allowing civilians to arm themselves, particularly those in war-torn states like the DRC, would virtually ensure the continuation of cycles of conflict.

Agreements made among states on arms trade have been threatened previously by loopholes, which arms dealers identify and exploit, especially in developing countries where the lack of controls and oversight ease their operations.[59] The same case applies to the UN arms protocol. One of the loopholes likely to cause problems is the issue of standardizing methods to track arms. This is an important aspect of the problem, because were the UN to impose an arms embargo against states experiencing civil war, like the DRC, such methods would make it possible to track the source. The imposition of sanctions and embargoes has been one of the methods applied by the international community to limit weapons availability during intrastate conflict. This method has failed in the past and even has compounded the problem by involving a criminal element in the arms trade. A good example is the arms embargo imposed against Rwanda in 1994 and Burundi in 1995 and 1996 by UN Security Council, which never served any useful purpose. Embargoes may also lead countries to develop costly indigenous arms production capabilities, as happened in South Africa.[60] Nonetheless, a stringent application of rules for tracking arms flows would go a long way in combating illegal transfers, as the states violating an obligation of international law or an embargo could be identified.

Another loophole easily taken advantage of involves the licensing of arms. The UN arms protocol already seems threatened because some member states appeared indecisive on whether to license the civilian possession of arms. The United States in particular registered reservations on measures that prohibit civilian possession of small arms.[61]

If the agreements and other documents arising from subregional and regional initiatives were implemented at the international level, the contribution of small arms proliferation to the problem of African conflicts could be mitigated. In the case of the Congo war, the first step would be to achieve agreement among the states intervening in the conflict to withdraw from the various battlefronts. The next step would be to realize a political *modus vivendi* among the main political actors within Congo, so that the state could once again be recognized as the sole possessor of the legitimate means of violence. In the medium term, however, the collection of arms from nonstate groups and the prevention of a new round of small arms proliferation are the only ways that the cycle of violence can be halted.

SYNTHESES AND CONCLUSION

The protracted conflict and war in the DRC is multifaceted, having been dubbed a conflict among regional warlords, a civil war, and Africa's first multiple-state international war. While the underlying causes of the conflict have been identified as the greed for natural resources, ethnic animosity, bad governance, and external aggression, it is clear that proliferation of arms in the Great Lakes has provided the means for the actual fighting. Accordingly, the latter must assume a fundamental position in any effort to resolve the conflict, since the possession of arms by many nonstate groups impedes peaceful resolution to any conflict. Arms serve as an impetus to conflict and war, as has clearly been demonstrated in the DRC since 1996. Intensive fighting has not delivered the benefit of peace or a resolution of political conflict. Instead, the war has only succeeded in attracting volumes of arms injected by all the parties on one side or the other. Needless to say, without an abundant arms supply, the war would not have dragged on for so long.

Arms proliferation has continued to impact negatively on the political culture of the DRC, as politics have been perpetually militarized. A culture of violence has slowly permeated into the social life of the Congolese people and their neighbors. President Laurent Kabila's own awareness of the problem of arms proliferation was reflected in his constant paranoia. It is not a surprise that, at the height of tension and suspicion, his own bodyguard murdered him. His murder reflected the magnitude of the problem facing the Congolese people. His successor has demonstrated a keen interest in peaceful resolution to the conflict, and he seems to have realized that no amount of fighting will deliver peace to his country. One must give due credit to the young Kabila for the peace initiatives he has taken since the demise of his father. The imminent total withdrawal of the foreign troops from the DRC is a positive indicator that there is hope for a total ceasefire, then a larger peace, and finally the curbing of arms proliferation in the region.

The problem of arms in the DRC affects every one there, civilians as much as armed combatants. Likewise, for arms collection initiatives to succeed, it is of paramount importance that the community gets involved. The members of local communities know who possesses arms, and if police in the DRC worked closely with them, they would benefit from authentic information. Such efforts in Congo only await the reconstruction of a civil order under which the police regain the trust of the local communities.

Because the problem of implementation of arms controls is a real issue in the DRC as well as in other states, governments need to set some funds aside to facilitate implementation of new controls at the subregional, regional, and international level. The DRC government also needs to set funds aside to increase public awareness of the problem of arms proliferation and its impact: economically, politically, socially, and in domestic and foreign policies. Also, there is the need to make public any information to do with small arms so that the public would feel involved. This would enhance community policing and increase desire among the people to share information with the police.

The UN Security Council has an obligation to increase the number of blue helmets on the ground under the MONUC, with the hope of ensuring the total withdrawal of the foreign troops and of implementing the long-dormant Lusaka Agreement. A large role for the UN in support of the efforts of the new Congolese government and other African countries will be necessary to bring peace to the DRC itself and to the wider region. Efforts must be made to bring Rwanda and Burundi on board while addressing the problem of arms proliferation and peace in the DRC, for events in any of these Great Lakes region states inevitably has a direct effect on the other countries.

The inter-Congolese dialogue under the facilitation of Ketumile Masire, former president of Botswana, has been one of the most hopeful steps toward restoring peace to Congo. There is room to hope that the Congolese will chart the way forward in subsequent Congolese national dialogues following the abortive one of October 2001 at Addis Ababa, Ethiopia. National dialogue will provide the Congolese with the best chance yet to address the problems facing their country and to work out sustainable solutions. While they do so, they will only ensure peace for the longer term if they include the problem of arms proliferation on the agenda. Otherwise, the circulation of arms will plague their efforts and prevent the possibility of achieving political stability and a sustainable peace. The same point applies to all peace initiatives directed to the current Congo war. A well-integrated approach to the peace initiatives must ensure that the problem of arms proliferation is addressed. The diplomatic or political approaches on their own will not succeed in resolving the conflict and bringing an end to the war. Indeed as the UN Special Envoy to DRC correctly observed, arms are an impediment to peace. "Every shot fired, regardless of where it originates, is a blow to our efforts towards peace."[62]

NOTES

1. Tom Porteous, "Briefing; The last three months in Africa," *BBC Focus on Africa* 10, no.3 (July–September 1999): 9.

2. See Jan Kamenju, "Small Arms and the Challenge to Conflict Prevention in Africa" (paper presented to UNITAR-RPTC Training Programme to Enhance Conflict Prevention and Peace Building in Southern Africa, held in Harare, 20–31 March 2000), 1–2.

3. United Nations General Assembly, "Report of Government Experts on Small Arms," 27 August 1997 referenced as A/52/298; see also, United Nations General Assembly A/54/258, 24.

4. Mike Bourne, "Militarization and Conflict in the Great Lakes," in Owen Green et al., *Light Weapons and Peacebuilding in Central and East Africa* (London: International Alert, 1998), 5.

5. Ibid.

6. Jos Havermans, "Africa's Most Worrying Battle Field," in Monique Mekenkamp, Paul van Tongeren, and Hans van de Veen, eds., *Searching for Peace in Africa: An Overview of Conflict Prevention and Management Activities* (The Hague: European Center for Conflict Prevention and Management Activities, 1999), 237.

7. T. Nyebirweki, "The Fire that Never Burns Out," *East & Central Africa Journal* (Nairobi) 3, no. 1, (January 2000), 8.

8. Gérard Prunier, *The Rwanda Crisis: History of a Genocide* (New York: Columbia University Press, 1995), 93–94.

9. Michael S. Lund, "A Region at War," in Mekenkamp, van Tongeren, and van de Veen, *Searching for Peace in Africa,* 187.

10. Ibid., 189.

11. For a general background on Burundi covering the period through the massacres of the 1990s, see René Lemarchand, *Burundi: Ethnocide as Discourse and Practice* (Washington: Wilson Center Press, 1994).

12. Jos Havermans, "Burundi: Peace-Initiatives Help Stem the Violence," in Mekenkamp, van Tongeren, and van de Veen, *Searching for Peace in Africa.*

13. Havermans, "Africa's Most Worrying Battle Field," 237.

14. Ibid., 238.
15. Nyebirweki, "The Fire that Never Burns Out," 8.
16. On this point, see chapter 9 in this volume.
17. Nyebirweki, "The Fire that Never Burns Out," 8.
18. Excerpts from Michela Wrong, *In the Footsteps of Mr. Kurtz*, serialized by *The East African*. (Nairobi), 16–22 October 2000, part 2, 1 and 11.
19. Lora Lumpe, "Introduction," in Lora Lumpe, ed., *Running Guns: The Global Black Markets in Small Arms* (London: Zen Books, 2000), 3.
20. Bourne, "Militarization and Conflict in the Great Lakes," 5.
21. The Reagan Doctrine was the Reagan's administration policy of providing arms to anti-communist insurgent groups fighting communist or left-wing governments in the developing world. It was applied in Afghanistan, Angola, Cambodia, and Nicaragua.
22. Bourne, "Militarization and Conflict in the Great Lakes," 5.
23. Ibid., 6.
24. Ibid.
25. Lumpe, "Introduction," 3.
26. See the July 1999 report by Stockholm International Peace Research Institute. [No more information available].
27. Ibid., 5.
28. Ibid., 6.
29. Ibid., 6–7.
30. Wairagala Wakabi and Ogoso Opolot, "Museveni Shopped for Guns in Belarus," *The East African*, 24–30 April 2000, 1–2.
31. Mohammed Ali, "Arms and Wars in Africa," *The African Herald* (Dallas, Texas) 2, no 1 (April/June 2000): 9.
32. Ibid.
33. Ibid.
34. Mwesiga Baregu, "Tanzania and the Rebels/Invaders in DRC," in Ibbo Mandaza, ed., *Reflections on the Crisis in the Democratic Republic of Congo* (Harare: Sapes Books, 1999), 39.
35. Ellen Knickmeyer, "City that Finances Congo's War Stays Poor," *Houston Chronicle*, 18 May 2001, available at http://www.HoustonChronicle.com (12 July 2001).
36. Ibid.
37. Levi Ochieng, "Uganda, Rwanda Push into Congo Driven by Greed," *The East African* (Nairobi) 17–23 July 2000, 9. Also see chapters 5, 6, 8, 9, and 12 in this volume.
38. L. Campbell, "Note on the Pace of the Struggle for a New Mode of Politics in the Congo," in Ibbo Mandaza, ed., *Reflections on the Crisis in the Democratic Republic of Congo*, 58.
39. See a detailed chronology in Africa Peace Forum, (APFO)-FEWER reports, "Early Warning Report on the Situation in the DRC," (Nairobi 1998 and "Background Report Great Lakes Early Warning Project," (Nairobi 1998). These reports were previously available at the FEWER Web site, www.fewer.org. (?) A staff member working with APFO and involved in compiling the FEWER Report is consulting with FEWER office for the current website if any. I shall furnish you with the information as soon as I get it [AM]. Also, see G. Punungwe, "Peace Initiatives in the DRC conflict," in Mandaza, ed., *Reflections on the Crisis in the Democratic Republic of Congo*, 145–153.
40. Havermans, "Africa's Most Worrying Battle Field," 237–257.
41. Ibid.
42. Integrated Regional Information Network for Central and Eastern Africa (Nairobi, 15 December 2000). p. 1. See also irin@ocha.union.org (15 December 2000) for further details on the Security council and MONUC.
43. Ed Laurence, "The OAS Agreement," *Small Arms Survey 2001* (Geneva: Graduate Institute of International Studies, 2001), 251–56.

44. Ibid., 252.
45. Anatole Ayissi, "The West African Moratorium," *Small Arms Survey 2001* (Geneva: Graduate Institute of International Studies, 2001), 258–261.
46. Ibid., 259.
47. Ibid., 260.
48. Andrew Mclean, "Tackling small arms in the Great Lakes region and the Horn of Africa," Presented 8 May 2000, Institute of African Studies, Dar es Salaam, Tanzania.
49. "Implementing the Nairobi Declaration on the Problem of the Proliferation of Illicit Small Arms and Light Weapons in the Great Lakes and the Horn of Africa," 15 March 2000. Accessed in the Ministry of Foreign Affairs and International Co-operation, Nairobi, July 2001.
50. The Coordinated Agenda for Action refers to an agreement by states in the subregion to promote human security and ensure that all states have in place adequate laws, regulations, and administrative procedures to exercise effective control over the possession and transfer of small arms and light weapons. "Implementing the Nairobi Declaration," p. 5.
51. Eunice Reyneke, *Small Arms and Light weapons in Africa: Illicit Proliferation, Circulation and Trafficking* (Proceedings of the OAU Experts Meeting and International Consultation, May–June 2000, Pretoria, South Africa, Institute of Security Studies).
52. Virginia Gamba, "An African Common Approach to small arms," *Small Arms Survey 2001* (Geneva: Graduate Institute of International Studies, 2001), 265–266.
53. Elizabeth Clegg, "European Measures," *Small Arms Survey 2001* (Geneva: Graduate Institute of International Studies, 2001), 268–272.
54. For a detailed account on the UN efforts see, Ed Laurence, "The Global Small Arms Process," *Small Arms Survey, 2001* (Geneva: Graduate Institute of International Studies, 2001), 276–278.
55. Ibid., 278.
56. See, "Report of the United Nations Conference on the Illicit Trade in Small Arms and Light Weapons in All Its Aspects," (United Nations; New York, 2001).
57. See organizer@iansa.org, 17 July 2001, Summary of day five from the conference room. [No more information available].
58. Ibid., 4.
59. Jakkie Cilliers and Christian Dietrich, "Introduction," in Cilliers and Dietrich, *Angola's War Economy: The Role of Oil and Diamonds* (Pretoria: Institute of Security Studies, 2000), 5.
60. Lora Lumpe, "Preliminary Policy Options for Monitoring/Restricting Exports of Light Arms," (presented at the UNIDIR Conference on Small Arms and Internal Conflict, 7–8 November 1994, Geneva, Switzerland); available on the Federation of American Scientists website at http://www.fas.org/asmp/campaigns/smallarms/options.html 7 (site accessed on 12 July 2001).
61. Ibid.
62. See Integrated Regional Information Network, englishservice@ocha.unon.org, accessed Friday, 22 December 2000.

CHAPTER 12

The Economic Impact of the Congo War

MUNGBALEMWE KOYAME AND JOHN F. CLARK

The war in the Democratic Republic of Congo (DRC) has certainly had devastating economic consequences for Congo itself, but it has also affected the whole of the central Africa region and even some countries not bordering on Congo, notably intervening Zimbabwe and Namibia. There can be no doubt that the economic potential of the entire African continent has been indirectly muted by the war's huge disruptive impact. At the same time, of course, narrow constituencies of individuals including smugglers, arms dealers, and corrupt military officials have profited handsomely from the war.

Yet such profits are not likely to disguise the overwhelmingly negative economic consequences of the war in general. Tens of millions of central Africans occupy an economic space at the extreme periphery of the new high-tech, global economy that has recently embraced so much of the world. Theirs is an economic life dominated by peasant agricultural production, with only fleeting and secondhand contacts with the industrial centers of the world. With so little capital at their disposal, even short-term disruptions in their normal economic activities can be devastating. By mid-2001, international non-governmental organizations (NGOs) were estimating that some 2.5 million persons had perished in Congo as the direct or indirect result of the war.[1] The large majority of these deaths were an indirect consequence of the war, stemming from malnutrition and disease. These in turn were primarily caused by the displacement of persons from their homes and fields, and by the utter disruption of health services, particularly in the occupied parts of the country. Large-scale death, it would seem, is the ultimate consequence of economic disruption for those living on the economic margins of a developing society.

Nevertheless, the calculation of the economic consequences of the war is an extremely daunting task. It is quite clear from the outset that a mere accounting exercise can reveal little about the economic costs of the war, and hence, the task can be carried out as well by political economists as by economists per se. First, as the illustration above suggests, many of the economic consequences of the war are indirect ones. Second, many of the economic consequences of the war are recorded only in the unofficial economy wherein dwell the criminal and quasicriminal elements, who seek to obscure or hide the scale of their economic activities. As a result, one must certainly look at the official figures, but one must look behind and between them, as well.

Any presentation of the economic consequences of the war also faces a daunting generic problem of social science causation, namely, that of establishing a reasonable baseline. It is widely appreciated that Congo itself contains an enormous economic potential, but it is also a harsh reality that its economic potential has scarcely been tapped in Congo's independent history. Of course, the extraction of Congo's mineral wealth was carried on at a moderately high rate during the first twenty-five years of the Mobutu reign, but virtually none of the profits from this exercise were reinvested in the country.[2] As a result, Congo endured a spiral of economic decline that accelerated downward during the 1990s, during which time even the extraction of minerals declined precipitously. Given this background, what should one have "normally" expected of Congo after the exile and death of Mobutu? Certainly, given Congo's grotesquely corrupt political culture and collapsed infrastructure, one could not reasonably have expected a sudden economic "take-off." On the other hand, some marginal improvements in economic life were certainly to have been expected. We can get a slight glimpse at what Congo's economic picture would have been without the war by examining the short period between May 1997, when Laurent Kabila seized power, and August 1998, which the current war began. Unfortunately, this window is far too narrow to give a clear picture of what Congo's "normal" post-Mobutu economic trajectory might have been.

Likewise, as we estimate the impact of the Congo war on other economies, we must imagine some kind of hypothetical, nonwar baseline. All of the neighboring countries have been affected in a variety of ways by the war. But the general economic stagnation of such countries as the Central African Republic or Zambia cannot be readily attributed to the war, for these countries had demonstrated an utter incapacity for economic development even prior to the war. On the other hand, a gradual economic stabilization and upswing in Congo would have provided some economic advantages for them. Another challenge is to perceive which observable effects are due to the war and which are due to unrelated causes. For Uganda, for instance, the world market prices for coffee may have a larger economic impact on its economy than any effects of the Congo war, positive or negative. While such problems cannot be entirely overcome, this chapter takes due account of them, starts with reasonable baseline expectations, and strives to separate war-related consequences from others related to other economic forces.

In attempting a survey of the economic consequences of the war, we begin with Congo itself. The economic impact on Congo itself is perhaps hardest to estimate because of the lack of accurate data, particularly from occupied parts of the country. The insecurity created by the war has reduced economic news coverage of the country and made systematic economic surveys impossible. Nonetheless, many fragments of evidence about the economic devastation of the war exist. In the section on Congo, we survey the different kinds of economic disruption of the war, both for the formal, externally directed parts of the economy, and for the informal economy of peasants and irregularly employed urban dwellers. With all of the countries affected by the war, we begin with some general macroeconomic data.

The second section of this chapter examines the economic impact of the war on the actively intervening states. These, in turn, may be divided into two different groups: those that intervened initially with the aim of overthrowing Laurent Kabila (Rwanda and Uganda), and those that intervened to support his regime (Angola, Zimbabwe, and Namibia).[3] For the latter group, we should recognize that the economic impact for Angola is fundamentally different than that for the other two because of its border with Congo, which increases the potential for smuggling. While the economic impact of war for Congo itself is undeniably negative, the overall economic impact on intervening states is doublesided, and therefore more controversial. All of the intervening states suffer some additional military costs associated with deploying and maintaining their troops in Congo. They also suffer a number of more obscure secondary economic effects of their participation in the war. On the other hand, all have enjoyed increased economic benefits, mostly in the form of access to natural resources or in the form of direct payments from the Congolese government. Hence, the challenge in this section is partly one of trying to understand the *net* economic impact on the economies in question.

The third and final section of this chapter briefly explores some of the economic consequences of the war for other African states with a stake, or potential stake, in Congo. These fall into two categories. The first is the category of neighboring states that are indirectly affected by the war. Some of the more obvious economic consequences for these states are disruptions in their trading patterns and the economic impact of refugees on the local economies. The second category is that of potential African capital-exporting states, in which we place a single country: South Africa. In this case, the negative economic impact is largely one of unrealized potential.

THE ECONOMIC IMPACT ON THE CONGO ITSELF

Since its outbreak in August 1998, the recent war in Congo has been devastating to the economy of this vast nation. While the ongoing conflict in the region can be blamed most directly for the country's current economic setback, one should note that the economic decline in Congo started decades before the war. In spite of the country's vast natural resource potential, the widespread corruption, economic controls, and the diversion of public resources for personal gain during the Mobutu era thwarted economic growth. Some of the blame should also be put on President Laurent Kabila's disastrous economic mismanagement, including the introduction of unrealistic price controls, regulation of foreign exchange markets, and the printing of money to finance government budget deficits.

Assessing the economic impact of the Congo war is a difficult task since the war itself has made it virtually impossible to collect data on most aspects of the Congolese economy for the past two years. Therefore, in this section, we undertake an overarching analysis of the economic impact of the war in the Congo using the limited economic data available. The review covers the effects of the war on Congo's gross domestic product (GDP), on the level of government revenue, on the informal economy, and on the socio-economic conditions of Congolese people.

Decline in Gross Domestic Product

One major economic impact of Congo's war has been a negative growth of real GDP. It is estimated that Congo's economy (real GDP growth) contracted by about 3.5 percent in 1998 and by 14.5 percent in 1999.[4] The Economist Intelligence Unit (EIU) also estimated that the economy contracted by a further 15 percent in 2000, probably because of the war. The negative growth of real GDP in Congo is a result of the decrease in production in almost all the sectors of the economy, especially mining and agriculture export crops (See Table 12.1). The drop in production is largely attributed to the loss of control by the government of a huge portion of the territory during the course of the war.

The production and exports of commodities and minerals in territories occupied by the Rwanda and Uganda rebel-backed political parties are not counted in the official statistics of Congo because they are being illegally done by Burundi, Rwanda, and Uganda.[5] This illegal extraction of minerals such as gold, diamonds, and columbo-tantalite (coltan) by the rebels and foreign soldiers is causing a decline in the production and exports of Congo while fueling the exports of Rwanda and Uganda. The EIU's economic data on Congo show a 27 percent drop in diamond exports from U.S.$717 million in 1997 to U.S.$520 million in 1999; meanwhile coffee exports dropped from U.S.$168 million in 1997 to U.S.$91 million in 1999, a 46 percent decrease.[6]

Statistics on the decline in Congo's production and exports of minerals such as coltan and gold are not readily available. Statistics provided by the United Nations Security Council (UNSC) on the suspicious increase in Rwandan and Ugandan exports of some minerals do suggest how much export revenue Congo is losing, however. The UNSC reports that the value of gold exported by Uganda, for example, nearly doubled from 1996 to 1997. Uganda exported U.S.$105 million in gold by September 1997 (during the first phase of the Congo war) compared with U.S.$60 million in 1996, a 43 percent increase. This trend continued in 1998 and 1999. Uganda exported 11.45 tons of gold in 1999 compared with 5.03 tons in 1998 and 0.22 in 1994. In addition, Uganda became a diamond-, niobium-, and cobalt-exporting country. The same is true for Rwanda, whose "production" of gold in 1997 was 10 times its 1996 level and its "production" of coltan more than double its 1996 level.[7]

There is also a decline in the production of goods such as timber (cut and uncut wood) and palm oil in Congo. Between 1998 and 1999, Congo experienced a 55 percent decline in its production of cut wood, a 66 percent decline in its production of

Table 12.1 Volume of Production, Democratic Republic of the Congo

Commodity (metric tons, unless otherwise noted)	Nov. 1998	Nov. 1999	Percent Change
Copper (metric tons)	36,086	23,804	−34
Cobalt (metric tons)	3,688	1,800	−51
Diamonds ('000 carats)	24,463	18,520	−24
Gold (kilos)	135	7	−94
Coffee	33,716	16,038	−52
Cut wood	34,268	15,386	−55
Uncut wood	79,656	27,226	−66
Palm oil	15,910	5,664	−64

Source: The Economist Intelligence Unit, "Country Report: Congo," 1st quarter, 2000, p. 40.

uncut wood, and a 64 percent decline in its production of palm oil (see Table 1.2). The production of these goods is in large part done in areas that are under the control of the rebels and their Rwandan and Ugandan protectors.[8] Even if production statistics from rebel-held areas were counted in the official national production figures of Congo, however, there would still be a drop in the level of Congo's production.

The drop in production is caused, among other things, by the destruction of resources of production, such as physical capital and human capital, and by the looting experienced by Congo at the outbreak of the war. The UNSC reported that Congo lost a considerable amount of its capital stock due to the destruction of industries, machines, and equipment in regions occupied by the rebels and their Rwandan and Ugandan allies. In some cases, factories were dismantled or machinery spare parts were taken away, as in the case of a sugar factory owned by Kaliba himself in South Kivu. Moreover, between September 1998 and August 1999, occupied regions of the Congo were drained of existing inventories, including minerals, agricultural and forest products, and livestock, by Burundian, Rwandan, and Ugandan forces. Stockpiles of minerals, coffee, wood, livestock, and money that were available in territories conquered by Burundi, Rwanda, and Uganda were taken and sent to those countries or sold in international markets by their forces and nationals.[9]

The loss in human capital also contributed to the contraction of Congo's economy. Loss in human capital in the country came from deaths and from the escape of civilians to neighboring countries. Although statistics in the Congo war are difficult to obtain, NGOs have been working hard to try to estimate the number of deaths and displaced people. The International Rescue Committee estimated that, by the end of April 2001, there have been about 2.5 million deaths since the second outbreak of the conflict in August of 1998, with the majority dying of malnutrition and disease.[10] The United Nations High Commissioner for Refugees (UNHCR) has been constantly documenting the number of civilians fleeing the Congo since 1998, estimating that more than half a million people have fled to the neighboring countries.[11]

Negative growth in Congo's real GDP is also the result of a sharp decrease in foreign direct investment that started decades before the war but was worsened by the outbreak of hostilities. Few foreign investors are willing to invest in a country with high political risk, let alone in a country at war. In addition, the war has had a negative effect on the savings and investment capacity of the nationals. The financial system of Congo was in part destroyed by the looting of money from domestic banks (including the central bank branches) and private businesses in the territories conquered by the armies of Burundi, Rwanda, and Uganda. Some of these monies were transferred to those countries, destroying the savings and investment potential of Congolese. Nowadays, local banks operating in occupied zones such as Goma, Bukavu, Kisangani, Bunia, and Gbadolite deal directly with Kigali or Kampala.[12]

The contribution of services, including tourism, to the economy of Congo has also been negatively affected by the war. The destruction of wildlife in occupied regions means no revenue from tourism either today or in the future. According to the UNSC report, numerous accounts and statistics from regional conservation organizations show that almost 4,000 out of 12,000 elephants were killed in the Garamba Park in northeastern Congo between 1995 and 1999. In the Kahuzi-Biega Park, a zone rich in coltan and controlled by Congolese rebels and their Rwandan allies, only 2 out of 350 elephant families remained in 2000. The Okapi Reserve and the Virunga Park are equally affected.[13]

Decrease in Government Revenue
and Increase in Military Spending

Since the outbreak of the war in 1998, Congo's government revenue has been falling while its military expenditures have been rising. The latter rose from 16.1 percent of total government expenditures in 1992 to about 41.4 percent in 1997.[14] This rise is a war-induced increase in military expenditures that any country at war would experience. For example, in its effort to defend its territory and secure a supply of military equipment, the government of Congo has signed a contract worth several million dollars with the government of China.[15] The decline in government revenue is caused by, among other things, the looting of all the government funds in occupied regions since the 1998 invasion; the fall in the production of minerals, particularly diamonds; the decline in government tax revenue; and the drop in international aid and grants.

According to the EIU, diamonds and copper constitute the government's two biggest sources of revenue. Officially the Congolese government earned about U.S.$500 million from diamonds in 2000.[16] This diamond revenue would have been much higher if the government had control over diamonds extracted in rebel-held areas. For example, the Rassemblement Congolaise pour la Démocratie-Goma (Congolese Rally for Democracy—RCD) reported that they were making about U.S.$1.5 million dollars a month in revenue in August 2001.[17] The UNSC estimated, however, that the Rwandan army could be making about U.S.$20 million a month from selling coltan alone.[18] In addition, further losses to government revenue from mineral production result from the government's granting of mining concessions to foreign powers (called "incentives for assistance" by the UNSC) in order to secure their engagement in the war.

Congo's main source of tax revenue, international trade taxes (export and import duties or tariffs), which represented about 34.4 percent of government tax revenue in 1997,[19] has been declining since the outbreak of the war in 1998. The UNSC reported that products entering or leaving Congo are mostly transported by air and are not being checked by custom services on either side of the transactions. "An increasing number of aircraft are utilized to transport products and arms into the Democratic Republic of the Congo, while transferring out vast quantities of agricultural products and minerals, in particular to Kampala and Kigali."[20] The loss in import duties is particularly large because of the vast amounts of arms and consumer goods entering the Congo from Rwanda and Uganda. In addition, Congo is faced with a well-organized smuggling of minerals, especially diamonds, which deprives the treasury of substantial tax revenue from export duties. The UNSC reports that most diamond dealers operating in the government-controlled area smuggled their diamonds to Brazzaville where they were able to sell them. The explosion in diamond smuggling was the result of the monopoly on the diamond trade that Laurent Kabila's government granted to the International Diamond Industries (IDI). The monopoly created artificially low prices for producers, which caused them to seek alternative buyers.

Aids and grants from the international community, which make up another large portion of government revenue, also stopped coming due to the ongoing political instability and the financial mismanagement in Congo. Laurent Kabila's government kept government finances largely off the books. Under those conditions, the IMF and the World Bank refused to extend credits to the Congolese government. These lenders were understandably suspicious that the Congolese government would use aid income to purchase arms. International grants, which represented 52 percent of Congo's total government revenue in 1996 and 44 percent in 1997,[21] began to decline after the outbreak of the war in 1998, and subsequently stopped altogether.

Rapid Growth of the Informal Sector

Informal economic activity has always been widespread in Congo. In the early 1990s, the illegal and unrecorded transactions of Congo's informal economy were estimated to be three times the size of the official GDP.[22] The ongoing war in Congo has further contributed to the growth of its informal economy. Indeed, the Congo war has created an economic environment in which the banking system has almost collapsed and in which individuals only feel safe to conduct business in the informal market.

According to the U.S. Department of State, the government of Congo has been unable to provide foreign exchange for economic transactions. Businesses rely on the black market to access foreign currency and to get a higher rate than the official exchange rate. In May 2001, the Congolese franc (FC) was currently traded at an official rate of FC50: U.S.$1, compared with a black market rate of FC255: U.S.$1.[23]

In addition, some of the economic policies introduced by the government of Congo in 1998 forced many business transactions into the illicit economy. For example, in 1998 the government introduced measures to enforce price control laws and to regulate foreign exchange markets. The introduced price controls were so unrealistic that they forced local traders to sell goods at prices lower than what they had paid for them.[24] Indeed, merchants who got foreign exchanges at a higher rate in the black market were forced to price their imported goods according to the official rate for buying local currency.[25] At the time, the exchange rate was fixed at a very unrealistic level of FC9: U.S.$1 compared with a parallel market rate of FC32: U.S.$1.[26] In addition, the printing of money by the government in order to finance its budget deficits has been putting more pressure on the exchange rate and on the inflation rate, sending more business underground. These same policies have driven the diamond trade almost totally underground.

The growth of the informal economy is, therefore, being fueled by the growth of the black market for foreign exchange. Moreover, the latter is in large part dominated by the inflow of counterfeited currencies (Congolese francs and U.S. dollars). According to the UNSC report, the counterfeited currencies are often used for transaction payments in the informal sector, especially in occupied territories. Counterfeited Congolese francs are, for example, used for the purchase of mineral and commercial crops, primarily coffee. Some traders not only produce counterfeited Congolese francs but also use them to purchase natural resources in the informal market.[27]

Socio-Economic Conditions

As in past Congolese conflicts, the civilians have suffered immensely in the current war. According to one human rights report on Congo's conflict, "all the many combatant forces have attacked civilians, killing, injuring, and raping thousands of persons and causing more than half a million others to flee their homes."[28] Aside from the threats of physical violence, however, more Congolese have actually suffered from the deterioration of socio-economic conditions in the country.

For instance, the Congolese must endure the very high inflation rates caused by the vast and uncontrolled black market for foreign exchange and the printing of money by the government. Higher inflation rates are also due to price-fixing by Rwandan and Ugandan monopolies operating in occupied zones. The inflation rate as measured by the Consumer Price Index (CPI) doubled from 147 percent in 1998 to 333 percent in 1999; it increased further to 540 percent in 2000.[29] Because of the continuing increase in the prices of goods and services, Congolese cannot afford to purchase basic necessities needed for everyday life. The United Nations Office for Coordination of Humanitarian Affairs (UNOCHA) estimates that about 33 percent of the population is now vulnerable to malnutrition and disease. Government spending on health has been cut to less than 1 percent of government expenditure. Another report estimates that an astounding 75 percent of children under five are malnourished and that 30 percent are severely malnourished.[30]

The economic conditions for ordinary people are also affected by the lack of commerce between rebel-held and government-held areas of the country. Travel along the Congo River, the main means of transportation for interregional trade, has become very unsafe and dangerous for the traders. Even within areas supposedly secured by one army or another, commerce has been rendered unsafe by the war. For example, the BBC news reported on 29 August 2001 that Mai-Mai warriors hijacked a boat traveling from Fizi to Uvira (in eastern Congo) with twenty-five people on board. Some of the people on board, mostly suspected Congolese Tutsi, were kidnapped and are assumed dead.[31]

The disruption in interregional trade has had a big negative impact on the country, particularly on the capital of Kinshasa. The economic and commercial links among the various sections of the country and Kinshasa are very important to the survival of the "Kinois" (Kinshasa residents), who depend on consumer products such as fish and beans coming from other parts of the country. Because of the disruption of trade between Kinshasa and the various parts of the country, there has been a shortage of foodstuffs in the capital. For example, due to the interruption of trade between Kinshasa and Kisangani, where most of Congo's beans are produced, there is a growing shortage of beans in Kinshasa. To meet the demand for beans, merchants have to import from abroad. The chronic shortage of foreign exchange and government regulation of foreign exchange markets, however, have impeded the ability of businesses to imports foodstuffs and other products. Consequently, food shortages in Kinshasa have become increasingly acute. International aid organizations are concerned that a humanitarian crisis may emerge in Kinshasa because of the growing food shortages and poverty. Indeed, a study by the NGO Action Against Hunger shows that there was an increase in the rate of malnutrition in Kinshasa's lower income suburbs after the war began.[32]

There is also a disruption of trade between the rebel-held territories of Congo and the neighboring countries because of the monopoly that Rwanda and Uganda have granted themselves in the regions they hold. According to the UNSC report, a Congolese woman explained how she and her husband could no longer sell their palm oil to the neighboring Central Africa Republic or ship it to Kinshasa for a better price.[33] Indeed, having total control of the commerce and trade system in eastern and northeastern Congo, Rwanda and Uganda impose prices and conditions such as forcing contracts on local farmers. For example, according to the UNSC report, a buyer of coffee from local farmers forced the latter to use a certain type of bag for coffee delivery, a bag that the coffee buyer sells to them.[34] Failure to use these bags causes an automatic reduction in the price of coffee. In addition to being sold at higher-than-market prices, these bags and most of the consumer goods sold in those areas are being imported from Burundi, Rwanda, or Uganda.

The ongoing exploitation of local farmers by Rwandan and Ugandan troops and their Congolese allies in the occupied territories has not been limited to trade but has spread to all areas of day-to-day life. For instance, local Congolese, who have been mining for years for their own benefit, are now forced to give the proceeds from the mining to the rebels and their counterparts. According to the UNSC report, local Congolese (adults and children) currently living in occupied regions are forced to mine gold, diamonds, and coltan for little or no pay, under the heavy guard of Rwandan and Ugandan soldiers.[35] Consequently, the income and consumption for local Congolese and their family has plummeted, leading to malnutrition and disease.

THE MIXED ECONOMIC CONSEQUENCES FOR THE INTERVENING STATES

As noted in the introduction to this chapter, we divide the intervening states into those intervening on behalf of the rebels (Uganda and Rwanda) and those intervening on behalf of the Congolese government (Angola, Namibia, and Zimbabwe). For the first group, the value of the amount of goods looted from Congo, or gotten from there by quasilegitimate commerce, must be balanced against the costs of the war. Many of these costs are indirect, as well as direct. For the second group, the gains derived from the special contracts given to them by the Congolese state, as well as direct payments, must be balanced against the costs of their military activities. In both sets of cases, some effort to distinguish between private gains, often sent abroad to foreign banks and bourses, and those accruing to the public good must be made. In other words, where gains are being made, some assessment of *who* is gaining, and what the larger economic consequences are, must be undertaken.

Uganda and Rwanda

It has long been appreciated that both Rwanda and Uganda have realized substantial benefits from their interventions in Congo, but many aspects of this situation remain controversial. Notably, there has been some debate about whether economic motives were the initial and primary reasons for Rwandan and Ugandan intervention in Congo, despite the cover of security rhetoric. Particularly, a number of French scholars have documented the economic gains realized by the armed forces of the two countries in Congo and have implied that these may have been their original motivations.[36] On the other hand, the chapters on Rwanda and Uganda in this volume both conclude that economic considerations were not the initial motivation for Rwandan and Ugandan intervention, though such considerations are likely a factor in the continuing occupation of parts of Eastern Congo by the countries in question.[37]

The recent report of the UNSC has revealed the extent of Rwandan and Ugandan plundering in Congo and put the fact of this plundering beyond dispute. This impressive report helps us to understand many economic aspects of the war's economic effects on Rwanda and Uganda, though it does not resolve all the economic questions. Here, we rely primarily on this report, while also introducing some other economic data on Rwanda and Uganda to put its findings in perspective.

The UNSC report documents a range of forms of illegal economic exploitation undertaken by the main two antigovernment interveners in Congo. The report begins by noting that much of the "infrastructure" of exploitation was already in place in August 1998, owing to Rwanda and Uganda's prior intervention on behalf of Laurent Kabila during the 1996–97 war. In fact, Rwanda and Uganda had engaged in considerable exploitation during that war, as well as during the interim period, between May 1997 and August 1998. Some continuing illegal and unwanted economic activities by these foreign states in Congo during the early months of 1998 may indeed have helped precipitate the fallout between Kabila, on the one hand, and Kagame and Museveni, on the other. The infrastructure put in place during these prior periods include financial institutions (notably the Banque de Commerce, du Développement et d'Industrie—BCDI, in Kigali), which served to fund AFDL rebel activities during the 1996–97 war through the laundering of Congo mineral profits and through transportation networks, including airline and trucking companies, set up during the earlier war.[38]

The report breaks down the economic activity into two periods. The first, lasting from September 1998 to August 1999, involved the "mass-scale looting" of Congolese cash and commodity stockpiles by foreign armed forces and/or Rassemblement Congolaise pour la Démocratie (RCD) commanders. Among the types of locations looted were banks, farms, storage facilities, and factories. In all cases, the local Congolese responsible for guarding or overseeing these goods were forced to relinquish them under the threat of violence. Besides cash, in both Congolese francs and U.S. dollars, taken from regional banks in Congo, a variety of different kinds of commodities were taken away. These included coltan, cassiterite from the SOMINKI mining operation in Kivu, timber stocks from the Amex-bois logging company, also in Kivu, and coffee from the SCIBE company in Équateur.[39] In other cases, such as that of the Kaliba sugar factory, in south Kivu, capital equipment used in manufacturing processes was simply taken away.[40] Innumerable banks throughout occupied North and South Kivu, Orientale, and Équateur were also looted. While the initial and large-scale looting was directed by senior commanders, and with the obvious knowledge of the respective foreign governments, small-scale looting by individual bands of lower-ranking soldiers eventually followed.[41]

The phase of mass-scale looting was followed by a second stage involving the "systematic exploitation" of resources by the occupying armies and rebel groups. In general, these practices involved the installation of non-Congolese companies in the occupied areas or the takeover of existing companies by the foreign armies and rebels. These companies then engaged in "normal" profit-making business activities, to the benefit of the foreign partners. To illustrate the phenomenon, the UNSC report takes the case of a Ugandan-Thai foresting company named DARA-Forest. This company had unsuccessfully sought to establish operations in Congo in the interim between the two recent Congo wars but was denied the right to do so by the Laurent Kabila government. After Uganda's invasion of the country in late August 1998, the company set up operations in the Ituri region of Orientale province. In 1999, the company also set up a sawmill in the town of Mangina to process some of the timber being harvested. Subsequently, satellite imagery of the region showed that huge areas of forest had been logged by the company. The timber and sawn wood from the factory were then exported from Congo via Uganda, with most finally leaving Africa through Kenyan ports. According to the report, taxes on the harvesting and transit of these products were not paid to either Congolese or Ugandan authorities.[42] The DARA-Forest case is representative of many other such operations run by Rwandans and Ugandans in Congo. These economic activities sometimes made use of forced or semiforced Congolese labor, as well as Rwandan prisoners, particularly in mining.[43] The "permits" for these operations were typically issued by one of the rebel groups, if any permits existed at all. Another form of economic exploitation was the creation and maintenance of monopolies in consumer goods, controlled by occupying forces. This was easily accomplished since the occupiers regulated the flow of traffic into and out of occupied areas. Yet another form of illegal exploitation of natural resources involved the poaching of wild animals. The rebels and foreign occupiers have slaughtered large elephant populations for their tusks, while other species have been killed for the meat.[44] Meanwhile, huge quantities of coltan, diamonds, gold, and other minerals and metals are mined in Congo and re-exported via Rwanda and Uganda. A myriad of other, specific forms of economic exploitation by Rwanda and Uganda, and a few by Burundi, are documented in the report.

That Rwanda and Uganda military forces have realized substantial economic gains in occupied regions is beyond dispute, but this fact only tells a small piece of the story of the economic consequences of their occupation. Rather, this observation raises a number of other economic questions, all related to the overall balance of costs and benefits: Who in the occupying countries ultimately benefits from the exploitation of Congolese resources? Do their economic benefits pay dividends to the national treasuries of the occupying countries? If so, do these benefits outweigh the extra military costs associated with the occupation? Do the ordinary citizens of the occupying countries ultimately benefit from the spoils of war? And the most daunting question of all: What hidden or obscure economic costs associated with the occupation must Uganda and Rwanda pay over the longer term?

The chain of answers to these questions differs somewhat between Rwanda and Uganda, as implied by the UNSC report. As portrayed in the report, Rwanda has taxed economic activities in Congo and channeled the profits into the hands of military authorities, who then use the income to finance Rwanda's continuing presence in the country. This suggests that Rwanda's ultimate purpose for being in Congo is primarily the security of the Tutsi-dominated regime of Paul Kagame. Through mid-2001, Rwanda was maintaining a large presence of some 25,000 troops across the vast parts of Congo that it occupied. The UNSC report estimated the costs of transporting these troops and their equipment came to some U.S.$26.1 million per year; the cost for pay and bonuses for the same soldiers came to about U.S.$30 million per year.[45] A great number of other expenses is also involved in the occupation. Meanwhile, the other 20,000 or so members of the Rwandan Patriotic Army (RPA) within Rwanda itself also must be maintained, and ready for operations, all on a meager annual military budget of less than U.S.$70 million. Given that its occupation of Congo is not only self-financing, but even pays much or all of the budget for the Rwandan army back at home, the UNSC report observes that this accounts for the "vicious circle of the war."[46]

Yet Rwanda's looting in Congo has not apparently redounded to the general benefit of the Rwandan economy, at least as recorded in official figures. Rwandan GDP figures recorded a steady decline for four straight years beginning in 1996. The average annual GDP growth for 1996 and 1997 was 14.3 percent, while the average annual growth for the subsequent three years was only 6.9 percent.[47] Of course, all of these numbers are high by historical standards, but then Rwanda was still in recovery, economic as well as emotional, from the 1994 genocide during these years. There is much evidence, unsurprisingly, that Rwanda's ill-gotten gains were mostly unrecorded in official figures. For instance, Rwandan exports averaged U.S.$77.45 million in 1996 and 1997, but only U.S.$65.1 for the next three years (1998 to 2000).[48] Had the staggering profits of pilfered minerals been added to Rwanda's exports, the figure for the latter three years would surely be much higher. While it is logical that Rwanda's ill-gotten gains in Congo were little recorded, the profits gained would have showed up, indirectly, in GDP growth had they been reinvested in the local Rwandan economy. This implies that Rwanda's economic gains from the war have been spent largely on the war effort, as the UNSC report asserts, or have gone directly into the pockets of Rwandan army officers. The overall point of this analysis is that war booty has not helped the overall Rwandan economy much, if at all, and has certainly not helped the average Rwandan citizen.

In the case of Uganda, the bulk of the "war profits" seem to be going to senior army commanders and to other friends and family members of President Yoweri Museveni who have been allowed to set up operations in Congo. The UNSC report focuses on three of the most infamous such actors: the president's younger brother, General Salim Saleh; Saleh's wife, Jovia Akandwanaho; and General James Kazini, a relative of Museveni's wife, Janet. These three figures, along with some others, are involved in the "purchase and the commercialization of diamonds, timber, coffee and gold" through companies that they have recently established.[49] Of Kazini, the UNSC report says, "He is the master in the field; the orchestrater, organizer and manager of most illegal activities related to the UPDF [Ugandan army] presence in north and north-eastern Democratic Republic of the Congo. He is the right hand of Salim Saleh."[50] These and other highly placed Ugandans have collaborated and shared profits with Congolese (rebel) allies, including Jean-Pierre Bemba, leader of the Mouvement pour la Libération du Congo (MLC).

Unlike the case of Rwanda, the UNSC report suggests that the millions in "war profits" have served to bolster the overall Ugandan economy. In assessing the impact of these profits on Uganda's defense budget, the report says that " . . . the Ugandan economy benefited from the conflict through the re-exportation economy. In turn, the treasury benefited and this allowed an increase in the defense budget."[51] At the end of this section, the assessment is repeated, claiming that war profits have " . . . had a trickle-down effect on the economy and permitted Uganda to improve its GDP in 1998 and maintain it somewhat in 1999."[52] But this assessment is *not* supported by general economic data on Uganda. The average growth of GDP for the 1995–97 period was 8.7 percent, while it only averaged 5.9 percent for the subsequent three year period (1998 to 2000).[53] Similarly, the average value of official exports for the 1995–97 period was U.S.$597 million per year, while the average for the 1998–2000 period was only U.S.$467 million.[54] Given that Uganda apparently reported all its mineral re-exports reliably to the UN team, these figures can be taken relatively seriously. Uganda's falling exports and rising trade deficits during the latter three-year period are also reflected in an escalating current account deficit. The 1995–1997 average was -U.S.$319 million, while the 1998–2000 average was -U.S.$535 million.

Thus, the overall health of the Ugandan economy cannot be said to have been improved by the indirect effects of war profits. As was the case for Rwanda, the occupation of Congo by Uganda was certainly a costly affair for the Ugandan treasury. The Ugandan military budget nearly *doubled* in the fiscal year ending on 30 June 1999, and remained at a high level the following year.[55] Thus, the Ugandan taxpayer bore most of the burden of the war's costs, while a few friends and family members of Museveni enjoyed most of the gains. Since the Ugandan economy did not flourish during the period in question, compared against its overall performance in the 1990s, one may assume that little of the war profits were invested locally. More likely, they found their way into foreign bank accounts and stock markets.

The long-term and indirect costs of the Congo war are much harder to document but perhaps ultimately more important. Before the war, the Museveni regime seemed to be steadily reducing the levels of corruption, militarism, and authoritarianism in Uganda's government; since the war renewed in 1998, all three negative phenomena seem to be on the rise. The increasing levels of corruption are well reflected in the illicit activities of Museveni's friends and family in Congo, as the UNSC report indicates. As for militarism, Uganda has had to maintain, and even increase somewhat, the size of its army due to the war, whereas it had been reducing the size of its military prior to the war. The conflicts with Rwanda in Kisangani in 1999 and 2000 are another aspect of Ugandan militarism. Finally, the Ugandan occupation of Congo has never been sanctioned by the Parliament but rather appears to be an affair primarily of the president and his close advisers.[56] The social costs of the war may also be high. One can only guess how many incidences of AIDS have been spread in Congo and back to Uganda by the occupying forces, but the incidence of sexual abuse of Congolese women is known to be high. Indeed, the general disruption of family life for all involved, Congolese, Ugandan, and Rwandan, certainly contributes to the spread of AIDS and other diseases. The economic costs of such negative social outcomes of the war will find their way stealthily into the national accounts for standards of living over many years to come.

Angola, Zimbabwe, and Namibia

The economic consequences for the three interveners on the side of the Congolese government are related to their differing individual motivations. Angola seems to have intervened primarily for security reasons and particularly its un-ending war against the União Nacional para a Independência Total de Angola (UNITA) for control of the country. Zimbabwe's motivations, on the other hand, seem to be primarily economic. Since Zimbabwe has no border with the Congo from which rebels could cross into its territory, it cannot even use the pretext of security concerns to disguise its motivations. Moreover, there is no ideological reason or justification for Zimbabwe's intervention, although it is able to use the international norm against unwanted intervention as a cover for its own "counter-intervention." Namibia's motivations are the most obscure in the conflict, but they seem to have to do with the residual loyalty that President Sam Nujoma has for the regime in Luanda and its own security problems with UNITA. Since UNITA often operates from Namibian territory and threatens the security of the Nujoma regime, it has the same security concern, though much less urgent, than Angola. Nujoma's continuing loyalty to the regime in Luanda owes partly to the political and even financial support the latter has rendered.

According to the UNSC report, Angola has not realized significant economic gains as a result of its operations in the Congo. Notably, the report states that the Angolan state has not registered increased exports of minerals or gemstones as a result of its army's presence in Congo.[57] Moreover, it notes only one new major investment initiative in Congo, the formation of a joint Angolan-Congolese petroleum services company called Sonangol.[58] The company, 60 percent of which is owned by Sonangol Angola, was set up to deliver Angolan oil to Congo, with a view toward joint explorations off the Congo-Angola coast in the future. The additional profits generated by this company would apparently be minimal.

Meanwhile, the *additional* costs to Angola of its deployment of 3,000 soldiers in the Congo appear to be relatively small. Given Angola's enormous military establishment, probably over 100,000 soldiers in total, the small contingent in Congo is not a major drain on resources. If these troops were not in Congo, they would likely be engaging with UNITA in some other locations, probably within Angola itself. To the extent to which these troops are successful in interrupting UNITA's supply chains and disrupting its military operations, they are in fact serving a positive economic function, namely, limiting the economic damage of UNITA's sabotage within Angola. The overall performance of the Angolan economy is closely tied to world oil prices and is virtually unrelated to its military presence in Congo.

For Namibia, on the other hand, the situation is somewhat different. The comparative costs of its operations in Congo represent a much heavier burden than for Angola. Like Angola, Namibia was not thought by the UN to have realized any meaningful benefits from its military presence in Congo. Namibia is commonly said to have sent about 2,000 troops to Congo beginning in 1998, but opposition forces have claimed that the real number was as high as 3,000.[59] By August 2001, most of these troops had been withdrawn, in keeping with the revival of the Lusaka peace accords. Interestingly, the UNSC report tried to downplay the costs to Namibia, indicating that the overall military budget had *declined* from U.S.$113 million in 1999 to U.S.$100 million in 2001.[60] But these figures mask the huge *increase* in military spending Namibia experienced against its pre-Congo war figures. According to a Namibian Finance Ministry statement given in November 2000, the Namibia's overall defense costs had *doubled* between 1998 and 2000. The ministry reported at that time that the government had spent some N$100 million (about U.S.$13 million) on allowances for its troops in the Congo in only seven months of 2000, and another N$41 (about U.S.$5 million) for equipment.[61] Meanwhile, a news report in the *Namibian* newspaper (Windhoek) reported that the families of each of the more than forty Namibian soldiers killed in the Congo were paid a compensation of N$250,000.[62] Thus, the taxpayers of Namibia paid at least N$10 million, or about U.S.$1.25 million, just to compensate the families of the killed. For a country with a GDP of less than U.S.$3 billion and a population of only 1.7 million, the war costs for Namibia were clearly substantial.

In contrast to the other two interveners, Zimbabwe's situation is much more analogous to that of Uganda, in that it has little at stake in Congo in terms of security, and much in terms of economics. Zimbabwe is maintaining a much larger force than the other two supporters of the regime in Kinshasa, about 10,000 troops according to most news accounts, but more than 13,000 according to the EIU.[63] Meanwhile, the army and some government officials have involved themselves in a number of illicit contracts and joint ventures with the Congolese government.

These serve primarily to enrich high army officers and members of Mugabe's government, and, to a lesser extent, to "buy" the loyalty of unmotivated Zimbabwean soldiers and pay their expenses. Accordingly, the overall economic consequence of Zimbabwe's participation in the war is much like that of Uganda: A few well-connected officials are enriched, while the treasury, and ultimately the Zimbabwean taxpayer, bears the financial burden of the war.

The UNSC report does an impressive job in describing some of the corrupt economic deals that were reached between the government of Laurent Kabila and various Zimbabwean individuals and companies. The report's section on Zimbabwe begins by noting that Gecamines, the Congolese mining giant, gave "bonuses" directly to individual Zimbabwean soldiers between May 1999 and October 2000. At the same time, Gecamines was involved in a contract with a Zimbabwean mining company, Ridgepoint, to exploit certain mineral resources.[64] But a far more notorious story is that of COSLEG, a joint company formed from a Congolese state import-export firm (COMIEX) and OSLEG, a Zimbabwean company owned by several businessmen, a former defense minister official, and a Zimbabwean Defence Forces (ZDF) lieutenant general. The purpose of these joint companies was to exploit "the various mining concessions given by the late President Kabila to ZDF as barter payment for its military support."[65] A number of other Zimbabwean companies became linked to this deal for the purposes of providing transportation, mining equipment, and financial and technical expertise.[66] Another deal, in which the Zimbabwean mining company KMC Group was to be given a cobalt and copper concession, was awaiting the signature of President Laurent Kabila at the time of his assassination in January 2001.

The exact amount of profits made from these illicit, inside business deals is likely to never be known. Likewise, how much of the profits were used to maintain Zimbabwean troops in Congo and how much went into the pockets of individuals officers and businessmen also cannot be reliably discerned. What is relatively certain, however, is that little if any of the proceeds found their way into the Zimbabwean (or Congolese) national treasury.

Despite the fact that the UNSC report serves chiefly as an indictment of Rwanda and Uganda's intervention in Congo, the report is admirably honest about the nefarious motives of Zimbabwe's involvement. It is rather naive, however, in estimating the costs of Zimbabwe's involvement, and therefore misleading in the economic consequences it suggests for Zimbabwe's involvement. The report blandly repeats Zimbabwe's official claim that it reduced its defense budget from Z$15.3 billion in 2000 to Z$ 13.3 billion in 2001 without further commentary.[67] In the same place, it estimates the cost of maintaining Zimbabwe's 10,000 troops in Congo at U.S.$3 million per month, for a total of U.S.$36 million per year. Yet the EIU wrote of Zimbabwe possibly *reducing* the number of its troops in Congo to "around 13,000 by the end of 2001."[68] This implies a much higher costs of troop maintenance in Congo. Moreover, the UNSC report apparently took its figures from the Zimbabwean government itself. According to independent sources, the true costs may be as much as U.S.$1 million per day, or ten times the amount of the official government figure.[69]

The report also fails to mention that Zimbabwe's budgeting and accounting processes virtually collapsed during 2000 and 2001. According to the EIU, in mid-2001, "In the case of budget data, there is a strong feeling among many economists that much government expenditure is now simply off-budget and not being captured in the official data. . . . As the Reserve Bank has not published an annual report [for 1999 or 2000] and is unwilling to offer a detailed explanation for the changes, such data tend to increase the feeling that the government is following some strange accounting methods, which undermines the credibility of the data."[70] Anecdotal evidence suggests that the official defense budget figures are indeed misleading. The *Zimbabwe Independent* revealed a government purchase of arms from China worth some Z$2.8 billion (or U.S.$72.3 million) in June 2000, all for use in the Congo war. Two weeks later (16 June 2000) the same paper reported a Z$18 million (U.S. $1.5 million) purchase of three Mig 23 fighter planes from Libya, again for use in Congo.[71] Earlier in the year, Britain approved the sale of £5–10 million worth of parts to service Zimbabwe's fleet of ten British-made Hawk jet-fighters.[72] These purchases alone, combined with the probable real costs of maintaining its troops in Congo, already exceed the official defense budget for 2000. There can be no doubt that much of the cost of the Congo war is off-budget and unrecorded.

Meanwhile, Zimbabwe entered its worst economic crisis of its independent history in 1999. The overall GDP, which was essentially flat in 1999, shrank by 6.0 percent in 2000 and was projected to fall another 5.6 percent in 2001.[73] The government budget deficit escalated dramatically from an already high –11.9 percent of GDP in 1999 to –22.7 percent in 2000. As investors lost faith in the previously sound Zimbabwean economy, the Zimbabwe dollar plummeted from a value of U.S.$1=Z$12.11 in 1997 to a rate of U.S.$1=Z$55 in June 2001.[74] The government's internal debt also escalated nearly out of control beginning in 2000, to some U.S.$4 billion in July 2001.[75] To what extent these financial woes are attributable to the costs of the Congo war cannot be accurately determined, but it is certain that they contributed to Zimbabwe's current economic crisis. This crisis has contributed, in turn, to the much-reported and high-profile political crisis in which President Mugabe is now embroiled.

In sum, then, those states intervening in Congo on behalf of the regime have borne substantial costs without noticeable rewards. While certain Zimbabwean military and business figures have reaped war-related windfalls, the overall economy has nearly collapsed. For Angola, it is impossible to determine whether the value of the added security it has gained by being in Congo is worth the costs of its mission there. For Namibia, it seems doubtful that the political gains of its military support for the regime were worth the financial outlay. Namibia's current process of withdrawal seems to suggest that the country's leadership has eventually come to this conclusion itself.

NON-INTERVENING STATES AND THE CONGO WAR

States that are not intervening directly in the Congo conflict are also affected by it. These states fall into two categories: those bordering Congo, and thereby suffering economic disruption as a result; and those states that have had trade and investment opportunities curtailed by the war. Since we have confined ourselves to the *African* stakes of the Congo war, the most affected state in the latter category is South Africa. We now take up these categories of states, in turn.

The Bordering States

Aside from the bordering countries that are also interveners in the war, probably the Central African Republic (CAR) has been the most affected by the war in Congo. These effects result chiefly from the facts that CAR is landlocked and that its primary trade linkages have traditionally been along the Congo River. While Zambia is another landlocked country affected by the Congo war, it has relatively good import-export linkages directly through Tanzania, and also through South Africa, via Zimbabwe. Fortunately for CAR, its primary export is diamonds, which can be easily exported without making use of land or river routes. For much of its trade, however, CAR had used the Congo Republic port of Pointe Noire until 1997, sending and receiving goods along the Oubangui and Congo Rivers to Brazzaville, and thence to Pointe Noire by train.[76] Due to the 1997 civil war in Congo-Brazzaville, and its attendant disruptions, CAR then shifted some of its exports to Douala. In March 2001, however, a border dispute between Cameroon and CAR also temporarily interrupted this trade route, as well.[77]

The price of imports in Bangui has been more dramatically affected by disruption on the Congo River caused by the rebellion of Jean-Pierre Bemba beginning in 1999. Given that Bemba established effective control over northern Équateur in mid-1999, CAR president Ange-Félix Patassé had little choice but to do business with him. Bemba had long-standing CAR contacts with whom he felt comfortable and once in power, Bemba both marketed his coffee through CAR and replenished his supplies of gasoline there.[78] As a result, Kinshasa cut off all remaining gasoline deliveries to Bangui via the river in the spring of 2000, causing a major fuel shortage by that summer.[79] CAR had to resort to much more expensive fuel brought in from Cameroon and to accept temporary gifts of fuel from Libya. More recently, in May 2001, Bemba came to the rescue of Patassé during an attempted coup d'état against the latter by former president André Kolingba. A rapid dispatch of troops by Bemba apparently saved the day for Patassé, but then the same troops apparently looted parts of the Central African capital.[80] Bemba's dispatch of aid to Patassé also caused a political standoff between Bangui and Kinshasa that remained unresolved in September 2001.

While CAR has suffered economic losses as a result of the war, it may have had some gains, as well. Notably, Central African traders may have been able to extract some profits from the coffee that Bemba smuggled through the country from 1999 to 2001. But the overall balance seems to be sharply negative. The country's overall growth of GDP averaged 4.85 percent for 1997 and 1998, the last two years before it was seriously affected by the Congo war; its growth of GDP in the subsequent two years, however, was only 1.1 percent. The EIU attributed this fallout partly to the war-related disruptions and predicted that CAR's growth would rebound with the implementation of the Lusaka Agreement and the resumption of trade along the Ubangui River.[81]

CAR and other neighboring countries were further affected economically by the flow of refugees into their countries. While international donors including the UNHCR and World Food Program (WFP) often finally take responsibility for the costs of maintaining refugees, they often take several weeks or months to establish operations. Even after they do so, these operations are sometimes disrupted, or insufficient to maintain the refugees. Finally, even when they function well, the presence of displaced persons can have important local economic consequences. Typical disruptions were well captured in a recent *Economist* article on the Karago refugee camp in Tanzania.[82] The article notes, "When there is a hiccup in delivery of food aid, many refugees rob nearby villages." More generally, the presence of the refugees often drives up the prices for local commodities and imports and sometimes drives down labor costs. Finally, the refugees often put pressure on local resources, including firewood. While the renowned generosity of Africans to refugees coming into their communities is heartening, it often puts families living on the margins under tremendous strain. This was precisely the effect that a mere 400 Congolese refugees had on the lives of 86 families living in Batalimo, CAR in late 2000.[83] The families shared their meager resources with the refugees, rendering themselves even more economically destitute than before. At that time, the CAR was home to over 7,000 Congolese refugees who were only sporadically cared for by the international community.

The numbers of refugees in other neighboring countries is typically much higher, but the level of international provision for them is also weak. For instance, the number of refugees from the DRC in the Congo Republic increased from about 73,000 to some 117,000 between July and October 2000. As the UNHCR admitted at the time, however, "only 50,000 refugees have access to UNHCR relief because DRC armed forces have blocked the only access route to the area."[84] Given that the Congo Republic was itself still recovering from its own civil wars of 1997 and 1998--1999, the burden of these refugees on the locals was no doubt tremendous.

The population of Brazzaville has also been negatively affected in other ways by the war. In the good times of the past, much food used to flow down the Oubangi and Congo Rivers to both Kinshasa and Brazzaville. During the recent war, however, the flow of local foodstuffs down the river has been hugely diminished. As a result, the population on both sides of the river has been adversely affected.

Another country heavily impacted by Congolese refugees is Zambia. The impact on Zambians, like Tanzanians, would be particularly heavily because the population is so poor. As of April 2001, about 255,000 refugees, of whom some 50,000 were Congolese, were in Zambia.[85] Early in April 2001, there was a riot at the Kala refugee camp among Congolese refugees, who had been put on one-half rations by the World Food Program because of a lack of provisions. One refugee was killed and twenty-eight injured in that incident.[86] Earlier in the year, there had been an outbreak of cholera at the same camp.[87] Interestingly, the Zambian government reportedly had already spent some U.S.$2 million for its role in mediating the Congo war in 1999, for which it was only partially compensated by the international community.[88] Hence, while the Congo war may have raised the international profile of Zambia, the country has paid a price both in terms of its diplomacy and maintenance of refugees.

South Africa

Finally, South Africa has been mainly affected by a loss of trade and investment opportunities. Since the end of the apartheid regime in 1991, South Africa has been expanding its economic and commercial ties with the rest of Africa and the world beyond. Mandela's administration (1994--99) started the reintroduction of South Africa into the global economy through its implementation of the Growth, Employment, and Redistribution plan (GEAR), a market-driven economic strategy.[89] Through this plan, the South African government committed itself to open markets, privatization, and the creation of a favorable investment climate. There have been efforts to reduce the government's role in the economy, to reduce tariffs and export subsidies, to loosen exchange rate control, to cut secondary tax on corporate dividends, and to improve enforcement of intellectual property laws. As a member of the World Trade Organization (WTO), South Africa has demonstrated its commitment to trade liberalization by reducing tariffs since the early 1990s; average import tariffs in South Africa have dropped from more than 30 percent in 1990 to about 14.3 percent in 1999.[90]

The government of South Africa is also dedicated to improving trade between South Africa and the other African countries. There has been a substantial increase in South African trade with other Sub-Saharan African countries, especially with southern African countries. South Africa is a member of the Organization of African Unity (OAU), the Southern African Customs Union (SACU) and the Southern African Development Community (SADC). Through such organizations, South Africa hopes to establish a major exporting and investment position in the member countries.

Regarding trade between South Africa and Congo, EIU estimated that 9.4 percent of Congolese exports went to South Africa in 1998, but that these had fallen to below 4 percent in 1999. Meanwhile, the percent of Congolese imports originating in South Africa increased from 25 percent to 28.4 percent over the same years.[91] Despite this slight increase, the two countries are currently losing in term of mutual business opportunities because of the war, and trade between them is expected to increase tremendously at the end of the war. South Africa played an important role in the signing and the enforcement of the ceasefire between the Congo government and the different rebel groups, insisting that this would help improve economic activities between South Africa and Congo.

Some efforts at economic cooperation have gone ahead in spite of the war, especially since it has entered a "dormant" phase. On 29 August 2001, the South African trade and industry minister, Alec Erwin, announced that South Africa and Congo agreed to set up a joint structure intended to promote mutual cooperation and the development of the economies of the two countries.[92] President Joseph Kabila, who was visiting with president Thabo Mbeki in Pretoria noted "the Congo has a variety of investment opportunities in areas such as hydro-electricity, agriculture, tourism, and eco-tourism."[93] His objective was clearly to lobby local South African investors to invest in Congo's most prominent sectors, such as hydro-electricity and mining. In a speech broadcast live across Zimbabwe, President Joseph Kabila said "Allow me to call upon the business communities of both countries [Zimbabwe and South Africa] to take advantage of the open market policies to develop the various opportunities that exist in mining, forestry, agriculture, and in other sectors such as textiles."[94]

Nonetheless, South Africa has been forced to forego many investment opportunities in Congo as a result of the war. South Africa is a world leader in several specialized sectors of the manufacturing industry, including railway rolling stock, synthetic fuels, and the mining equipment and machinery.[95] These are precisely the type of investments that Congo needs for the growth of its economy. Most of Congo's main import commodities, including many foodstuffs, transport and mining equipment, other machinery, and fuels, are also produced in South Africa.

Directly investing in the production of these goods in Congo would benefit the two countries in terms of job creation for Congo and business expansion for South African companies. As a result of the high political risk in the country, however, virtually all of the plans that South African businessmen had for investment in Congo in 1997 have been scrapped.

CONCLUSION

Almost all states involved seem to have suffered economic losses as a result of the Congo war. With regard to Congo itself, there is no gainsaying the huge and devastating consequences of the war for the state's economy and its people, even taking account of the fact that Congo would have confronted major economic difficulties after May 1997 in any case. Although the intervening states have certainly enjoyed some economic benefits from their interventions, the costs of their interventions are also not inconsiderable, even if they are less visible. In the case of Angola, the country's government is willing to bear the costs in order to prosecute the war against UNITA, and in the case of Zimbabwe, President Mugabe is simply buying the support of his most important generals at the expense of the state treasury. Among the other interveners, only Uganda and Namibia may be realizing a net economic gain from their participation in the war, but this is far from certain. While Rwanda "reinvests" much of its gains in the costs of prosecuting the war itself, Uganda is experiencing an erosion of domestic political legitimacy that may outweigh the value of its ill-gotten gains in Congo. In any case, these gains hardly redound to the economic benefit of ordinary Ugandans. As we saw just above, even the neighboring, nonintervening states are suffering economic losses from the war, as is South Africa, though the loss of investment income. In sum, then, we conclude that the Congo war has impeded the entire process of economic development in central Africa and indeed, throughout the Africa continent. Only an end to the fighting and a restoration of internal political order to Congo can provide any hope for the success of new development initiatives in the region.

NOTES

1. *Marchés Tropicaux et méditerranéens* (MTM) (Paris), 11 May 2001, p. 988.
2. For a splendid general account of the political economy of Zaire under Mobutu, see Crawford Young and Thomas Turner, *The Rise and Decline of the Zairian State* (Madison: University of Wisconsin Press, 1985). For shorter accounts, see John F. Clark, "The Nature and Evolution of the State in Zaire," *Studies in Comparative International Development* 32, no.4 (winter 1998), and chapter 3 in this volume.
3. Although Burundi has deployed a small number of its forces in Congo along with Rwanda, the economic impact of this deployment on Burundi is not profound. Accordingly, we do not treat Burundi here.
4. Economist Intelligence Unit (EIU), "Country Report: Democratic Republic of Congo [DRC]," (London: EIU, May 2001).
5. United Nations Security Council (UNSC), "Report of the Panel of Experts on the Illegal Exploitation of Natural Resources and Other Forms of Wealth of the Democratic Republic of the Congo (S/2001/357)," April 12, 2001.

6. EIU, "Country Report: DRC," 1st quarter, 2000; and EIU, "Country Report: DRC," May 2001.
7. See UNSC, "Report of the Panel of Experts," tables 1–4, following para. 99. The domestic "production" of these minerals is claimed by the Rwandan Official Statistics office.
8. UNSC para. 5, 32, and 36; For more detail, see below.
9. For more detail, see below in this chapter.
10. The International Rescue Committee (IRC), "Preliminary Findings Indicate Some Two and a Half Million Deaths in Eastern Congo Conflict," available at http://www.theIRC.org/news/ display.cfm?newsID=479, 30 April 2001; also see, Global Issues, "Conflicts in Africa," available at http://www.Globalissues.com/ Geopolitics/Africa/ DRC.asp, 11 July 2001.
11. United Nations High Commissioner for Refugees (UNHCR), "DR Congo: The impact on Refugees," UNHRC Nairobi, Kenya, 24 January 2001, available at http://www.unhcr.ch/cgi-bin/texis/vtx/home/+VwwBmrevEudwwwwn-wwwwwwwhFqnNobItFqnDni5AFqnNobIcFqVy2agdDtdeuGmDRrnaoMpwqB-Dzmxwwwwwww/opendoc.pdf.
12. UNSC para. 77 and 78; also, see below.
13. UNSC, para. 61.
14. World Bank, "World Development Indicators" (Washington, D.C.: World Bank, 2001).
15. UNSC, para. 167–68.
16. BBC News, "Congo Economy Ravaged by Conflict," 18 January 2001, available at http://news.bbc.co.uk/hi/english/business/newsid_1123000/1123779.stm.
17. Yahoo News, "Rwandan-Backed Rebels in DR Congo Declare Monthly Earning," available at: sg.news.yahoo.com/010829/1/1dnql.html, August 29, 2001.
18. UNSC, para. 130.
19. International Monetary Fund (IMF), "Government Finance Statistics Yearbook: Country Pages, Democratic Republic of Congo," (Washington, D.C: IMF, 2000).
20. UNSC, para. 72.
21. IMF, "Government Finance Statistics Yearbook."
22. U.S. Department of State (USDS), "Background Notes: Congo, Democratic Republic of," January 2000, Bureau of African Affairs; available at www.state.gov/ r/pa/bgn/index.cfm?docid=2823.
23. EIU, "Country Report: DRC," May 2001, 28.
24. BBC News, "Congo Economy Ravaged by Conflict."
25. USDS, "Background Notes: Congo."
26. EIU, "Country Report: DRC," 1st quarter 2000, 26.
27. UNSC, para. 67 and 80.
28. Global Issues, "Conflicts in Africa."
29. EIU, "Country Report: DRC," May 2001, 28.
30. MTM, no.2878, 5 January 2001, 27. Cf. the only slightly less alarming figures given by Oxfam Great Britain, "A Forgotten War—A Forgotten Emergency: The Democratic Republic of Congo," Oxfam GB Policy Paper, December 2000, available at www.Oxfam.org.uk/policy/papers/drc.html, accessed July 21 2001.
31. Integrated Regional Information Network [IRIN] of the UN Office for the Coordination of Humanitarian Affairs, "Boat in Kivu Hijacked by Mayi-Mayi with 25 People on Board," 30 August 2001.
32. EIU, "Country Report: DRC," 1st quarter 2000, 40.
33. UNSC, para. 66.
34. UNSC, para. 65.
35. UNSC, para. 58–59.

36. Sandrine Perrot, "Entrepreneurs de l'insécurité: La Face Cachée de l'Armée Ougandaise," *Politique Africaine* 75 (October 1999).
37. See chapters 8 and 9, in this volume.
38. UNSC, para. 29–31.
39. Ibid., para. 33–35.
40. Ibid., para. 36.
41. Ibid., para. 43–45.
42. Ibid., para. 47–48.
43. Ibid., para. 58–60.
44. Ibid., para. 61–62.
45. Ibid., para. 112–113.
46. Ibid., para. 30.
47. EIU, "Country Report: Rwanda and Burundi," (London: EIU, May 2001), 6.
48. Ibid.
49. UNSC, para. 88.
50. Ibid., para. 89
51. Ibid., para. 135.
52. Ibid., para. 142.
53. EIU, "Country Report: Uganda," (London: EIU, July 2001), 5.
54. It should be noted, however, that the export of diamonds, among other minerals taken from Congo, do not appear in the official statistics that Uganda disseminates. UNSC, para. 107.
55. See Clark's chapter 9 in this volume.
56. See John F. Clark, "Explaining Ugandan Intervention in Congo: Evidence and Interpretations," *Journal of Modern Africa Studies* 39, no.2 (2001).
57. UNSC, para. 106.
58. Ibid., para. 171.
59. IRIN, 25 November 2000.
60. UNSC, para. 121; in mid-2001, U.S.$1 traded for approximately N$8.
61. Werner Menges, "Military Budget Grows," *Namibian*, 9 November 2001.
62. Chrispin Inambao, "Heroes' Welcome for Returning DRC Troops," *Namibian*, 22 June 2001.
63. EIU, "Country Report: Zimbabwe," (London: EIU, June 2001), 8.
64. UNSC, para. 156.
65. Ibid., para. 160.
66. Ibid., para. 161–65.
67. The exchange rate in mid-2001 was about Z$55= U.S.$1 in mid-2001, but the Zimbabwe dollar has been rapidly depreciating since 1998.
68. EIU, "Country Report: Zimbabwe," June 2001, 8.
69. Dumisani Muleya and Brian Hungwe, "Govt Orders $3b Arms [sic] from China," *Zimbabwe Independent* (Harare), 2 June 2000.
70. EIU, "Country Report: Zimbabwe," June 2001, 24.
71. See Dumisani Muleya and Brian Hungwe, "Govt Orders $3b Arms [sic] from China," and Dumisani Muleya and Vincent Kahiya, "Airforce Buys More Fighter Planes from Libya," *Zimbabwe Independent*, 16 June 2000.
72. EIU, "Country Report: Zimbabwe," 1st quarter, 2000, 13.
73. EIU, "Country Report: Zimbabwe," June 2001, 5 and 11.
74. Ibid., 5.
75. *Financial Gazette* (Harare), 12 July 2001.
76. Agence France Presse [AFP], 16 July 2001.
77. EIU, "Country Report: Cameroon, CAR, Chad," (London: EIU, May 2001), 34.
78. AFP, 19 June 2001.

79. IRIN, "Central African Republic: Fuel Crisis Threatens Economic Recovery," 4 July 2000.

80. *L'Avenir* (Kinshasa), 5 July 2001.

81. EIU, "Country Report: Cameroon, CAR, Chad."

82. "Tanzania: The Plenty of Kindness," *Economist*, 25–31 August 2001, 40.

83. IRIN, "Central African Republic: Security and Shelter Concerns for Refugees," 23 November 2000.

84. United Nations High Commissioner for Refugees [UNHCR], "UNHCR Refugee Newsnet," available at www.unhcr.ch/ref/newscountry/CongoRepublic, accessed on 17 July 2001.

85. IRIN, "Zambia: EU Provides Food Aid for Refugees in Zambia," 27 April 2001.

86. IRIN, "Zambia-DRC: Congo Refugees Riot in Zambian camp," 16 April 2001.

87. IRIN, "Nchelenge, Zambia: Kala Refugee Camp Health Update," 31 January 2001.

88. UNHCR, "UNHCR Country Profiles: Zambia," available at www.unchr.ch/world/afri/zambia.htm, accessed on 17 July 2001.

89. U.S. Department of State [USDS], "Background Notes: South Africa," Bureau of African Affairs; available at www.state.gov/r/pa/bgn/index.cfm?docid–2898, May 2001, accessed July 12, 2001.

90. Ibid.

91. EIU, "Country Report: DRC," 1st quarter 2000, 26, and "Country Report: DRC," May 2001, 28.

92. "South Africa, Democratic Republic of Congo Set Up Joint Structures," *The Sowetan* (Johannesburg), available at allAfrica.com/stories/200108300447.html, August 30, 2001.

93. "Kabila to Lobby for Support," *Business Day* (Johannesburg), available at allAfrica.com/stories/200108300229.html, August 30, 2001.

94. Ibid.

95. USDS, "Background Notes: South Africa."

CHAPTER 13

The Politics of Refugees and Internally Displaced Persons in the Congo War

JUDE MURISON[1]

INTRODUCTION

Since 1994, the Democratic Republic of Congo (DRC) has seen a mass movement of refugees and internally displaced persons (IDPs) within its borders. The impact of more than 1.2 million Rwandan refugees coming into Congo following the Rwandan genocide in 1994 drastically affected the eastern region and brought international media attention with it. The internal politics of the DRC have been significantly transformed since that time with the end of Mobutu's "kleptocratic" regime, the sudden rise to power of Laurent Désiré Kabila, and finally the new leadership of his son, Joseph Kabila. Subsequently, the DRC has witnessed its own movement of populations, stimulated by internal violence and civil war.

This chapter examines forced migration in the DRC. It takes as its focus two groups of forced migrants. The first is the Rwandan refugees who came as a result of both the genocide and the Rwandan Patriotic Front's (RPF) victory in Rwanda in 1994. The second is the Congolese who are internally displaced persons, those who have remained within Congo rather than move outside but who have been forced to flee their usual home because of war in the country.

This chapter argues that forced migration in the DRC during the Congo wars has differed from the forced migration in Rwanda in 1994 because the majority of Congolese displaced by the war have remained inside the DRC. These people are classed as "internally displaced persons" rather "refugees" because they have not crossed an international border.[2] Consequently, for these Congolese IDPs, remaining in the DRC has had a significant impact on the dynamics of their displacement as well as the level of international assistance being given to them. In both cases, local political actors have used the forced migrants for their own narrow ends. As a result, their suffering has been much more severe than it might otherwise have been. The chapter begins by giving the background leading to the exodus of the Rwandan refugees into Congo in 1994 and the later displacement of the Congolese due to conflict within the DRC. The second section discusses the movement of the refugees and the IDPs, and how the shape of the Congo war affected the regions of the DRC at different times and to varying degrees. The third section considers the way in which the refugees and displaced population were used politically by various governments and rebel groups for their own benefit. The final section looks at some of the consequences for the displaced themselves.

Rwandan refugees arriving in 1994 comprised the second major wave of Rwandan refugees to flee their homeland for Congo (then Zaire). The first wave arrived as a result of the 1959 "social revolution" in Rwanda, when violence erupted following political change in the country. Thousands of Rwandan refugees also fled to Tanzania, Uganda, and Burundi at that time. It is estimated that 60,000 Rwandan refugees went to Congo during this period.[3] They were settled in the Kivu region of eastern Zaire, mainly in the areas of Goma, Bukavu, Nyangezi, and Luvangi.[4] The fact that the 1994 (predominantly Hutu) Rwandan refugees sought asylum in the Kivus, the same area of Congo as the (mainly Tutsi) Rwandan refugees had more than thirty years earlier, had a significant impact on the Kivu region. First, the sheer number of refugees was overwhelming. Knowledgeable observers estimate that 850,000 refugees arrived in Goma, 332,000 in Bukavu, and 62,000 in Uvira.[5] These vast numbers later increased with the 1994–95 influxes of more than 90,000 Burundian refugees following political killings in their country.[6]

Second, the arrival of the new Rwandan refugees created insecurity in the region. This was partly because of the environmental impact that the refugees had on the area, the emerging competition between nationals and refugees for local resources, and tensions arising from the influx of international humanitarian aid organizations responding to the refugee influx in the area. The most serious threat, however, was the fact that the Rwandan refugee camps housed Hutu militia who had been involved in organizing and orchestrating the Rwandan genocide. These militias were essentially able to control the refugee camps because the political structures of individual communes in Rwanda were replicated in the refugee camps.[7] The rearming and training of the ex-Forces Armées Rwandaises (ex-FAR) and Interahamwe became a serious threat to the Rwandan government, which was fearful that the Hutu militia would use Congo as a base to effectively organize a reinvasion of Rwanda.

There had been no screening of refugees to identify members of the ex-FAR and Interahamwe at the time of the influx. Subsequently, it was easy for the militia to disguise themselves among the mélange of refugees and Hutu militia within the refugee camps. They consequently were able to use the camps as a recruiting ground for soldiers and as a territory within which to train their members. The insecurity that the Hutu militias created was so great that in 1996 Rwanda repeatedly demanded that the Congolese government either shut the refugee camps or face a Rwandan use of force. Consequently the desire of the Rwandan government to rid the Congo/Rwanda frontier of any potential military threat from the ex-FAR and Interahamwe is said to be the reason why Rwanda gave support and backing to Laurent Kabila and the rebel movement, the Alliance des Forces Démocratiques pour la Libération du Congo-Zaïre (Alliance of Democratic Forces for the Liberation of Congo-Zaire—ADFL) in 1996.[8]

The impact of the Rwandan refugees in the DRC was not the catalyst for the present wars in Congo, although it must be acknowledged that it contributed to them.

Prior to the arrival of the Rwandan refugees in 1994, there had been instances of sudden increases in political tensions. For example, the introduction of the new citizenship act in 1981 that deliberately withdrew citizenship rights for the Banyarwanda (including the 1960s Rwandan refugees) created tremendous social stress in the Kivus.[9] In 1993 there had also been localized fighting in North Kivu between the *autochtones* ("natives") and the Banyarwanda. Later, this fighting took on a more ethnic dimension as the conflict segregated the groups united under the label "Banyarwanda" into the "Hutu" and "Tutsi," pitting the *autochtones,* the Hutu, and the Tutsi against each other.[10]

In considering the events in the DRC, it is important to recognize that the current conflict is not just one war but is in fact many wars that involve multilayered and multidimensional conflict. The conflicts are multidimensional in that they comprise many different rebel groups and splintered rebel groups from Congo, Rwanda, and Burundi. The Congolese rebel groups include the Mouvement pour la Libération du Congo (MLC), the Rassemblement Congolais pour la Démocratie-Goma (RCD-Goma), and the RCD-Mouvement de Libération (RCD-ML), as well as the Mai-Mai.[11] The Rwandan rebel groups include the aforementioned ex-FAR and *Interahamwe,* and the Burundian element is composed of the Front pour la Défense de la Démocratie (FDD).[12] The war is multilayered in that it engages actors at both a local and a regional level. It involves localized fighting between communities, such as the Lendu and the Hema, as was the case with fighting in early 2001 in Ituri province,[13] and fighting between regional forces, such as that between the armies of Uganda and Rwanda in Kisangani in the DRC in August 1999 and May--June 2000.[14]

MOVEMENT OF REFUGEES AND INTERNALLY DISPLACED PERSONS

The multidimensional and multilayered nature of war in the DRC has affected regions of the country at different times and to varying degrees. Localized fighting in the north between the Lendu and Hema in Ituri intensified in early 2001 and is estimated to have killed between 7,000 and 10,000 people and displaced a further 50,000 to 125,000.[15] The clashes between the Ugandan People's Defence Forces (UPDF) and the Rwandan Patriotic Army (RPA) in Kisangani in 1999 and 2000 displaced approximately 60,000 with an estimated 1,000 having died during the fighting. In the southern region of Katanga, it is estimated that 150,000 to 200,000 Congolese were forced to flee their homes between October and December 2000 because of RPA and RCD-Goma clashes with the Congolese government forces.[16]

The mass outpouring of refugees, epitomized by the Rwandan exodus in July 1994, has not been repeated in the DRC. The influx of Rwandan refugees into the DRC was intense—more than 1.2 million Rwandans entered Congo in the space of four days in 1994.[17] The movement of Congolese out of Congo has been less dramatic. In fact, statistics show that a much greater percentage of Congolese have remained within their country, choosing to move internally rather than move outside. Statistics from 1999 show that there were three times as many internally displaced Congolese as there were Congolese refugees. According to UN figures, in 1999 there were 221,000 Congolese refugees in neighboring countries, compared with 775,000 internally displaced persons in Congo.[18]

The number of IDPs continues to rise as conflict in the DRC persists. Between 1999 and 2001, the number of IDPs in the DRC has more than trebled. Statistics for 2001 suggest that there are now more than 2,335,000 IDPs and 330,000 Congolese refugees outside the DRC.[19] Physically, the DRC is large enough to accommodate such a mass population displacement, compared to Rwanda, which is much smaller. Finding an alternative place of refuge within the country was more difficult for Rwandans after July 1994, especially given that the RPF controlled the country. Another reason for mass displacement rather than exodus is the nature of the war, which changes in location and intensity over time. As a result the Congolese are able to move in and out of areas between rounds of fighting. Between July 1999 and December 2000 the number of IDPs in Katanga and Orientale Province doubled, tripled in Équateur province, quadrupled in North Kivu, and increased nearly sevenfold in Maniema. While elsewhere the number of IDPs increased between July 1999 and December 2000, Eastern Kasai was the only area where the number of IDPs fell—the number of IDPs there fell by half.[20]

The rise and fall in the number of IDPs has also varied according to region. Although the number of IDPs in Équateur, Katanga, Maniema, South Kivu, and especially North Kivu increased between June and December 2000, the number of IDPs in Orientale Province and Western Kasai actually decreased.[21] For those who are displaced by the conflict and chaos in the DRC, the complex nature of the war means that there is not "one enemy" but that there are a number of actors whose fighting, kidnapping, raiding, looting, and destruction creates reason to move. One of the changing characteristics of the displacement of Congolese within the DRC is the increased distance they are being displaced from their homes. It has been noted that as the war continues, the internally displaced are being forced to move further away from their place of normal residence. There has also been a tendency to move into unpopulated or forest areas to avoid potential conflict areas.[22]

The Burundian and Rwandan refugees in camps in eastern Congo had been forced out prior to the beginning of the second Congo war in 1998. The RPF and the ADFL believed that these camps posed too high a security risk because of the militia operating within them. The RPF and the ADFL tried to eliminate this security threat by dismantling the refugee camps that housed the militia.

Although the FDD is a Burundian rebel group opposed to the Burundian government, like the ex-FAR and *Interahamwe,* it operates from within the DRC. The inability to separate the Rwandan refugees from the ex-FAR and *Interahamwe* and the Burundian refugees from the FDD within the camps had a detrimental impact on the refugees. In October and November 1996, the RPA and the ADFL forcibly closed the Burundian refugee camps in Uvira that housed members of the FDD,[23] as well as the Rwandan refugee camps in Goma and Bukavu that accommodated members of the *Interahamwe* and ex-FAR.[24] The attacks on the refugee camps forced UN High Commissioner for Refugees (UNHCR) and aid organizations to withdraw from the area and compelled UNHCR to admit that it was unable to ensure the protection of refugees.[25] The closure of the camps left the refugees with three options: It either forced them back to their country of origin, pushed them deeper into the Congo interior, or induced them to seek refuge in a third country.[26]

It is difficult to gauge the precise number of those Burundian and Rwandan refugees who left Congo or the number of those who remained. It has been suggested that 40,000 Burundian refugees were repatriated, and 100,000 moved deeper into Congo.[27] According to UNHCR statistics, there were 1,100,600 Rwandan refugees in Congo in December 1995. By December 1996, the number had been reduced to 423,600.[28] It is estimated that between 500,000 and 700,000 refugees returned to Rwanda from Congo in November 1996,[29] while others went to third countries such as Cameroon, Gabon, Congo-Brazzaville, Central African Republic, Angola, and Zambia.[30]

This section has illustrated the complex nature of refugee and IDP movements within the DRC. One of the difficulties in understanding such population movements is that they occur suddenly and involve such a large mass of people. The closure of the refugee camps in 1996 led to discussions on the whereabouts of a large number of Rwandan refugees who were not accounted for. These became known as the "lost" refugees and were later the subject of an international investigation.[31] The refugees were deliberately targeted by the ADFL and the RPA. Evidence suggests that more than 200,000 Rwandan refugees died[32] and also that the refugees were effectively chased from east to west Congo and killed as the ADFL advanced to Kinshasa. The proposition that the ADFL and RPA deliberately targeted the Rwandan refugees is succinctly summed up by the journalist Howard French: "[A]n investigation in Mbandaka[33] was particularly threatening. Killings in the east, near Rwanda, could perhaps be written off as random acts of overzealous or vengeful Tutsi soldiers. But for Hutu refugees to be tracked down and killed at the opposite end of this huge country, when Kabila's victory in the war was already assured, would strongly suggest deliberate extermination."[34] In a similar way, it is very difficult to identify what has happened to the two million plus Congolese who are now displaced. Some information exists about the estimated number of displaced and the direction they are moving in to escape the continuing conflict, but more detailed data is lacking. The following section considers the political use of refugees and IDPs within the context of the Congo wars.

THE POLITICAL USE OF REFUGEES AND IDPS

The dynamics of the influx of Rwandan refugees into Congo allowed both Mobutu Sese Seko and Laurent Kabila to use the refugees politically to their own advantage. In both instances Mobutu and Kabila attempted to gain the support of the international community. In Mobutu's case, he openly acknowledged the international community's concerns about the rearming of the Rwandan militia within the camps while simultaneously giving them support. Gérard Prunier proposes that Mobutu's actions on the international arena were an attempt to use the refugees as a "reintegration ticket into the international community."[35] Mobutu's manipulation of the refugee problems is also affirmed by UNHCR: " . . . President Mobutu was able to continue to play a double game, publicly accepting UNHCR's concerns about growing violence in the border zones and privately tolerating or even supporting it."[36]

If Mobutu realized the benefit his involvement in negotiating the Rwandan refugee problem would have for his international reputation, Laurent Kabila also recognized the gains from selective negotiations with UNHCR. In 1996, when Mobutu was still in power, the ADFL under Kabila had control over eastern Congo. An agreement was made that allowed UNHCR to resume its humanitarian operations in the region under ADFL control. According to UNHCR, "The ADFL, adopting a tactic which was to be used over and over again in the following months, announced that it would allow UNHCR to have access to refugees, while in reality it limited access to areas that had come under its control. Invariably, UNHCR only gained access after suspected armed elements had been killed. Often refugees were also killed in the process."[37]

In both instances, Mobutu and Kabila were able to use the issue of the Rwandan refugees to their own advantage, gaining international favor by appearing to be sympathetic to the refugees' cause while actually implicating the refugees in political violence. The fact that the majority of Congolese have remained within the DRC rather than move outside, and that it is the warring groups in the DRC who are responsible for their displacement, has meant that the same approach has not been possible for the different warring groups during the second Congo war. In the two examples above, Mobutu and Kabila were able to disguise their involvement in human rights violations behind a curtain of concern for the Rwandan refugees. During the second Congo war, the human rights violations have been blatant on both sides. Human rights violations within the DRC have been identified in reports by the UN Special Rapporteur for Human Rights, Amnesty International, and Human Rights Watch.[38] These reports identify examples of human rights abuses that have been carried out by the various armed actors in the Congo war as they vie for power to extend their control over geographical territory or to extract economic resources from the DRC. Arbitrary detention, killing, and torture are used as tools of war to eliminate enemies or prevent people from acting in a particular way.

Another example of the way in which refugees are used for political ends has been in the recruitment of refugees to rebel groups. For any ongoing war there is the need to attain resources, whether it be through the recruitment of soldiers or the collection of food and medical supplies. Recruitment from among the refugee diaspora has been a tactic used earlier by both the RPF prior to its 1990 invasion of Rwanda and the Rwandan Hutu militia recruiting from the Rwandan refugee camps within Congo after 1994. The RPF recruited from among the Rwandan diaspora that had been displaced since the 1960s. Refugees from Uganda and Burundi were among the first to join,[39] and some were trained in refugee settlements in southwestern Uganda. Nakivale, a refugee settlement in Mbarara, was used as a training ground for RPF soldiers during the 1990–93 civil war in Rwanda.[40] The arming and training of the Hutu militia within the Rwandan refugee camps in Congo, such as Mugunga camp, became known internationally and led to the withdrawal of humanitarian organizations such as Care International and Médecins sans Frontières (MSF) in 1995.[41] They realized that not only were the militias controlling the distribution of food and basic commodities but also that those intent on re-organizing incursions on Rwanda were using the refugee camps as a recruitment ground for soldiers and that the refugees were being coerced into joining the militias.[42]

Less well publicized was the recruitment of Congolese refugees living outside the DRC to rebel groups such as the ADFL. One such example was the recruitment of Congolese refugees living in Kabarole district, Uganda. These refugees left Congo in the 1960s and were originally settled in Agago-Acholpii and Nakapiripirit in northern Uganda.[43] Due to political problems in the north, in 1980 the refugees were transferred to Kyaka I.[44] In the early 1980s Kyaka II settlement was established, and by 1995 more than 12,000 Congolese refugees had settled there. Fieldwork conducted in Kyaka I, Kyaka II and Kabarole district in late 2000 suggested that Ugandan officials were aware of refugee activities. One source indicated that in December 1996, refugees who were "well trained" were being transported from the refugee settlement to Ishasha on the Uganda/Congo border.[45] Another example is a letter from a district official in Fort Portal to the settlement commandants of Kyaka I and Kyaka II,[46] instructing them not to issue Congolese refugees with travel documents allowing travel to Congo because they are committing "acts of insecurity" there.[47] Later, the assistant resident district commissioner instructed the district police commissioner that "Due to the present security alert in the region, I have decided to suspend all movements of [Congolese] refugees out of Kyaka until further notice."[48] One government official likened the behavior of the Congolese refugees in his settlement to that of the Rwandan refugees when they were organizing under the RPF. He compared the actions of the Congolese refugees to the "Rwandese clandestine movements" by describing them as "rampant" and "unidentified movements." The government official remarked that, "Since the return of the Rwandese mid last year, [Congolese] refugees have expressed deeper enthusiasm for the same act."[49] That is, the Congolese also expressed a desire to return to their homeland as part of a rebel group, as the Rwandan refugees had done in 1990 with the RPF invasion into Rwanda.

Another example of recruitment from camps in Uganda is that of André Kisasse-Ngandu, a commander in the ADFL who was killed in 1997 and who came from Kyaka I. The recruitment and training of rebel groups within refugee camps continues to be a contentious issue. In September 2001, Rwanda accused Uganda of using its refugee camps to train Rwandese rebel groups. Rwanda maintained that rebels opposed to the government of Rwanda were being trained in refugee camps, such as Nakivale in Mbarara district and others in Masindi district. At the same time, Uganda accused Rwanda of training Ugandan rebels in Goma, which is occupied by the Rwandan army.[50] While the governments of Rwanda and Uganda may still be training rebels to help with the war in Congo, the populations within Congo are forced to deal with the horrendous consequences that the impact of the war has brought upon them.

CONSEQUENCES FOR THE DISPLACED

Since the beginning of the second Congo war in August 1998, it is estimated that up to 2.5 million people have died.[51] It has been suggested that the majority of deaths have been the result of inadequate basic needs, such as food and medical supplies, rather than the direct result of being caught in the armed conflict. This is largely because there has been a collapse in the supply of food in Congo, and, consequently, what is available has a high market price.

The lack of adequate food supplies is a serious problem affecting the DRC as a whole and is not specific to the internally displaced. Statistics issued by the World Food Program (WFP) in 2000 indicated that one third of people in the DRC do not have enough food—this equates to almost 16 million people.[52] In an attempt to address the problem of food security, the UN Food and Agricultural Organization instigated a program in March 2001 to encourage food production and to re-establish the food market supplies in urban areas of the DRC, such as Lubumbashi and

Kinshasa.[53] Humanitarian organizations have attempted to address this food crisis, but there have been many obstacles. First, the rapid increase in the number of displaced persons, as discussed earlier, has meant that it is difficult for organizations to keep up with the numbers who need assistance. Second, there are logistical problems because of the collapse of Congolese transport networks, and the fact that many displaced people are hiding in forest areas to avoid the rebel groups. Third, the insecurity of the region has proved hazardous for aid workers. Last, less international assistance has been donated than is actually needed.

The dangerous conditions of working in a war zone have led to a number of attacks on humanitarian workers. In March 2001 a UNHCR employee was shot dead in Kimpese while working with Angolan refugees in Lower Congo.[54] In April 2001 six members of the International Committee of the Red Cross were killed in an ambush close to Bunia, eastern Congo, while transporting medical supplies,[55] and in July 2001, five members of the World Health Organization were reportedly "arrested and beaten" by soldiers belonging to RCD-Goma while carrying out an antipolio immunization program in Équateur province.[56] These conditions have led to a number of nongovernmental organizations withdrawing from conflict areas. For example, in January 2000 Médecins sans Frontières withdrew from Bunia and Ituri districts because of fighting between the Hema and Lendu on one hand, and rebels and government soldiers on the other.[57]

Organizations such as Oxfam, the WFP, and the United Nations have highlighted the lack of humanitarian assistance being given to the Congolese.[58] There has been relatively little international aid donated to the DRC compared to other international areas in need of assistance. In 1999 Western governments gave more than twenty-five times more money per person in humanitarian assistance to the former Yugoslavia than to the DRC,[59] and in 2000 the United Nations failed to raise nearly 40 percent of the targeted funds for operations in the DRC.[60] This lack of assistance has had a dramatic impact on the people of the DRC. It has been suggested that half of the displaced population in the DRC has not received any humanitarian assistance at all.[61] These statistics show that the international response to the humanitarian crisis in the DRC is hugely inadequate, given the number of people affected by the war. The inadequate supply of food by aid organizations cannot meet demand, and this has led to programs being temporarily halted, or to organizations prioritizing the needs of some Congolese over others. For example, in September 2000, Refugee International reported that both the WFP and UNICEF were experiencing distribution problems. According to Refugee International, UNICEF had insufficient milk supplies to distribute to children and consequently, only IDPs in rural (rather than urban) areas were being assisted. Refugee International also stated that lack of WFP supplies would temporarily force the WFP to halt food distribution programs in eastern DRC between September and November 2000.[62] In early 2001, the WFP began work on its Protracted Relief and Rehabilitation Operation (PRRO), which will provide food to more than a million people in the DRC. However, the WFP admitted that less than ten percent of the quantity of food aid that the WFP estimates is needed in the DRC has actually been donated.[63] Until the magnitude of the humanitarian crisis in the DRC is recognized, and adequately addressed by both international governments and the warring groups in the DRC, the humanitarian suffering of its people will continue to increase.

CONCLUSION

Given the intensity and level of warfare, together with the number of Congolese displaced by the fighting, the response of the international community to this humanitarian crisis has been significantly less than the international response to the Rwandan refugee crisis in 1994. One of the reasons for this is that those forced to move because of the war have remained within the DRC rather than move outside. Knowing exactly what is occurring in the vast territory of the Congo, especially within the forests and remote areas to which the displaced have fled, is significantly more difficult than when there is a mass refugee exodus to another country. In the latter case, access is usually more attainable, especially if the refugees move to a country at peace. This problem is further compounded when instances of insecurity prevent humanitarian organizations from operating in the areas where their assistance is needed. Another reason for the difficulty in addressing the needs of the displaced within Congo is that the safety of their physical locality changes with the changing political nature of the war from which they are fleeing. Therefore, rather than move from their country of origin to a host country and then remain in one physical location (as is the case with most refugee outflows to camps), the internally displaced in DRC are constantly living under the possibility that if fighting begins in the new area where they have sought safety, then they will be forced to move on. Internally displaced persons are living with the consequences of the war in Congo, not only through the lack of food, shelter, and medical facilities, but through displacement from their communities, as well.

The 1994 influx of Rwandan refugees, together with elements of the ex-FAR and *Interahamwe*,[64] had a significant impact on the subsequent wars in the DRC. Not only did the influx intensify local ethnic tensions, but the existence of a Rwandan militia intent on destabilizing Rwanda provided justification for the Rwandan army to close the Rwandan refugee camps in DRC in 1996. The influx also provided the justification for the more recent Rwandan occupation of DRC territory in an attempt to eliminate the insecurity that the presence of the ex-FAR and *Interahamwe* in the DRC created.

The nature of war in the DRC is multilayered and multidimensional. The impact it has had on the Congolese people is massive but unquantifiable. The governments of Congo, Rwanda, and Uganda may alter their alignment with one another, and rebel groups may splinter or amalgamate to form other alliances all to ensure their stakes in the Congo war. But one feature of the war is clear: that forced displacement will continue to be a consequence of politics within the DRC and of a war in which the internally displaced have realized no gains. The war has brought with it a host of issues that have so far remained under-researched, including the militarization of refugee camps and the political use of the displaced during war by different actors vying for greater power and territory. Joseph Kabila, the new president of the DRC, hinted at this himself when he discussed the Congo war in an interview with the Belgian newspaper *Le Soir*: "This too is a genocide against the Congolese this time, but no one cares. . . . It's true that in the forests in the east of the country, there are no CNN cameras."[65] Recent figures indicate that the number of internally displaced is continually increasing as the conflict persists, and the examples given suggest that aid organizations have inadequate resources to respond to the level of assistance needed.

1. Jude Murison would like to thank and acknowledge the financial support of the Economic and Social Research Council, U.K.
2. For a discussion of this point see Guy S. Goodwin-Gill, *The Refugee in International Law*, 2nd ed. (Oxford: Oxford University Press, 1998), 14.
3. UNHCR, *The State of the World's Refugees: Fifty Years of Humanitarian Action* (Oxford: Oxford University Press, 2000), 50. It should be noted that prior to this, there had been economic migration between Rwanda and Congo since the 1920s. See Catharine Newbury, *The Cohesion of Oppression* (New York: Columbia University Press, 1988), 161–171, and Jean-Pierre Pabanel, "La question de la nationalité au Kivu," *Politique Africaine*, no. 41 (mars 1991): 32–40.
4. UNHCR, *The State of the World's Refugees*, 50. It is estimated that a further 90,000 Rwandans fled to Uganda, Burundi, and Tanzania (then Tanganyika), ibid., 49. For greater detail of the events surrounding the refugee exodus from Rwanda in the 1960s see André Guichaoua, *Le problème des réfugiés Rwandais et des populations Banyarwanda dans la région des Grands Lacs Africains* (Geneva: UNHCR, 1992), M. d'Hertefelt and D. Lame, *Société, culture et histoire du Rwanda. Encyclopédie bibliographique (1963–1980/87)* (Tervuren: MRAC, 1987), and Rachel Yeld, *Rwanda: Unprecedented Problems Call for Unprecedented Solutions* (Oxford: Refugee Studies Programme, 1996).
5. Gérard Prunier, *The Rwanda Crisis: History of a Genocide* (London: Hurst & Co., 1998), 312, and Abbas H. Gnamo, "The Rwandan Genocide and the Collapse of Mobutu's Kleptocracy," in Howard Adelman and Astri Suhrke, eds., *The Path of a Genocide: The Rwanda Crisis from Uganda to Zaire* (New Jersey: Transaction Publishers, 1999), 324, use the same figures, although Prunier suggests these figures may be inflated. For figures concerning the influx of Rwandan refugees to other neighboring countries, UNHCR estimates that 270,000 Rwandan refugees went to Burundi, 580,000 to Tanzania, and 10,000 to Uganda; see UNHCR, *The State of the World's Refugees*, 246.
6. UNHCR, *Background Paper on Refugees and Asylum Seekers from the Democratic Republic of the Congo* (Geneva: UNHCR, 2000), 29. Prunier, *The Rwanda Crisis*, 373–374, estimates that by 1996 there were 144,000 Burundian refugees in the Kivus, situated only in the Uvira area with none in Goma or Bukavu.
7. For a more detailed analysis of this point see Fiona Terry, *Condemned to Repeat? The Paradoxes of Humanitarian Action* (Ph.D. diss., Australian National University, Canberra, 2000), and Kate Halvorsen, "Protection and Humanitarian Assistance in the Refugee Camps in Zaire: The Problem of Security," in Howard Adelman and Astri Suhrke, eds., *The Path of a Genocide: The Rwanda Crisis from Uganda to Zaire* (New Jersey: Transaction Publishers, 1999).
8. This point will be discussed later in this chapter.
9. Mahmood Mamdani, *When Victims Become Killers: Colonialism, Nativism, and the Genocide in Rwanda* (Oxford: James Currey, 2001), chapter 8.
10. Gnamo, "The Rwandan Genocide and the Collapse of Mobutu's Kleptocracy," 323.
11. The first two groups are headed by Jean-Pierre Bemba and Professor Wamba dia Wamba respectively, while the latter is an indigenous militia group based in eastern Congo. For more on the rebel groups, see Osita Afoaku's chapter in this volume.
12. Jean-Bosco Ndayikengurukiye heads the FDD.
13. Integrated Regional Information Network (IRIN) of the U.N. Office for the Coordination of Humanitarian Affairs, "DRC: Garreton Concerned by Ituri Situation," 21 March 2001; IRIN, "DRC: Rival Hema and Lendu Communities Sign Peace Pact," 19 February 2001; and IRIN, "DRC: Bunia Situation 'Critical,'" 31 January 2001.

14. "We Will Stay in Congo, Says Rwanda," *The New Vision* (Kampala daily), 16 June 2000; "Uganda to Quit DRC—Museveni," *The New Vision*, 16 June 2000; "Unilateral Cease-fire in Kisangani," *The New Vision*, 9 June 2000; "UN Faces Obstacles on Congo," *The New Vision*, 6 June 2000.

15. Figures taken from United Nations Economic and Social Council (ECOSOC), *Report on the Situation of Human Rights in the Democratic Republic of the Congo, Submitted by the Special Rapporteur, Mr. Roberto Garretón, in accordance with Commission on Human Rights Resolution 2000/15* (New York: ECOSOC, 2001), para. 31 and Global IDP Database, "Violent Conflict between the Hema and Lendu People in the Orientale Province Has Caused Major Displacements since June 1999," *Democratic Republic of Congo Section: Causes and Background of Displacement*, available at web site http://www.db.idpproject.org/Sites/idp.

16. All figures taken from International Crisis Group (ICG), *Scramble for the Congo: Anatomy of an Ugly War* (Nairobi/Brussels: ICG: 2000), 67.

17. Halvorsen, "Protection and Humanitarian Assistance in the Refugee Camps in Zaire," 308.

18. Figures taken from UNHCR, *Background Paper on Refugees and Asylum Seekers from the Democratic Republic of the Congo*, 29, and Global IDP Database, "Distribution of IDPs by Province (July 1999, July 2000 and December 2000)," *Democratic Republic of Congo Section: Population Profile and Figures*, available at http://www.db.idpproject.org/Sites/idp.

19. Figures taken from IRIN, "Kivu IDPs Increased Fourfold in 12 Months," 15 February 2001, and IRIN, "UNHCR Urges Restraint On All Sides," 22 January 2001.

20. Global IDP Database, "Distribution of IDPs by province (July 1999, July 2000, and December 2000)."

21. Ibid.

22. United Nations Office for the Coordination of Humanitarian Affairs (UNOCHA), *DRC Monthly Humanitarian Bulletin, January–February 2000* (New York: UNOCHA, 15 February 2000).

23. Gérard Prunier, "The Geopolitical Situation in the Great Lakes Area in light of the Kivu Crisis," *WRITENET Country Papers* (Geneva: UNHCR, February 1997).

24. ICG, *Scramble for the Congo*, 68.

25. For example, see UNHCR, *The State of the World's Refugees*, 263.

26. Prunier, "The Geopolitical Situation in the Great Lakes Area in Light of the Kivu Crisis."

27. Ibid.

28. UNHCR, *The State of the World's Refugees*, 250.

29. Kisangani N. F. Emizet, "The Massacre of Refugees in Congo: A Case of UN Peacekeeping Failure and International Law," *Journal of Modern African Studies* 38, no. 2 (2000): 163–202.

30. Ibid., 174–176.

31. See ECOSOC, *Report on the Situation of Human Rights in Zaire, Prepared by the Special Rapporteur, Mr. Roberto Garretón, in Accordance with Commission on Human Rights Resolution 1996/77* (New York: ECOSOC, 1997).

32. See Emizet, "The Massacre of Refugees in Congo," for an excellent analysis of these events. See 173–179 for calculations on establishing the number of refugees killed.

33. Mbandaka is in western Congo.

34. Quoted in Emizet, "The Massacre of Refugees in Congo," 171

35. Prunier, *The Rwanda Crisis*, 376.

36. UNHCR, *The State of the World's Refugees*, 255.

37. Ibid., 264. This example is taken from events in 1996 when Mobutu was still in power and Kabila the leader of the ADFL rebel group in eastern Congo.

38. See, respectively, ECOSOC, *Report on the Situation of Human Rights in the Democratic Republic of the Congo, Resolution 2000/15*; Amnesty International, *DRC: A Long-standing Crisis Spinning Out of Control*, AI Index: AFR 62/33/98 (London: Amnesty International, 1998); and Human Rights Watch, *Uganda in Eastern DRC: Fueling Political and Ethnic Strife*, March 2001, available at http://www.hrw.org.

39. Mamdani, *When Victims Become Killers*, 255; Prunier, *The Rwanda Crisis*, 116.

40. This point was discussed openly on many occasions during interviews conducted with members of parliament, government officials, and refugees in Uganda during 2000. For further details concerning the establishment of the RPF see Wm. Cyrus Reed, "Exile, Reform, and the Rise of the Rwandan Patriotic Front," *The Journal of Modern African Studies* 34, no. 3 (1996): 479–501, and Gérard Prunier; "Eléments pour une histoire du Front Patriotique Rwandais," *Politique Africaine*, no. 51 (Octobre 1993): 121–138.

41. In an interview with the *New York Times*, the MSF Secretary-General during the refugee crisis said, "We can't be a party to slaughter in Rwanda. International aid has allowed the militias to reorganize, stockpile food and recruit and train new members. . . . Agencies like ours are caught in a lose-lose situation; either continue being reluctant accomplices of genocidal warmongers or withdraw from the camps, leaving the refugee population to the mercy of their jailers." Quoted in Thomas G. Weiss and Cindy Collins, *Humanitarian Challenges and Intervention* (Oxford: Westview, 1996), 101.

42. Weiss and Collins, *Humanitarian Challenges and Intervention*, 101; Prunier, *The Rwanda Crisis*, 374–375.

43. In 1967 there were approximately 33,576 Congolese refugees in Uganda. See John B. Kabera, "The Refugee Problem in Uganda," *Refugees: A Third World Dilemma* (New Jersey: Rowman & Littlefield, 1987), 73. In 1983, there were 1700 Congolese refugees in Kyaka I, *Statistics collected Kyaka I Refugee Settlement*, November 2000.

44. *Kyaka II Refugees Settlement Annual Report for the Year Ending 31st December 1995.*

45. Confidential letter, dated 5 December 1996.

46. Settlement commandants are appointed by the Office of the Prime Minister, Refugee Section. They are in charge of the administration of the settlements.

47. Confidential letter on illegal issue of travel documents to Settlement Commandants of Kyaka I and II, dated 15 May 1996.

48. Letter on movement of Congolese refugees out of Kyaka I and Kyaka II settlements to District Police Commissioner, dated 16 December 1996.

49. Confidential letter to Ministry of Local Government, dated 9 January 1995.

50. "Uganda Training Rebels in Mbarara—Rwanda," *The East African* (Nairobi weekly), 17 September 2001.

51. International Rescue Committee (IRC), *Mortality in Eastern Democratic Republic of Congo* (New York: IRC, 2001).

52. ICG, *Scramble for the Congo*, 67.

53. IRIN, "FAO Announces $10 Million Food Security Plan," 28 March 2001. U.S.$10 million was donated to various projects.

54. IRIN, "UNHCR Worker Killed in Bas-Congo," 28 March 2001.

55. IRIN, "UN Calls for Justice after ICRC Killings," *IRIN-CEA Weekly Round-up* 71, 28 April–4 May 2001.

56. IRIN, "Anti-Polio Campaign Workers Arrested, Released," *IRIN-CEA Weekly Round-up* 81, 7–13 July 2001. An RCD-Goma spokesman later refuted the allegations.

57. Global IDP Database, "Violent Conflict between the Hema and Lendu People in the Orientale Province Has Caused Major Displacements since June 1999," *Democratic Republic of Congo Section: Causes and Background of Displacement*, available at http://www.db.idp-project.org/Sites/idp.

58. For example, see Oxfam, *A Forgotten War—A Forgotten Emergency* (Oxford: Oxfam, 2000); ECOSOC, *Report on the Situation of Human Rights in the Democratic Republic of the Congo, Resolution 2000/15;* IRIN, "'Very Concerned' over Humanitarian Situation," 16 October 2000.

59. Oxfam, *A Forgotten War—A Forgotten Emergency.*

60. Ibid.

61. ECOSOC, *Report on the Situation of Human Rights in the Democratic Republic of the Congo, Resolution 2000/15,* 17.

62. Refugee International, "Food Pipeline Break Threatens Internally Displaced in Eastern Democratic Republic of Congo," *Relief Web,* available at http://www.reliefweb.int/w/rwb, 14 September 2000.

63. IRIN, "WFP to Provide over 130,000mt of Food to the Needy," 19 February 2001. The PRRO is also operational in other states in the Great Lakes region.

64. It should be noted that Emizet, "The Massacre of Refugees in Congo," 186 estimates that probably less than 6 percent of those in the Rwandan refugee camps in Congo were ex-FAR or *Interahamwe.*

65. Quoted in IRIN, "President Says His People Victims of 'Genocide,'" 8 March 2001.

Notes on the Contributors

JOHN F. CLARK is associate professor and chairperson of the International Relations Department at Florida International University, Miami. He is coeditor, with David E. Gardinier, of *Political Reform in Francophone Africa* (1997). He has also published in the *Journal of Modern African Studies, African Affairs, Studies in Comparative International Development, Journal of Democracy,* and *Africa Today,* among others. From September 1999 to July 2000, he was a Fulbright lecturer/research professor at Makerere University, Uganda.

OSITA AFOAKU is associate professor and chairperson of the Department of Africana Studies at the University of Northern Colorado, Greeley. He is the 1998 recipient of the Lawrence Dunbar Reddick Memorial Scholarship Award from the Association of Third World Studies. His works have appeared in the *Journal of Conflict Studies,* the *Western Journal of Black Studies,* and the *Journal of Third World Studies.*

KEVIN C. DUNN is assistant professor of political science at Hobart and William Smith Colleges in Geneva, NY. He is coeditor of *Africa's Challenge to International Relations Theory* (with Timothy Shaw, Palgrave, 2001). He has published in such journals as *Millennium, Geopolitics,* and the *Journal of Third World Studies.*

MUNGBALEMWE KOYAME is assistant professor of economics at Florida Memorial College in Miami. She received her doctorate in 1996 from the University of Illinois, Champaign-Urbana. From 1996 to 1997, she reviewed four articles for the African Economic Research Consortium. In 1999, she submitted a paper entitled "Income Tax Evasion in Developing Countries: A Panel Study of African countries" that is being revised for publication in the *Journal of African Economies.* She is currently working on a study of corruption in Sub-Saharan African countries.

CHRIS LANDSBERG is senior lecturer in international relations and codirector of the Center for African International Relations (CAIR) at Witwatersrand University in Johannesburg, South Africa. He was a Rhodes Scholar at Oxford University, where he read for both his M. Phil. and D. Phil. international relations degrees. During 1999 and 2000 he was a Hamburg Scholar at Stanford University's Center for International Security and Co-operation. He has published widely on South Africa's foreign policy and international relations and is currently coediting a volume entitled *From Cape to Congo: Southern Africa's Evolving Security Architecture.*

TIMOTHY LONGMAN is on leave from Vassar College, where he is an assistant professor of Africana studies and political science. He is directing the Rwanda portion of a research project on social reconstruction after genocide at the Human Rights Center of the University of California, Berkeley. His book on the role of Christian churches in the Rwanda genocide, *Commanded by the Devil: Christianity and Genocide in Rwanda,* is forthcoming.

JERMAINE O. MCCALPIN is a Ph.D. student in the Department of Political Science at Brown University, where he is studying African politics and political theory. He holds an M.A. from the University of the West Indies in Jamaica. His previous work was on the South African Truth and Reconciliation Commission and the moral dilemmas that accompany such an enterprise as a truth commission. He has been studying in the United States as a Fulbright student since August 2000.

AUGUSTA MUCHAI received a master's degree from the Institute of Diplomacy and International Studies, University of Nairobi, and works as a Research Fellow with the Security Research and Information Center (SRIC), a Nairobi-based NGO. Her research there involves collecting data on gun-related incidences and analyzing the impact of arms proliferation on conflict situations in the Horn of Africa and the Great Lakes region. Ms. Muchai also lectures part time in the Social Science Department at the Catholic University of Eastern Africa, Nairobi. She hopes to commence doctoral studies abroad in the coming year.

JUDE MURISON is a doctoral candidate in the Department of Politics and International Studies, University of Warwick, U.K. During the 1999–2000 academic year she was a research associate at the Makerere Institute for Social Research (MISR), Makerere University, Kampala, and conducted fieldwork on Rwandan refugee settlements in Uganda. The research was undertaken as part of a larger project on comparative politics of refugee policy funded by the Economic and Social Research Council, U.K.

MARTIN RUPIYA is founder and executive director of the Centre for Defence Studies (CDS) and senior lecturer in war and strategic studies at the University of Zimbabwe, Harare. Dr. Rupiya's research examines the history of military institutions and how they relate to one another in the political arena, as well as their approach to the utilization of economic resources. He is author of *Landmines in Zimbabwe: A Deadly Legacy* (1998), as well as a number of journal articles, book chapters, and working papers.

THOMAS TURNER is the author of *Ethnogenese et nationalisme en Afrique Centrale: aux racines de Patrice Lumumba* (2000) and coauthor of *The Rise and Decline of the Zairian State* (1985). He is teaching at the National University of Rwanda and at the University of Tunis, El Manar.

CRAWFORD YOUNG is Rupert Emerson and H. Edwin Young professor of Political Science at the University of Wisconsin-Madison. Emeritus since 2001, he is the author of *Politics in the Congo* (1965), *The Politics of Cultural Pluralism* (1976), *Ideology And Development in Africa* (1982), *The Rise and Decline of the Zairian State* (1985, with Thomas

Turner), and *The African Colonial State in Comparative Perspective* (1994), among other publications. A former president of the African Studies Association, he received the Distinguished Africanist Award in 1991 and is a fellow of the American Academy of Arts and Sciences. He has served as visiting professor in Congo-Kinshasa, Uganda, and Senegal.

Index

CPSIA information can be obtained at www.ICGtesting.com
Printed in the USA
LVOW07s1951230915

455421LV00002B/181/P